The Chicago Guide to Writing about **Multivariate Analysis**

Chicago Guides
to *Writing*, Editing,
and Publishing

Doing Honest Work in College
  Charles Lipson

How to Write a B.A. Thesis
  Charles Lipson

The Chicago Guide to Writing about Numbers
  Jane E. Miller

Mapping It Out
  Mark Monmonier

The Chicago Guide to Communicating Science
  Scott L. Montgomery

Indexing Books
  Nancy C. Mulvany

Getting into Print
  Walter W. Powell

A Manual for Writers of Term Papers, Theses, and Dissertations
  Kate L. Turabian

Tales of the Field
  John Van Maanen

Style
  Joseph M. Williams

A Handbook of Biological Illustration
  Frances W. Zweifel

The
Chicago
Guide to
Writing
about
Multivariate
Analysis

JANE E. MILLER
The University of Chicago Press
Chicago and London

Jane E. Miller is
on the faculty at
the Institute for
Health, Health
Care Policy, and
Aging Research
and the Edward J.
Bloustein School
of Planning and
Public Policy at
Rutgers University.
Trained as a
demographer at
the University of
Pennsylvania,
she has taught
research methods
and statistics for
more than a
decade.

The University of Chicago Press, Chicago 60637
The University of Chicago Press, Ltd., London
© 2005 by The University of Chicago
All rights reserved. Published 2005
Printed in the United States of America

14 13 12 11 10 09 08 07 06 05   1 2 3 4 5

ISBN: 0-226-52782-4 (cloth)
ISBN: 0-226-52783-2 (paper)

Library of Congress Cataloging-in-Publication Data
Miller, Jane E. (Jane Elizabeth).
    The Chicago guide to writing about multivariate
analysis / Jane E. Miller.
        p.   cm.
    Includes bibliographical references and index.
    ISBN 0-226-52782-4 (alk. paper)—ISBN 0-226-52783-2
(pbk. : alk. paper)
    1. Technical writing.   2. Multivariate analysis.
I. Title.
T11.M484 2005
808′.066519535—dc22   2004026821

To my sons,

Ian and Colin,

with whom I share

a love of numbers

CONTENTS

LIST OF TABLES

LIST OF FIGURES

LIST OF BOXES

PREFACE

The Chicago Guide to Writing about Multivariate Analysis is intended for people who estimate and present multivariate models, focusing on writing about ordinary least squares (OLS), logistic regression, and related methods such as survival analysis or multilevel models. Although measures of association are interpreted differently for probit models, log-linear models, principal components analysis, and other multivariate statistical methods, many of the other principles and tools described here also apply to these types of analyses. In addition to covering basic aspects of writing about numbers, this book shows how to explain why multivariate regression is needed for your research question and data, and how to present the results effectively to both statistical and nonstatistical ("applied") audiences.

Although I review some basic concepts about OLS and logistic regression, this book is not a substitute for a statistics textbook or a course on regression analysis. To take full advantage of this book, you should have a solid grounding in those methods, ideally including hands-on experience estimating models and interpreting their output. *The Chicago Guide to Writing about Multivariate Analysis* can be used as a companion volume in courses on regression analysis, research methods, or research writing, or as a shelf reference for experienced multivariate analysts who seek to improve their communication about these models and their application. For a study guide with problem sets and suggested course applications, see http://www .press.uchicago.edu/books/miller/.

If you write about numbers but do not work with multivariate analyses, see Miller (2004) for guidance on writing about elementary statistics and mathematical concepts.

ACKNOWLEDGMENTS

This book is the product of my experience as a student, practitioner, and teacher of multivariate analysis and its presentation. Thinking back on how I learned to write about numbers, I realized that I acquired most of the ideas from patient thesis advisors and collaborators who wrote comments in the margins of my work to help me refine my presentation of quantitative material. This book was born out of my desire to share the principles and tools for writing effectively about multivariate analyses.

Foremost, I would like to thank the members of my doctoral dissertation committee from the University of Pennsylvania, who planted the seeds for this book nearly two decades ago. Samuel Preston was the source of several ideas in this book and the inspiration for others. He, Jane Menken, and Herbert Smith not only served as models of high standards for communicating results of quantitative analyses to varying audiences, but also taught me the skills and concepts needed to meet those standards.

Many colleagues and friends offered tidbits from their own experience that found their way into this book, or provided thoughtful feedback on early drafts. In particular, I would like to thank Louise Russell, Deborah Carr, Donald Hoover, Julie Phillips, Ellen Idler, Julie McLaughlin, Dawne Harris, Diane (Deedee) Davis, Usha Sambamoorthi, Lynn Warner, and Tami Videon. Susan Darley and Ian Miller taught me a great deal about effective analogies and metaphors. Jane Wilson, Kelli Regan, Lori Glickman, and Charles Field gave invaluable advice about the organization, writing, and graphic design, and four reviewers offered insightful suggestions of ways to improve the book. Kathleen Pottick, Keith Wailoo, and Allan Horwitz provided indispensable guidance and support for bringing this project to fruition. As director of the Institute for Health, Health Care Policy, and Aging Research, David Mechanic generously granted me the time to work on this project. Partial funding for this work was provided by a Rutgers Undergraduate Curriculum Seed Grant.

Finally, I would like to thank my students—especially those from Rutgers University's Project L/Earn—for providing a steady stream of ideas about what to include in the book, as well as opportunities to test and refine the methods and materials.

Introduction

Writing about multivariate analyses is a surprisingly common task. Results of ordinary least squares (OLS) and logistic regression models inform decisions of government agencies, businesses, and individuals. In everyday life, you encounter forecasts about inflation, unemployment, and interest rates in the newspaper, predictions of hurricanes' timing and location in television weather reports, and advice about behaviors and medications to reduce heart disease risk in magazines and health pamphlets. In many professional fields, multivariate analyses are included in research papers, grant proposals, policy briefs, and consultant's reports. Economists and meteorologists, health researchers and college professors, graduate students and policy analysts all need to write about multivariate models for both statistical and nonstatistical audiences. In each of these situations, writers must succinctly and clearly convey quantitative concepts and facts.

Despite this apparently widespread need, few people are formally trained to write about numbers, let alone multivariate analyses. Communications specialists learn to write for varied audiences, but rarely are taught specifically to deal with statistical analyses. Statisticians and researchers learn to estimate regression models and interpret the findings, but rarely are taught to describe them in ways that are comprehensible to readers with different levels of quantitative expertise or interest. I have seen poor communication of statistical findings at all levels of training and experience, from papers by students who were stymied about how to put numbers into sentences, to presentations by consultants, policy analysts, and applied scientists, to publications by experienced researchers in elite peer-reviewed journals. This book is intended to bridge the gap between correct multivariate analysis and good expository writing, taking into account your intended audience and objective.

■ AUDIENCES FOR MULTIVARIATE ANALYSES

Results of multivariate analyses are of interest to a spectrum of audiences, including:

- legislators, members of nonprofit organizations, the general public, and other "applied audiences" who may have little statistical training but want to understand and apply results of multivariate analyses about issues that matter to them;
- readers of a professional journal in your field who often vary substantially in their familiarity with multivariate models;
- reviewers for a grant proposal or article involving a multivariate analysis, some of whom are experts on your topic but not the methods, others of whom are experts in advanced statistical methods but not your topic;
- an audience at an academic seminar or workshop where everyone works with various regression methods and delights in debating statistical assumptions and dissecting equations.

Clearly, these audiences require very different approaches to writing about multivariate analyses.

Writing for a Statistical Audience

When writing for statistically trained readers, explain not only the methods and findings but also the reasons a multivariate model is needed for your particular study and how the findings add to the body of knowledge on the topic. I have read many papers and sat through many presentations about statistical analyses that focused almost solely on equations and computer output full of acronyms and statistical jargon. Even if your audience is well versed in multivariate techniques, do not assume that they understand why those methods are appropriate for *your research question and data.* And it behooves you to make it as easy as possible for reviewers of your paper or grant proposal to understand the point of your analysis and how it advances previous research.

Another important objective is to avoid a "teaching" style as you write about multivariate analyses. Although professional journals usually require that you report the detailed statistical results to show the basis for your conclusions, reading your paper should not feel like a refresher course in regression analysis. Do not make your readers slog through every logical step of the statistical tests or leave it to them to interpret every number for themselves. Instead, ask and answer the research question, using the results of your analysis as quantitative evidence in your overall narrative.

Writing for a Nonstatistical Audience

Although researchers typically learn to explain multivariate models to other people with training equivalent to their own, those who write for applied or lay audiences must also learn to convey the findings to folks who have little if any statistical training. Such readers want to know the results and how to interpret and apply them without being asked to understand the technical details of model specification, coefficients, and inferential statistics. Just as most drivers don't have the faintest idea what goes on under the hood of a car, many people interested in multivariate statistical findings don't have a clue about the technical processes behind those findings. They don't need to, any more than you need to understand your car's engineering to be able to drive it.

When writing for an applied audience, make it easy for them to grasp the questions, answers, and applications of your study, just as car manufacturers make it easy for you to operate your car. Translating your findings in that way forces you to really understand and explain what your multivariate model means "in English" and as it relates to the concepts under study, which ultimately are important messages for any audience. Throughout this book I point out ways to explain various aspects of multivariate analyses to applied audiences, with all of chapter 16 devoted to that type of communication.

■ OBJECTIVES OF MULTIVARIATE ANALYSES

Multivariate models can be estimated with any of several objectives in mind. A few examples:

- To provide information to an applied audience for a debate about the issue you are analyzing. For example, findings about whether changing class size, teachers' qualifications, or curriculum yields the greatest improvement in math skills are relevant to education policy makers, teachers, and voters.
- To test hypotheses about relationships among several variables. For instance, the net effects of exercise, diet, and other characteristics on heart disease risk are of interest to the general public, professionals in the food and exercise industries, and health care providers.

- To generate projections of expected economic performance or population size over the next few years or decades. For example, forecasted employment and interest rates are widely used by businesses and government agencies in planning for the future.
- To advance statistical methods such as testing new computational algorithms or alternative functional forms. Information on the statistical derivation, software, and guidelines on how to interpret and present such findings will be useful to statisticians as well as researchers who later apply those techniques to topics in other fields.

The audience and objective together determine many aspects of how you will write about your multivariate analysis. Hence, a critical first step is to identify your audiences, what they need to know about your models, and their level of statistical training. That information along with the principles and tools described throughout this book will allow you to tailor your approach to suit your audience, choosing terminology, analogies, table and chart formats, and a level of detail that best convey the purpose, findings, and implications of your study to the people who will read it.

If you are writing for several audiences, expect to write several versions. For example, unless your next-door neighbor has a doctorate in statistics, chances are he will not want to see the derivation of the equations you used to estimate a multilevel discrete-time hazards model of which schools satisfy the No Child Left Behind regulations. He might, however, want to know what your results mean for your school district—in straightforward language, sans Greek symbols, standard errors, or jargon. On the other hand, if the National Science Foundation funded your research, they will want a report with all the gory statistical details and your recommendations about research extensions as well as illustrative case examples based on the results.

■ WRITING ABOUT MULTIVARIATE ANALYSES

To write effectively about multivariate models, first you must master a basic set of concepts and skills for writing about numbers. As you write, you will incorporate numbers in several different ways: a few carefully chosen facts in an abstract or the introduction to a journal article; a table and description of model estimates in the analytic section of a scientific report; a chart of projected patterns in the slides for a speech or poster; or a statistic about the overall impact of a proposed policy in an issue brief or grant proposal. In each of these contexts, the numbers support other aspects of the written work. They are not taken in isolation, as in a simple arithmetic problem. Rather, they are applied to some larger objective, as in a math "word problem" where the results of the calculations are used to answer some real-world question. Instead of merely estimating a model of out-of-pocket costs of prescription medications under the 2003 Medicare prescription drug act, for instance, the results of that analysis would be included in an article or policy statement about insurance coverage for prescription medications. Used in that way, the numbers generate interest in the topic or provide evidence for a debate on the issue.

In many ways, writing about multivariate analyses is similar to other kinds of expository writing. It should be clear, concise, and written in a logical order. It should start by stating a hypothesis, then provide evidence to test it. It should include examples that the expected audience can follow and descriptive language that enhances their understanding of how the evidence relates to the question. It should be written at a level of detail that is consistent with its expected use. It should set the context and define terms the audience might not be expected to know, but do so in ways that distract as little as possible from the main thrust of the work. In short, it will follow many of the principles of good writing, but with the addition of quantitative information.

When I refer to writing about numbers, I mean "writing" in a broad sense: preparation of materials for oral or visual presentation as well as materials to be read. Most of the principles outlined in this book apply equally to creating slides for a speech or a research poster. Other principles apply specifically to either oral or visual presentations.

Writing effectively about numbers also involves *reading* effectively about numbers. To select and explain pertinent numbers for your work, you must understand what those numbers mean and how they were measured or calculated. The first few chapters provide guidance on important features such as units and context to watch for as you garner numeric facts from other sources.

■ A WRITER'S TOOLKIT

Writing about numbers is more than simply plunking a number or two into the middle of a sentence. You may want to provide a general image of a pattern or you may need specific, detailed information. Sometimes you will be reporting a single number, other times many numbers. Just as a carpenter selects among different tools depending on the job, people who write about numbers have an array of tools and techniques to use for different purposes. Some approaches do not suit certain jobs, whether in carpentry (e.g., welding is not used to join pieces of wood), or in writing about numbers (e.g., a pie chart cannot be used to show trends). And just as there may be several appropriate tools for a task in carpentry (e.g., nails, screws, glue, or dowels to fasten together wooden components), in many instances any of several tools could be used to present numbers.

There are three basic tools in a writer's toolkit for presenting quantitative information: prose, tables, and charts.

Prose

Numbers can be presented as a couple of facts or as part of a detailed description of findings. A handful of numbers can be described in a sentence or two, whereas a complex statistical analysis can require a page or more. In the body of a paper or book, numbers are incorporated into full sentences. In slides, the executive summary of a report, or a research poster, numbers may be reported in a bulleted list, with short phrases used in place of complete sentences. Detailed background information is often given in footnotes (for a sentence or two) or appendixes (for longer descriptions).

Tables

Tables use a grid to present numbers in a predictable way, guided by labels and notes within the table. A simple table might present high school graduation rates in each of several cities. A more complicated table might show relationships among three or more variables such as graduation rates by city over a 20-year period, or results of statistical models analyzing graduation rates. Tables are often used to organize a detailed set of numbers in appendixes, to supplement the information in the main body of the work.

Charts

There are pie charts, bar charts, line charts, scatter charts, and the many variants of each. Like tables, charts organize information into a predictable format: the axes, legend, and labels of a well-designed chart lead the audience through a systematic understanding of the patterns being presented. Charts can be simple and focused, such as a pie chart showing the racial composition of your study sample. Or they can be complex, such as charts showing confidence intervals around estimated coefficients or projected patterns based on a multivariate model.

As an experienced carpenter knows, even when any of several tools could be used for a job, often one of those options will work better in a specific situation. If there will be a lot of sideways force on a joint, glue will not hold well. If your listening audience has only 30 seconds to grasp a numerical relationship, a complicated table showing results of five regression models with up to 20 variables apiece will be overwhelming. If kids will be playing floor hockey in your family room, heavy-duty laminated flooring will hold up better than parquet. If your audience needs many detailed numbers, a table will organize those numbers better than sentences.

With experience, you will learn to identify which tools are suited to different aspects of writing about numbers, and to choose among the workable options. Those of you who are new to writing about multivariate analysis can consider this book an introduction to carpentry—a way to familiarize yourself with the names and operations of each of the tools and the principles that guide their use. Those of you who have experience writing about such models can consider this a course in advanced techniques, with suggestions for refining your approach and skills to communicate reasons for and results of multivariate analyses more clearly and systematically.

■ IDENTIFYING THE ROLE OF THE NUMBERS YOU USE

When writing about numbers, help your readers see where those numbers fit into the story you are telling—how they answer some question you have raised. A naked number sitting alone and uninterpreted is unlikely to accomplish its purpose. Start each paragraph with a topic sentence or thesis statement, then provide evidence that supports or refutes that statement. An issue brief about wages might report an average wage and a statistic on how many people earn the minimum wage. Longer, more analytic pieces might have several paragraphs or sections, each addressing a different question related to the main topic. An article on wage patterns might present overall wage levels, then describe a model of how they vary by educational attainment, work experience, and other factors. Structure your paragraphs so your audience can follow how each section and each number contribute to the overall scheme.

To tell your story well, you, the writer, need to know *why* you are including a given fact or set of facts in your work. Think of the numbers as the answer to a word problem, then step back and identify (for yourself) and explain (to your readers) both the question and the answer. This approach is much more informative for readers than encountering a number without knowing why it is there. Once you have identified the objective and chosen the numbers, convey their purpose to your readers. Provide a context for the numbers by relating them to the issue at hand. Does a given statistic show how large or common something is? How small or infrequent? Do trend data illustrate stability or change? Do those numbers represent typical or unusual values? Often, numerical benchmarks such as thresholds, historical averages, highs, or lows can serve as useful contrasts to help your readers grasp your point more effectively: compare current average wages with the living wage needed to exceed the poverty level, for example.

■ ITERATIVE PROCESS IN WRITING

Writing about multivariate analyses is an iterative process. Initial choices of tools may later prove to be less effective than some alternative. A table layout may turn out to be too simple or too complicated, or you may conclude that a chart would be preferable. You may discover as you write a description of the patterns in a table that a different table layout would highlight the key findings more efficiently. You may need to condense a technical description of patterns for a research report into bulleted statements for an executive summary, or simplify them into charts for a speech or issue brief.

To increase your virtuosity at writing about numbers, I introduce a wide range of principles and tools to help you assess the most effective way to present your results. I encourage drafting tables and charts with pencil and paper before creating the computerized version, and outlining key findings before you describe a complex pattern, allowing you to separate the work into distinct steps. However, no amount of advance analysis and planning can envision the perfect final product, which likely will emerge only after several drafts and much review. Expect to have to revise your work, considering along the way the variants of how numbers can be presented.

■ OBJECTIVES OF THIS BOOK

How This Book Is Unique

Writing about numbers—particularly multivariate analysis—is a complex process. It involves finding data, creating variables, estimating statistical models, calculating net effects or projected patterns, organizing ideas, designing tables or charts, and finally, writing prose. Each of these tasks alone can be challenging, particularly for novices. Adding to the difficulty is the final task of integrating the products of those steps into a coherent whole while keeping in mind the appropriate level of detail for your audience. Unfortunately, these steps are usually taught separately, each covered in a different book or course, discouraging authors from thinking holistically about the writing process.

This book integrates all of these facets into one volume, pointing out how each aspect of the process affects the others. For instance, the patterns in a table are easier to explain if that table was designed with both the statistics and writing in mind. An example will work better if the objective, audience, and data are considered together. By teaching all of these steps in a single book, I encourage you to consider both the "trees" (the tools, examples, and sentences) and the "forest" (your overall research question and its context). This approach will yield a clear, coherent story about your topic, with numbers playing a fundamental but unobtrusive role.

What This Book Is Not

Although this book deals with both writing and multivariate statistical analysis, it is neither a writing manual nor a statistics book. Rather than restate principles that apply to other types of writing, I concentrate on those that are unique to writing about numbers and those that require some translation or additional explication. I assume a solid grounding in basic expository writing skills such as organizing ideas into a logical paragraph structure and use of evidence to support a thesis statement. For good general guides to expository writing, see Strunk and White (1999) or Zinsser (1998). Other excellent resources include Lanham (2000) for revising prose, and Montgomery (2003) for writing about science.

I also assume a good working knowledge of ordinary least squares (OLS) and logistic regression, although I explain some statistical concepts along the way. See Fox (1997), Gujarati (2002), or Kleinbaum et al. (1998) for detailed information about the derivation and estimation of OLS models; Powers and Xie (2000) or Long (1997) for logistic models and other methods of analyzing categorical dependent variables. Allison (1999) offers an excellent primer on multiple regression and its interpretation. See also Kornegay (1999) for a dictionary of mathematical terms, Utts (1999) or Moore (1997) for good introductory guides to statistics, and Schutt (2001) or Lilienfeld and Stolley (1994) on study design. If you are not familiar with multivariate regression but need to write about more elementary statistics, see Miller (2004).

How This Book Is Organized

Writing about multivariate analyses requires a good foundation in quantitative writing, starting with presentation of one or two simple numeric facts, progressing through distributions and associations among two or three variables, and finally to results of statistical models involving many variables. To provide an underpinning for these tasks, I begin by describing some fundamental principles and tools that apply to all quantitative writing, illustrated with examples drawn from a range of topics and disciplines. I then trace one research question and data set through the chapters related to multivariate analysis to show how the various pieces fit together to create a complete article, grant proposal, or speech.

This book encompasses a wide range of material, from broad planning principles to specific technical details. The first section of the book, "Principles," lays the groundwork, describing a series of guidelines which form the basis for planning and evaluating your writing about numbers. The next section, "Tools," explains the nuts-and-bolts tasks of selecting, calculating, and presenting the numbers you will describe in your prose. The third section, "Pulling It All Together," demonstrates how to apply these principles and tools to write about multivariate analysis for both scientific and applied audiences.

Principles

PART I

In this section, I introduce a series of fundamental principles for writing about numbers, ranging from setting the context to concepts of statistical significance to more technical issues such as examining distributions and using standards. These principles lay the groundwork for writing about multivariate analyses by introducing concepts and vocabulary used throughout the book. To illustrate these ideas, I include "poor/better/best" versions of sentences—samples of ineffective writing annotated to point out weaknesses, followed by concrete examples and explanations of improved presentation. The poor examples are adapted from ones I have encountered while teaching research methods, writing and reviewing research papers and proposals, or attending and giving presentations to academic, policy, and business audiences. These examples may reflect lack of familiarity with quantitative concepts, poor writing or design skills, indoctrination into the jargon of a technical discipline, or failure to take the time to adapt materials for the intended audience and objectives. The principles and better examples will help you plan and evaluate your writing to avoid similar pitfalls in your own work.

Seven Basic Principles

In this chapter, I introduce seven basic principles to increase the precision and power of your quantitative writing. I begin with the simplest, most general principles, several of which are equally applicable to other types of writing: setting the context; choosing simple, plausible examples; and defining your terms. Next, I introduce principles for choosing among prose, tables, and charts. Last, I cover several principles that are more specific to quantitative tasks: reporting and interpreting numbers, specifying direction and magnitude of associations, and summarizing patterns. I accompany each of these principles with illustrations of how to write (and how not to write) about numbers.

▨ ESTABLISHING THE CONTEXT FOR YOUR FACTS

"The W's"

Context is essential for all types of writing. Few stories are told without somehow conveying "who, what, when, and where," or what I call the W's. Without them your audience cannot interpret your numbers and will probably assume that your data describe everyone in the current time and place (e.g., the entire population of the United States in 2004). This unspoken convention may seem convenient. However, if your numbers are read later or in a different situation without information about their source, they can be misinterpreted. Don't expect your readers to keep track of when a report was issued to establish the date to which the facts pertain. Even using such tricks, all they can determine is that the information predated publication, which leaves a lot of room for error. If you encounter data without the W's attached, either track down the associated contextual information and report it, or don't use those facts.

To include all of the W's, some beginners write separate sentences for each one, or write them in a stilted list: "The year was 2004.

The place was the United States. The numbers reported include everyone of all ages, racial groups, and both sexes. [Then a sentence reporting the pertinent numbers]." Setting the context doesn't have to be lengthy or rote. In practice, each of the W's requires only a few words or a short phrase that can be easily incorporated into the sentence with the numbers. Suppose you want to include some mortality statistics in the introductory section of a paper about the Black Plague in fourteenth-century Europe.

Poor: "There were 25 million deaths."
This statement lacks information about when and where these deaths occurred, or who was affected (e.g., certain age groups or occupations). It also fails to mention whether these deaths were from the Black Plague alone or whether other causes also contributed to that figure.
Better: "During the fourteenth century, 25 million people died in Europe."
Although this statement specifies the time and place, it still does not clarify whether the deaths were from all causes or from the plague alone.
Best: "When the Black Plague hit Europe in the latter half of the fourteenth century, it took the lives of 25 million people, young and old, city dwellers and those living in the countryside. The disease killed about one-quarter of Europe's total population at the time (Mack, n.d.)."
This sentence clearly conveys the time, place, and attributes of the people affected by the plague, and provides information to convey the scale of that figure.

Despite the importance of specifying context, it is possible to take this principle too far: in an effort to make sure there is absolutely no confusion about context, some authors repeat the W's for every numeric fact. I have read papers that mention the date, place, and group literally in every sentence pertaining to numbers—a truly mind-numbing experience for both writer and reader. Ultimately, this obscures the meaning of the numbers because those endless W's clutter up the writing. To avert this problem, specify the context for the first number in a paragraph, then mention it again in that paragraph only if one or more aspects of the context change.

"When the Black Plague hit Europe in the latter half of the fourteenth century, it took the lives of 25 million people. The disease killed about one-quarter of Europe's total population at the time." [*Add*] "Smaller epidemics occurred from 1300 to 1600."

The last sentence mentions new dates but does not repeat the place or cause of death, implying that those aspects of the context remain the same as in the preceding sentences.

If you are writing a description of numeric patterns that spans several paragraphs, occasionally mention the W's again. For longer descriptions, this will occur naturally as the comparisons you make vary from one paragraph to the next. In a detailed analysis of the plague, you might compare mortality from the plague to mortality from other causes in the same time and place, mortality from the plague in other places or other times, and a benchmark statistic to help people relate to the magnitude of the plague's impact. Discuss each of these points in separate sentences or paragraphs, with introductory topic phrases or sentences stating the purpose and context of the comparison. Then incorporate the pertinent W's into the introductory sentence or the sentence reporting and comparing the numbers.

Units

An important aspect of "what" you are reporting is the units in which it was measured. There are different systems of measurement for virtually everything we quantify—distance, weight, volume, temperature, monetary value, and calendar time, to name a few. Although most Americans continue to be brought up with the British system of measurement (distance in feet and inches; weight in pounds and ounces; liquid volume in cups, pints, and gallons; temperature in degrees Fahrenheit), most other countries use the metric system (meters, grams, liters, and degrees Celsius, respectively). Different cultural and religious groups use many different monetary and calendar systems.

Scale of measurement also varies, so that population statistics may be reported in hundreds, thousands, millions, or even billions of people, according to whether one is discussing local, national, or international figures. Because of these variations, if the units of measurement are not reported along with a fact, a number alone is virtually useless, as you will see in some amusing examples in chapter 4, where I discuss this important principle in depth.

■ PICKING SIMPLE, PLAUSIBLE EXAMPLES

As accomplished speakers know, one strong intuitive example or analogy can go a long way toward helping your audience grasp quantitative concepts. If you can relate calories burned in a recommended exercise to how many extra cookies someone could eat, or translate a tax reduction into how many dollars a typical family would save, you will have given your readers a familiar basis of comparison for the numbers you report.

Most people don't routinely carry scales, measuring cups, or radar guns with them, so if you refer to dimensions such as weight, volume, or speed, provide visual or other analogies to explain particular values. In a presentation about estimating the number of people attending the Million Man March, Joel Best held up a newspaper page to portray the estimated area occupied by each person (3.6 square feet).[1] This device was especially effective because he was standing behind the page as he explained the concept, making it easy for his audience literally to see whether it was a reasonable approximation of the space he—an average-size adult—occupied.

The choice of a fitting example or analogy is often elusive. Finding one depends on both the audience and the specific purpose of your example.

Objectives of Examples

Most examples are used to provide background information that establishes the importance of the topic, to compare findings with earlier ones, or to illustrate the implications of results. Your objectives will determine the choice of an example. For introductory information, a couple of numerical facts gleaned from another source usually will do. In a results section, examples often come from your own analyses, and appropriate contrasts within your own data or comparisons with findings from other sources become critical issues. Below I outline a set of criteria to get you started thinking about how to choose effective examples for your own work.

The logic behind choosing numeric illustrations is similar to that for selecting excerpts of prose in an analysis of a literary work or case examples in a policy brief. Some examples are chosen to be representative of a broad theme, others to illustrate deviations or exceptions from a pattern. Make it clear whether an example you are writing about is typical or atypical, normative or extreme. Consider the following ways to describe annual temperature:

Poor: "In 2001, the average temperature in the New York City area was 56.3 degrees Fahrenheit."
From this sentence, you cannot tell whether 2001 was a typical year, unusually warm, or unusually cool.

Better: "In 2001, the average temperature in the New York City area was 56.3 degrees Fahrenheit, 1.5 degrees above normal."
This version clarifies that 2001 was a warm year, as well as reporting the average temperature.

Best: "In 2001, the average temperature in the New York City area was 56.3 degrees Fahrenheit, 1.5 degrees above normal, making it the seventh warmest year on record for the area."
This version points out not only that temperatures for 2001 were above average, but also just how unusual that departure was.

Principles for Choosing Examples

The two most important criteria for choosing effective examples are simplicity and plausibility.

Simplicity

The oft-repeated mnemonic KISS—"Keep It Simple, Stupid"—applies to both the choice and explication of examples and analogies. Although the definition of "simple" will vary by audience and length of the work, your job is to design and explain examples that are straightforward and familiar. The fewer terms you have to define along the way, and the fewer logical or arithmetic steps you have to walk your readers through, the easier it will be for them to understand the example and its purpose. The immensity of the Twin Towers was really driven home by equating the volume of concrete used in those buildings to the amount needed to build a sidewalk from New York City to Washington, D.C. (Glanz and Lipton 2002)—especially to someone who recently completed the three-hour train ride between those cities.

Plausibility

A comparison example must be plausible: the differences between groups or changes across time must be feasible biologically, behaviorally, politically, or in whatever arena your topic fits. If you calculate the beneficial effects of a 20-pound weight loss on chances of a heart attack but the average dieter loses only 10 pounds, your projection will not apply to most cases. If voters are unlikely to approve more than a 0.7% increase in local property taxes, projecting the effects of a 1.0% increase will overestimate potential revenue.

This is an aspect of choosing examples that is ripe for abuse: advocates can artificially inflate apparent benefits (or understate liabilities) by using unrealistically large or small differences in their examples. For example, sea salt aficionados tout the extra minerals it provides in comparison to those found in regular ol' supermarket salt (sodium chloride). Although sea salt does contain trace amounts of several minerals, closer examination reveals that you'd have to eat about a quarter pound of it to obtain the amount of iron found in a single grape (Wolke 2002). The fact that two pounds of sodium chloride can be fatal provides additional perspective on just how problematic a source of iron sea salt would be.

Other factors to consider include relevance, comparability, target audience, and how your examples are likely to be used, as well as a host of measurement issues. Because the choice of examples has many subtle nuances, I devote the whole of chapter 7 to that subject.

■ SELECTING THE RIGHT TOOL FOR THE JOB

The main tools for presenting quantitative information—prose, charts, and tables—have different, albeit sometimes overlapping, advantages and disadvantages. Your choice of tools depends on several things, including how many numbers are to be presented, the amount of time your audience has to digest the information, the importance of precise versus approximate numeric values, and, as always, the nature of your audience. Chapters 5 and 6 provide detailed guidelines and examples. For now, a few basics.

How Many Numbers?

Some tools work best when only a few numbers are involved, others can handle and organize massive amounts of data. Suppose you are writing about how unemployment has varied by age group and region of the country in recent years. If you are reporting a few numbers to give a sense of the general pattern of unemployment for a short piece or an introduction to a longer work, a table or chart would probably be overkill. Instead, use a sentence or two:

> "In December 2001, the unemployment rate for the United States was 5.8%, up from 3.9% a year earlier. Unemployment rates in each of the four major census regions also showed a substantial increase over that period (U.S. Bureau of Labor Statistics 2002a)."

If you need to include ten years' worth of unemployment data on three age groups for each of four census regions, a table or chart is efficient and effective.

How Much Time?

When a presentation or memo must be brief, a chart, simple table, or series of bulleted phrases is often the quickest way of helping your audience understand your information. Avoid large, complicated tables: your audience won't grasp them in the limited time. For a memo or executive summary, write one bullet for each point in lieu of tables or charts.

Are Precise Values Important?

If in-depth analysis of specific numeric values is the point of your work, a detailed table is appropriate. For instance, if your readers need to see the coefficients on each of a dozen predictors of unemployment trends, a table reporting those coefficients to a couple of decimal places would be an appropriate choice. However, if your main objective is to compare the actual and predicted patterns of unemployment over the period for which you have data, a chart would work better: all those numbers (and extra digits) in a table can distract and confuse.

"A chart is worth a thousand words," to play on the cliché. It can capture vast amounts of information far more succinctly than prose, and illustrate the size of a difference or the direction of a trend more powerfully than a sentence or a table. There is a tradeoff, however: it is difficult to ascertain exact values from a chart; avoid them if that is your objective.

Mixing Tools

In most situations, you will use a combination of tables, charts, and prose. Suppose you were writing a scholarly paper on unemployment patterns. You might include a few statistics on current unemployment rates in your introduction, charts to illustrate 10-year trends in unemployment by age group and region, and a table of multivariate model results. To explain patterns in the tables or charts and relate them to the main purpose of the paper, describe those patterns in prose. For oral presentations, chartbooks, or automated slide shows, use bulleted phrases next to each chart or table to summarize the key points. Examples of these formats appear in later chapters.

As a general rule, don't duplicate information in both a table and a chart; you will only waste space and test your readers' patience. For instance, if I were to see both a table and a chart presenting unemployment rates for the same three age groups, four regions, and 10-year period, I would wonder whether I had missed some important point that one but not the other vehicle was trying to make. And I certainly wouldn't want to read the explanation of the same patterns twice— once for the table and again for the chart.

There are exceptions to every rule, and here are two. First, if both a quick sense of a general pattern *and* access to the full set of exact numbers matter, you might include a chart in the text and tables in an appendix to report the detailed numbers from which the chart is constructed. Second, if you are presenting the same information to different audiences or in different formats, make both table and chart versions of the same data. You might use a table of unemployment statistics in a detailed academic journal article but show the chart in a presentation to your church's fundraising committee for the homeless.

■ DEFINING YOUR TERMS (AND WATCHING FOR JARGON)

Why Define Terms?

Quantitative writing often uses technical language. To make sure your audience comprehends your information, define your terms, acronyms, and symbols.

Unfamiliar Terms

Don't use phrases such as "opportunity cost" or "hierarchical linear model" with readers who are unfamiliar with those terms. Ditto with abbreviations such as SES, LBW, or PSA. If you use technical language without defining it first, you run the risk of intimidating an applied or lay audience and losing them from the outset. Or, if they try to figure out the meaning of new words or acronyms while you are speaking, they will miss what you are saying. If you don't define terms in written work, you either leave your readers in the dark, send them scurrying for a textbook or a dictionary, or encourage them to disregard your work.

Terms That Have More Than One Meaning

A more subtle problem occurs with words or abbreviations that have different meanings in other contexts. If you use a term that is defined differently in lay usage or in other fields, people may *think* they know what you are referring to when they actually have the wrong concept.

- To most people, a "significant difference" means a large one, rather than a difference that meets certain criteria for inferential statistical tests.[2] Because of the potential for confusion about the meaning of "significant," restrict its use to the statistical sense when describing statistical results. Many other adjectives such as "considerable," "appreciable," or even "big" can fill in ably to describe large differences between values.
- Depending on the academic discipline and type of analysis, the Greek symbol α (alpha) may denote the probability of Type I error, inter-item reliability, or the intercept in a regression model—three completely different concepts (Agresti and Finlay 1997).
- "Regression analysis" could mean an investigation into why Johnny started sucking his thumb again. Among statisticians, it refers to a technique for estimating the net effects of several variables on some outcome of interest, such as how diet affects child growth when illness and exercise are taken into account.
- The acronym PSA means "public service announcement" to people in communications, "prostate specific antigen" to health professionals, "professional services automation" in the business world, among more than 80 other definitions according to an online acronym finder.

These examples probably seem obvious now, but can catch you unaware. Often people become so familiar with how a term or symbol is used in a particular context that they forget that it could be confused with other meanings. Even relative newcomers to a field can become so immersed in their work that they no longer recognize certain terms as ones they would not have understood a few months before.

Different Terms for the Same Concept

People from different fields of study sometimes use different terms for the same quantitative concept. For example, what some people call an "interaction" is known to others as "effect modification," and what are termed "hierarchical linear models" in some quarters are referred to as "multilevel models" in other fields. Even with a quantitatively sophisticated audience, don't assume that people will know the equivalent vocabulary used in other fields. The journal *Medical Care* recently published an article whose sole purpose was to compare statistical terminology across various disciplines involved in health services research, so that people could understand one another (Maciejewski et al. 2002). After you define the term you plan to use, mention the synonyms from other fields represented in your audience to make sure they can relate your methods and findings to those from other disciplines.

To avoid confusion about terminology, scan your work for jargon before your audience sees it. Step back and put yourself in your readers' shoes, thinking carefully about whether they will be familiar with the quantitative terms, concepts, abbreviations, and notation. Show a draft of your work to someone who fits the profile of one of your future readers in terms of education, interest level, and likely use of the numbers and ask them to flag anything they are unsure about. Then evaluate whether those potentially troublesome terms are necessary for the audience and objectives.

Do You Need Technical Terms?

One of the first decisions is whether quantitative terminology or mathematical symbols are appropriate for a particular audience and objective. For all but the most technical situations, *you* need to know the name and operation of the tools you are using to present numeric concepts, but your readers may not. When a carpenter builds a deck for your house, she doesn't need to name or explain to you how each of her tools works as long as she knows which tools suit the task and is adept at using them. You use the results of her work but don't need to understand the technical details of how it was accomplished.

To demonstrate their proficiency, some writers, particularly novices to scientific or other technical fields, are tempted to use only complex quantitative terms. However, some of the most brilliant and effective writers are so brilliant and effective precisely because they can make a complicated idea easy to grasp. Even for a quantitatively adept audience, a well-conceived restatement of a complex numeric relation underscores your familiarity with the concepts and enlightens those in the audience who are too embarrassed to ask for clarification.

When to Avoid Jargon Altogether

For nonscientific audiences or short pieces where a term would be used only once, avoid jargon altogether. There is little benefit to introducing new vocabulary or notation if you will not be using it again. And for nonstatisticians, equations full of Greek symbols, subscripts, and superscripts are more likely to reawaken math anxiety than to promote effective communication. The same logic applies to introductory or concluding sections of scientific papers: using a new word means that you must define it, which takes attention away from your main point. If you will not be repeating the term, find other ways to describe numeric facts or patterns. Replace complex or unfamiliar words, acronyms, or mathematical symbols with their colloquial equivalents, and rephrase complicated concepts into more intuitive ones.

Suppose an engineering firm has been asked to design a bridge between Littletown and Midville. To evaluate which materials last the longest, they use a statistical technique called failure time analysis (also known as hazards analysis, survival modeling, and event history analysis). They are to present their recommendations to local officials, few of whom have technical or statistical training.

Poor: "The relative hazard of failure for material C was 0.78."
The key question—which material will last longer—is not answered in ways that the audience will understand. Also, it is not clear which material is the basis of comparison.

Better: "Under simulated conditions, the best-performing material (material C) lasted 1.28 times as long as the next best choice (material B)."
This version presents the information in terms the audience can comprehend: how much longer the best-performing material will last. Scientific jargon that hints at a complicated statistical method has been translated into common, everyday language.

Best: "In conditions that mimic the weather and volume and weight of traffic in Littletown and Midville, the best-performing material (material C) has an average expected lifetime of 64 years, compared with 50 years for the next best choice (material B)."
In addition to avoiding statistical terminology related to failure time analysis, this version gives specific estimates of how long the materials can be expected to last, rather than just reporting the comparison as a ratio. It also replaces "simulated conditions" with the particular issues involved—ideas that the audience can relate to.

When to Use and Then Paraphrase Jargon

Many situations call for one or more scientific terms for numeric ideas. You may refer repeatedly to unfamiliar terminology. You may use a word or symbol that has several different meanings. You may refer to a concept that has different names in different disciplines. Finally, you may have tried to "explain around" the jargon, but discovered that explaining it in nontechnical language was too convoluted or confusing. In those instances, use the new term, then define or rephrase it in other, more commonly used language to clarify its meaning and interpretation. Suppose a journalist for a daily newspaper is asked to write an article about international variation in mortality.

Poor: "In 1999, the crude death rate (CDR) for Sweden was 11 deaths per 1,000 people and the CDR for Ghana was 10 deaths per 1,000 people (World Bank 2001a). You would think that Sweden—one of the most highly industrialized countries— would have lower mortality than Ghana—a less developed country. The reason is differences in the age structure, so I calculated life expectancy for each of the two countries. To calculate life expectancy, you apply age-specific death rates for every age group to a cohort of . . . [You get the idea . . .]. Calculated life expectancy estimates for Sweden and Ghana were 78 years and 58 years."
This explanation includes a lot of background information and jargon that the average reader does not need, and the main point gets lost among all the details. Using many separate sentences, each with one fact or definition or calculation, also makes the presentation less effective.

Better (For a nontechnical audience): "In 1999, people in Ghana could expect to live until age 58, on average, compared to age 78 in Sweden. These life expectancies reflect much lower mortality rates in Sweden (World Bank 2001a)."
This version conveys the main point about differences in mortality rates without the distracting detail about age distributions and how to calculate life expectancy.

Better (For a longer, more technical article): "In 1999, the crude death rate (CDR) for Sweden was 11 deaths per 1,000 people and the CDR for Ghana was 10 deaths per 1,000 people, giving the appearance of slightly more favorable survival chances in Ghana (World Bank 2001a). However, Sweden has a much higher share of its population in the older age groups (17% aged 65 and older, compared to only 3% in Ghana), and older people have higher death rates. This difference pulls up the average death rate for Sweden. Life expectancy—a measure of mortality that corrects for differences in the age distribution—shows that in fact survival chances are much better in Sweden, where the average person can expect to live for 78 years, than in Ghana (58 years)." *This version conveys the main point about why life expectancy is the preferred measure and rephrases it in ways that introduce the underlying concepts (that older people have higher mortality, and that Sweden has a higher share of older people).*

When to Rely on Technical Language

Although jargon can obscure quantitative information, equations and scientific phrasing are often useful, even necessary. When tradesmen talk to one another, using the specific technical names of their tools, supplies, and methods makes their communication more precise and efficient, which is the reason such terms exist. Being familiar with a "grade 8 hex cap bolt," they know immediately what supplies they need. A general term such as "a bolt" would omit important information. Likewise, if author and audience are proficient in the same field, the terminology of that discipline facilitates communication. If you are defending your doctoral dissertation in economics, using the salient terminology demonstrates that you are qualified to earn your PhD. And an equation with conventional symbols and abbreviations provides convenient shorthand for communicating statistical relationships, model specifications, and findings to audiences that are conversant with the pertinent notation.

Even for quantitatively sophisticated audiences, define what you mean by a given term, acronym, or symbol to avoid confusion among different possible definitions. I also suggest paraphrasing technical language in the introductory and concluding sections of a talk or paper, saving the heavy-duty jargon for the methodological and analytic portions. This approach reminds the audience of the purpose of the analyses, and places the findings back in a real-world context—both important parts of telling your story with numbers.

▓ REPORTING *AND* INTERPRETING

Why Interpret?

Reporting the numbers you work with is an important first step toward effective writing about numbers. By including the numbers in the text, table, or chart, you give your readers the raw materials with which to make their own assessments. After reporting the raw numbers, interpret them. An isolated number that has not been introduced or explained leaves its explication entirely to your readers. Those who are not familiar with your topic are unlikely to know which comparisons to make or to have the information for those comparisons immediately at hand. To help them grasp the meaning of the numbers you report, provide the relevant data and explain the comparisons. Consider an introduction to a report on health care costs in the United States, where you want to illustrate why these expenditures are of concern.

Poor: "In 1998, total expenditures on health care in the United States were estimated to be more than $1.1 trillion (Centers for Medicare and Medicaid Services 2004)."
From this sentence, it is difficult to assess whether total U.S. expenditures on health care are high or low, stable or changing quickly. To most people, $1.1 trillion sounds like a lot of money, but a key question is "compared to what?" If they knew the total national budget, they could do a benchmark calculation, but you will make the point more directly if you do that calculation for them.

Better: "In 1998, total expenditures on health care in the United States were estimated to be more than $1.1 trillion, equivalent to $4,178 for every man, woman, and child in the nation (Centers for Medicare and Medicaid Services 2004)."
This simple translation of total expenditures into a per capita figure takes a large number that is difficult for many people to fathom and converts it into something that they can relate to. Readers can compare that figure with their own bank balance or what they have spent on health care recently to assess the scale of national health care expenditures.

Best (To emphasize trend): "Between 1990 and 1998, the total costs of health care in the United States rose to $1,150 billion from $699 billion—an increase of 65%. Over that same period, the share of gross domestic product (GDP) spent for health care increased to 13.1% from 12.0% (Centers for Medicare and Medicaid Services 2004)."
By discussing how health care expenditures have changed across time, this version points out that the expenditures have risen markedly in recent years. The sentence on share of GNP spent on health care shows that these expenditures comprise a substantial portion of the national budget—another useful benchmark.

Best (To put the United States in an international context): "In the United States, per capita health expenditures averaged $4,108 in the 1990s, equivalent to 13.0% of gross domestic product (GDP)—a higher share of GDP than in any other country in the same period. In comparison, Switzerland—the country with the second highest per capita health expenditures—spent approximately $3,835 per person, or 10.4% of GDP. No other country exceeded $3,000 per capita on health expenditures (World Bank 2001b)."

This description reveals that health care expenditures in the United States were the highest of any country and reports how much higher compared to the next highest country. By using percentage of GDP as the measure, this comparison avoids the issue that countries with smaller populations would be expected to spend fewer total dollars but could still have higher per capita or percentage of GDP expenditures on health.

Why Report the Raw Numbers?

Although it is important to interpret quantitative information, it is also essential to report the numbers. If you *only* describe a relative difference or percentage change, for example, you will have painted an incomplete picture. Suppose that a report by the local department of wildlife states that the density of the deer population in your town is 30% greater than it was five years ago but does not report the density for either year. A 30% difference is consistent with many possible combinations: 0.010 and 0.013 deer per square mile, or 5.0 and 6.5, or 1,000 and 1,300, for example. The first pair of numbers suggests a very sparse deer population, the last pair an extremely high concentration. Unless the densities themselves are mentioned, you can't determine whether the species has narrowly missed extinction or faces an overpopulation problem. Furthermore, you can't compare density figures from other times or places.

■ SPECIFYING DIRECTION AND MAGNITUDE OF AN ASSOCIATION

Writing about numbers often involves describing relationships between two or more variables. To interpret an association, explain both its shape and size rather than simply stating whether the variables are correlated.[3] Suppose an educational consulting firm is asked to compare the academic and physical development of students in two school districts, one of which offers a free breakfast program. If the consultants do their job well, they will report which group is bigger, faster, and smarter, as well as *how much* bigger, faster, and smarter.

Direction of Association

Variables can have a *positive* or *direct* association (as the value of one variable increases, the value of the other variable also increases) or a *negative* or *inverse* association (as one variable increases, the other decreases). Physical gas laws state that as the temperature of a confined gas rises, so does pressure; hence temperature and pressure are positively related. Conversely, as physical exercise increases, body weight decreases (if nothing else changes), so exercise and weight are inversely related.

For nominal variables such as gender, race, or religion that are classified into categories that have no inherent order, describe direction of association by specifying which category has the highest or lowest value (see chapter 4 for more about nominal variables, chapter 13 for more on prose descriptions of associations). "Religious group is negatively associated with smoking" cannot be interpreted. Instead, write "Mormons were the group least likely to smoke," and mention how other religious groups compare.

Size of Association

An association can be large (a given change in one variable is associated with a big change in the other variable) or small (a given change in one variable is associated with a small change in the other. A 15-minute daily increase in exercise might reduce body weight by five pounds per month or only one pound per month, depending on type of exercise, dietary intake, and other factors. If several factors each affect weight loss, knowing which make a big difference can help people decide how best to lose weight.

To see how these points improve a description of a pattern, consider the following variants of a description of the association between age and mortality. Note that describing direction and magnitude can be accomplished with short sentences and straightforward vocabulary.

Poor: "Mortality and age are correlated."
   This sentence doesn't say whether age and mortality are positively or negatively related or how much mortality differs by age.
Better: "As age increases, mortality increases."
   Although this version specifies the direction of the association, the size of the mortality difference by age is still unclear.
Best: "Among the elderly, mortality roughly doubles for each successive five-year age group."

This version explains both the direction and the magnitude of the age/mortality association.

Specifying direction of an association can also strengthen statements of hypotheses: state which group is expected to have the more favorable outcome, not just that the characteristic and the outcome are expected to be related. "Persons receiving Medication A are expected to have fewer symptoms than those receiving a placebo" is more informative than "symptoms are expected to differ in the treatment and control groups." Typically, hypotheses do not include precise predictions about the size of differences between groups.

■ SUMMARIZING PATTERNS

The numbers you present, whether in text, tables, or charts, are meant to provide evidence about some issue or question. However, if you provide only a table or chart, you leave it to your readers to figure out for themselves what that evidence says. Instead, digest the patterns to help readers see the general relationship in the table or chart.

When asked to summarize a table or chart, inexperienced writers often make one of two opposite mistakes: (1) they report every single number from the table or chart in the text, or (2) they pick a few arbitrary numbers to contrast in sentence form without considering whether those numbers represent an underlying general pattern. Neither approach adds much to the information presented in the table or chart and both can confuse or mislead the audience. Paint the big picture, rather than reiterating all of the little details. If readers are interested in specific values within the pattern you describe they can look them up in the accompanying table or chart.

Why Summarize?

Summarize to relate the evidence back to the substantive topic: do housing prices change across time as would be expected based on changing economic conditions? Are there appreciable differences in housing prices across regions? Summarize broad patterns with a few simple statements instead of writing piecemeal about individual numbers or comparing many pairs of numbers. For example, answering a question such as "are housing prices rising, falling, or remaining stable?" is much more instructive than responding to "what were housing prices in 1980, 1981, 1982 . . . 1999, 2000 in the Northeast?" or "how much did housing prices in the Northeast change between 1980 and 1981? Between 1981 and 1982? . . . "

Generalization, Example, Exceptions—
An Approach to Summarizing Numeric Patterns

Here is a mantra I devised to help guide you through the steps of writing an effective description of a pattern involving three or more numbers: "generalization, example, exceptions," or GEE for short. The idea is to identify and describe a pattern in general terms, give a representative example to illustrate that pattern, and then explain and illustrate any exceptions. This approach works well for describing interactions among variables, which can be characterized as exceptions to a general pattern (see chapter 13). It can also be used to compare results across models that test similar hypotheses for different subgroups, time periods, dependent variables, or statistical specifications (see "GEE Revisited" in chapter 14) or to synthesize findings or theories in previous literature (see "Literature Review" in chapter 11).

Generalization

For a generalization, come up with a description that characterizes a relationship among most, if not all, of the numbers. In figure 2.1, is the general trend in most regions rising, falling, or stable? Does one region consistently have the highest housing prices over the years? Start by describing one such pattern (e.g., trends in housing prices in the Northeast) then consider whether that pattern applies to the other regions as well. Or figure out which region had the highest housing prices in 1980 and see whether it is also the most expensive region in 1990 and 2000. If the pattern fits most of the time and most places, it is a generalization. For the few situations it doesn't fit, you have an *exception* (see below).

"As shown in figure 2.1, the median price of a new single-family home followed a general upward trend in each of the four major census regions between 1980 and 2000. This trend was interrupted by a leveling off or even a decline in prices around 1990, after which prices resumed their upward trajectory. Throughout most of the period shown, the highest housing prices were found in the Northeast, followed by the West, Midwest, and South (U.S. Census Bureau 2001a)."

This description depicts the approximate shape of the trend in housing prices (first two sentences), then explains how the four regions compare to one another in terms of relative price (last sentence). There are two generalizations: the first about how prices changed across time, the

Median sales price of new single-family homes, by region, United States, 1980–2000

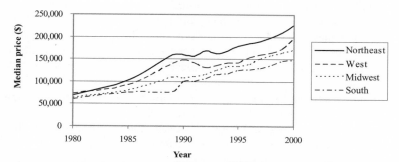

Figure 2.1. Generalizing patterns from a multiple-line trend chart.
Source: U.S. Census Bureau 2001a.

second about regional differences in price. Readers are referred to the accompanying chart, which depicts the relationships, but no precise numbers have been reported yet.

Example

Having described your generalizable pattern in intuitive language, illustrate it with numbers from your table or chart. This step anchors your generalization to the specific numbers upon which it is based. It ties the prose and table or chart together. By reporting a few illustrative numbers, you implicitly show your readers where in the table or chart those numbers came from as well as the comparison involved. They can then test whether the pattern applies to other times, groups, or places using other data from the table or chart. Having written the above generalizations about figure 2.1, include sentences that incorporate examples from the chart into the description.

(To follow the trend generalization): "For example, in the Northeast region, the median price of a new single-family home rose from $69,500 in 1980 to $227,400 in 2000, more than a three-fold increase in price."
(To follow the across-region generalization): "In 2000, the median prices of new single-family homes were $227,400, $196,400, $169,700, and $148,000 in the Northeast, West, Midwest, and South, respectively."

Exceptions

Life is complicated: rarely will anything be so consistent that a single general description will capture all relevant variation in your data. Tiny blips can usually be ignored, but if some parts of a table or chart depart substantially from your generalization, describe those departures. When portraying an exception, explain its overall shape and how it differs from the generalization you have described and illustrated in your preceding sentences. Is it higher or lower? By how much? If a trend, is it moving toward or away from the pattern you are contrasting it against? In other words, describe both direction and magnitude of change or difference between the generalization and the exception. Finally, provide numeric examples from the table or chart to illustrate the exception.

> "In three of the four regions, housing prices rose throughout the 1980s. In the South, however, housing prices did not begin to rise until 1990, after which they rose at approximately the same rate as in each of the other regions."
>
> *The first sentence describes a general pattern that characterizes most of the regions. The second sentence describes the exception and identifies the region to which it applies. Specific numeric examples to illustrate both the generalization and the exception could be added to this description.*

Other types of exceptions include instances where prices in all four regions were rising but at a slower rate in some regions, or where prices rose over a sustained period in some regions but fell appreciably in others. In other words, an exception can occur in terms of magnitude (e.g., small versus large change over time) as well as in direction (e.g., rising versus falling, or higher versus lower) (see chapter 13). Because learning to identify and describe generalizations and exceptions can be difficult, in appendix A you will find additional pointers about recognizing and portraying patterns and organizing the ideas for a GEE into paragraphs, with step-by-step illustrations from several different tables and charts.

▓ CHECKLIST FOR THE SEVEN BASIC PRINCIPLES

- Set the context for the numbers you present by specifying the W's.
- Choose effective examples and analogies.
  - Use simple, familiar examples that your audience will be able to understand and relate to.
  - Select contrasts that are realistic under real-world circumstances.
- Choose vocabulary to suit your readers.
  - Define terms and mention synonyms from related fields for statistical audiences.
  - Replace jargon and mathematical symbols with colloquial language for nontechnical audiences.
- Decide whether to present numbers in text, tables, or figures.
  - Decide how many numbers you need to report.
  - Estimate how much time your audience has to grasp your data.
  - Assess whether your readers need exact values.
- Report and interpret numbers in the text.
  - Report them and specify their purpose.
  - Interpret and relate them back to your main topic.
- Specify both the direction and size of an association between variables.
  - If a trend, is it rising or falling?
  - If a difference across groups or places, which has the higher value and by how much?
- To describe a pattern involving many numbers, summarize the overall pattern rather than repeating all the numbers.
  - Find a generalization that fits most of the data.
  - Report a few illustrative numbers from the associated table or chart.
  - Describe exceptions to the general pattern.

Causality, Statistical Significance, and Substantive Significance

A common task when writing about numbers is describing a relationship between two or more variables, such as the association between math curriculum and student performance, or the associations among diet, exercise, and heart attack risk. After portraying the shape and size of the association, interpret the relationship, assessing whether it is "significant" or "important."

Although many people initially believe that importance is based only on the size of an association—the bigger the difference across groups, the more important the association—in practice, this appraisal involves a bit more thought. There are three key questions to consider. First, is the association merely a spurious correlation, or is there an underlying causal relationship between the variables? Second, is that association statistically significant? And third, is it substantively significant or meaningful? Only if all three criteria are satisfied does it make sense to base programs or policy on that association, seeking to improve student performance by changing math curriculums, for example. To provide a common basis for understanding these principles, below I review some needed statistical terms and concepts of study design and provide references that treat these concepts in greater depth.

■ CAUSALITY

Many policy issues and applied scientific topics address questions such as, If we were to change x, would y get better? Will a new curriculum improve math comprehension and skills? If we dye white-haired people's hair some other color, will it increase their life spans? For permanent characteristics like gender, the question is slightly different: is the difference across groups real, such that targeting cases based on those traits would be an appropriate strategy? Is it really gender that explains lower average income among women (implying gender discrimination), or are differences in work experience the cause?

Explanations for Associations

Anyone with even a passing acquaintance with statistics has probably heard the phrase "correlation does not necessarily mean causation." If an association between two variables x and y is statistically significant (see below), that does not necessarily mean that x caused y or that y caused x. An association between two variables can be due to causality, confounding, bias, or simple happenstance.

Causal Associations

A causal association means that if the ostensible cause ("predictor" or "independent" variable) is changed, the hypothesized effect ("outcome" or "dependent" variable) will change in response. If a new curriculum is really the cause of better math performance, then adopting that curriculum should improve test scores. Establishing a plausible mechanism by which the first variable could affect the second helps build the case for a causal association. If you can show that the new math curriculum improves test scores by addressing previously neglected math facts or skills, that information strengthens the argument that the new curriculum is the reason for the better performance. To identify such mechanisms, know the theoretical context and base of existing knowledge for your topic.

Reverse causation occurs when what was believed to be the cause is actually the effect. For example, newspaper vendors are among the least healthy of all workers. How could that be? Selling newspapers doesn't seem like a very risky enterprise. It turns out that people who are too ill or disabled to perform other jobs are more likely than other people to become newspaper vendors because they are able to sell papers despite health problems that would prevent them from doing other jobs. Hence the ill health is what causes the occupation choice, not the reverse. To detect reverse causation, consider the time sequence of the two variables: which occurred first?

Confounding

If two variables are associated because of their mutual association with another variable, that relationship is confounded by that third variable (Abramson 1994). In some relationships affected by confounding, the third variable completely explains the association between the other two, in which case we say that association is spurious. People with white hair have higher mortality than people with other hair colors, but dyeing their hair black or blond is unlikely to improve their survival chances. Why? Because both the white hair and higher mortality are caused by old age (with some variation, of course), so the association between hair color and mortality is spurious rather than causal—it is wholly explained by the fact that both are associated with age.

In other associations, confounding is only a partial explanation: taking into account one or more confounding factors reduces the size of the association between a predictor and outcome, but the predictor retains some explanatory role. For example, both a high salt diet and a lack of exercise are associated with higher risk of a heart attack, but diet and exercise are correlated. Thus when both are considered simultaneously, the size of the association between each predictor and heart attack risk is reduced; each of those variables confounds the relationship between the other predictor and heart attacks. Again, consider the theoretical and empirical context of your topic to assess whether confounding might be occurring.

Bias

Bias is a systematic error in the observed patterns of one or more variables relative to their true values. In contrast to random error, where some measured values are higher than their actual values and some are lower, bias means that measurements consistently deviate from the true value in the same direction (Moore 1997). Bias can occur for several reasons, broadly classified into problems related to sampling, measurement, and those that arise in the specification and estimation of regression models.

Sampling issues affect how cases are selected for a study. For instance, people who volunteer and qualify for a study are often different from nonparticipants. To be eligible for the Women's Health Initiative study of hormone replacement therapy (HRT), participants had to be free of heart disease at the start of the study, never have used HRT previously, and be willing to take HRT for several years—much longer than is typically prescribed (Kolata 2003). Hence the study findings might not apply to all women considering HRT. In these situations, the apparent association does not reflect the real pattern because the sample is not representative of the population of interest (see "Representativeness" in chapter 12).

Measurement problems relate to the ways data are collected,

whether due to subjective reporting or bias in objective measurement. Respondents may shape their answers to more closely conform to social norms—playing down stigmatizing traits such as mental illness or exaggerating desirable attributes like income, for example. Or an improperly calibrated scale might falsely add to the measured weights of every specimen.

Estimation or specification biases can arise in multiple regression if the model is not correctly specified. If important independent variables are omitted from the model, estimated coefficients on other variables may be biased, leading to spurious conclusions. For instance, if a measure of age were omitted from a model relating hair color to mortality, white hair might appear to have a large, positive, statistically significant coefficient. Another form of estimation bias occurs when a model is specified as linear in the independent variables but the underlying relationship is curvilinear, as in the example of the relationship between the income-to-poverty ratio and birth weight portrayed in chapters 6 and 9.

As you interpret model results related to an association between two or more variables, be alert to possible sampling, measurement, or specification biases that might cause the estimated association to differ from the pattern in the population from which your sample is drawn. See Schutt (2001) or Moore (1997) for more on bias in sampling and measurement, Allison (1999) for more on bias in estimation of regression models.

Assessing Causality

How can you tell whether a relationship between two or more variables is causal? In the mid-1960s an advisory committee to the surgeon general agreed upon five criteria for establishing causality in epidemiologic studies (Morton, Hebel, and McCarter 2001). Four of those criteria are applicable to evaluating associations in other disciplines,[1] and similar principles have been established for the social sciences and other fields (Schutt 2001).

- Consistency of association. The association is observed in several different populations using different types of study design.
- Strength of association. A bigger difference in outcomes between cases with and without the purported causal factor indicates a stronger association.
- Temporal relationship. The cause preceded the effect. A correlation between two variables measured at the same time

gives weaker evidence than one measuring the relationship between changes in the supposed cause and subsequent responses in the outcome.

- Mechanism. There is a plausible means by which the alleged cause could affect the outcome.

Much scientific research aims to assess whether relationships are causal, using empirical evidence as the basis of evaluation. Certain types of data are better for evaluating a potentially causal relationship. Data from a randomized experiment or other "before and after" design provide more convincing evidence of a causal relationship than data where both the hypothesized cause and the hypothe-sized effect are measured at the same time ("cross-sectional" data). For situations in which random assignment isn't possible, "quasi-experimental" conditions can be simulated using multivariate regression. For example, observational studies of different math curriculums compare performance by controlling statistically for potential confounding factors—running a regression that "holds all other variables constant" to estimate the effect of the new curriculum.

Consider three approaches to evaluating whether a new math curriculum *causes* better math scores.

- An experimental study comparing math scores from schools with similar demographic and social makeup can provide convincing causal evidence. In an experiment, schools are randomly assigned either the new or the old math curriculum, using a coin toss, lottery, or random number table to decide which school gets which curriculum. Random assignment ensures that other possible causes of improved math scores are equally distributed among schools with both new and old curriculums, so those other factors cannot explain differences in observed test scores.
- Even in the absence of an experimental study, an improvement in math test scores after introduction of a new curriculum can lend support for the curriculum as the reason for better performance. The time sequence (temporal relationship) of curriculum adoption and math performance is unambiguous. However, other concurrent changes such as a decrease in class size or increase in teacher experience could be the reason for the better scores, and should be taken into account before inferring cause in either this or the preceding situation.
- A cross-sectional comparison of math scores for two schools, each of which happens to use one type of math curriculum, is

less compelling because other factors that affect test scores could affect curriculum choice: an innovative school with involved parents or a larger budget might be more likely to adopt the new curriculum and to have better math scores regardless of curriculum, confounding the association between curriculum and math performance. Because it is impossible to measure all ways in which schools differ, however, evidence of causality from quasi-experimental studies is weaker than evidence from randomized experiments.

See Lilienfeld and Stolley (1994), Davis (1985) or Morton et al. (2001) for a thorough discussion of study design and causal inference.

Causality as the Basis for Interventions

If confounding, bias, or reverse causality explains a correlation between variables, that association is not a good basis for policies or interventions aimed at changing the outcome. However, if a residual association remains after you take confounding, bias, and reverse causation into account, then evaluate both the substantive and statistical significance of the remaining association to determine its policy relevance. For example, if exercise retains a large, statistically significant association with lowered heart attack risk even after the effect of diet has been considered, exercise programs could be an appropriate intervention against heart attacks.

Writing about Causality

How does knowledge about causality affect the way you write about relationships among the concepts under study? For analyses intended to inform policy or other interventions, convey whether the association is causal and describe possible causal mechanisms. Discuss alternative explanations such as bias, confounding, or reverse causation, indicating whether or not they are taken into account in your analysis. For noncausal relationships, explain the confounders, biases, or reverse causation that gave rise to the observed association.

Vocabulary Issues

Carefully select the words you use to describe associations: verbs such as "affect" or "cause" and nouns such as "consequences" or "effects" all imply causality. "Correlated" or "associated" do not.

Poor: "The effect of white hair on mortality was substantial, with five times the risk of any other hair color."

Poor (version 2): "White hair increased the risk of dying by 400%."
The active verb ("increased") suggests that white hair brought about the higher mortality. The phrase "effect of x [white hair] on y [mortality]" also implies causality. Avoid such wording unless you have good reason to suspect a causal association.

Slightly Better: "The whiter the hair, the higher the mortality rate" or "As hair gets whiter, mortality increases."
These versions are written in neutral, purely descriptive language, failing to provide guidance about whether these patterns are thought to be causal.

Better: "People with white hair had considerably higher mortality rates than people with a different color hair. However, most people with white hair were over age 60 — a high-mortality age group — so the association between white hair and high mortality is probably due to their mutual association with older age."
Both the more neutral verb ("had") and linking both white hair and high mortality with old age help the audience grasp that white hair is not likely to be the cause of higher mortality. In this explanation, the focus is shifted from the attribute (white hair) to other possible differences between people who do and do not have that attribute that could explain (confound) the hair color/mortality pattern.

Similar considerations apply to statements of hypotheses: phrase your statement to convey whether you believe the relationship to be causal or merely a correlation.

Poor: "We expect that the new math curriculum will be associated with higher math scores."
In the absence of a statement to the contrary, most readers will interpret this to mean that the new curriculum is expected to cause better math performance.

Better: "We expect that adoption of the new mathematics curriculum will improve math scores."
By using an active verb ("improve"), this statement explicitly conveys that the curriculum change is an expected cause of better math performance.

Limitations of Study Design for Demonstrating Causality
While causality can be disproved by showing that even one of the causal criteria listed above is *not* true, it is much more difficult for

one study to simultaneously show that all four criteria *are* true. It may be impossible to establish which event or condition occurred first, and often there are numerous potential unmeasured confounders and biases. For study designs that do not allow a cause-effect pattern to be tested well, point out those weaknesses and their implications for inferring causality; see "Data and Methods in the Discussion Section" in chapter 12 for additional guidelines.

Poor: "In 1999, School Q, which adopted the new math curriculum
   two years ago, averaged 10 percentiles higher on a standardized
   math test than School R, which continued to use an older
   curriculum."
   *By omitting any reference to the way the study was conducted and how
   that might affect interpretation of the data, this explanation implies that
   the new curriculum is the cause of Q's better performance.*
Better: "In 1999, School Q, which adopted the new math
   curriculum two years ago, averaged 10 percentiles higher on a
   standardized math test than School R, which continued to use an
   older curriculum. However, School Q is in a higher income
   district which could afford the new curriculum and has smaller
   average class sizes and more experienced teachers than School R.
   Consequently, School Q's better performance cannot be
   attributed exclusively to the new curriculum."
   *By mentioning alternative explanations for the observed cross-sectional
   differences in math performance, this version explains that the evidence
   for beneficial effects of the new curriculum is relatively weak. A
   discussion of other study designs that could better assess causality
   would further strengthen this explanation.*

■ STATISTICAL SIGNIFICANCE

Statistical significance is a formal way of assessing whether observed associations are likely to be explained by chance alone. It is an important consideration for most descriptions of associations between variables, particularly in scientific reports or papers. In the absence of disclaimers about lack of statistical significance, readers tend to interpret reported associations as "real" and may use them to explain certain patterns or to generate solutions to problems. This is especially true if the association has already been shown to be causal.

In most instances, avoid a complicated discussion of the logic behind your statistical conclusions. Your statistics professor aside, many readers neither want nor need to hear how you arrived at your conclusions about statistical significance for every variable and model. Readers with statistical training will know how it was done if you name the statistical methods you used. Those without such training don't need the details. As in the carpenter analogy, the quality of the final product is affected by work done behind the scenes, but many consumers are interested only in that final product. It is up to you—the tradesperson—to ensure that appropriate steps were done correctly and to present the results in a neat, finished form.

An Aside on Descriptive and Inferential Statistics

As background for the remainder of this section, here's a quick review of the logic behind how statistical significance is assessed, to show how it relates to the other two aspects of "significance" discussed in this chapter. In chapter 10, I return to the topic of inferential statistics as I discuss how to present results of statistical tests.

Inferential statistical tests evaluate how likely it would be to obtain the observed difference or a larger difference between groups under the assumption (called the *null hypothesis; H_0*) that there is no difference. In the math example, the null hypothesis would state that average test scores for schools using the new and old math curriculums are equal. Most studies are based on a sample of all possible cases; thus random error affects estimates of average test scores and must be taken into account when assessing differences between groups. For example, inferences about the benefits of the math curriculum might be based on comparison of scores from a random sample of students rather than from all students following those curriculums. Because of random variation, the average scores in each of the curriculum groups will vary from one sample to the next. The extent of variation around the sample average is measured by the standard error of that estimate, which is affected by the number of cases used in the calculation (see below).

In a twist of logic that many novice statisticians find perplexing, the next step is to try to reject the null hypothesis by posing the question "If the null hypothesis were true, how likely would it be to observe associations as large as or larger than those seen in the current analysis simply by chance alone?" To answer this question, a *test statistic* such as the *t*-test statistic or *z*-statistic is computed from the estimate and its standard error. A *p-value* is then obtained by comparing the test statistic against the critical value of the pertinent statistical distribution. (See "Concepts behind Inferential Statistics," in chapter 10.)

The p-value gives the probability of obtaining a score difference at least as large as that observed in the sample, if in fact there is no difference between all students following the two curriculums. The lower the p-value, the lower the chance of falsely rejecting the null hypothesis. Put differently, a very small p-value corresponds to a very low probability of incorrectly concluding that there is a difference in achievement under the new versus old curriculum if in reality the two yield the same student performance. So, to conclude that a difference is statistically significant, we want a low p-value.

The "p < 0.05 Rule"

The standard criterion for "statistically significant" is a p-value < 0.05 on the pertinent statistical test, although this convention (also known as the α-level or Type I error) varies somewhat by discipline. That $p < 0.05$ means that if the null hypothesis were true, we would observe a difference as large as or larger than the sample value in fewer than 5 out of 100 samples (less than 5%) drawn from the same population. Suppose a study of the two math curriculums obtained a p-value of 0.001 for an estimated difference in test scores. This means that if in truth there was no real difference in math performance between the old and new curriculums and we were to obtain 1,000 different samples, in only *one* of these samples would the score differences be at least as large as in the sample we studied. This p-value of 0.001 is less than 0.05, so by the $p < 0.05$ rule we reject the null hypothesis of no difference between old and new curriculums. In other words, this p-value suggests that it is extremely unlikely that the observed difference in test scores could be due only to random variation between samples, lending support to the idea that there is a "real" difference in how the students perform under the two different curriculums.

Sample Size and Statistical Tests

The number of cases affects the related statistical tests: the more cases used to calculate the average score, the smaller the standard error of that average. A smaller standard error reflects less chance variability in the estimate. Hence a two-point difference in average test scores between groups might not be statistically significant if only a few students in each school were involved in the study, but the same two-point difference might be statistically significant if more students were tested.

How Statistical Significance (or Lack Thereof)
Affects your Writing

How should you write about results of statistical tests? The answer depends on whether findings are statistically significant, your audience, the length and detail of the work, and the section of the paper. Here I provide a few general rules, then return to address these issues more closely in chapters 11 and 14 (for statistical audiences) and chapter 16 (for applied or lay audiences).

Statistically Significant Results

Many academic journals specify that you use a table to report statistical test results for all variables, but then limit your text description to only those results that are statistically significant, in most cases using $p < 0.05$ as the criterion. The $p < 0.05$ rule of thumb also applies for lay audiences, although you will use and present the statistical information differently. Emphasizing statistically significant findings is especially important if you are investigating several different independent variables, such as estimating a multivariate model of how gender, race, class size, teacher's experience, and teacher's major field of study each affected students' math test scores. If only some traits associated with math scores are statistically significant, focus your discussion on those rather than giving equal prominence to all factors. This approach helps readers answer the main question behind the analysis: which factors can help improve math performance the most?

When to Report Results That Are Not Statistically Significant

The $p < 0.05$ rule notwithstanding, a nonstatistically significant finding can be highly salient if that result pertains to the main variable you are investigating: if the lack of statistical significance runs contrary to theory or previously reported results, report the numbers, size of the association, and the lack of statistical significance. In such situations, the lack of a difference between groups answers a key question in the analysis, so highlight it in the concluding section of the work (see "Numeric Information in a Concluding Section" in chapter 11).

Suppose earlier studies showed that students in School A were more likely to pass a standardized math test than students in School B. After a new math curriculum was implemented in School B, you find no difference between math scores in the two schools, or that the observed difference is not statistically significant. Mention the change in both size and statistical significance of the difference between the schools' scores compared to before the curriculum change, then explicitly relate the new finding back to theoretical expectations and results of previous studies. This approach applies to a short general-interest article or a policy brief as well as to scientific reports or papers.

"Borderline" Statistical Significance

A controversial issue is what to do if the p-value is only slightly above 0.05, say $p = 0.06$ or $p = 0.08$. Such values fall in a gray area: strictly speaking they are not statistically significant according to conventional criteria, but they seem oh-so-close that they are difficult to ignore. How you handle such findings depends on several factors that influence statistical tests:

- The effect size
- The sample size
- The value of the test statistic and its associated p-value

If the effect size (e.g., the difference in math test scores between two schools, or the coefficient on exercise in a model of heart attack risk) is very small, a larger number of cases is unlikely to increase the statistical significance of the association. Such associations are unlikely to be of substantive interest even if they are real and causal (see "Substantive Significance" below), so treat them as if they were not statistically significant. On the other hand, if the effect size is moderate to large, the p-value is in the gray area between $p < 0.05$ and $p < 0.10$, *and* the sample size is small, report the effect and its p-value, and mention the small sample size and its effect on the standard error. Unfortunately, all of these criteria are subjective (What is a "moderate effect size?" A "small sample size?") and opinions vary by discipline, so learn the conventions used in your field.

■ SUBSTANTIVE SIGNIFICANCE

The third aspect of the "importance" of a finding is whether the size of an association is substantively significant, which is just a fancy way of asking "So what?" or "How much does it matter?" Is the cholesterol reduction associated with eating oatmeal large enough to be clinically meaningful? Is the improvement in math performance large enough to justify the cost of adopting the new curriculum? Statistical significance alone is not a good basis for evaluating the importance of some difference or change. With a large enough sample size, even truly microscopic differences can be statistically significant.

However, tiny differences are unlikely to be meaningful in a practical sense. If every fourth grader in the United States were included in a comparison of two different math curriculums, a difference of even half a point in average test scores might be statistically significant because the sample size was so large. Is it worth incurring the cost of producing and distributing the new materials and training many teachers in the new curriculum for such a small improvement?

To assess the substantive importance of an association, place it in perspective by providing evidence about how that half-point improvement translates into mastery of specific skills, the chances of being promoted to the next grade level, or some other real-world outcome to evaluate whether that change is worthwhile. Report and evaluate both the prevalence and consequences of a problem: preventing a rare but serious health risk factor may be less beneficial than preventing a more common, less serious risk factor. For scientific audiences, consider including attributable risk calculations (see chapter 8), cost-effectiveness analysis (e.g., Gold et al. 1996), or other methods of quantifying the net impact of proposed health treatments, policies, or other interventions as a final step in the results section. For others, integrate results of those computations into the discussion and conclusions.

Address substantive significance in the discussion section as you consider what your results mean in terms of your original research question.

Poor: "The association between math curriculums and test scores was not very substantively significant."
Most people won't know what "substantively significant" means. In addition, this version omits both the direction and size of the association, and doesn't help readers assess whether the change is big enough to matter.

Better (for a scientific audience): "Although the improvement in math test scores associated with the new math curriculum is highly statistically significant, the change is substantively inconsequential, especially when the costs are considered: the half-point average increase in math scores corresponds to very few additional students achieving a passing score, or mastering important fourth-grade math skills such as multiplication or division. Spending the estimated $40 million needed to implement the new curriculum on reducing class sizes would likely yield greater improvements."

This description puts the results back in the context of the original research question. Both substantive and statistical significance are explicitly mentioned; causality is implicitly addressed using words such as "change" and "increase."

■ RELATIONS AMONG STATISTICAL SIGNIFICANCE, SUBSTANTIVE SIGNIFICANCE, AND CAUSALITY

The consequence of a numeric association depends on whether that association is causal, statistically significant, and substantively meaningful. All three conditions are often necessary, and none alone may be sufficient to guarantee the importance of the association. Avoid a long discussion of how much something matters substantively if the association is not causal or the difference between groups is not statistically significant. In scientific papers, review the evidence for statistical and substantive significance and explain that those two perspectives have distinctly different purposes and interpretations, devoting a separate sentence or paragraph to each.

As you evaluate these criteria for the associations you are writing about, remember that even if one condition is satisfied, the others may not be.

- In nonexperimental studies, a statistically significant association does not necessarily mean causation: white hair and high mortality could be correlated 0.99 with a $p < 0.001$, but that does not make white hair a cause of high mortality. In experiments, where cases are randomized into treatment and control groups, however, confounding is ruled out, and statistically significant findings are usually interpreted as causal.
- Conversely, a causal relationship does not necessarily guarantee statistical significance: e.g., random error or bias can obscure effects of the curriculum change on math performance.
- Statistical significance does not necessarily translate into substantive importance: the new math curriculum effect could be statistically significant at $p < 0.05$, but the increment to math scores might be very small.
- Conversely, substantive importance does not ensure statistical significance: a large effect might not be statistically significant due to wide variation in the data or a small sample size.
- Causality does not automatically mean substantive

importance: the new curriculum may improve math scores, but that change may be so slight as to be unworthy of investment.

- Substantive importance (a "big effect") does not automatically translate into causality, as in the white hair example.

■ CHECKLIST FOR CAUSALITY, STATISTICAL SIGNIFICANCE, AND SUBSTANTIVE SIGNIFICANCE

As you write about associations, discuss each of the following criteria as they pertain to your research question:

- Causality

    Describe possible mechanisms linking the hypothesized cause with the presumed effect.

    Discuss and weigh the merits of other, noncausal explanations, identifying sources of bias, confounding, or reverse causation.

    Explain the extent to which your statistical methods overcome drawbacks associated with observational (nonexperimental) data, if applicable.

- Statistical significance

    For a scientific audience,

    —report statistical significance in the results section (see chapters 13 and 14 for illustrative wording), mentioning p-values or confidence intervals in the text and reporting other types of statistical test results in a table (see chapter 10);

    —return to statistical significance in the discussion, especially if findings are new or run counter to theory or previous studies. Restate findings in words, not numeric test results or p-values.

    For a nontechnical audience, use the results of statistical tests to decide which findings to emphasize, but don't report the numeric details of the test results (see chapter 16).

- Substantive significance

    Evaluate the substantive importance of a finding by translating it into familiar concepts such as overall cost (or cost savings) or improvements in specific skills.

    For a technical audience, consider quantifying the difference using z-scores.

- Integration of the three elements

  In your discussion or closing section, relate the findings
  back to the main research question, considering
  causality, statistical significance, and substantive
  significance together.

  For an observed numeric association to be used as the basis
  for a policy or intervention to improve the outcome
  under study, all three criteria should be satisfied.

Five More Technical Principles

In addition to the principles covered in the previous two chapters, there are a handful of more technical issues to keep in mind as you write about numbers: understanding the types of variables you're working with, specifying units, examining the distributions of your variables, and finding standards against which to compare your data. These are important background steps before you decide which kinds of calculations, model specifications, tables, and charts are appropriate, or select suitable values to contrast with one another. The final principle—choosing how many digits and decimal places to include—may seem trivial or merely cosmetic. However, measurement issues and ease of communication dictate that you select a level of numeric detail that fits your data and your audience.

■ UNDERSTANDING TYPES OF VARIABLES

Information about types of variables affects your choice of comparisons. Some calculations and types of statistical models make sense only for variables measured in continuous units, others only for those classified into categories. You cannot calculate a mean test score if those data were collected as "pass/fail," and an ordinary least squares model of passing the test may not model the relationship correctly (Aldrich and Nelson 1984). Some variables allow only one response for each case, others permit more than one response. You cannot analyze patterns of multiple insurance coverage if each person was allowed to report only one type.

Choice of tools for presenting numbers also is affected by type of variable and number of responses. In chapter 6, I explain why line or scatter charts are suitable for some types of variables, and bar or pie charts for others, and why some charts accommodate multiple responses per case while others work for only single-response variables.

In chapter 13, I show how to describe distributions for different types of variables. For now, I introduce the vocabulary and properties of each kind of variable.

There are two main characteristics of each variable to consider: Was it measured in continuous or categorical fashion? And was each case allowed only one response or several responses?

Continuous and Categorical Variables

The type of variable—continuous or categorical—affects a variety of issues related to model specification and interpretation which are described in chapter 9. Below I give basic definitions of these types of variables and how they relate to measurement issues and mathematical consistency checks.

Continuous Variables

Continuous variables are measured in units such as years (e.g., age or date), inches (e.g., height or distance), or dollars (e.g., income or price), including those with decimal or fractional values. Continuous dependent variables are modeled using ordinary least squares (OLS) regression, analysis of variance (ANOVA), or related techniques. Continuous variables are one of two types: *interval* and *ratio* (Chambliss and Schutt, 2003).

Interval variables can be compared using subtraction (calculating the interval between values; also known as the "absolute difference"; see chapter 8) but not division (calculating the ratio of two values; also known as "relative difference"). Temperature as we conventionally measure it (whether Fahrenheit or Celsius)[1] is an interval variable: if it was 30°F yesterday and 60°F today, it makes sense to say that it is 30 degrees hotter today, but not that it is twice as hot. And using a ratio to compare temperatures above and below zero (e.g., −20°F versus +20°F) would be truly misleading.

Ratio variables can be compared using either subtraction or division because a value of zero can be interpreted as the lowest possible value. Weight is an example of a ratio variable: if one infant weighed 2,000 grams and another weighed 4,000 grams, you could either say the second baby "weighed 2,000 grams more than" or "was twice as heavy as" the first.

Categorical Variables

Categorical variables classify information into categories such as gender, race, or income group. They come in two flavors: *ordinal* and *nominal.* Ordinal ("ordered") variables have categories that can be ranked according to the values of those categories. A classic example is letter grades (A, B+, etc.). Income grouped into ranges of several thousand dollars is another ordinal variable. Nominal ("named") variables include gender, race, or religion, for which the categories have no inherent order.[2] Both ordinal and nominal dependent variables can be modeled using logistic regression (for binary variables), multinomial logit (for multichotomous variables), and related statistical methods. For ordinal dependent variables with more than two categories, ordered logit regression can also be used (Powers and Xie 2000).

Continuous and categorical variables are not completely different animals. Continuous variables can be classified into categories. You can create a "low birth weight" indicator variable out of a variable measuring weight in grams: A 2,000 gram baby would be classified low birth weight (LBW < 2,500 grams or 5.5 pounds). However you can't create a detailed continuous birth weight variable from a categorical variable that encompasses several values in each weight category: knowing that a baby was low birth weight does not tell you whether he weighed 900 or 1,234 or 2,499 grams.

Categorical versions of continuous variables are useful for simplifying information (by grouping birth weight into 500 gram categories, for example), or for indicating whether values of a continuous variable fall above or below a cutoff like the Federal Poverty Level. They also can be used to test for nonlinear patterns of association, such as whether birth weight increases at a constant rate across the entire income range or exhibits an accelerating, decelerating, or nonmonotonic relationship.

Defining Sensible Categories

Creating good categorical variables takes careful thought. If each case can have only one valid value, then every case should fall into exactly one group—no more, no less. Each person is either male or female, and has only one age and one total income at a time. In addition, every person has a gender, age, and income (even if it is $0.00 or negative). In set theory, classifications such as these are known as *mutually exclusive* (nonoverlapping) and *exhaustive* (encompassing all possible responses). "Under 18 years," "18–64," and "65 and older" are mutually exclusive and exhaustive age groups because the youngest age group starts at zero and the oldest has no upper age limit, covering the full range of relevant answers.

Although mutually exclusive and exhaustive seem like straightforward concepts, they can be difficult to implement. Through 1990, the U.S. Census question on race allowed each respondent to mark only one answer. For people who considered themselves to be multiracial, however, marking one race was not sufficient—the race categories weren't mutually exclusive. To resolve this issue, the 2000 census permitted respondents to classify themselves as more than one race, and tabulations of race include both single- and multiple-race categories. These new categories allowed each person to be counted once and only once. According to the new tabulations, multiple-race individuals accounted for about 2.4% of the total population (U.S. Census Bureau 2002a).

A second problem arose for people of Hispanic origin: the Census Bureau treats Hispanic origin and race as separate characteristics covered in separate questions. According to Census Bureau definitions, Hispanic persons can be of any race, and persons of any race can be of Hispanic origin. However, many people of Hispanic origin consider their race to be Hispanic, not white, black, Asian, or Native American, so they often left the race question blank or checked "other" (Navarro 2003). For them, the list of categories was incomplete—in other words, it was not exhaustive.

"Other." A common practice when collecting or classifying data is to create a category for "other" responses, allowing for answers researchers didn't anticipate. A survey question about the primary reason someone did not seek prenatal care might list financial costs, travel issues, and the belief that pregnancy is a healthy condition, but overlook child care issues and language barriers, for example. An "other" category also permits us to combine uncommon responses instead of creating separate categories for reasons mentioned by only a small share of respondents. Everyone's response fits somewhere, but there needn't be dozens of tiny categories to record and present in every table or chart.

If "other" encompasses a large share of cases, however, it can obscure important information, as when many Hispanics mark "other" for race on the census. Sometimes the response "none of the above" is used to indicate "other," but that approach misses the opportunity to find out what answer does apply. To avoid this problem, often questionnaires include a blank for respondents to specify what "other" means in their case. If many respondents list similar answers, they can be grouped into a new category for analysis or future data collection.

Missing values. If you've ever collected data, you know that people sometimes skip questions, refuse to respond, write something illegible or inappropriate, or mark more answers than are allowed. To account for all cases, an "unknown" or "missing" category is used to tabulate the frequency of missing information—an important fact when assessing whether your data are representative of the population under study (chapter 12).

"Not applicable." Some questions pertain only to some cases. In a survey asking whether someone has changed residences recently and if so when, the "when" question does not apply to those who did not move. To make sure every case is accounted for, such cases are classified "not applicable." Differentiating "not applicable" from "missing" makes it easier for cases to be omitted from calculations that don't pertain to them, leaving out those who didn't move from an analysis of timing of moves rather than incorrectly lumping them in with people who did move but neglected to report when.

Single versus Multiple-Response Questions

For characteristics like gender or current age, each case has only one value. Other situations call for more than one answer per respondent. In a school board election, each voter is asked to select three candidates, or a survey asks respondents to list all types of health insurance coverage within their families, for example. The number of possible responses does not determine the type of variable—both single- and multiple- response items can be either continuous or categorical.

For many multiple-response questions, some people mark no responses, others mark several, and a few mark all possible answers. In some families, everyone has the same kind of health insurance, such as employer-sponsored or Medicaid. For those families, one response characterizes their insurance coverage. Some families have several kinds of health insurance, such as both employer-sponsored and Medicare, or both Medicaid and Medicare. Two or three responses are needed to characterize their coverage. Families that lack health insurance do not fit any categories. (On some surveys, "uninsured" might be listed as an option, in which case every family would have at least one response.)

Why does it matter that the number of answers to a question can vary from none to many? Because the principles of "mutually exclusive" and "exhaustive" don't apply to variables created from those questions. Having employer-sponsored health insurance does not preclude a family from also having Medicare for its elderly or disabled members, for example. If you tally up the total number of responses in all categories, they will exceed the number of families surveyed. For cases where none of the responses apply, the total number of responses can be less than the number of families surveyed. Consequently, the kinds of mathematical consistency checks used to evaluate the distribution of a single-response variable cannot be used for multiple-response questions. For single-response questions with an exhaustive set of response categories, the frequencies of all responses will add up to 100% of the cases. For multiple-response questions, that total could range from 0% (if no one marked any of the categories) to several hundred percent (if many people marked several categories).

Before you analyze and write about numbers, familiarize yourself with how the data were collected, to ensure that you make sensible choices about calculations, creation of new variables, consistency checks, and ways of presenting the information.

▪ SPECIFYING UNITS

To interpret and compare your numbers, specify the units of observation and the units and systems of measurement. Make a note of the units for any numeric facts you collect from other sources so you can use and interpret them correctly.

Dimensions of Units
Unit of Analysis
The unit of analysis (also known as the "level of aggregation") identifies the level at which numbers are reported. If you measure poverty in number of persons with income below some threshold, your unit of analysis is a person. If you count families with income below a threshold, your unit of analysis is a family. Poverty can also be calculated at the census tract, county, state, or national level. Each approach is valid, but values with different levels of aggregation cannot be compared with one another. In 2001, there were 32.9 million poor *people* but 6.8 million poor *families* in the United States (Proctor and Dalaker 2002). When collecting information to compare against your data, look for a consistent level of aggregation.

Level of aggregation pertains to most quantitative topics. For instance, cancer penetration can be measured by the number of cells affected within a particular organ, cancerous organs in a patient, people afflicted within a family or town, or the number of towns with cases. Avoid confusion by stating the level of aggregation along with the numbers:

"Mr. Jones's cancer had metastasized, affecting three major organ systems."
"Breast cancer is widespread in the area, with at least five towns having prevalence rates well above the national average."

Units of Measurement
There are two aspects of units of measurement: scale and system of measurement. Both are critical for your model results to be interpretable.

Scale. Scale, or order of magnitude, refers to multiples of units. Are you reporting number of people, number of *thousands* of people, *millions* of people? Consider the following error of omission, which had data analysts scratching their heads: a utility company observed a sudden and substantial drop-off in demand for electricity at the end of 1978 between periods of fairly steady demand (figure 4.1). At first, researchers looked for a real, causal explanation. The region had several major industrial clients. Had one of them closed? Had a com-

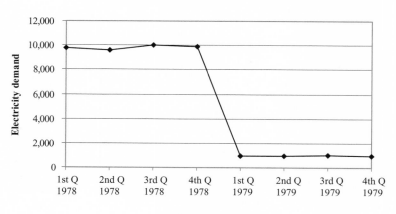

Electricity demand, Industrytown, 1978–1979

Figure 4.1 Effect of a change in scale of reported data on apparent trends.

peting electricity provider opened up shop? In fact, the apparent drop was due to a change in the scale of units used to report electricity demand, from hundreds of megawatt-hours to thousands of megawatt-hours. The actual amount of electricity used was fairly stable.

System of measurement. There is plenty of room for confusion in a world where metric, British, and other systems of measurement co-exist. Virtually every dimension of our experience that is quantified— distance (feet or meters), mass (pounds or kilograms), velocity (miles per hour or kilometers per hour), volume (quarts or liters), money (dollars or euros or pesos or yen), dates (Christian or Jewish or other calendar), and time (standard time or daylight saving time or military time)—can be measured using any of several systems.

The embarrassing experience of the Mars Climate Orbiter in 1999 is a classic illustration of what can happen if units are not specified. Engineers who built the spacecraft specified the spacecraft's thrust in pounds, which are British units. NASA scientists thought the information was in newtons, which are metric units. The miscalculation went overlooked through years of design, building, and launch, and the spacecraft missed its target by roughly 60 miles (Pollack 1999). Even rocket scientists make basic, easily avoidable mistakes about units. Don't emulate them.

Several common variants of regression analysis introduce the possibility of even more confusion about units. Standardized coefficients and logarithmic or other transformations of the independent or dependent variables change the units of measurement away from their original forms. If you estimate such models or conduct such transformations, either convey the new units as you interpret the coefficients or transform the values back to the original units; see chapter 9 for guidelines and examples.

Writing about Units

Incorporate units of observation and measurement into the sentence with the pertinent numbers.

"In 1998, per capita income in the United States was $20,120 (U.S. Census Bureau 1999a)."
This sentence includes information on units of measurement (dollars), units of observation (per capita means "for each person") and the W's (what, when, where).

Definitions of Units

Familiar units such as dollars, numbers of people, and degrees Fahrenheit can be used without defining them first. Likewise, if you are writing for experts in your field, you can usually skip an explanation of commonly used units in that field. However, remember that what is familiar to a group of experts might be completely Greek to people from other disciplines or to an applied audience; adjust your explanations accordingly. For instance, measures such as constant dollars, age-standardized death rates, or seasonally adjusted rates will need to be defined for people who do not work with them routinely. Regardless of audience, provide a standard citation to explain the calculation.

Inexperienced writers often fail to explain their units precisely or completely, particularly for common but tricky measures that express relationships between two quantities such as parts of a whole, the relative size of two groups, or rates. For variables that are measured in percentages, proportions, rates, or other types of ratios, include phrases such as "of ___," "per ___," or "compared to ___" so your figures can be interpreted.

Ratios. Ratios are simply one number divided by another. They measure the relative size of two quantities. Sometimes the quantities in the numerator and denominator are mutually exclusive subsets of the same whole. For instance, the sex ratio is defined as number of males per 100 females. Some ratios divide unrelated quantities. For example, population density is number of people per land area (e.g., per square mile).

Proportions, percentages, and fractions. Proportions (and their cousins, percentages) are a special type of ratio in which a subset is divided by the whole, such as males divided by total population. Percentages are simply proportions multiplied by 100. If the proportion male is 0.50, then 50% of the population is male. Do not make the all-too-common mistake of labeling proportions and percentages interchangeably; they differ by a factor of 100.

For measures such as proportions, percentages, and fractions that compare parts to a whole, make it clear what "the whole" comprises. In technical terms, what does the denominator include? If I had a nickel for every time I have written "percentage of what?" in the margins of a paper, I would be rich. Consider the following statistics on voter turnout from figure 4.2:

**a. Voter participation,
1996 U.S. presidential election
% of voting age population**

**b. Voter participation,
1996 U.S. presidential election
% of registered voters**

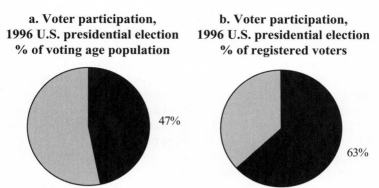

Figure 4.2. Effects of different referent group definitions on percentage calculations.
Source: Institute for Democracy and Electoral Assistance 1999.

Poor: "In 1996, the voter turnout for the presidential election was 63%."
   Is voter turnout measured as a percentage of the voting age population (figure 4.2a), or as a percentage of all registered voters (figure 4.2b)? Because some people of voting age are not registered to vote, the two measures cannot be directly compared, but to avoid that mistake, readers need to know which measure is reported.
Better: "In 1996, of the 146 million registered voters, 63% participated in the U.S. presidential election."
   Here, number of registered voters is identified as the basis of comparison, so this number can be compared with equivalently defined voter participation rates for other years or places.
Best: "In 1996, of the 146 million registered voters, 63% participated in the U.S. presidential election. As a percentage of the voting age population (197 million people), however, voter turnout was only 47%, revealing a large pool of potential voters who did not participate."
   By specifying the denominator for each statistic, this version gives the information needed to assess comparability of numbers from other sources. The description is enhanced by contrasting the two measures of voter participation and explaining how they are different.

When relationships involve two or more variables, such as the association between poverty and age group, "percentage of what?" is more complicated. In cross-tabulations like table 4.1, there are several possible definitions of the whole against which some part is being compared. Depending on the question you are asking, you might report the percentage *of the total population* that is in each of the six possible poverty/age group combinations (table 4.1a), the percentage of *each poverty category* that falls into each age group (table 4.1b), or the percentage *of each age group* that is poor (table 4.1c).

Approximately one-third of the poor are children (<18 years old; table 4.1b), but one-sixth of children are poor (table 4.1c).[3] These values have completely different meanings, so specify what subgroup is being compared to what whole entity.

Poor: "In 2002, there were a lot of poor children in the United States (16.7%)."
> Does 16.7% *refer to poor children out of* all people, *poor children out of* all poor people *(both incorrect in this case), or poor children out of* all children *(correct)?*

Better: "In 2002, 16.7% of children in the United States were poor."
> *The referent group (children) for the percentage is stated, clarifying interpretation of the statistic.*

Best: "In 2002, 16.7% of children were poor, compared to 10.6% of people aged 18 to 64, and 10.4% of those aged 65 or older."
> *This sentence makes it clear that the observed poverty rate among children is higher than that for other age groups. Both the units of observation (persons) and measurement (percentage of the age group) are specified and are consistent with one another, hence the comparison is correctly done.*

Rates. Rates are a type of ratio with the added element of time. For example, velocity is often measured in miles per hour, death rates as number of deaths per 100,000 people within a specified period of time (Lilienfeld and Stolley 1994). Report the time interval to which the rate pertains along with the units and concepts in both the numerator and denominator.

A common error is to confuse a death rate for a particular subgroup with deaths in that group as a proportion of all (total) deaths, as in the following example.

Poor: "In the United States in 1999, one-third died from heart disease."
> *One-third of what? Deaths (correct, in this case)? People? By failing to specify one-third of what, the author leaves this sentence open to*

Table 4.1. Three tables based on the same cross-tabulation: (a) Joint distribution, (b) Composition within subgroups, (c) Rates of occurrence within subgroups

a. Poverty by age group, United States, 2002

Age group (years)	Thousands of persons (% of total population)		
	Poor	Non-poor	Total
<18	12,133 (4.3%)	60,520 (21.2%)	72,653 (25.5%)
18–64	18,861 (6.6%)	159,073 (55.8%)	177,934 (62.4%)
65+	3,576 (1.3%)	30,809 (10.8%)	34,385 (12.1%)
Total	34,570 (12.1%)	250,402 (87.9%)	284,972 (100.0%)

b. Age distribution (%) by poverty status, United States, 2002

Age group (years)	Poor		Non-poor		Total	
	Number (1,000s)	% of all poor	Number (1,000s)	% of all non-poor	Number (1,000s)	% of total pop.
<18	12,133	35.1	60,520	24.2	72,653	25.5
18–64	18,861	54.6	159,073	63.5	177,934	62.4
65+	3,576	10.3	30,809	12.3	34,385	12.1
Total	34,570	100.0	250,402	100.0	284,972	100.0

c. Poverty rates (%) by age group, United States, 2002

Age group (years)	# Poor (1,000s)	Total pop. (1,000s)	% Poor within age group
<18	12,133	72,653	16.7
18–64	18,861	177,934	10.6
65+	3,576	34,385	10.4
Total	34,570	284,972	12.1

Source: Proctor and Dalaker 2003

misinterpretation: the fraction of all deaths that occurred due to heart disease is not the same as the death rate (per population) from heart disease.

Poor (version 2): "One-third of people died from heart disease in the United States in 1999."

This version is even worse because it implies that one out of every three living people died of heart disease in 1999—a figure that would translate into roughly 84 million heart disease deaths in the United States that year. In fact, the actual death toll from all causes combined was only 2.3 million. Don't make the mistake of thinking that "one-third is one-third," without specifying the "of what?" part of the fraction.

Best: "In 1999, the number of people who died of heart disease in the United States was 725,000, accounting for roughly one out of every three deaths that year. The death rate from heart disease was 265.9 deaths per 100,000 people (Anderson 2001)."

This version conveys that heart disease accounted for approximately one-third of deaths that year. Mentioning the death rate clarifies the other perspective on heart disease—the annual risk of dying from that cause.

■ EXAMINING THE DISTRIBUTION OF YOUR VARIABLES

As you write about numbers, you will use a variety of examples or contrasts. Depending on the point you want to make, you may need

- a typical value, such as the average height or math score in a sample;
- an expected change or contrast, such as a proposed increase in the minimum wage;
- the extremes; for example, the maximum possible change in test scores.

To tell whether a given value is typical or atypical or a change is large or modest, you need to see how it fits in the distribution of values for that variable *in your data and research context.* For instance, the range of math scores will be smaller (and the average higher) in a group of "gifted and talented" students than among all students in an entire school district; which you would use depends on your research question and the available data. Before you select values for calculations or as case examples, use exploratory data analytic techniques such as frequency distributions, graphs, and simple descriptive statistics to familiarize yourself with the distributions of the variables in question.

Minimum, Maximum, and Range

The first aspects of a distribution to consider are the minimum and maximum observed values and the range—the difference between them. Examine the actual range of values taken on by your variables, not just the theoretically possible range. For example, the Center for Epidemiological Studies of depression (CESD) scale is an index composed of 20 questions about frequency of certain symptoms, each scaled from 0 to 3. Although in theory the CESD scale could range from 0 to 60, in the general population the mean is between 8 and 10 and scores above 20 are rarely observed (Radloff and Locke 1986). Thus using a change of 25 points as an illustrative example would be unrealistic. See chapter 7 for more discussion of out-of-range values and contrasts.

Measures of Central Tendency

The second aspect of distribution to consider is central tendency—the mean, median, and/or modal values, depending on the type of variable in question. The mean is usually the arithmetic average of the values under study, calculated by adding together all values and dividing that sum by the number of cases.[4] The median is the middle value (at the 50th percentile) when all values are ranked in order from lowest to highest. The mode is the most common value—the value observed the most frequently of all values in the sample. Any of the measures of central tendency can be used for continuous variables, but neither the mean nor the median makes sense for categorical (nominal or ordinal) variables.

Although the mean is the most widely used of the three measures of central tendency for continuous variables, before you rely on it to characterize your data, observe the distribution of values. The mean does not always represent the distribution well. In figures 4.3a, b, and c, the mean value (6.0) would be an appropriate example, although in figure 4.3c it is no more typical than any of the other observed values. (See "Variability" below for an explanation of "SD.")

In figure 4.3d, however, the mean (still 6.0) is not observed for any cases in the sample and hence is not a representative value. Likewise, in figure 4.3e, the mean (again 6.0) is atypical. If such a pattern characterizes your data, the mode would be a better choice of a typical value.

Another caution: the mean can be biased if your sample has one or two outliers—values that are much higher or much lower than those

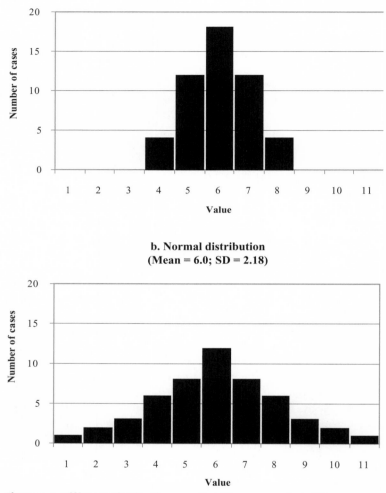

Figure 4.3. Different distributions, each with a mean value of 6.0.
(a) Normal distribution; (b) Normal distribution, same mean, higher SD.

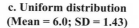

c. Uniform distribution
(Mean = 6.0; SD = 1.43)

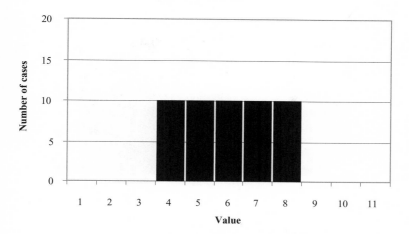

d. Polarized bimodal distribution
(Mean = 6.0; SD = 4.71)

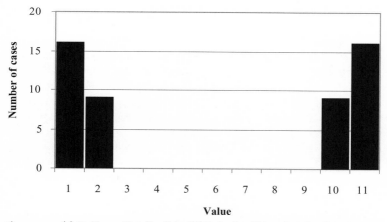

Figure 4.3. (c) Uniform distribution; (d) Polarized bimodal distribution.

e. Skewed distribution
(Mean = 6.0; SD = 1.76)

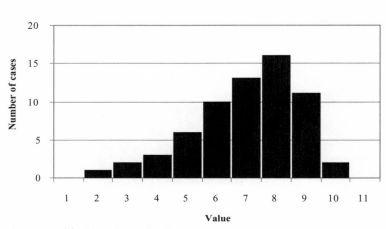

Figure 4.3. (e) Skewed distribution.

in the rest of the sample. Use Tukey's box-and-whisker or stem-and-leaf techniques to display deviation from the mean or identify the presence of outliers (see chapter 6 or Hoaglin et al. 2000). See also chapter 12 for how to describe your treatment of outliers.

Variability

Another important consideration is the variability in your data, the extent to which values are spread around the mean. It is usually summarized by the variance or standard deviation (SD). For example, an absolute difference of 2 points is "bigger" or more meaningful in a distribution that is tightly clustered around the mean (e.g., SD = 1.07; figure 4.3a) than in one with more spread (e.g., SD = 2.18; figure 4.3b). In the first instance, 2 points is 1.86 standard deviations from the mean, placing it farther out in the distribution than in the second instance, where 2 points is less than one standard deviation. To convey the position of a given value in the overall distribution, report its rank, percentile, or z-score (see chapter 8).

Alternatively, use the "five number summary" (Moore 1997)—the minimum value, first quartile value (Q1), median, third quartile (Q3), and maximum value—to illustrate the spread. The minimum and maximum values encompass the range, while the interquartile range (Q1 to Q3) shows how the middle half of all values are distributed within the full span of the data. These numbers can be reported in tabular form or a box-and-whisker chart.

Transformed Variables

In some applications, you may decide to transform your independent or dependent variables, using multiples of the original units or taking logarithms, for example. If so, examine the distribution of the transformed variable before you select examples and contrasts.

■ DEFINING STANDARD CUTOFFS AND PATTERNS

Comparison against a standard is a useful way of assessing whether a particular value is commonplace or exceptional, or an observed pattern typical or unusual for the topic under study.

What Is a Standard?

Standards include cutoffs, patterns, and records that define the highest and lowest observed values. Some cutoffs are based on physical principles: the properties of water change below 32°F. Other cutoffs are based on social or legal convention: 21 as the minimum drinking age in most states, a specified dollar amount as the Federal Poverty Level for a family of certain size and age composition, adjusted annually for inflation. Commonly used standard patterns include the J-shaped age pattern of mortality, the seasonal pattern of employment for a given occupation, and growth charts for height and weight of children from birth to adulthood.

Some standard patterns are empirically derived, like the mean temperature for New York City on January 1 calculated from several decades of data, or the median height for 12-month-old girls computed from a national sample. Other standards are conventions agreed upon by experts in the field. The Bureau of Labor Statistics calculates the Consumer Price Index (CPI) with 1982–1984 as the base period when CPI = 100 (U.S. Bureau of Labor Statistics 2001b). Demographers and epidemiologists at the Census Bureau and Centers for Disease Control recently replaced the 1940 age structure with that for 2000 as the basis for their "standard million" for all age adjustments (Anderson and Rosenberg 1998; CDC 1999).

Often the initial choice of a standard is somewhat arbitrary—it doesn't really matter which year or population is chosen. However, the same convention must be used to generate all numbers to be compared because the results of an age adjustment or a constant dollar calculation vary depending which standard was used. As always, read for and specify the context (W's), units, and methods used to apply the standard to ensure comparability.

Although the term "standard" implies uniformity of definition, there is a striking variety and malleability of standards. As of January 1, 2002, the National Weather Service began using the average conditions from 1971 through 2000 to assess temperatures, replacing the relatively cool decade of the 1960s with the relatively warm decade of the 1990s. Thus a temperature that would have been interpreted as unusually warm if it had occurred on December 31, 2001, when the old standard was in use might have been considered normal or even cool if it had occurred one day later, when the new standard was in place. Periodically, the standard referent year for constant dollars, the standard population for age adjustment of death rates, and human growth standards are also updated.

Standards also vary by location. What constitutes a normal daytime high temperature in Los Angeles in January is quite different from the normal daytime high for that month in Chicago or Sydney. A different age pattern of mortality is observed in the United States and other developed countries today (where chronic diseases account for most deaths) than in Afghanistan and other less developed countries (where infectious and accidental causes of death predominate; Omran 1971, Preston 1976). In addition, standards or thresholds may differ according to other characteristics. For instance, Federal Poverty Levels ("poverty thresholds") vary by family size and age composition: the threshold for a single elderly person is lower than for a family with two adults and two children.

Why Use Standards?

Standards are used to assess a given value or pattern of values by comparing against information about pertinent physical or social phenomena. Such comparisons factor out some underlying pattern to help ascertain whether a given value is high, low, or average.

Does a particular value exceed or fall below some cutoff that has important substantive meaning? For instance, alcohol consumption is illegal only below a certain age.

- Is an observed trend consistent with other concurrent changes? Did college tuition rise faster than the general rate of inflation, for example?
- Is the pattern for a given case typical or unusual? For instance, is a child growing at the expected rate? Is he significantly

above or below the average size for his age? If so, is that gap increasing, decreasing, or stable as he gets older?

- Is a particular change expected based on cyclical patterns or due to some other factor? Did a new law reduce traffic fatalities, or is such a decline expected at the time of the year the law took effect, for example?

In addition to some measure of average value, standards frequently include information on range or other aspects of distribution. Weather standards mention record high and low temperatures as well as averages. Growth charts for children typically show the 10th, 25th, 50th, 75th, and 90th percentiles for age and sex.

Selecting an Appropriate Standard

For many nontechnical topics, cutoffs and patterns are part of cultural literacy: most Americans grow up knowing they'll have the right to vote when they turn 18 and can retire at 65. The freezing point of water, the concept of 50% or more as a democratic majority, and that it is warmer in summer than winter are also generally known. For more technical issues or if precise values are needed, read the related literature to become familiar with standard cutoffs, patterns, or standardization calculations. See chapter 8 for additional discussion of how to use standards in numeric contrasts.

Where and How to Discuss Standards

For a lay audience, use of standards is a behind-the-scenes activity. Report the conclusions but not the process. Do children from low-income families grow normally? Did this year's employment follow the typical cyclical pattern? Because standards vary, mention the time, place, and other attributes of the standard you are using: "in constant 1990 dollars," "compared to the normal daily high for November in Chicago," or "below the 2002 poverty threshold for a family of two adults and one child."

For a scientific audience, specify which standard has been applied. Explain cutoffs, standard patterns, or standardization processes that are unfamiliar to your audience, and consider using diagrams (see "Reference Lines" in chapter 6) or analogies (chapter 7) to illustrate. If you have used a cutoff to define a categorical variable, explain that in your data and methods section. If the approach is new or unusual, include the formula and a description in the methods section, a footnote, or an appendix. For lengthy calculations or explanations, cite a published source where readers can find the details.

■ CHOOSING A FITTING NUMBER OF DIGITS
AND DECIMAL PLACES

How many digits and decimal places should you include as you write about numbers? Too many are cumbersome and uninformative and may overstate the precision with which the data were originally measured. Too few may not meet your readers' objectives.

Precision of Measurement and Number of Significant Digits

Established scientific guidelines specify how the precision of measurement limits the appropriate number of digits to report for both measured values (raw data) and calculations (Logan 1995; NIST 2000)—a concept referred to as "significant digits" or "significant figures."[5] If a ruler is marked with increments for each millimeter (tenth of a centimeter or 0.1 cm), one can "eyeball" to approximate halfway between those marks, or to the nearest 0.05 cm. All values measured with that ruler and all calculations based on those data should be reported with no more than two decimal places. Likewise, if you are averaging income that was originally collected in multiples of thousands of dollars, you can report one level down (e.g., hundreds of dollars), but not single dollars and cents.

It is surprising how often calculators and computers seem to magically enhance the implied level of detail and precision of numeric information. Just because your calculator or computer output displays eight or more digits or decimal places does not mean that information is accurate. Make sure the number of decimal places in reported calculations is consistent with the precision of the original measurement. See Logan (1995) for a comprehensive discussion of how measurement and calculations determine the appropriate number of significant digits.

The number of significant digits is often fewer than the total number of digits displayed because of the presence of leading or trailing zeroes. Leading zeroes are those found to the right of the decimal point, before the first "significant" (nonzero) numeral, e.g., the five zeroes between the decimal point and the 2 in the numeral "0.0000023." They serve as placeholders that convey the scale of the number, in this case, millionths. Likewise trailing zeroes are placeholders for thousands, millions, or billions. For example, the six zeroes used to convey the scale in "285,000,000" rarely reflect an exact count down to the single unit. Eliminate them by rounding to that scale—just write "285 million."

Number of Digits

Guidelines about significant digits set an upper limit on the appropriate number of digits and decimal places for your data. Rarely, however, are all those digits needed to make your point. For most purposes, "approximately six billion persons" is an adequate description of the world's population at the turn of the millennium. The number "6,049,689,552 persons" is more detail than all but the most persnickety demographer could want to know, and almost certainly exaggerates the precision of the estimate. To provide a bit more detail, write "6.0 billion" or "6.05 billion" persons. Information about the last few hundred persons is not very informative when the overall scale is in the billions. Often, the main point is the similarity of two or more numbers; if so, don't display extra digits merely to reveal tiny differences. And you don't want your readers pausing to count commas to figure out the scale of the number: "Let's see. Three commas . . . that's billions."

In most prose, two to four digits are enough to illustrate your point without too much detail. Consider these three ways of reporting results of a very close election:

Poor: "In the recent election, Candidate A received 2,333,201 votes while Candidate B received 2,333,422 votes."
To figure out who won and by how much, readers must wade through a lot of digits and then do the math themselves.

Better: "Candidate B won the recent election over Candidate A, with 2,333,422 votes and 2,333,201 votes, respectively."
This version conveys who won, but readers must still calculate the margin of victory.

Best: "In an extremely close election, Candidate B eked out a victory over Candidate A, receiving only 221 more votes out of more than 4.6 million votes tallied—a margin of less than 100th of 1% of the total votes."
By presenting the calculations, the key point is far more accessible than in the previous two versions. Who won and by how much? Phrases such as "extremely close" and "eked" communicate how narrow the victory was much more effectively than just reporting the numbers, and none of the numbers presented include more than three digits. If the exact number of votes is needed, accompany the description with a simple table reporting the tallies.

Number of Decimal Places

In general, include the smallest number of decimal places that suit the scale of your numbers—in many cases, none. If most of the variation is in the thousands, millions, or billions, detail in the second decimal place won't add much to the main point: do we really need to know the federal budget down to the penny? On the other hand, for numbers less than 1.0, a couple of decimal places are needed for the variation to be visible: because of rounding, differences between coefficients of 0.072 and 0.068 won't be evident unless you show three decimal places. And p-values or test statistics can't be evaluated if they are rounded to the nearest whole number.

Having chosen an appropriately modest number of digits and decimal places for the text, do not turn around and report a zillion digits in your accompanying tables. Yes, tables are good for detail, but there is a limit to what is useful. If you are creating a table of coefficients and standard errors for six models with up to 20 variables apiece, don't overwhelm your readers by reporting each number to eight digits and six decimal places, particularly if your associated narrative discusses each of those numbers rounded to the nearest two digits.

Use the recommendations in table 4.2 to decide what level of detail is suitable for the types of numbers you report, then design your tables and prose accordingly. On occasion, you might exceed the recommended number of digits or decimal places, but do so only if fewer will not accomplish your purpose. For some types of numbers, there are well-established conventions about how many decimal places to include:

- Monetary denominations include two decimal places to show value to the nearest cent, except for values of $1 million or greater, when decimal places are usually superfluous. Even on my bank statement (with a balance far below a million dollars), I rarely look at how many cents I have.
- Proportions include three decimal places if several values presented are less than 0.10; otherwise, two will suffice.
- Percentages often don't need any decimal places unless the values are very similar to one another (e.g., 5.9 and 6.1, or 66.79 and 67.83). In such cases, include one or two decimal places, as shown.
- Estimated coefficients and standard errors can include up to four decimal places if needed to display at least two significant digits. For coefficients with many leading zeroes,

consider changing the scale of your variables; see "Transforming Variables" below.

- Odds ratios often need only two significant digits (e.g., 1.7 or 0.22) to convey the size of the difference across groups. An exception is continuous independent variables, where the odds ratio measures the effect of a one-unit increase in that variable. Again, consider changing scale or classifying values into groups to reduce the need to report three or more decimal places.
- Test statistics (e.g., t-statistic, χ^2, or F-statistic) require two decimal places to compare them against critical values.
- p-values conventionally include two decimal places, although three may be shown if $p < 0.01$, to display one significant figure.

In general, I recommend choosing the numbers of digits and decimal places depending on the scale of the numbers, aiming for no more than four total digits in prose and no more than six (ideally fewer) in tables. Possible exceptions include tables of raw data in reports intended as standard data sources for public use, and "dazzle" statistics to catch your audience's attention with a single showy number. In the latter case, you might report the federal budget down to the last cent, then remind them that such detail may be fun but is probably unwarranted. Report fewer digits for general background statistics than for detailed quantitative analyses, and use a consistent scale and number of decimal places within a series of numbers to be compared.

Changing Scale, Rounding, and Scientific Notation

One way to reduce the number of digits you report is to change the scale of the numbers, rounding to the nearest million or thousandth, for example. To decide on an appropriate scale, consider the highest and lowest values you need to report, then choose a scale that gracefully captures most values using three to four numerals. In 1999, the populations of the 50 United States ranged from approximately 480 thousand people in Wyoming to 33.1 million people in California (U.S. Census Bureau 1999b). Because most states' populations exceed one million, round the figures to the nearest million with one or two decimal places to accommodate both small and large states' populations: 0.5 million people in Wyoming, 33.1 million in California.

Changing scale also can help reduce the number of digits for proportions or other statistics that have several leading zeroes without

Table 4.2. Guidelines on number of digits and decimal places for text, charts, and tables, by type of statistic

Type of Statistic	Text or Chart			Table		
	Total digits[a]	Decimal places	Examples	Total digits	Decimal places	Examples
Integer[b]	3 to 4	Not applicable	7 million 388	Up to 6	Not applicable	7,123 thousand[c] 388
Rational number	3 to 4	1 to 2	32.1 −0.71	Up to 6	Up to 4; enough to show 2 significant digits	32.1 −0.71 0.0043
Percentage	3 to 4	1 if several #s would round to same value; otherwise none	72% 6.1%	3 to 4	2 if several #s would round to same value; otherwise 1	72.1% 6.12%
Proportion	Up to 3	3 if several #s <0.10; otherwise 2	.36 .0024	Up to 3	3 if several #s <0.10; otherwise 2	.36 0.024
Monetary value	3 to 4	None for large denominations; 2 for small	$5 million $12.34	3 to 4	None for large denominations; 2 for small	$5 million $12.34
Estimated coefficient	Up to 4	1 to 2	−2.13 0.16	Up to 5	Up to 4; enough to show 2 significant digits[d]	−2.13 0.0021

Ratio (includes odds ratios)	Up to 3	1 to 2	12.7 0.83	Up to 4	Up to 3; enough to show 2 significant digits[d]	12.71 0.83
Standard error	Up to 4	1 or 2	1.25 0.02	Up to 5	Up to 4; enough to show 2 significant digits	1.25 0.027
Test statistic	3 to 4	2	$\chi^2 = 12.19$ $t = 1.78$	3 to 4	2	$\chi^2 = 12.19$ $t = 1.78$
p-value	Up to 3	2	$p = 0.06$ $p < 0.01$	Up to 3	2 for values $\geq$ 0.01 3 for values $<$ 0.01	$p = 0.06$ $p < 0.001$
Model goodness-of-fit statistic (GOF)	3 to 4	2 for R^2 1 or 2 for other GOFs	$R^2 = 0.08$ $-2 \log L = 61.9$	3 to 4	2	$R^2 = 0.08$ $-2 \log L = 61.91$

Note: See Logan (1995) for considerations on appropriate number of digits for calculations.

[a] Including decimal places. If number of digits exceeds this value, round or change scale.

[b] Integers include the positive and negative counting numbers and zero (Kornegay 1999). By definition, they have no decimal places.

[c] The word "thousand" (or other unit name) would appear only in the column head, not in the table cells; see table 4.1 for an example.

[d] For very small coefficients or odds ratios on continuous variables, consider changing the scale of the independent or dependent variable before estimating the model (see text).

losing any meaningful information. Convert proportions to percentages to save two decimal places, sparing readers the chore of counting zeroes to assess scale. For instance, a proportion of 0.0007 becomes 0.07% or could be rounded to 0.1%. This averts the common mistake of calling proportions percentages, and makes the scale of the numbers easier to grasp. Or, for a chemical sample weighing 0.0000023 grams, report it as 2.3 micrograms; in a nonscientific piece, include a note that one microgram equals one millionth of a gram. In a lab report or other document for a biological or physical science audience, use scientific notation—another convention for succinctly presenting only the meaningful digits of a number; write 2.3×10^{-6} grams.

Transforming Variables

When working with continuous independent variables for which a one-unit increase or difference has only a small effect on the dependent variable, consider changing the scale or conducting another transformation of one or both variables. For example, measure income in hundreds or thousands of dollars instead of single dollar increments, or take logarithms of income or other continuous variables that have a range of several orders of magnitude. See chapter 7 for a discussion of choosing an appropriate increment or scale for each variable, chapter 9 for how to interpret coefficients on continuous variables.

Numbers versus Numerals

A few more technical points: some editors require that numbers under 10 and units (e.g., "percent," "million") be spelled out rather than reported in numeral form. These guidelines vary across disciplines, so consult a manual of style for your field. Spell out numbers at the beginning of a sentence: "Thirty percent of all deaths were from heart disease," rather than "30 percent of all deaths were from heart disease." Or rephrase the sentence to put the number later in the sentence. "Heart disease accounted for 30% of all deaths." Whenever possible, separate distinct numeric values with more than a comma, using symbols or names for units (e.g., %, grams) or adverbs (e.g., "approximately," "nearly") to help readers distinguish where one number ends and the next begins. For instance, replace "100, 320, and 799 grams, respectively" with "100 grams, 320 grams, and 799 grams, respectively." See University of Chicago Press (2003) or Alred et al. (2000) for additional technical writing guidelines.

■ CHECKLIST FOR FIVE MORE BASIC PRINCIPLES

- Familiarize yourself with each of your variables.
    Are they categorical or continuous?
        −If categorical, are they nominal or ordinal?
        −If continuous, are they ratio or interval?
    Are they single or multiple response?
- Know the units of measurement for each variable.
    Check units:
        −Level of aggregation or unit of analysis.
        −Scale or order of magnitude.
        −System of measurement, such as British, metric, or other.
        −Standardized or transformed variables.
    Check comparability within your work and with that of others.
- Examine the distribution of your variables: range, central tendency, variance, and symmetry in order to identify typical and atypical values or contrasts.
- Consider standard cutoffs, distributions, or historic records.
    Find out which are used for your topic.
    Cite references for standards.
    Put details in appendixes or footnotes.
- Pick an appropriate number of digits and decimal places, taking into account
    Precision with which the data were originally measured, and
    Objectives of your work.
        −Aim for four digits with up to two decimal places in the text and charts, one to two more in tables (see table 4.2 for guidelines).
        −Round or change the scale to reduce number of digits or leading or trailing zeroes.

Tools

In this section, I introduce some basic tools for designing tables and charts, choosing quantitative examples and analogies, calculating and comparing numbers, and deciding how to present results of statistical tests. Used in concert with the principles described in the previous few chapters, these tools will help you develop effective ways to present quantitative information from multivariate models.

To explain the purpose and application of the tools, I have written these chapters in a "teaching" style. In general, this is *not* how you will write about numbers. For example, your readers don't need to know why you decided to present confidence intervals instead of standard errors, the steps to calculate excess risk, that you right-justified the numbers in your table, or why you chose a chart to illustrate an interaction. Make those decisions, do those calculations, and create your charts or tables to function well, but don't write about how or why you did so. Instead, present the fruits of those labors, following the examples and guidelines throughout this book.

An important exception is when you are writing about multivariate analysis for a problem set or course paper for a research methods or statistics course. In those instances you may be asked to show your calculations and explain your thought process to demonstrate that you have mastered the corresponding concepts and skills. The methods section of a scientific paper also often includes a description of analytic strategy; see chapters 12 and 14. Check with your professor to find out whether to include this information in your course assignments. If you later revise a course paper for publication or presentation to another audience, remove most of the "teaching statistics" material and focus instead on the products of that behind-the-scenes work.

Creating Effective Tables

Good tables complement your text, presenting numbers in a concise, well-organized way to support your description. Make it easy for your audience to find and understand numbers within your tables. Design table layout and labeling that are straightforward and unobtrusive so the attention remains on the substantive points to be conveyed by your data rather than on the structure of the table. In this chapter, I explain the following:

- How to create tables so readers can identify the purpose of each table and interpret the data simply by reading the titles and labels
- How to make tables self-contained, including units, context, source of the data, types of statistics or models, and definitions of abbreviations
- How to design a layout that contributes to the understanding of the patterns in the table and coordinates with your written description

The first section gives principles for planning effective tables. The second explains the "anatomy of a table"—the names and features of each table component. The third gives guidelines on how to design tables to display univariate, bivariate, three-way, and multivariate statistics. The final sections offer advice about how to draft a table and create it on a computer.

■ PRINCIPLES FOR PLANNING EFFECTIVE TABLES

Creating Focused Tables

Most reports and papers about multivariate analyses include several tables, each of which reports one aspect of the overall research question. Typically, such papers include a table of descriptive statistics, some tables showing bivariate or three-way associations, and one or more tables of parameter estimates and goodness-of-fit statistics from the multivariate models. Additional tables might elucidate interaction effects or present predicted values for a few case examples (chapter 9). See "Building the Case for a Multivariate Model" in chapter 14 for guidelines on designing a logical sequence of tables for your analysis.

Creating Self-Contained Tables

Often tables are used separately from the rest of the document, either by readers in a hurry to extract information or as data sources that become detached from their origins. For journals with very low word limits, readers must be able to distinguish among roles and interpretation of different variables with little if any explanation. Label each table so your audience can understand the information without reference to the text. Using the title, row and column headings, and notes, they should be able to discern the following:

- The purpose of the table
- The context of the data (the W's)
- The location of specific variables within the table
- Coding or units of measurement for every number in the table
- For multivariate models of a categorical dependent variable, the identity of the category or categories being modeled
- The type of statistics or statistical model
- Data sources
- Definitions of pertinent terms and abbreviations

The units and sources of data can be specified in any of several places in the table depending on space considerations and whether the same information applies to all data in the table (see next section).

■ ANATOMY OF A TABLE

Title

Write a title for each table to convey the specific topics or questions addressed in that table. In documents that include several tables or charts, create individualized titles to differentiate them from one another and to convey where each fits in the overall scheme of your analysis.

Topic

In the title, name each of the major components of the relationships illustrated in that table. To avoid overly long titles, use summary phrases or name broad conceptual categories such as "demographic characteristics," "physical properties," or "academic performance measures" rather than itemizing every variable in the table. (The individual items will be labeled in the rows or columns; see below). The title to table 5.1 mentions both the outcome (number of households) and the comparison variables (household type, race, and Hispanic/non-Hispanic origin).

Types of Statistics

If only one type of statistic is reported in the table, mention it in the table title.

- For a univariate table, state whether it reports distribution or composition, mean values, or other descriptive statistics.
- For a bivariate table, indicate whether it reports correlations, differences in means, cross-tabulations, or other measure of association.
- For a table of multivariate model results, mention the type of statistical model such as ordinary least square regression (OLS), logistic regression, Cox proportional hazards model, or multilevel model.

For tables that include several types of statistics, provide a summary moniker in the title and identify the types of statistics in column, row, or panel headings. See "Common Types of Tables" below for illustrative titles.

Context

Specify the context of the data by listing the W's in the table title: where and when the data were collected, and if pertinent, restrictions on who is included in the data (e.g., certain age groups). If the data are from a specific study (such as the National Survey of America's Families or the Human Genome Project) or institution (e.g., one college or hospital), include its name in the title or in a general note below the table. Minimize abbreviations in the title. If you must abbreviate, spell out the full wording in a note.

Units

State the units of measurement, level of aggregation, and system of measurement for every variable in the table. This seemingly lengthy list of items can usually be expressed in a few words such as "household income ($)," or "birth weight in grams." Whenever possible,

Table 5.1. Anatomy of a table

Households by type, race and Hispanic origin (thousands), United States, 1997

Characteristic	All households	Family households					Nonfamily households		
		Total	Married couple	Other families			Total	Female householder	Male householder
				Female householder	Male householder				
Race/ethnicity									
White	86,106	59,511	48,066	8,308	3,137		26,596	14,871	11,725
Non-Hispanic White	77,936	52,871	43,423	6,826	2,622		25,065	14,164	10,901
Black	12,474	8,408	3,921	3,926	562		4,066	2,190	1,876
All other[a]	3,948	2,961	2,330	418	212		986	455	532
Origin									
Non-Hispanic	93,938	63,919	49,513	11,040	3,366		30,018	16,762	13,258
Hispanic[b]	8,590	6,961	4,804	1,612	545		1,630	754	875
Total	102,528	70,880	54,317	12,652	3,911		31,648	17,516	14,133

Source: U.S. Census Bureau 1998.

[a] "All other" races includes Asians, Pacific Islanders, Native Americans, and those of unspecified race.

[b] People of Hispanic origin may be of any race.

generalize units for the table rather than repeating them for each row and column. If the same units apply to most numbers in the table, specify them in the title. If there isn't enough space in the title, or if the units vary, mention units in the column or row headings. In table 5.1, the title states that all statistics are reported as number of thousands of households. Tables of descriptive statistics and multivariate results often involve different units for different variables; in those instances, specify the units for each variable in the associated column or row headings (see related sections below).

In tables presenting multivariate models, report the units or coding of the dependent variable in the title—usually the only place in the table to put such information. For example, a model of birth weight should indicate whether it is measured in ounces or grams. Models of dichotomous (two-category) or multichotomous (multiple category) dependent variables such as "birth weight status" should indicate which category is being modeled: low or normal birth weight, for example. Verify this information against the computer output of model results to make sure your labels and units are consistent with those in the estimated model; see appendix B.

Use of Sampling Weights

If some or all of the statistics in a table are weighted, state so in the table title or a footnote and cite a reference for the source of the weights.

Row Labels

Name the concept for each row and column in its associated label so readers can interpret the numbers in the interior cells of the table. The identity and meaning of the number in the most heavily shaded cell of table 5.1 is households of all types (known from the column header) that include black persons (row label), with population measured in thousands of households (title).

If the units of measurement differ across rows or columns of a table, mention the units in the pertinent row or column label. A table of descriptive statistics for a study of infant health might include mean age (in days), weight (in grams), length (in centimeters), and gestational age (in weeks). With different units for each variable, the units cannot be summarized for the table as a whole. Do not assume that the units of measurement will be self-evident once the concepts are named: without labels, readers might erroneously presume that age was measured in months or years, or weight and length reported in British rather than metric units.

Minimize use of abbreviations or acronyms in headings. If space is tight, use single words or short phrases. Explain the concepts measured by each variable as you describe the table so the brief labels will become familiar. Do not use eight-character variable names from statistical packages—your audience will not know what they mean. If readers need to see the long or complex wording of a question to understand the meaning or source of a variable, refer them to an appendix that contains the pertinent part of the original data collection instrument.

Indenting

When organizing rows in a table, place categories of a nominal or ordinal variable in consecutive rows under a single major row header with the subgroups indented. Counts and percentages for subgroups that are indented equally can be added together to give the total. In table 5.1, for example, "White," "Black" and "All other" together comprise all households. Row labels that are indented farther indicate subgroups and should not be added with the larger groups to avoid double counting. "Non-Hispanic white" is indented in the row below "White," showing that the former is a subgroup of the latter. In the terminology of chapter 4, "white" and "non-Hispanic white" are not mutually exclusive, so they should not be treated as distinct groups when calculating totals or frequency distributions.[1] To indicate that Hispanics should not be added to the other racial groups within the table, the Hispanic origin contrast is given a separate left-justified row label with rows for Hispanics and non-Hispanics below. Finally, a footnote explains that Hispanics can be of any race, indicating that they should not be added to the racial categories.

Labels for Categorical Independent Variables

In tables of multivariate model results, identify both the included and omitted (or reference) categories of each nominal or ordinal variable. As obvious as this may seem, it is probably the single most common basic error in tables of multivariate model results. In both linear and logistic regression models the estimated coefficients compare each of the included categories against the reference category. Without information on which category was omitted, readers cannot interpret the effects correctly (see "Coefficients on Categorical Independent Variables" in chapter 9). Name each "dummy" variable (also known as "binary" or "indicator" variable) after the category it embodies rather than the general concept measured by the categorical variable: "Married" not "Marital status," for example.

There are several conventions for identifying the reference category in a table. Usage varies, so check the guidelines in your discipline before you construct your table.

- Put parentheses around the row label for the omitted category of each variable.
- Place a symbol next to the row label for the omitted category.
- Identify the reference category in parentheses next to the row header for that variable, followed by indented row(s) naming the other categories. See table 9.1 for an example.
- Report an effect estimate of 0.00 (for an OLS or logit coefficient) or 1.00 (for relative risk or odds ratio), with "NA" or "—" in the corresponding column for statistical significance.

If you use one of the above conventions, explain it in a footnote to the table. Alternatively, you can include a footnote describing the omitted category for all variables combined, e.g., "the reference category is girls born to non-Hispanic white women with at least some college who did not smoke." Examples of these conventions appear in chapters 9 and 14.

Panels

Use panels—blocks of consecutive rows within a table separated by horizontal lines ("rules") or an extra blank row—to organize material within tables. Arrange them one above another with column headings shared by all panels. Panels can introduce another dimension to a table, show different measures of the relationship in the table, or organize rows into conceptually related blocks.

Adding a dimension to a table. Examples of tables that use panels to introduce an additional dimension to a table:

- Separate panels for different years. For example, the relationship between race, ethnic origin, and household structure (table 5.1) might be shown at 10-year intervals from 1960 through 2000 with each year in a separate panel, labeled accordingly. The panels introduce a third variable to a two-way (bivariate) table, in this case adding year to a cross-tabulation of household structure and race or origin. The panels would share the column headings (household structure), but repeat the row headings (for race and ethnic origin) in each panel.

- Separate panels for other characteristics. For instance, the relationship between household structure and race and ethnic origin might be shown for each of several regions or income levels.

Different measures for the same relationship. Also use panels to organize a table that presents different measures of the same concept, such as number of cases or events, along with measures of distribution or rate of occurrence:

- Table 5.1 could be modified to include a second panel reporting the *percentage* of households in each category to supplement the first panel showing the *number* of households.
- A table might present *number of deaths* according to cause or other characteristics in one panel and *death rates* in another, as in many Centers for Disease Control reports.

For these types of applications, repeat the row headings within each panel and specify the units separately in a header for each panel.

Organizing conceptually related blocks. When a table contains many related variables in the rows, use panels to organize them into blocks of similar items. In table 5.2 rather than lump all 10 questions on AIDS transmission into one section, the table is arranged into two panels—the top panel on knowledge of ways AIDS is likely to be transmitted, the bottom panel on ways it is unlikely to be transmitted—each labeled accordingly. Within each panel, results are shown separately for each specific question, followed by a summary statistic on that broad knowledge area. In a table presenting results of one or more multivariate models, organize the independent variables into conceptually related blocks, with major row headers to identify those concepts; see "Organizing Tables to Coordinate with Your Writing" below.

If two small, simple tables have the same column headers and address similar topics, you can combine them into a single table with panels, one panel for the set of rows from each of the smaller tables. Although table 5.2 could have been constructed as two separate tables — one on likely modes of AIDS transmission and the other on unlikely modes, creating a single table facilitates comparison across topics, such as pointing out that the likely modes are all better understood than the unlikely modes.

For tables that you describe in your text, avoid using more than two or three panels per table, and try to fit each table onto one page or on facing pages. Refer to each panel in your written description to direct readers to specific concepts and numbers as you mention them. Appendix tables that organize data for reference use can include more panels and spill onto several pages. For multipage tables, repeat the table number and column headings on each page, and label the panels (topics, units) so that your readers can follow them without written guidance.

Column Headings

Each column heading identifies the variable or measure (e.g., odds ratio, standard error) in that column. The guidelines listed above for labeling abbreviations, notes, and units in rows also apply to columns. If most numbers in a large table are measured in the same unit, use a spanner across columns to generalize with a phrase such as "percentage unless otherwise specified," then name the units for variables measured differently (e.g., in years of age or price in dollars) in the pertinent column heading.

Column Spanners

Column spanners (also known as "straddle rules") show that a set of columns is related, much as indenting shows how a set of rows is related. In table 5.1, households fall into two broad categories—family households and nonfamily households—each of which is demarcated with a column spanner. Beneath the spanners are the associated household subtypes: "Family households" comprise "Married couple" and "Other families," with "Other families" further subdivided into "Female householder" and "Male householder." Nonfamily households include those headed by a "Female householder" and those headed by a "Male householder." Each column spanner also encompasses a column for the total number of households of that type: the "Total" column under the "Family households" spanner is the sum of the "Married couple" and the two "Other families" columns.

Column Spanners to Organize Multivariate Model Output

In tables that report results of more than one multivariate model, use column spanners to group the columns with the effect estimates

Table 5.2. Use of panels to organize conceptually related sets of variables

Knowledge about AIDS transmission, by language spoken at home and ability to speak English, New Jersey, 1998

| Mode of transmission | Language spoken at home/ language used on questionnaire | | | Chi-square | (p-value) |
	English (N = 408)	Spanish/ English ques. (N = 32)	Spanish/ Spanish ques. (N = 20)		
Likely modes of transmission[a]					
Sexual intercourse with an infected person	93.6	87.5	95.0	1.9	(.39)
Shared needles for IV drug use	92.4	90.6	65.0	17.6	(.000)
Pregnant mother to baby	89.5	75.0	80.0	7.2	(.03)
Blood transfusion from infected person	87.5	81.3	60.0	12.5	(.002)
Mean percentage of "likely" questions correct	91.7	83.6	75.0	8.3[b]	(.000)

Unlikely modes of transmission[a]

Working near someone with the AIDS virus	81.6	75.0	35.0	25.4	(.000)
Using public toilets	66.4	53.1	30.0	12.7	(.002)
Eating in a restaurant where the cook has AIDS	61.3	50.0	35.0	3.7	(.04)
Being coughed or sneezed on	57.8	50.0	25.0	8.8	(.01)
Sharing plates, cups or utensils	56.4	46.9	25.0	8.3	(.02)
Visiting an infected medical provider	35.0	34.4	25.0	0.8	(.65)
Mean percentage of "unlikely" questions correct	59.8	51.6	29.2	8.2[b]	(.000)
Mean percentage of all questions correct	72.1	64.4	47.5	11.7[b]	(.000)

Source: Miller 2000a.

[a] Percentage of respondents answering AIDS transmission questions correctly.

[b] Test for difference based on ANOVA. Reported statistic is the *F*-statistic with 2 degrees of freedom.

and statistical test results for each model. There are several variants, including tables that present a series of nested models, tables with the same model specification for different subgroups, and tables with alternative model specifications. Label each column spanner to show which of these applications are displayed in that table. See illustrative applications under "Tables of Multivariate Models" below.

Interior Cells

Report your numbers in the interior cells of the table, following the guidelines in table 4.2 for number of digits and decimal places. Many disciplines omit numeric estimates based on only a few cases, either because of the substantial uncertainty associated with those estimates or to protect confidentiality of human subjects (appendix 1 in Benson and Marano 1998; NCHS 2002). Conventions about minimum sample sizes vary by discipline, so follow the standards in your field. If there is an insufficient number of cases to report data for one or more cells in your table, type a symbol in place of the numeric estimate and include a footnote that specifies the minimum size criterion and a pertinent citation.

Notes to Tables

Put information that does not fit easily in the title, row, or column labels in notes to the table. Spell out abbreviations, give brief definitions, and provide citations for data sources or other background information. To keep tables concise and tidy, limit notes to a simple sentence or two, referring to longer descriptions in the text or appendixes if more detail is needed. If a table requires more than one note, label them with different symbols or letters rather than numbers (which could be confused with exponents), then list the notes in that order at the bottom of the table following the conventions for your intended publisher. Labeling the notes with letters also allows the reader to distinguish table notes from text notes.

If you are using secondary data, provide a note to each table citing the name and date of the data set or a reference to a publication that describes it. If all tables in your article, report, or presentation use data from the same source, you might not need to cite it for every table. Some journals or publishers require the data source to be specified in every chart or table, however, so check the applicable guidelines.

■ COMMON TYPES OF TABLES

This section describes common variants of univariate, bivariate, three-way, and multivariate tables. See also Nicol and Pexman (1999) for guidance on tables to present specific types of statistics.

Univariate Tables

Univariate tables show information on each variable alone rather than associations among variables. Common types of univariate tables include those that present the distribution of a variable or composition of a sample (table 5.3) or descriptive statistics on the key independent variables and dependent variable for your study (table 5.4).

A univariate table can include more than one type of numeric information for each variable. Table 5.3 includes separate columns

Table 5.3. Univariate table: Sample composition

Demographic characteristics of study sample, Faketown, 2000

Demographic characteristic	Number of cases	Percentage of sample
Gender		
Male	1,000	48.6
Female	1,058	51.4
Age group (years)		
18–39	777	37.8
40–64	852	41.4
65+	429	20.8
Education		
<High school	358	17.4
=High school	1,254	60.9
>High school	446	21.7
Race/ethnicity		
Non-Hispanic white	1,144	55.6
Non-Hispanic black	455	22.1
Hispanic	328	15.9
Asian	86	4.2
Other race	45	2.2
Overall sample	2,058	100.0

Table 5.4. Univariate table: Descriptive statistics

Descriptive statistics on infant health and maternal characteristics, 1988–1994 NHANES III

	Mean	Standard deviation	Minimum	Maximum
Birth weight (grams)	3,379.2	37,877.3	397	5,896
Age of mother at child's birth (years)	26.0	339.7	11	49
Mother's education (years)	12.6	187.3	0	17
Income-to-poverty ratio[a]	2.28	91.51	0.00	8.47

Source: U.S. DHHS 1997.
Notes: Unweighted N = 9,813. Statistics weighted to national level using sampling weights provided with the NHANES (U.S. DHHS 1997). NHANES III = Third U.S. National Health and Nutrition Examination Survey, 1988–1994.
[a] Income-to-poverty ratio = family income divided by the Federal Poverty threshold for a family of that size and age composition.

for the number and percentage of cases with each attribute, labeled accordingly. Table 5.4 presents the mean, standard deviation, minimum, and maximum values for birth weight and several maternal characteristics.

A table can also be used to compare composition of a sample and target population (or universe), as in table 5.5, where characteristics of the NHANES III survey sample used to study birth weight are compared against those among all births that occurred nationally at about the same time. This type of comparative table could also present information on alternative measures of a concept, such as ratings of items at several points in time or from each of several sources (not shown).

Bivariate Tables

Bivariate, or two-way, tables show the relationship between two variables. Common types of bivariate tables are cross-tabulations, those that present differences in means or other statistics for one variable according to values of a second variable, and correlations. The

Table 5.5. Comparison of sample with target population

Birth weight, socioeconomic characteristics, and smoking behavior, NHANES III sample, 1988–1994, and all U.S. births, 1997

	NHANES III sample [abc]	All U.S. births, 1997 [d]
Birth weight		
Median (grams)	3,402	3,350
% Low birth weight (<2,500 grams)	6.8	7.5
Race/ethnicity		
Non-Hispanic white	73.4	68.4 [e]
Non-Hispanic black	16.9	17.0
Mexican American	9.7	14.6
Mother's age		
Median (years)	26.0	26.7
% Teen mother	12.5	12.7
Mother's education		
Median (years)	12.0	12.8
% < High school	21.6	22.1
% = High school	35.0	32.4
Mother smoked while pregnant (%)	24.5	13.2
Number of cases	9,813	3,880,894

[a] Weighted to population level using weights provided with the NHANES III (Westat 1996); sample size is unweighted.

[b] Information for NHANES III is calculated from data extracted from National Center for Health Statistics (U.S. DHHS 1997).

[c] Includes non-Hispanic white, non-Hispanic black, and Mexican American infants with complete information on family income, birth weight, maternal age, and education.

[d] Information for all U.S. births is from Ventura et al. (1999) except median mother's age (Mathews and Hamilton 2002).

[e] For consistency with the NHANES III sample, racial composition of U.S. births is reported as a percentage of births that are non-Hispanic white, non-Hispanic black, or Mexican American, excluding births of other Hispanic origins or racial groups. When all racial/ethnic groups are considered, the racial composition is 60.1% non-Hispanic white, 15.0% non-Hispanic black, 12.9% Mexican American, 5.4% other Hispanic origin, and 6.6% other racial groups.

Table 5.6. Bivariate table: Rates of occurrence based on a cross-tabulation

Percentage low birth weight by race/ethnicity, 1988–1994, NHANES III

	Non-Hispanic white	Non-Hispanic black	Mexican American	Total
Unweighted cases	3,733	2,968	3,112	9,813
% low birth weight[a]	5.8%	11.3%	7.0%	6.8%

Source: U.S. DHHS 1997.
Notes: Weighted to national level using sampling weights provided with the NHANES (U.S. DHHS 1997). NHANES III = Third U.S. National Health and Nutrition Examination Survey, 1988–1994.
[a] LBW $<$ 5.5 pounds or 2,500 grams.

nature of your variables—categorical or continuous—will determine which type of table applies to your topic.

Cross-Tabulations

A cross-tabulation shows the joint distribution of two categorical variables — how the overall sample is divided among all possible combinations of those two variables. Table 5.6 shows how the rate of low birth weight differs by race/ethnicity, calculated from a cross-tabulation of two variables: race/ethnicity and low birth weight status. The number of births that are low birth weight (LBW) in each racial/ethnic group can be calculated from the total number of births and the percentage LBW in each group (see "Which Numbers to Include" below).[2]

Differences in Means

Bivariate tables are also used to present statistics for one or more continuous variables according to some categorical variable. Table 5.2 shows how AIDS knowledge varies by language group, presenting mean scores for two topic areas ("likely" and "unlikely" modes of AIDS transmission) for each of three language groups.

Correlations

A bivariate table can present correlations among continuous variables. In table 5.7, each interior cell holds the pairwise correlation between the variables named in the associated row and column. For instance, in the late 1990s, the correlation between the child poverty rate and the unemployment rate in New Jersey's 21 counties was 0.75. Notes to the table show calculations and cite sources to define potentially unfamiliar measures used in the table.

To present more detailed information about the joint distribution of two continuous variables, use a line graph or scatter chart (see chapter 6).

Three-Way Tables

Three-way tables present information on associations among three variables or sets of related variables, such as the joint distribution of three categorical variables. One way to show a three-way relationship is to use column spanners. In table 5.8, the columns contain two categorical variables—race/ethnicity and mother's education—with rows to display the weighted mean and standard deviation of birth weight and the unweighted number of cases. The upper spanner divides the table into three mother's education groups, each of which encompasses columns for the three racial/ethnic groups. The interior cells present mean birth weight for each race/education combination. Placing educational attainment in the spanners facilitates comparison across race/ethnicity within each educational level because the races are in adjacent columns. To emphasize educational attainment differences within each racial/ethnic group, rearrange the table with race/ethnicity in the column spanner with the educational attainment groups underneath.

This type of design works only if the two variables used in the column spanners and the columns below have no more than a few categories apiece. For variables with more categories, use panels or a chart to present three-way relationships.

Tables of Multivariate Models

Follow the guidelines earlier in this chapter for effective titles, row and column labels, interior cells, and footnotes. A few special considerations for multivariate tables:

- In the title, name the type of model, the dependent variable and its units or coding, and a phrase summarizing the concepts captured by the independent variables.
- Label each column of effect estimates to convey whether it contains standardized or unstandardized coefficients, log-odds or odds ratios, etc.

Table 5.7. Bivariate table: Pairwise correlations

Correlations among county-level demographic and economic characteristics, New Jersey, 1999–2001

Characteristics	Demographic characteristics					Economic characteristics		
	Black pop.	Black ID[a]	Pop. density	Total pop.	Non-English speakers (%)	Unemp. rate (%)	Income inequality[b]	Child pov. rate (%)
Demographic								
Black population	1.00							
Black ID[a]	0.15	1.00						
Population density (persons/mi.²)	0.39	0.12	1.00					
Total population	0.31	0.12	0.58[d]	1.00				
Non-English speakers (%)	0.39	0.05	0.91[d]	0.49[c]	1.00			
Economic								
Unemployment rate (%)	0.31	−0.17	0.22	−0.16	0.33	1.00		
Income inequality[b]	0.10	0.94[d]	0.10	0.09	−0.02	−0.15	1.00	
Child poverty rate (%)	0.69[d]	−0.07	0.53[c]	0.12	0.61[d]	0.75[d]	−0.06	1.00

Source: Quality Resource Systems 2001.

Note: $N = 21$ counties.

[a] ID = Index of dissimilarity, a measure of residential segregation; see James and Taeuber (1985).

[b] Gini coefficient, a measure of income inequality; see Levy (1987).

[c] $p < 0.05$.

[d] $p < 0.01$.

Table 5.8. Three-way table with nested column spanners

Descriptive statistics on birth weight (grams) by race/ethnicity and mother's educational attainment, 1988–1994 NHANES III

	Mother's education								
	<High school			High school grad, no higher			>High School		
	Non-Hispanic white	Non-Hispanic black	Mexican American	Non-Hispanic white	Non-Hispanic black	Mexican American	Non-Hispanic white	Non-Hispanic black	Mexican American
Mean birth weight	3,299.9	3,089.9	3,345.2	3,361.5	3,177.5	3,365.1	3,506.9	3,283.4	3,384.1
Standard deviation	51,604.9	28,120.5	21,829.7	49,252.6	28,485.5	20,314.5	50,155.2	30,801.6	21,161.3
Unweighted N	596	903	1662	1309	1219	712	1762	725	446

Notes: Data are from U.S. DHHS 1997. Weighted to national level using sampling weights provided with the NHANES (U.S. DHHS 1997). NHANES III = Third U.S. National Health and Nutrition Examination Survey, 1988–1994.

- Label columns of statistical test results to identify which variant is presented—t-statistic, standard error, p-value, etc.
- Report and name goodness-of-fit (GOF) statistics for each model, either in a row at the bottom of the table or in a footnote. If more than one type of statistic is commonly used to assess or compare model fit (e.g., the F-statistic, adjusted and unadjusted R^2 for OLS models) label separate rows for each.
- Report number of degrees of freedom (df) in each model in another row or in parentheses next to the GOF statistic.
- Report the unweighted final sample size (N = number of cases with valid data; see chapter 12) for each model in the table. (A reminder: A multivariate model should be based on the same sample of cases as the accompanying univariate and bivariate analyses. Likewise, a series of nested models should be based on a consistent sample. Check the respective Ns in your computer output *before* you type your tables.)

Tables of multivariate models can show results of one model, results of several models for the same sample, or results of the same model specification for several samples or subgroups.

One Model

To present the results of one multivariate model, create a table with columns for the effect estimates and statistical test results, and a row for each independent variable. Tables 5.9a and 5.9b illustrate poor and better tables to present results of the same multivariate model. Numbers in parentheses within each table are keyed to the statements below. The poor version has so many problems that the results are at best subject to considerable misinterpretation, and at worst, almost completely inaccessible. Even if you are a veteran quantitative analyst, do not assume that you are immune to such errors: I collected these examples not only from student papers, but also from articles by senior researchers published in elite peer-reviewed journal articles.

Statement 1

Poor: "Model of insurance"

In addition to lacking information about the context (W's), this title has more problems than it has words.

- First, it is not clear what kind of insurance (life? health? auto?) or which aspect of insurance this model is analyzing:

Table 5.9a. Table of multivariate model results: Poor version

(1) Model of insurance

	Effect estimate (8)	Sig. (9)
Intercept		
Income (2)	0.0008 (3)	3.20
Gender (4)	1.21	1.71
Empstat1 (5)	0.92	1.88
Empstat2	0.52	5.51*
Q727a (6)	1.70	3.87*
Q727b	1.02	0.80
Model GOF (7)	88.1	0.001

Table 5.9b. Table of multivariate model results: Better version

(1) Estimated odds ratios from a logistic regression of lacking health insurance, by sociodemographic factors and attitudes about insurance, Mystate, 1999

	Odds ratio (8)	χ^2 (9)
Intercept		
Income ($10,000s) (2)	0.80 (3)	3.20
Male (4)	1.21	1.71
Employment status (5) (Unemployed)		
Part time	0.92	1.88
Full time	0.52	5.51**
Attitudes about health insurance (6)		
Willing to risk low health care needs	1.70	3.87*
Don't like available insurance options	1.02	0.80
−2 Log likelihood vs. null (7)	88.1** (6 df)	

Notes: $N = 7{,}244$; df = number of degrees of freedom relative to the null model.

*$p < 0.05$. **$p < 0.01$.

Type of insurance (e.g., employer-based versus Medicaid versus . . .)? The dollar value of the policy? The cost of the premium? Insurance status (e.g., insured versus uninsured)? The latter is the one that is modeled here, but that is not conveyed by the title.

- Second, even knowing that in this case "insurance" is a categorical measure of health insurance status, the model could have been estimated with any of several statistical methods (e.g., logit, probit, or log-linear). Because the output and interpretation differ for each of these methods, state which was used to generate the results in the table.
- Third, even for a logistic regression of insured versus uninsured, without knowing which category is being modeled, readers can't tell whether the reported effects are odds ratios for *being uninsured* (as in table 5.9a) or of *being insured*—diametrically opposite interpretations.
- Finally, no information is given about what explanatory variables or concepts are included in the model. Use the title to orient readers to the specific aspects of the research question presented in the table.

Better: "Estimated odds ratios from a logistic regression of lacking health insurance, by sociodemographic factors and attitudes about insurance, Mystate, 1999."
This version names the dependent variable (health insurance) and which category is being modeled ("lacking"), statistical method (logistic regression), independent variables (sociodemographic factors and attitudes about insurance), and the W's.

Statements 2 and 3
Poor: "Income"
There are two issues here:
- Statement 2: Income appears to have been specified as a continuous variable, so readers will probably assume the "income effect" is that of a one-unit ($1) increase in income. To eliminate ambiguity, specify the units in the row label.
- Statement 3: The income coefficient is displayed with many more digits than the other variables in the model because the effect of a $1 increase in income is quite small. With such variables, consider reestimating the model with income

measured in increments of $1,000 or even $10,000—a substantively meaningful difference that will produce a more easily measured (and reported) effect size. Or use logged income as the predictor.

Better: "Income ($10,000s)"

Units are specified, and the new scale of income measurement yields an effect size consistent with others in the model and of greater real-world interest.

Statement 4

Poor: "Gender"

Gender is obviously a categorical variable, but this label doesn't identify the reference category. Without such information, how is the reader to know whether males are being compared to females (in which case an odds ratio of 1.21 would indicate higher odds among males), or females to males (meaning higher odds among females)?

Better: "Male"

By naming the included category of a binary variable, this label clearly conveys the direction of the comparison.

Statement 5

Poor: "Empstat1, Empstat2"

Eight-character variable names from software are poor ways to identify variables in your tables. Whoever created the dummy variables and specified the model hopefully remembers what Empstat1 and Empstat2 mean, but readers won't, nor should they have to search in the text to find out. In this example, the categories of employment status and the identity of the reference category are unspecified. Moreover, because their row labels aren't indented or grouped, any relationship between those two variables is ambiguous.

Better: "Part time; Full time"

Each employment status category is named in the table. The reference category (unemployed) is identified in parentheses and further signaled by the lack of a parameter estimate. A major row header coupled with indented categories show that these variables together comprise the categories of employment status.

Statement 6

Poor: "Q727a; Q727b"

Variable names based on question number can help you remember which questionnaire items were the original source of the data, but obscure the variables' identities. Feel free to use such shorthand in your data sets and in initial drafts of your tables, but replace them with meaningful phrases in the version your audience will see.

Better: "Attitudes about health insurance: Willing to risk low health care needs; Don't like available insurance options."

The new section of rows, its label, and the row labels for these variables clarify that they are measures of attitudes about health insurance. Each attitude is named in easily understood terms and the values being modeled ("willing to risk"; "don't like") are specified so that direction of association can be interpreted. If the names are too long to fit in a row label, create a footnote or refer to the data section or an appendix that contains a more detailed description or the wording of the original question.

Statement 7

Poor: "Model GOF"

There are several GOF (goodness-of-fit) statistics for most types of statistical models, so a general label like "Model GOF" is uninformative. Moreover, the acronym isn't defined within the table and degrees of freedom aren't reported.

Better: " −2 Log likelihood vs. null"

This version identifies the specific goodness-of-fit test. The asterisk next to the numeric test result is keyed to a footnote explaining the associated p-value, and the number of degrees of freedom for the model is shown in parenthesis next to the associated GOF statistic.

Statement 8

Poor: "Effect estimate"

For a logistic model, the coefficient is the log-odds, but some authors transform the log-odds into odds ratios. If some of the "effect estimates" in table 5.9a were negative, they would have to be log-odds because an odds ratio cannot be less than 0.0, but why make your readers work that hard to figure out what type of statistic you are reporting? You are trying to convey results, not give a statistics quiz.

Better: "Odds ratio"

This label removes any uncertainty about which measure of effect size is being reported. In conjunction with information on which category of the dependent variable is being modeled and the units or omitted categories of the independent variables, readers can interpret the findings without outside guidance.

Statement 9

Poor: "Sig."

"Sig." is a reasonable abbreviation for "significance," but which type of statistical significance test result is being shown? With some thought, a statistically savvy reader could tell that this column is not reporting a p-value (which must fall between 0 and 1) or a confidence interval (requiring two values, one each for the lower and upper confidence limits). Don't make them speculate — just tell them.

Better: "χ^2"

This label clarifies that the column is reporting a test statistic and specifies which one. If your audience is unfamiliar with Greek symbols, you might spell out "chi-square statistic" in lieu of "χ^2."

Several Models

Most of the above guidelines also apply to tables that present results of several multivariate models. A few additional considerations:

- Include a phrase in the title to convey how the models differ, or at least that the table presents results of more than one model. Examples:

    ". . . from a series of nested models."

    ". . . for each of [N] age/sex groups."

    ". . . using three alternative parametric specifications of . . ."

- Use column labels or spanners to differentiate among the models in the table, giving each a different name in both the table and associated text. See examples below.
- Report sample size for each model in the table.

    For nested models or alternative specifications for a given sample, the number of cases should be consistent for all models in the table (check your output), and can be reported just once in a table footnote or row near the GOF statistics.

    In a table showing the same model for several subgroups, places, or dates, sample sizes usually vary. Create a row labeled "sample size" or "unweighted N" to report the sample sizes for each subgroup in the pertinent column, or put the value in the associated column header.

Common variants of tables presenting more than one model include nested models, alternative specifications, and separate models for different subgroups. Avoid mixing these different objectives within one table. For example, do not compare a model for one sub-group with a different statistical model for a different subgroup within one table. If your objectives include *both* comparing models across subgroups and testing out alternative statistical specifications for one or more of those groups, design two separate tables, each of which presents the relevant models for one of those contrasts.

Nested models. Nested models are often used to test for potential mediating or confounding factors, starting with a model with only the key predictor, then adding successive variables thought to mediate or confound its relation with the dependent variable (see "Comparing a Series of Nested Models" in chapter 14). To present results of that type of analysis, state in the title that the table presents a series of nested models, then organize the models using column spanners to cluster the effect estimate and statistical test result for each model. If possible, label each spanner with a short name summarizing the specification for each model, as shown below. If such labels are too long to fit in the column spanner, name each model with a number (e.g., Model I, Model II, etc.), then explain the contents and sequence of models in your methods section (see chapter 14). Refer to each model by name in the associated descriptions of the results.

Estimated coefficients from a series of OLS models of birth weight (grams), United States, 1988–1994

	Model I Infant traits only		Model II Infant traits & SES		Model III Infant traits, SES & smoking	
Variable	Coeff.	s.e.	Coeff.	s.e.	Coeff.	s.e.
Name of variable	##	##	##	##	##	##

In a table of nested models, some interior cells will be empty, reflecting the inclusion of different sets of independent variables in each of the models. For example, neither model I nor model II would include coefficients or standard errors for the maternal smoking variable.

Same model specification for different subgroups. To compare results of the same model specification for different subgroups (e.g., stratified models), title each column spanner after the respective subgroup. The example below shows how these spanners can be nested further to display several levels of clustering—in this case different models for each of four age/sex groups. Depending on your analytic strategy, you might include the same set of independent variables for all subgroups or estimate parsimonious models for each subgroup. Include a row for every variable that appears in at least one of the models. Report sample sizes and GOF statistics for each model at the bottom of the table.

Ordinary least squares regression of income ($) by gender, age group, and background characteristics, New York State, 1999

	Men				Women			
	<35 years		35−64 years		<35 years		35−64 years	
Variable	Coeff.	s.e.	Coeff.	s.e.	Coeff.	s.e.	Coeff.	s.e.
Name of variable	#	#	#	#	#	#	#	#

A similar structure could be used to compare models for different places or dates.

Alternative functional forms. To present results for models with alternative specifications (e.g., different parametric hazards models of the age pattern of mortality, or a comparison of fixed-effects and random-effects models), title the table accordingly, then label each column spanner with the name of the specification used in that model.

Different parametric specifications of a continuous-time hazards model of the age pattern of mortality, United States, 2003

	Exponential		Weibull		Gompertz	
Variable	Log-hazard	z-statistic	Log-hazard	z-statistic	Log-hazard	z-statistic
Name of variable	#	#	#	#	#	#

If your main objective is to compare overall model goodness-of-fit, create a table with one column per model with rows to report only degrees of freedom and GOF statistics—no spanners needed. If evaluating the robustness of individual coefficients is your main objective, report effect estimates and statistical tests for the independent variables in each model in the rows below, with additional rows for overall model GOF statistics.

Models of multinomial dependent variables. Models involving multinomial dependent variables contrast more than two categories of outcomes. They comprise ranked (ordinal) dependent variables and unordered (nominal) dependent variables, including competing risks models. For example, you might estimate models of heart disease, cancer, and all other causes of death. These analyses involve estimating a separate model for each outcome, with all other alternatives as the omitted category of the dependent variable for that model (Powers and Xie 2000). To organize a table of results for multinomial models, name each column after the category being modeled. For ordinal dependent variables, organize the columns in the ranked order of the categories. For nominal variables, use theoretical or empirical criteria to determine the order of outcome categories in the columns.

Competing risks model of cause of death by socioeconomic and behavioral factors, United States, 2000

	Heart disease		Cancer		All other causes	
	Relative risk	z-statistic	Relative risk	z-statistic	Relative risk	z-statistic
Name of variable	#	#	#	#	#	#

■ ORGANIZING TABLES TO COORDINATE WITH YOUR WRITING

As you write about the patterns shown in your tables, proceed systematically. Decide on the main point you want to make about the data using one or more of the principles described below. Arrange the rows and columns accordingly, then describe the numbers in the same order they appear in the table. If possible, use the same organizing principles in all the tables within a document, such as tables reporting descriptive statistics and multivariate results for the same set of variables. In most cases, theoretical criteria will determine the order in which you include variables in your multivariate models, so use those same criteria to organize the associated univariate, bivariate, and three-way tables.

When reporting results for ordinal variables, the sequence of items in rows or columns will be obvious. List the possible response categories in their ranked order: from "Excellent" to "Poor" or from "Agree strongly" to "Disagree strongly," for example, either in ascending or descending order, depending on how you prefer to discuss them. Arrange information for each of several dates in chronological order.

For nominal variables (such as religion or race), tables that encompass several different variables (such as AIDS knowledge topics), or tables of multivariate results, the categories or variables do not have an inherent order. In those instances, use one or more of the following principles to organize them.

Theoretical Grouping

Arranging items into theoretically related sets can be very effective. Using panels to separate likely and unlikely modes of AIDS transmission in table 5.2 reveals important distinctions between the items that would be obscured if they were listed in one undifferentiated block. The accompanying discussion can then emphasize that the former topics were much better understood than the latter without asking readers to zigzag through the table to find the pertinent numbers.

In a multivariate model specification, first organize your variables into conceptually similar groups such as demographic traits, socioeconomic characteristics, and behaviors. Then arrange those blocks in the table to match their roles in your analysis, position in the causal sequence, or order of importance for your research question. Most analyses concern relationships among two or three variables, with other variables playing a less important role. Logically, you will discuss the key variables first, so put them at the top of your table. For instance, a table of univariate descriptive statistics for a study of how race and socioeconomic characteristics relate to birth weight might put the dependent variable (birth weight) in the top row, followed by the main independent variable or variables (race and socioeconomic status), and then other factors considered in the study (e.g., smoking behavior; see table 5.5). For journals that permit only limited description of model results, this kind of organization and labeling is essential, as readers must be able to discern the roles of the variables solely from the table.

Empirical Ordering

For many tables presenting distributions or associations, an important objective is to show which items have the highest and the lowest values and where other items fall relative to those extremes. If this is your main point, organize your univariate or bivariate table in ascending or descending order of numeric values or frequency. An international health report might list countries in rank order of infant mortality, life expectancy, and death rates from AIDS or other causes of death, for example. If the ranking varies for different variables shown in the table, decide which you will emphasize, then use it as the basis for organizing the rows.

Alphabetical Ordering

Few substantively meaningful patterns happen to occur alphabetically, hence alphabetical order is usually a poor principle for arranging items within tables to be discussed in the text. On the other hand, alphabetical order is often the best way to organize data in appendix tables or other large data tabulations that are not accompanied by written guidance. In such cases, using a familiar convention helps readers find specific information quickly. The daily stock market report of opening, closing, high, and low prices of thousands of stocks is a well-known example.

Order of Items from a Questionnaire

Unless your analysis is mainly concerned with evaluating the effects of questionnaire design on response patterns, do not list items in the order they appeared on the questionnaire. Again, this order is unlikely to correspond to underlying empirical or theoretical patterns, so your table and description will not match.

Multiple Criteria for Organizing Tables

For tables with more than a few rows of data, a combination of approaches may be useful for organizing univariate or bivariate statistics. You might group items according to their characteristics, then arrange them *within* those groups in order of descending frequency or other empirical consideration. In table 5.2, knowledge of AIDS transmission is first grouped into likely and unlikely modes of transmission, then in descending order of knowledge within each of those classifications.

Sometimes it makes sense to apply the same criterion sequentially, such as identifying major theoretical groupings and then minor topic groupings within them. Political opinion topics could be classified into domestic and foreign policy, for example, each with a major row heading. Within domestic policy would be several items apiece on education, environment, health, transportation, and so forth, yielding corresponding subcategories and sets of rows. Foreign policy would also encompass several topics.

If you have organized your table into several theoretically or empirically similar groups of items, alphabetical order can be a logical way to sequence items *within* those groups. For example, data on the 50 United States are often grouped by major census region, then presented in alphabetical order within each region. Alphabetical order within conceptual or empirical groupings also works well if several items have the same value of the statistics reported in the table (e.g., mean or frequency). Conventions about placement of "total" rows vary, with some publications placing them at the top of the table or panel, others at the bottom. Consult your publisher's instructions to decide where to place your total row.

■ TECHNICAL CONSIDERATIONS

Which Numbers to Include

A table is a tool for presenting numeric evidence, not a database for storing data or a spreadsheet for doing calculations. Except for a data appendix or a laboratory report, omit the raw data for each case: readers don't need to wade through values of every variable for every case in a large data set. Generally you will also leave out numbers that represent intermediate steps in calculating your final statistics. Like a carpenter, do the messy work (data collection and calculations) correctly, then present a clean, polished final product. Decide which numbers are needed to make the table's substantive points, then keep the other data out of the table, where your readers don't trip over it on their way to the important stuff.

The output from a statistical program is usually a poor prototype of a table for publication: such output often includes information that isn't directly relevant to your research question and thus should be omitted from your table. For example, output from a cross-tabulation usually shows the count (number of cases), row percentage, column percentage, and percentage of the overall (grand) total for every cell. Determine which of those statistics answer the question at hand—usually *one* of the percentages and possibly the number of cases for each cell—and report only those numbers in your table. In most instances, report the number of cases only for the margins of a cross-tabulation (as in table 5.6), because the counts for interior cells can be calculated from the marginals (the row and column subtotals found at the edges, or margins, of the cross-tabulation) and the interior percentages.

Cross-tabulations of dichotomous variables in particular include a lot of redundant information. If you report the percentage of cases that are male, the percentage female is unnecessary because by definition, it is 100% minus the percentage male. Likewise for variables coded true/false, those that indicate whether some event (e.g., a divorce, cancer incidence) did or did not happen, whether a threshold was or wasn't crossed (e.g., low birth weight, the legal alcohol limit), or other variants of yes/no.[3] Hence a tabulation of approval of legal abortion (a yes/no variable) by a six-category religion variable will yield 12 interior cells, eight marginals, and the grand total, each of which contains counts and one or more percentages. In your final table, only seven of those numbers are needed to compare abortion attitudes across groups: the share of each religious group that believes abortion should be legal and the approval rate for all religions combined; subgroup sample sizes could also be included if they aren't reported elsewhere.

Similarly, regression output from a statistical package typically includes far more information than you need to communicate your findings. See chapter 10 and appendix B for suggestions on creating an effective table from multivariate regression output.

Number of Decimal Places and Scale of Numbers

Within each column, use a consistent scale and number of decimal places. For instance, do not switch from grams in one row to kilograms in other rows. Likewise, keep the scale and number of decimal places the same for all columns reporting numbers measured in similar units: if all your columns show death rates, use a uniform scale (e.g., deaths per 100,000 persons across the board, not per 1,000 in some columns).

Follow the guidelines in chapter 4 regarding the following:

- Number of digits and decimal places that inform but do not overwhelm. Change the scale or use scientific notation to avoid presenting overly long numbers or those with many zeros as placeholders.
- Conventions about decimal places for certain kinds of numbers: two decimal places for small monetary denominations, none for integers
- Precision of measurement that is consistent with the original data collection

- Sufficient detail to evaluate statistical test results (e.g., for p-values or test statistics)

Alignment

There are certain standard or sensible ways to align the contents of different table components:

- Left-justify row labels, then use indenting to show subgroups.
- Use decimal alignment in the interior cells to line up the numbers properly within each column, especially if symbols are used in some but not all rows (e.g., to denote statistical significance). Right alignment works too, assuming you have used a consistent number of decimal places for all numbers in the column and no symbols are needed.
- Center column titles over the pertinent column and column spanners over the range of columns to which they apply.

Portrait versus Landscape Layout

Tables can be laid out in one of two ways: *portrait* (with the long dimension of the page vertical, like table 5.3), or *landscape* (with the long dimension horizontal, like table 5.1). For print documents and Web pages, start with a portrait layout because the accompanying text pages are usually vertical. For slides or chartbooks, start with a landscape layout to match the rest of the document.

These general considerations aside, pick a layout that will accommodate the number of rows and columns needed to hold your information. If you have more than a dozen rows, use a portrait layout or create a multipanel landscape table that will flow onto more than one page. Unless your column labels and the numbers in the corresponding interior cells are very narrow, four to five columns are the most that can fit in a portrait layout, up to 12 narrow columns in a landscape layout.

Consider alternative arrangements of variables in the rows and columns. If you are cross-tabulating two variables, there is no law that decrees which variable must go in the rows. Take, for example, a table comparing characteristics of geographic entities: the 50 United States are virtually always listed in the rows because a 50-column table would be ungainly. On the other hand, the six populated continents easily fit within the columns of a landscape table. Which variable to put in the rows is determined by the number of categories (countries or continents), not the concept being measured. A long, skinny table can be revised by bringing the bottom half up alongside the top half.

Repeat the column heads side by side and separate the two halves by a vertical rule.

Layouts for Reporting Coefficients and Statistical Test Results

Two different table layouts are commonly used for presenting coefficients and their associated inferential test results (e.g., standard errors, test statistics, confidence intervals, or p-values):

- Adjacent columns, as in table 5.9. To present more than one model within a single table using this type of layout, create a column spanner to show which statistics pertain to each model.
- Consecutive rows, with the statistical test result typed in parentheses beneath the estimated coefficient, as in the example below. For this layout, label the column to identify the type of statistic, and to illustrate the convention that it is reported in parentheses.

Estimated coefficients and standard errors (s.e.) from an OLS model of birth weight (grams) by racial/ethnic, socioeconomic, and smoking characteristics, United States, 1988–1994

Variable	Coeff. (s.e.)
Intercept	3,039.8 (39.2)

To choose between these two layouts, consider how many models and variables you need to present. The two-row-per-variable approach creates a longer table that can accommodate results of several models if each contains relatively few variables. The two-column-per-variable approach yields a wider table that is better suited to fewer models or those with many independent variables. Some journals specify a particular layout, so check the requirements for authors.

Type Size

For your tables, use a type size consistent with that in your text—no more than one or two points smaller. With the possible exception of reference tables, tiny scrunched labels with lots of abbreviations and microscopically printed numbers are usually a sign that you are trying to put too much into one table. Redesign it into several tables, each of which encompasses a conceptually related subset of the original table. Arrange a large appendix table into a few panels per page using one or more of the criteria explained above to divide and organize the variables so readers can find information of interest easily.

Table and Cell Borders

Many word processing programs initially create tables with gridlines delineating the borders between cells. However, once you have typed in the row and column labels, most of those lines are no longer needed to guide readers through your table. Places where it *is* useful to retain lines within a table include borders between panels, and lines to designate a column spanner.

Word processing programs offer table templates or auto formatting—predesigned formats complete with fancy colors, fonts, shading, and lines of different thickness. While some lines and other features can make it easier to read a table, others simply add what Edward Tufte (2001) refers to as "nondata ink": aspects of the design that distract readers rather than adding to the function of the table. Design your tables to emphasize the substantive questions and pertinent data, not superfluous eye candy.

Formatting for Different Publications

Table formatting varies by discipline and publisher. Some require titles to be left-justified, others centered. Some require all capital letters, others mixed upper- and lowercase. Many journals have specific guidelines for labeling footnotes to tables and using other symbols within tables. Requirements for punctuation and use of lines within the table also vary. Consult a manual of style for your intended publisher before you design your tables. Even if you aren't required to follow specific guidelines, be consistent as you format your tables: do not left-justify one table title, then center the title for the next table, or label footnotes to one table with letters but use symbols to denote footnotes in a second.

■ DRAFTING YOUR TABLES

Conceptualize the contents and layout of a table early in the writing process, certainly before you start typing the information into a word processor and possibly even before you collect or analyze the data. Identifying the main question to be addressed by each table helps you anticipate the statistics to be calculated. Thinking ahead about the specific points you will make about patterns in the table helps you design a layout that coordinates with the description.

Drafting Your Table with Pencil and Paper

To create an effective table, plan before you type. Separating these steps helps you think about a layout and labels that emphasize the substantive concepts to be conveyed before you get caught up in the point-and-click task of creating the table on a computer. By not planning ahead, you are more likely to write incomplete titles or labels, create too few columns or rows, overlook important features like column spanners or footnotes, and arrange these elements poorly. You must then go back and reconstruct the table on the screen—quite a hassle if the numbers have already been typed in—increasing the risk that numbers end up in the wrong cells of the table.

To test possible layouts for your tables, use scrap paper, a pencil, and an eraser. Don't skimp on paper by trying to squeeze drafts of all four (or however many) tables you need to plan onto one page. Use a full page for each table. Expect to have to start over a couple of times, especially if you are new to planning tables or are working with unfamiliar concepts, variables, or types of statistical analyses.

Determining the Shape and Size of Your Table

Create one column for each set of numbers to be displayed vertically, then add a column for row labels. Make the column for row labels wide enough to accommodate a short, intelligible phrase that identifies the contents (and sometimes units) in each row. Most numeric columns can be narrower (see below).

Count how many variables you will be displaying in the rows, then add rows to accommodate the table title and column headings. Depending on the content and organization of your table, you may need additional rows to fit column spanners, labels for panels, information on the overall sample (e.g., total sample size), results of statistical tests, or simply white space to increase ease of reading.

Once you know how many rows and columns you need, assess whether a landscape or portrait layout will work better. For tables with approximately equal numbers of rows and columns, try it both ways to see which fits the information better and is easier to read. Orient your scrap paper accordingly, then draw in gridlines to delineate the rows and columns. Erase gridlines to show column spanners and draw in horizontal lines to differentiate panels. The idea is to have a grid within which you can test out the labels and other components of the table. You will probably redesign and redraw it a couple of times before you are satisfied, so don't bother to measure exact spacing or draw perfect, straight lines in your rough drafts. The software will that do for you, once you have decided what the table should look like.

Interior Cells

The interior cells of the table are where your numbers will live. When planning column widths, consider the following questions:

- What is the maximum number of digits you will need in each column?
- Do you need to include unit indicators (e.g., $, %), thousands' separators (e.g., the comma in "1,000"), or other characters that will widen your column?
- Will you be using symbols within the table cells, to key them to a footnote or indicate statistical significance, for example?

Evaluating Your Table Layout

Before you type your table into a word processor, evaluate it for completeness and ease of understanding. To test whether your table can stand alone, pick several cells within the table and see whether you can write a complete sentence describing the identity and meaning of those numbers using only the information provided in the table. Better yet, have someone unfamiliar with your project do so.

Creating your Table in a Word Processor

Word processing software can be a real boon for creating a table: simply tell your computer to make a seven-column by 12-row table on a landscape page and voilà! However, some word processors think they know what you want better than you do, and will automatically format aspects of your table such as page layout, alignment, type size, and whether text wraps to the next line. After you have created the basic table structure on the computer, save it, then check carefully that each part of the table appears as you showed it on your rough draft. Occasionally, the computer's ideas will improve upon yours, however, so consider them as well.

A few hints:

- *Before* you begin to create the table, inform the word processor whether you want a portrait or landscape page layout, then save the document. Then when you specify the desired number of columns, their width will be calculated based on the full available width (usually 6.5″ for portrait, 9.5″ for landscape, assuming 1″ margins all around). Much easier than manually resizing columns from portrait to landscape after the fact . . .
- Specify alignment for each part of the table after creating the initial grid. An alternative in some software programs is to impose a selected, preformatted design for your table (see your software manual or Help menu for more information).
- Alter appearance of table and cell borders.

    Once titles and labels are in place, omit many cell borders for a cleaner look.

    Resize column widths to accommodate row labels and numbers.

    Delineate panels within the table. If you have omitted most row borders, use a single, thin line or a blank row to separate panels; if you have retained borders between all rows, use a thicker line, a double line, or a blank row between panels.

As you transfer your design into the word processor, you may discover that a different layout will work better, so learn from what appears on the screen and then revise it to suit.

■ CHECKLIST FOR CREATING EFFECTIVE TABLES

- Title: write an individualized title for each table.
    State the purpose or topic of that table.
    Include the context of the data (the W's).
    Mention the type of statistical model, the dependent variable, and the conceptual groups of key independent variables.
    For models of categorical dependent variables, name the category being modeled.
- Other labeling
    Label each row and column.
    −Briefly identify its contents.
    −Specify units or coding if not summarized in table title.
    −Identify reference categories of dummy variables.
- Footnotes
    Identify the data source (if not in table title).
    Define all abbreviations and symbols used within the table.
- Structure and organization
    Use indenting or column spanners to show how adjacent rows or columns relate.
    Apply theoretical and empirical principles to organize rows and columns.
    −For text tables, coordinate row and column sequence with order of discussion.
    −For appendix tables, use alphabetical order or another widely known principle for the topic so tables are self-guiding.
    Report the fewest number of digits and decimal places needed for your topic, data, and types of statistics.
    Use consistent formatting, alignment, and symbols in all tables in a document.
- Check that the table can be understood without reference to the text.

Creating Effective Charts

Charts have some real advantages for communicating statistical findings, making it easy to observe direction and magnitude of trends and differences, assess statistical significance of effects, or synthesize net patterns of multiterm calculations. The many uses of charts in articles or speeches about multivariate analyses include the following:

- Displaying sample composition in terms of the key variables in your analysis
- Portraying bivariate or three-way associations among your dependent and independent variables
- Illustrating net effects for patterns that involve several terms such as polynomials or interactions
- Showing the shapes of other nonlinear functions such as those involving logarithmic transformations
- Facilitating visual hypothesis-testing with the addition of confidence intervals around point estimates
- Conveying results of competing risks models or other analyses that compare multiple outcomes
- Presenting model fit diagnostics such as fitted lines against observed values or plots of residuals
- Showing the sensitivity of results to alternative assumptions, definitions, or model specifications

Although these benefits are most pronounced for speeches and lay audiences, they are often underutilized in scientific papers. In any of those contexts, charts are an effective, efficient way to convey patterns, keeping the focus on your story line rather than requiring readers to do a lot of mental gymnastics to calculate or compare numbers.

I begin this chapter with a quick tour of the anatomy of a chart followed by general guidelines about features shared by several types of charts. Using examples of pie, bar, line, and scatter charts and their variants, I then show how to choose the best type of chart for different topics and types of variables. Finally, I discuss additional design considerations and common pitfalls in chart creation. For other resources on chart design, see Tufte (1990, 1997, 2001), Briscoe (1996), and Zelazny (2001).

■ ANATOMY OF A CHART

Many of the principles for designing effective tables apply equally to charts.

- Label the chart so readers can identify its purpose and interpret the data from the titles and labels alone.
- Make the chart self-contained, including units, context, data sources, and definitions of abbreviations.
- Design each chart to promote understanding of the patterns in that chart and to coordinate with your written description.
- Create charts that emphasize the evidence related to your research question rather than drawing undue attention to the structure of the charts themselves.

Chart Titles

The same principles that guide creation of table titles also work for charts.

- Specify the topic and W's in each chart title. A short restatement of the research question or relationships shown in the chart often works well.
- Use the title to differentiate the topic of each chart from those of other charts and tables in the same document.

Axis titles, labels, and legends identify the concepts and units of the variables in charts, much as row and column labels do in tables.

Axis Titles and Axis Labels

Charts that illustrate the relations between two or more variables usually have an x (horizontal) axis and a y (vertical) axis. Give each axis a title that identifies its contents and units of measurement, and include labels for categories or values along that axis. Write brief but informative axis titles and labels, using short phrases or single words instead of acronyms whenever possible. In the axis *title* name the overall concept ("Year" for the x axis title in figure 6.1), then assign axis *labels* to identify values (1990, 2010, 2030 . . . ; figure 6.1) or category names (Saudi Arabia, Russia, etc.; figure 6.4) along the axis.

For continuous variables, minimize clutter by marking major in-

Projected population under low, middle, and high growth rates, United States, 2000–2100

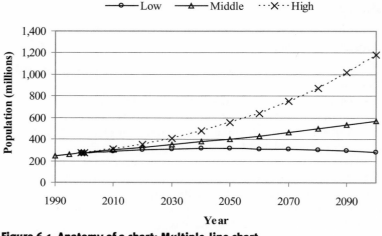

Figure 6.1. Anatomy of a chart: Multiple-line chart.
Source: U.S. Census Bureau 2000a.

crements of the units, aiming for 5 to 10 value labels on each axis. Remember, charts are best used when precise values aren't important, so your axis labels need only show approximate values. To choose an appropriate increment for the axis scale, consider the range, scale, precision of measurement, and how the data were collected. To present census data for 1950 through 2000, for example, make those dates the limits of the axis values and label 10-year increments to match the data collection years.

In the chart title name the general concepts or variables ("projected population" in figure 6.1), then give specific units for that dimension (millions) in the axis title. For pie charts, which don't have axes, identify units in the title, footnote, or data labels.

Legends

Use a legend to identify the series or categories of variables that are not labeled elsewhere in the chart. In figure 6.1, the legend specifies which line style corresponds to each of the three growth rates. See below for how to use legends in other types of charts.

Data Labels

Data labels are typed numeric values adjacent to the pertinent slice, point, or bar in a chart (e.g., the reported percentages in figure 6.2b). To keep charts simple and readable, use data labels sparingly. Again, the main advantage of a chart is that it can illustrate general levels or patterns, which will be evident without data labels if your chart has adequate titles. Complement the general depiction in the chart with your text description, reporting exact values of selected numbers to document the patterns (see appendix A for guidelines). If your audience requires exact values for all numbers in the chart, replace the chart with a table or include an appendix table rather than putting data labels on every point.

Reserve data labels for reference points or for reporting absolute level associated with a pie or stacked bar chart, such as total number of cases or total value of the contents of the pie or stacked bar (e.g., total dollar value of annual outlays in figures 6.2 and 6.9b). See pertinent sections below for more on data labels.

▪ CHART TYPES AND THEIR FEATURES

Charts to Illustrate Univariate Distributions

Univariate charts present data for only one variable apiece, showing how cases are distributed across categories (for nominal or ordinal variables) or numeric values (for interval or ratio variables).

Pie Charts

Most people are familiar with pie charts from elementary school. A pie chart is a circle divided into slices like a pizza, with each slice representing a different category of a variable, such as expenditure categories in the federal budget (figure 6.2). The size of each slice illustrates the relative size or frequency of the corresponding category. Identify each slice either in a legend (figures 6.2a and b) or in a value label adjacent to each slice (figure 6.2c). Although you can also label each slice with the absolute amount or percentage of the whole that it contributes (figure 6.2b), the basic story in the chart is often adequately illustrated without reporting specific numeric values: is one slice much larger (or smaller) than the others, or are they all about equal? Pie charts also work well to display the composition of a study sample in terms of nominal characteristics. Create one pie to illustrate each trait (e.g., one for race composition, another for gender).

To compare two or three pie charts that differ in the total quantity

a. U.S. federal outlays by function, 2000

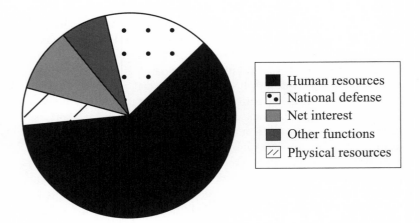

Total outlays: $1.8 trillion

b. U.S. federal outlays by function, 2000

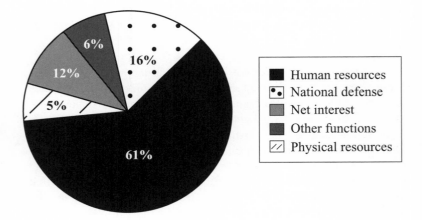

Total outlays: $1.8 trillion

Figure 6.2. Pie charts to illustrate composition, (a) without data labels, (b) with data (numeric value) labels.

Source: U.S. Office of Management and Budget 2002.

c. U.S. federal outlays by function, 2000

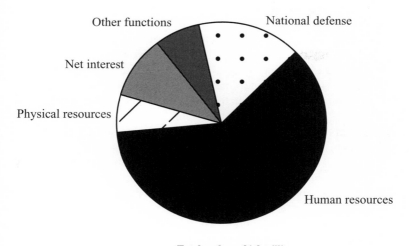

Total outlays: $1.8 trillion

Figure 6.2. (c) with value labels.

they represent, you can make them proportionate to their respective totals. For instance, if the total budget in one year was twice as large as in another, create the former pie with twice the area of the latter.

Use pie charts to present composition or distribution—how the parts add up to the whole. Each pie chart shows distribution of a single variable, such as racial composition of the study sample. Because they illustrate composition, pie charts can be used only for variables whose values are mutually exclusive—after all, the slices of a single pizza don't overlap one another in the pan.

- Display only one variable per pie chart: either age or gender distribution—not both.[1]
- Don't use pie charts to compare averages or rates across groups or time periods. Those dimensions don't have to add up to any specifiable total, so a pie chart, which shows composition, doesn't fit the topic.

  Rates of low birth weight for boys and for girls don't add up to the rate of low birth weight for the two genders combined.

  Average temperatures in each of the 12 months of the year are not summed to obtain the average temperature for the year. Such logic would yield an average annual temperature of 664° F for the New York City area.

- Don't use a pie chart to contrast measures of quantitative comparison such as rates, ratios, percentage change, or average values of some outcome; instead, use a bar or line chart.
- Don't use a pie chart to present multiple-response variables; those responses are not mutually exclusive. Instead, create a different pie chart for each possible response, or use a bar chart to show frequency of each response.
- Avoid pies with many skinny slices. Consider combining rare categories unless one or more of them are of particular interest to your research question. Or create one pie that includes the most common responses with a summary slice for "other," then a second pie that shows a detailed breakdown of values within the "other" category.

In addition to the above pie-chart no-nos, some aspects of composition are more effectively conveyed with a different type of chart.

- Use a histogram to present the distribution of values of an ordinal variable, especially one with many categories. Histograms show the order and relative frequency of those values more clearly than a pie.
- To compare composition across more than three groups (e.g., distribution of educational attainment in each of 10 countries), use stacked bar charts, which are easier to align and compare than several pie charts. Or create a multipanel histogram.

Histograms

Histograms are a form of simple bar chart used to show distribution of variables with values that can be ranked along the *x* axis. Use them to present distribution of an ordinal variable, such as the share of adults that fall into each of several age groups (figure 6.3), or an interval (continuous) variable with 20 or fewer values. For a ratio variable or interval variable with more than 20 values, such as IQ score, use a line chart to present distribution.

Array the values of the variable across the *x* axis and create a bar to show the frequency of occurrence of each value, either number of cases or percentage of total cases, measured on the *y* axis. To accurately portray distribution of a continuous variable, don't leave horizontal space between bars for adjacent *x* values. Bars in a his-

Age distribution of U.S. adults, 2000

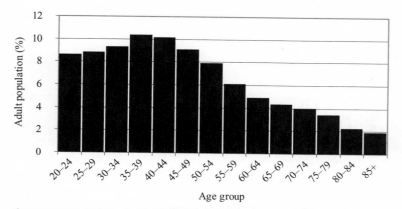

Figure 6.3. **Histogram to illustrate distribution of an ordinal variable.**
Source: U.S. Census Bureau 2002d.

togram should touch one another (as in figure 6.3) unless there are intervening *x* values for which there are no cases. For example, in figure
4.3d, no cases have any of the values 3 through 9, so there is a gap
above the labels for those values, between the bars showing frequency
of the *x* values 2 and 10. Alternatively, use a line chart or box-and-
whisker plot to illustrate distribution of a single variable (see respective sections below).

Don't use histograms to display distribution of nominal variables
such as religion or race, because their values do not have an inherent
order in which to arrange them on the *x* axis. Instead, use a pie chart.

A histogram can be used to display distribution of an ordinal variable with unequal width categories; see cautions under "Line Chart
for Unequally Spaced Ordinal Categories" in the section on "Common Errors in Chart Creation" below.

Charts to Present Relationships among Variables
Bar Charts

Simple bar chart. A simple bar chart illustrates the relationship
between two variables—a categorical independent variable on the
x axis, and a continuous dependent variable on the *y* axis. Most dimensions of quantitative comparison—value, absolute difference,
ratio, or percentage change—can be shown in a bar chart, making it
an effective tool for comparing values of one variable across groups

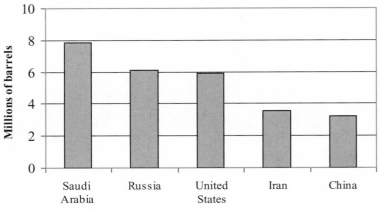

Daily crude oil production in the five leading countries, 1999

Figure 6.4. Simple bar chart.
Source: U.S. National Energy Information Center 2003.

defined by a second variable. Create one bar for each group with the height of the bar indicating the value of the dependent variable for that group, such as mean crude oil production (y axis) for each of five countries (x axis, figure 6.4).

To format a simple bar chart, place the continuous variable on the y axis and label with its units. The variable on the x axis is usually nominal or ordinal. Arrange the categories of nominal variables such as race or country of residence in meaningful sequence, using theoretical or empirical criteria. Display the categories of ordinal variables or values of a continuous variable in their logical order (e.g., income group, letter grades). Simple bar charts don't need a legend because the two variables being compared are defined by the axis titles and labels; hence the same color is used for all the bars.

Clustered bar chart. Use a clustered bar chart to introduce a third variable to a simple bar chart, illustrating relationships among three variables—a continuous dependent variable by two categorical independent variables. Variants include portraying patterns for multiple-response items, illustrating an interaction between two categorical variables, or showing results of competing risks models.

To show patterns across groups for multiple-response items (how votes for the top three candidates for school board varied according to voter's party affiliation) or a series of related questions, create a cluster for each topic and a bar for each group. For example, figure 6.5 includes one cluster for each of 10 AIDS knowledge topics, with a bar for each language group. The height of each bar shows the percentage of the pertinent language group that answered that question correctly.

Clustered bar charts can also be used to display patterns of change or difference, where some values are negative and some are positive. For example, figure 6.6 presents changes in average percentile rank for 7th though 11th grade students in Los Angeles and Houston between 1999 and 2000. In Houston, students in grades 9 through 11 decreased in average rank compared to national norms, yielding bars that fall below the reference line indicating zero change. In contrast, Los Angeles's students in those grades showed an average improvement of one to two percentiles, with bars above the reference line.

A clustered bar chart can also show the simple (unadjusted) three-way association among variables or illustrate an interaction between

Knowledge of AIDS transmission modes by topic, language spoken at home, and language of questionnaire (Q), New Jersey, 1998

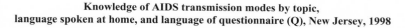
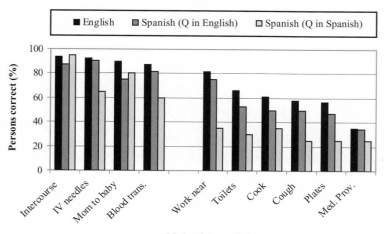

Mode of transmission

Figure 6.5. Clustered bar chart: Series of related outcomes by a nominal variable.
Source: Miller 2000a.
Note: See table 5.2 for detailed wording of questions.

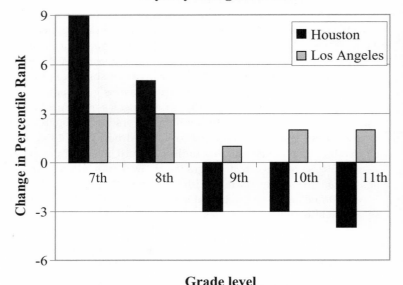

Change in average percentile rank, 1999–2000, by city and grade level

Figure 6.6. Clustered bar chart to illustrate change or difference in several outcomes by a nominal variable.
Source: Schemo and Fessenden 2003.

two categorical independent variables based on coefficients from a multivariate model, complementing tabular presentation of the pertinent main effects and interaction terms from the full model. For instance, figure 6.7a shows how emergency room (ER) use for asthma varies according to race and income level simultaneously. One independent variable (income group) is shown on the x axis, the other (race) in the legend, and the dependent variable and its units (relative odds of ER use for asthma) on the y axis. A footnote lists the other variables that were controlled in the model from which the estimates were derived.

A similar design can present results of competing risks models—models that compare predictors of several mutually exclusive outcome categories such as cause of death (e.g., heart disease, cancer, or other causes) according to some other variable. For example, figure 6.8 presents log-odds of three different reasons for disenrollment

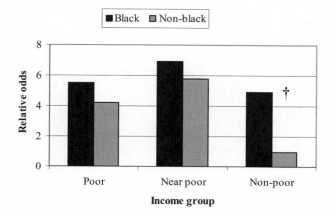

a. Relative odds of emergency room visits for asthma, by race and income, United States, 1991

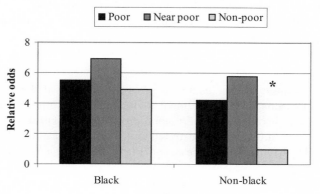

b. Relative odds of emergency room visits for asthma, by race and income, United States, 1991

Figure 6.7. Two versions of clustered bar chart to illustrate an interaction: Patterns by two nominal variables, (a) by income group, and (b) by race.
Source: Miller 2000b; data are from U.S. DHHS 1991.
Notes: Taking into account mother's age, educational attainment, and marital history; number of siblings; presence of smokers in the household; low birth weight (<2,500 grams) and preterm birth (<37 weeks' gestation).
*Difference across income groups significant at $p < 0.05$ for non-blacks only.
†Difference across racial groups within income group significant at $p < 0.05$ for non-poor only.

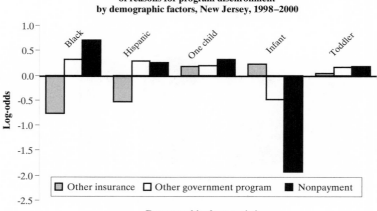

Figure 6.8. Clustered bar chart to portray results of competing risks model.
Source: Birch and Davis Health Management Corporation 2000.
Note: Compared to non-Hispanic white children aged five years or older with one or more enrolled siblings.

from a public health insurance program for several demographic traits. Reasons for disenrollment included finding other insurance, placement in another government program, and failure to pay a monthly premium, each illustrated with a different bar color (defined in the legend). The reference category is identified in a footnote to the chart.

By plotting all three outcomes on the same chart and using a reference line to differentiate positive from negative log-odds, this design makes it easy to distinguish characteristics that have the same direction of effect on different values of the dependent variable from those that have opposite effects on different values. For instance, being from a one-child family is associated with increased odds of all three reasons for disenrollment, whereas black race is associated with increased odds of placement in a government program or nonpayment, but decreased odds of disenrollment because of a switch to other health insurance. The chart also conveys the relative sizes of the effects. For example, the decrease in odds of disenrollment among infants compared to older children was much larger for nonpayment (black bar) than for placement in another government program (white bar). (See chapter 9 for an explanation of odds and log-odds.)

Finally, clustered bar charts can be used to show distribution of one variable for each of two or three groups, with the histogram for each group comprising one cluster within the chart.

To format a clustered bar chart, place one categorical independent variable on the x axis, the other in the legend, and the dependent variable on the y axis. Label each cluster on the x axis for the corresponding category, then include a legend to identify values of the second predictor. To decide which variable to show on the x axis and which to put in the legend, anticipate which contrast you want to emphasize in your description. Although the description of each version of figure 6.7 would include both the income pattern and the racial pattern of ER use for asthma, each arrangement highlights a different contrast. Figure 6.7a underscores the pattern of ER use across income groups (on the x axis). Figure 6.7b presents the same data but reverses the variables in the legend (income group) and the x axis (race), highlighting the comparisons across racial groups.

Stacked bar chart. Create a stacked bar chart to show how the distribution of a variable differs according to another characteristic, such as how age composition varies by race, or how different causes of death add up to the respective overall death rates for males and for females. Because they illustrate the contribution of parts to a whole (composition), stacked bar charts can be used only for variables with mutually exclusive categories, just like pie charts. For multiple-response items, use a clustered bar chart.

There are two major variants of stacked bar charts: those that show variation in level and those that show only composition. To emphasize differences in level while also presenting composition, construct a stacked bar chart that allows the height of the bar to reflect the level of the dependent variable. Figure 6.9a shows how total federal outlays were divided among major functions with data at 10-year intervals. For each year, the dollar value of outlays in each category is conveyed by the thickness of the respective slice (defined in the legend), and the value of total outlays for all functions combined by the overall height of the stack.

If there is wide variation in the level of the dependent variable, however, this type of stacked bar chart can obscure important inter-group differences in the distribution of those components. For ex-

a. U.S. federal outlays by function, 1950–2000

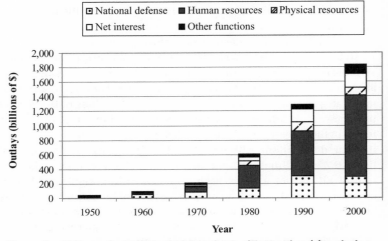

Figure 6.9. Two versions of stacked bar charts, illustrating (a) variation in level.
Source: U.S. Office of Management and Budget 2002.
Note: Human resources include education, training, employment, and social services; health; Medicare; income security; Social Security; and veterans benefits and services. Physical resources include energy; natural resources and environment; commerce and housing credit; transportation; and community and regional development. Other functions include international affairs; general science, space, and technology; agriculture; administration of justice; general government; and allowances.

ample, with more than a forty-fold increase in total outlays between 1950 and 2000, it is virtually impossible to assess the relative contribution of each category in the early years based on figure 6.9a.

To compare composition when there is more than a three-fold difference between the lowest and highest *y* values across groups or periods, create a stacked bar chart with bars of equal height, and show percentage distribution in the stacked bar. This variant of a stacked bar chart highlights differences in composition rather than level. Figure 6.9b shows that the share of outlays for defense dropped from roughly 50% in 1960 to 16% in 2000. Because this version of a stacked bar chart does not present information on absolute level (e.g.,

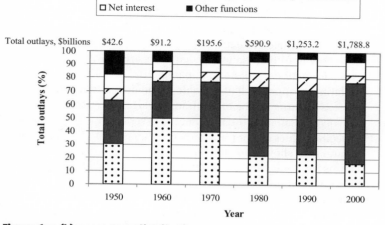

Figure 6.9. (b) percentage distribution.

outlays in billions of dollars) on the *y* axis, report that information in a separate table, at the top of each stack (as in figure 6.9b), or in a footnote to the chart.

In formatting stacked bar charts, the variables on the *x* axis and in the slices (legend) must be categorical; the variable on the *y* axis is continuous. On the *x* axis, put the variable that is first in the causal chain, then show how the legend variable differs within those categories. For stacked bar charts in which the height of the bar reflects the level of the dependent variable, the units on the *y* axis are those in which the variable was originally measured. In figure 6.9a, for example, the *y* axis shows federal outlays in billions of dollars. For stacked bar charts that emphasize composition (e.g., figure 6.9b), the *y* axis units are percentage of the overall value for that stack, and by definition, the height of all the bars is the same since each bar reflects 100% of that year's outlays.

Line Charts

Single-line charts. Simple line charts are invaluable for portraying distributions, bivariate relationships, and predicted patterns calculated from estimated coefficients from a multivariate model. Use single-line charts for the following purposes:

- To show distribution of a continuous variable, like the familiar "bell-curve" of the IQ distribution
- To illustrate the relationship between two continuous variables. For example, figure 6.10 shows the age pattern of mortality, in this case plotted on a logarithmic scale from simple bivariate tabulations.
- To show nonlinear patterns such as logarithmic transformations, polynomial, parametric, or spline functions relating an independent variable to the dependent variable. These patterns can be difficult to visualize because they involve calculating the net effect of several terms or plugging specific values into a transformation (chapter 9). For instance, figure 6.11 shows the net effect of the linear and quadratic terms for the income-to-poverty ratio from an OLS model of birth weight (table 9.1).

For all charts based on coefficients from multivariate models, refer to a table that reports the pertinent coefficients and identifies reference categories for categorical variables, or explain in the text or a footnote which other variables were controlled in the model. Except for lengthy statistical papers or reports, don't include charts of patterns for control variables, as they will distract from your main story.

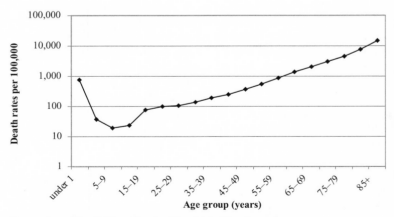

Figure 6.10. Single-line chart with a logarithmic scale.
Source: Peters et al. 1998, table 2.

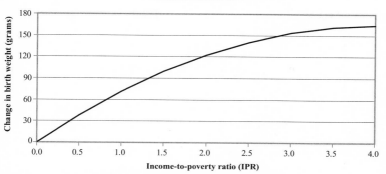

Figure 6.11. **Single-line chart to illustrate projected pattern for continuous independent variable.**
Source: Data are from U.S. DHHS 1997.
Notes: Relative to IPR = 0. Based on multivariate model with controls for gender, race/ethnicity, mother's age, educational attainment, and smoking status. See table 9.3.

As in the other types of *xy* charts, typically the independent variable is shown on the *x* axis and the dependent variable on the *y* axis, along with their associated units. No legend is needed in a single-line chart because the two variables are identified in the respective axis labels. If you plot smoothed data (such as moving averages of temporal data, or seasonally adjusted patterns), or other transformations of the original variable, report those transformations in a footnote and refer to the text for a more detailed explanation.

Multiple-line charts. Create a multiple-line chart to add a third dimension to a single-line chart. For instance, present projected population under several different scenarios (e.g., figure 6.1), with a separate line for each scenario. Or illustrate an interaction between categorical and continuous independent variables, with a different line style for each category.

To display an interaction between continuous and categorical predictors, create a line chart with the continuous variable on the *x* axis and a line for each value of the categorical variable (identified in the legend). Figure 6.12 shows how the effects of income-to-poverty ratio (IPR) on birth weight vary by race/ethnicity, based on the estimated

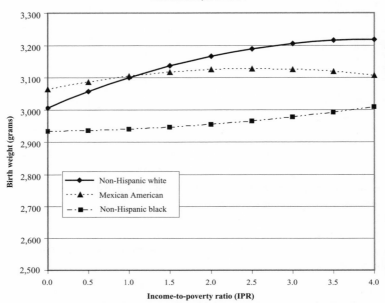

Predicted birth weight by race/ethnicity and income-to-poverty ratio,
United States, 1988–1994

Figure 6.12. Multiple-line chart to illustrate an interaction between a continuous and a categorical independent variable.
Notes: Data are from U.S. DHHS 1997. Based on multivariate model with controls for gender, mother's age, educational attainment, and smoking status. See table 9.3.

coefficients from the model shown in table 9.3. The interaction appears as differences in the levels and shapes of the lines, which are curved in this case because of quadratic specification of the IPR/birth weight relationship. The *y* axis starts at 2,500 grams on this chart—the low end of the plausible range for mean birth weight for large subgroups.

Place the continuous dependent variable on the *y* axis, the continuous independent variable on the *x* axis, and identify the different values of the categorical independent variable in the legend.

Multiple-line charts with two different y scales. Line charts can also show relations between a continuous variable (on the *x* axis) and

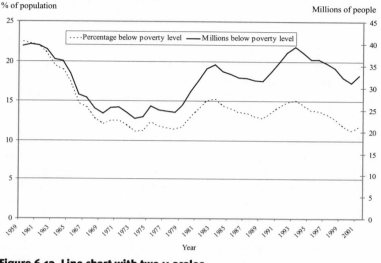

Figure 6.13. Line chart with two *y*-scales.
Source: Proctor and Dalaker 2002.

each of two closely related continuous variables that are measured in different units (on the *y* axes). Figure 6.13 shows trends in the number and percentage poor in the United States. Because the units differ for the two outcome variables, one is presented and identified by the title on the left-hand *y* axis (in this case the percentage of the population that is poor), the other on the right-hand *y* axis (millions of people in poverty). Use the legend to convey which set of units pertains to each line: the dotted line shows poverty rate and is read from the left-hand *y* axis (sometimes called the *Y*1 axis), while the solid line shows the number of poor persons, on the right-hand (*Y*2) axis.

Charts that use two different *y* axes are complicated to explain and read, so reserve them for relatively savvy audiences and only for variables that are closely related, such as different measures of the same concept. Explicitly refer to the respective *y* axes' locations and units as you describe the patterns.

XYZ line charts. To illustrate the relationship among three continuous variables, such as age, income, and birth weight, create a three-dimensional line chart, sometimes called an *xyz* chart after the three axes it contains. Label each axis with the name and units of the pertinent variable.

High/Low/Close Charts

High/low/close charts present three *y* values for each *x* value. They are probably most familiar as ways to present stock values, but can also be used to compare distributions or present confidence intervals around point estimates.

Comparing distributions. Use a high/low/close chart to compare the distribution of a continuous variable across categories of an ordinal or nominal variable. In figure 6.14, for example, the median socioeconomic index (SEI) for each of three racial/ethnic groups is plotted by a horizontal dash above its label, along with a vertical bar showing the first and third quartiles (the interquartile range).

Error bars or confidence intervals. Use a high/low/close chart to show error bars or confidence intervals around point estimates from multivariate models; see "Confidence Intervals" in chapter 10 for calculations and interpretation. A chart permits much more rapid

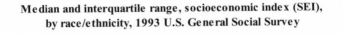

**Median and interquartile range, socioeconomic index (SEI),
by race/ethnicity, 1993 U.S. General Social Survey**

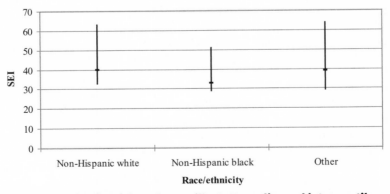

Figure 6.14. High/low/close chart to illustrate median and interquartile range.
Source: Davis, Smith, and Marsden 2003.

Odds ratios and 95% confidence intervals of low birth weight
for selected maternal and infant characteristics,
United States, 1988–1994

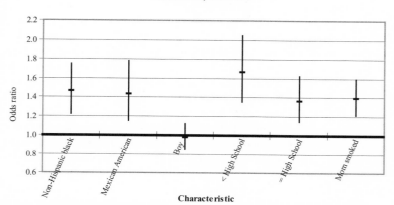

Figure 6.15. High/low/close chart to illustrate confidence intervals around estimated odds ratios.

Source: Data are from U.S. DHHS 1997.

Note: Compared to non-Hispanic white girls whose mother had more than a high school education and did not smoke. See table 9.4.

comparison of confidence intervals against the null hypothesis than a tabular presentation of the same numbers. Figure 6.15 plots the estimated odds ratio of low birth weight for each of several categorical independent variables with a horizontal dash, accompanied by a vertical line showing the 95% confidence interval.[2]

Figure 6.15 is designed so the x axis crosses at $y = 1.0$, indicating equal odds of low birth weight in the group shown compared to the reference category (identified in the footnote). By comparing each point estimate against that reference line, it is easy to see whether that characteristic is associated with increased or decreased odds of low birth weight. If both upper and lower 95% confidence limits are on the same side of that reference line, the effect is statistically significant at $p < 0.05$. Confidence intervals for subgroups of the same categorical variable can also be contrasted. For instance, the confidence intervals for "< high school" and "= high school" substantially overlap, indicating that they are not statistically significantly different from one another; see chapter 10 for more on testing differences between coefficients from within one model.

Use *confidence bands* in conjunction with line graphs of predicted values for continuous variables. For each series, create one line based on the point estimate and two additional lines corresponding to the upper and lower 95% confidence limits based on the associated standard errors. For example, addition of confidence bands to figure 6.11 would show the 95% confidence interval of predicted birth weight for each value of the income-to-poverty ratio.

Tukey box-and-whisker plots. Statistician John Tukey developed another variant of this type of chart, now widely known as "box-and-whisker" plots (Tukey 1977; Hoaglin, Mosteller, and Tukey 2000). The "box" portion of the graph shows the distance between the first and third quartiles, with the median shown as a dot inside the box. "Whiskers" (vertical lines) extend upward and downward from those points to illustrate the highest and lowest values in the distribution. Outliers—highest or lowest values that are distant from the next closest values—are graphed with asterisks.

Use box-and-whisker techniques to become acquainted with your data, assess how well measures of central tendency (e.g., mean or median) represent the distribution, and identify outliers. Such exploratory graphs are rarely shown in final written documents, but can be invaluable background work to inform how you classify data or choose example values.

In formatting high/low/close charts or error bars, ensure that the values to be plotted for each x value are measured in consistent units—all in dollars, for example. The x variable should be either nominal or ordinal; for a continuous x variable, create a line chart with confidence bands. Identify the meaning of the vertical bars either in the title (as in figure 6.15) or a legend.

Scatter Charts

Use scatter charts to depict the relationship between two continuous variables when there is more than one y value for each x value, such as several observations for each year. A point is plotted for each x/y combination in the data, creating a "scatter" rather than a single line. In figure 6.16, each point represents the percentage increase in the adult obesity rate between 1992 and 2002 in one state, plotted against that state's adult obesity rate in 2002. Although both the obesity rate and increase in obesity rate are well above zero in every state, both axis scales start at 0 to avoid misrepresenting the levels of those variables (see "Common Errors in Chart Creation" below).

Scatter charts can be combined with other formats or features,

Adult obesity rate (%) versus percentage increase in obesity rate, United States, 1992–2002, by state

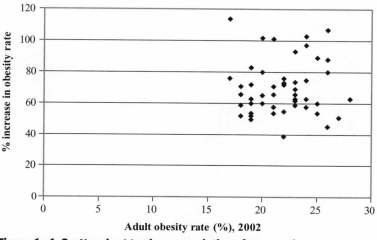

Figure 6.16. Scatter chart to show association of two continuous variables.

Source: Johnson 2004.

such as to show points from two different sets on the same scatter chart, using different symbols to plot points from each set. For example, an asterisk could be used to show data for men, a pound sign for women. Or show a regression line fitted through a set of points, combining line and scatter chart features on the same chart.

For a simple scatter chart, no legend is needed because the two variables and their units are identified in the axis titles and labels. For a scatter chart showing more than one series, provide a legend to identify the groups associated with different plotting symbols.

Maps of Numeric Data

Maps are superior to tables or other types of charts for showing data with a geographic component because they show the spatial arrangement of different cases. They can display most types of quantitative comparison, including level, rank, percentage change, rates, or average values for each geographic unit. For example, figure 6.17 displays average annual pay for each of the lower 48 United States in 1999, revealing a cluster of states with pay in the top quartile in the Northeast and a cluster of bottom-quartile states in the northern

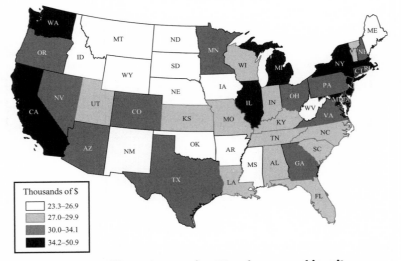

Average annual pay ($1,000s) by state,
United States, 1999

Thousands of $
	23.3–26.9
	27.0–29.9
	30.0–34.1
	34.2–50.9

Figure 6.17. Map to illustrate numeric pattern by geographic unit.
Source: U.S. Census 2002c. Average annual pay grouped into quartiles.

Rockies and upper Midwest. These patterns would be much more difficult to visualize from other types of charts or tabular presentation of data.

Maps can also convey location, distance, and other geographic attributes. Include a legend to explain shading or symbols used on the map and a ruler to show scale. Most of the basic principles mentioned above for effective titles and layout also apply to maps. See Monmonier (1993) or Slocum (1998) for in-depth guides to using maps to display numeric data.

■ ADDING DIMENSIONS TO CHARTS

Most of the chart types described above can display relationships among two or at most three variables. Use panels or combine formats to include additional variables.

- To illustrate the age distribution for each of three countries, for instance, create one panel like that in figure 6.3 for each country, then display all the panels on a single page or on facing pages. Use a uniform axis scale and chart size for all panels of the chart to avoid misleading viewers.

- To compare changes across time in the distribution of federal outlays for several countries—as in figure 6.9, but with more countries—create a cluster for each year with a stack for each country and slices for each category of outlay.

■ ADVANCED CHART FEATURES

If your analysis involves comparing your data against standard values or patterns or identifying exceptions to a general pattern, consider using reference points, lines, regions, or annotations in your chart. Include these features only if they are vital to illustrating a pattern or contrast, then refer to them in the accompanying narrative. Many charts work fine without these extra bells and whistles, which can distract your readers and clutter the chart.

Annotations

Annotations include labels to guide readers to specific data values or to provide information to help interpret the chart. On a graph showing a skewed distribution you might report and indicate the median or mean with arrows and a short note or label, for instance. Reserve such annotations for when they convey information that is otherwise not evident from the chart. If the distribution is a symmetric bell curve, keep the graph simple and report median and mean in the text or a table. Annotations can also be used to show outliers or values you use as illustrative examples. In that case, omit data labels from all other values on the chart, naming only those to which you refer in the text.

Another useful type of annotation is denoting statistical significance with symbols accompanied by a footnote to define their meaning; see "Symbols" in chapter 10. If a chart involves a three-way association, assign different symbols for each contrast, then use a footnote to specify the meaning of each symbol. In figure 6.7a, for example, there are two possible contrasts: emergency room use *within race across income,* and emergency room use *within income across race,* requiring two different symbols to communicate the patterns of statistical significance. The asterisk indicates that among non-blacks, the non-poor group is statistically significantly different from the other two income groups, while the dagger indicates that among the non-poor, risks for blacks and non-blacks are statistically significantly different from one another. Racial differences in odds for the other two income groups are not statistically significant, nor are differences across income groups among blacks.

Reference Points, Lines and Regions

Include reference points, lines, or regions in your chart to call attention to one or more important values against which other numbers are to be evaluated.

Reference Points

Reference points are probably most familiar from spatial maps. A famous example of the analytic importance of a reference point is the spot map created by John Snow (1936) in his investigation of the London cholera epidemic of 1854. By mapping the location of water pumps where many residents obtained their drinking and cooking water along with the residence of each cholera case, he was able to demonstrate a link between water source and cholera.

Reference Lines

Use reference lines to show the position of a threshold level or other reference value against which to compare data on individual cases or groups.

Horizontal reference lines. On an xy chart, a horizontal reference line identifies a value of the dependent variable that has an important substantive interpretation.
- On a scatter chart with birth weight on the y axis, cases below a line showing the 2,500 gram cutoff would be classified as low birth weight.
- On a bar chart showing change or difference, a reference line at $y = 0.0$ differentiates positive from negative change (figure 6.6).
- On a bar chart showing odds ratios, a line at $y = 1.0$ differentiates cases with higher and lower odds than the odds for the reference group (ratios >1.0 and <1.0, respectively). The addition of 95% confidence intervals for each point estimate allows readers to detect which estimates are statistically significant at $p < 0.05$ (figure 6.15).
- For OLS models, where the estimated coefficient is the absolute difference between the groups or values being compared, have the x axis cross at $y = 0$ (figure 15.16). This

design corresponds to the null hypothesis of no difference between the groups.

Vertical reference lines. To identify pertinent values of a continuous independent variable, include a reference line emanating upward from the x axis. For example, show the date of a change in legislation on a trend chart.

Nonlinear reference lines. Some standard patterns yield curvilinear reference lines. For example, to contrast the age pattern of specific causes of death against that for overall mortality, use the J-shaped reference curve for all-cause mortality (figure 6.10). A trend chart of employment patterns over the past few years might include a recurrent (cyclical) reference curve for the long-term average seasonal pattern.

Reference Regions
Use a reference region to locate a range of values on the x axis (a vertical region) or y axis (horizontal band) that are relevant to your analysis. In figure 6.18, shading periods of recession facilitates com-

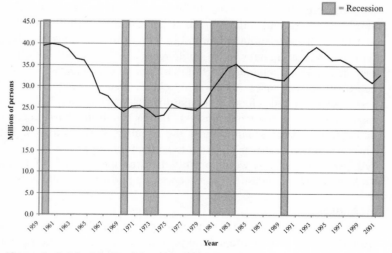

Figure 6.18. Line chart with reference regions.
Source: Proctor and Dalaker 2002.

parison of how the number of poor persons increased and decreased during and between those periods.

Reference regions can also enhance spatial maps: analyses of effects of nuclear accidents like Chernobyl included maps with concentric circles to show geographic extent of different levels of exposure. In a study of whether to merge local emergency services, you might show which locations can be reached within five minutes by a local police or fire company, which you also plot on the map.

■ CHOOSING AN APPROPRIATE CHART TYPE

To choose among the many types of charts to present your numbers, first figure out how many and what types of variables you are working with, then consider your audience.

Number and Types of Variables in a Chart

Table 6.1 summarizes the different types of charts for presenting distribution of a single variable, relationships between two variables, and relationships among three variables. Within each of those broad categories, chart types are organized according to whether they involve categorical (nominal or ordinal) or continuous variables, or a mixture of the two types. Start by finding the row that matches the type of task and the number and kinds of variables for your chart (leftmost column), then read across to find suggested chart types with examples of topics and comments on chart design and application.

Unless otherwise noted in the column for example topics, the chart type can accommodate only single-response items; for multiple-response items, a separate chart of that type must be created for each category of response. Accompany charts that present multiple-response items with a footnote explaining that each respondent could have given more than one answer, hence the sum of frequencies across all categories can exceed the number of respondents. For charts based on multivariate model results, include a footnote specifying which variables were controlled in the model, and refer to a table in the same document that reports the pertinent coefficients.

Audience

For nonscientific audiences, keep graphs as simple and familiar as possible. Most people understand pie charts, line charts, and simple bar charts. Reserve complicated three-dimensional charts, logarithmic scales, and charts with two different y scales for audiences that

CREATING EFFECTIVE CHARTS : 149

have worked with them before. For speeches, design most slides with simple, focused charts even for scientific audiences; complicated charts are often hard to read from slides and take longer to explain well.

■ **OTHER CONSIDERATIONS**

Design charts so the order in which you mention variables or values in the text matches the order in which they appear in the chart, following the principles for coordinating tables with your writing described in chapter 5. For nominal variables, identify the main point you want to make about the data, then arrange the values on the axes or in the legend accordingly. For ordinal, interval, or ratio variables, retain the natural order of values on your axes.

Use of Color

Graphics software often automatically uses different colors for each line or bar in a chart. Although slides and some publications permit use of color, in many instances you will need to replace colors with different patterns or shades of gray.

- Most documents are printed in grayscale, meaning that the only colors available are black, white, and shades of gray.
- Even if your original will be printed in color, it may be photocopied into black and white.
- Handouts printed from slides are often distributed in black and white.

What appear as different primary hues or pastel tints on a computer screen can become virtually indistinguishable tones in a black and white rendition. Choose a color or shading scheme that will remain evident and interpretable regardless of how your chart is reproduced. For color documents or slides, select colors with maximum contrast such as yellow, red, and blue, then make a second version in black and white for other uses. For black-and-white documents, replace colors with one of the following:

- For line charts, pick a different style (solid, dashed, dotted) for each line. If data points are plotted, also vary the plotting symbol, using a circle for one group, a diamond for another, etc.
- For pie charts, bar charts, or maps that include shaded regions, use a different type of shading for each group.
  If there are only two or three groups (slices or bar colors),

Table 6.1. Choice of chart type for specific tasks and types of variables

Task	Type of chart	Example topic	Comments
Distribution of one variable			
Nominal with ≤5 categories	Pie	Religious affiliation, major religions	Arrange categories by theoretical criteria or in order of frequency.
Nominal with >5 categories	Simple bar	Religious affiliation, major and minor religious groups	
Ordinal	Histogram	Distribution of letter grades	Arrange categories in numeric order.
Continuous with ≤20 values	Histogram or line	Birth weight distribution in 500-gram categories.	Arrange values in numeric order.
Continuous with >20 values	Line	Distribution of birth weight in grams	Arrange values in numeric order.
Continuous with summary measures of range or variance	Box-and-whisker	Distribution of birth weight in grams	Use to illustrate minimum, maximum, interquartile range, or other summary measures of variance.

Relationships between two variables

Both categorical	Simple bar	For a dichotomous dependent variable, show frequency of one value for each categorical predictor; unadjusted or adjusted.[a]
		Percentage low birth weight (LBW) by race
	Clustered bar or clustered histogram	For distribution of one variable within each of two or three groups, use a clustered bar to create a histogram for each group.
		Educational attainment (3 levels) by race/ethnicity
	Stacked bar	To compare distribution of a variable across more than three groups of a second variable, use a stacked bar.
		Educational attainment (7 levels) by race/ethnicity
One categorical, one continuous	Simple bar	Illustrate one y value for each x value. Unadjusted or adjusted.[a]
		Mean birth weight (grams) by race
	High/low/close	Illustrate distribution of y values for each x value (e.g., race). See Box-and-whisker.
		Birth weight distribution by race

(continued)

Table 6.1. (continued)

Task	Type of chart	Example topic	Comments
One categorical, one continuous (*continued*)	High/low/close (*continued*)	Confidence interval around birth weight coefficients for non-Hispanic black and Mexican American dummy variables	Estimated coefficient for categorical independent variable with confidence interval.
Both continuous	Single line	Trend in annual percentage low birth weight	Use a line chart if there is only one y value for each x value or to show a summary (e.g., regression line).
		Predicted birth weight by income from a regression model	
	Scatter	Association between birth weight and gestational age for sample of 200 infants	Use a scatter chart to show individual points or more than one y value for each x value.
Relationships among three variables			
All categorical	Two-panel stacked bar	Educational attainment composition (3 levels) by race and region	Use one panel for each value of one categorical independent variable, one bar for each category of the other independent variable, and slices for each category of dependent variable.

Variable types	Chart type	Example	Description
Two categorical, one continuous	Clustered bar	Mean birth weight by race and educational attainment	Illustrate an interaction between two categorical independent variables and a continuous dependent variable; unadjusted or adjusted.[a]
		Multiple response: average scores for different topics by type of school	Create a separate cluster for each item with bars for each group.
		Odds ratios of each of three causes of death by race	Create one cluster for each categorical predictor, one bar color for each outcome category; unadjusted or adjusted.[a]
Two continuous, one categorical	Multiple line	Birth weight by income and race	Use to illustrate an interaction between one continuous and one categorical independent variable and a continuous dependent variable; unadjusted or adjusted.[a]
		Multiple response: trend in income components by age group	To compare multiple-response continuous variables across groups, create a separate line for each response.

(continued)

Table 6.1. (*continued*)

Task	Type of chart	Example topic	Comments
Two continuous, one categorical (*continued*)	Multiple line	Predicted birth weight by income, with confidence bands	Create one line for predicted birth weight, other lines for upper and lower confidence limits for each x value.
	Scatter	Birth weight and gestational age by gender for each of 200 infants	Use different symbols to plot values from the different series.
All continuous	Three-dimensional line (xyz)	Relationships among height, weight, and age of children	Use to illustrate interactions among three continuous variables; unadjusted or adjusted.[a]

[a]"Unadjusted" refers to simple bivariate or three-way association; "adjusted" refers to estimates from a multivariate model that controls for other attributes. For adjusted estimates, include a footnote or text description identifying the table from which estimates were taken or listing the other variables controlled in the model.

use white for one, black for the second, and gray for a third. Avoid using color alone to contrast more than three categories in grayscale, as it is difficult to discriminate among light, medium, and dark gray, particularly if the graph has been photocopied from an original.

For four or more slices or bar colors, use different shading schemes (e.g., vertical, horizontal, or diagonal hatching, dots) in combination with solid black, white, and gray to differentiate among the groups to be compared.

- For scatter charts, use a different plotting symbol to plot values for each group. For more than two or three groups create separate panels of a scatter plot for each group, as patterns for more than three types of symbols become difficult to distinguish on one graph.

Once you have created your chart, print it out to evaluate the color or shading scheme: check that line styles can be differentiated from one another, that different slices or bars don't appear to be the same shade, and that your shading combinations aren't too dizzying.

Three-Dimensional Effects

Many graphing software programs offer the option of making bars or pie slices appear "3-D." Steer clear of these features, which tend to disguise rather than enhance presentation of the data. Your objective is to convey the relative values for different groups or cases in the chart—a task accomplished perfectly well by a flat (two-dimensional) bar or slice. By adding volume to a two-dimensional image, 3-D effects can distort the relative sizes of values by inflating the apparent size of some components. Also avoid tilted or other angled perspectives on pie or bar charts, which can misrepresent proportions. See Tufte (2001) for more details and examples.

Number of Series

For legibility, limit the number of series, particularly if your chart will be printed small. On a multiple-line chart, aim for no more than eight categories (corresponding to eight lines on the chart)—fewer if the lines are close together or cross one another. In a clustered bar chart, consider the total number of bars to be displayed, which equals the number of clusters multiplied by the number of groups in the legend. To avoid overwhelming your readers with too many comparisons, display no more than 20 bars in one chart. An exception: if you will be generalizing a pattern for the entire chart (e.g., "the black bar is higher than the gray bar in every subgroup") with little attention to individual bars, you can get away with more bars.

To display a larger number of comparisons, use theoretical criteria to break them into conceptually related blocks, then make a separate chart or panel for each such block. For example, the questions about knowledge of AIDS transmission shown in figure 6.5 comprise 10 out of 17 AIDS knowledge questions from a survey. A separate chart could present patterns of general AIDS knowledge as measured by the other seven questions, which dealt with disease characteristics, symptoms, and treatment. Remember, too, that a chart is best used to convey general impressions, not detailed values; if more detail is needed, substitute a table.

Landscape versus Portrait Layout

Some charts work well with a portrait (vertical) layout rather than the traditional landscape (horizontal) chart layout. Revising figure 6.5 into a portrait layout (figure 6.19) leaves more room to label the AIDS knowledge topics (now on the vertical axis).

Knowledge of AIDS transmission modes by topic, language spoken at home, and language of questionnaire (Q), New Jersey, 1998

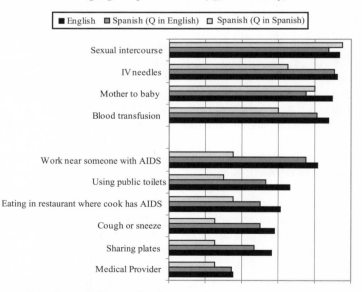

Figure 6.19. Portrait layout of a clustered bar chart.
Source: Miller 2000a.

Death rates by age, United States, 1996

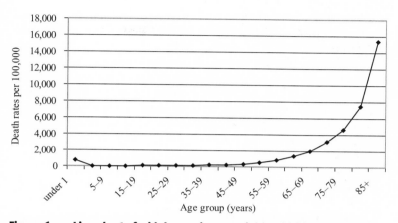

Figure 6.20. Line chart of widely ranging *y*-variable with linear scale.
Source: Peters et al. 1998, table 2.

Linear versus Logarithmic Scale

If the range of values to be plotted spans more than one or two orders of magnitude, consider using a logarithmic scale. On a logarithmic scale, the distance between adjacent tick marks on the axis corresponds to a 10-fold *relative* difference or multiple: in figure 6.10, for example, the first three tick marks on the *y* axis are for 1, 10, and 100 deaths per 1,000, instead of the uniform 2,000-unit *absolute* difference between tick marks in figure 6.20.

Because of the very high mortality rates among the elderly, when mortality rates across the life span are plotted on a linear scale (figure 6.20), mortality differences among persons aged 1 to 55 are almost imperceptible, although there is a nearly 40-fold difference between the lowest and highest death rates in that age range. Plotted on a logarithmic scale (figure 6.10), differences among the low-mortality age groups are easily perceived, yet the much higher mortality rates among the oldest age groups still fit on the graph.

Charts to Display Logistic Regression Results

If your logistic model yields a mixture of odds ratios (OR) above and below 1.0 for categorical variables, design the chart to preserve symmetry in the interpretation of the effect sizes. For example, an OR of 5.0 for group A compared to group B is equivalent to an OR of 0.20 for group B compared to group A (simply reversing the reference category). Although these comparisons differ only in the choice of a reference category, with a linear y scale the former difference appears much larger than the latter (figure 6.21a). To minimize this visual misinterpretation either:

- Plot the odds ratios on a logarithmic y scale, as in figure 6.21b.
- Reestimate your model, coding all dummy variables so that the reference category is the lowest risk category, producing odds ratios greater than 1.0 for each independent variable. This approach may not work for plots of competing risks, where one group could have increased odds of some outcomes but decreased odds of others (e.g., black children in figure 6.8).
- To accommodate a mixture of increased and decreased odds, plot the log-odds instead of the odds ratios as in figure 6.8. Groups with lower odds than the reference category will have bars that drop below the reference line at $y = 0.0$ (negative log-odds), while those with higher odds will have bars that rise above the line (positive log-odds).

A warning: many nonscientific audiences may not be comfortable with logarithmic scales or log-odds, so avoid their use for such readers. If you must use a log scale in those contexts, mention that differences between some values are larger than they appear and use a couple of numeric examples to illustrate the range of values before describing the pattern shown in your data.

Digits and Decimal Places

Charts are best used to illustrate general patterns rather than to present exact data values. Choose a level of aggregation with at most five or six digits to avoid illegible axis labels.

■ COMMON ERRORS IN CHART CREATION

Watch out for some common errors that creep into charts—particularly those produced with computer software. Graphing applications seem to be programmed to visually maximize the difference between displayed values, resulting in misleading axis scales and design that varies across charts. Check your charts for the following design issues before printing your final copy.

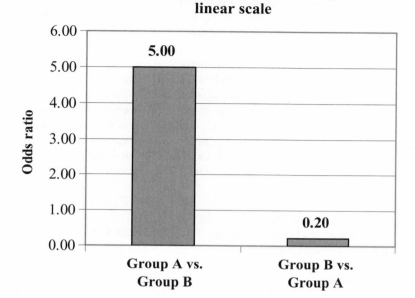

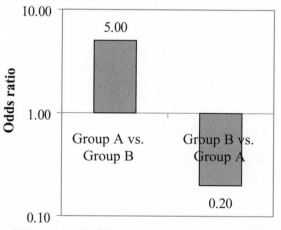

Figure 6.21. Odds ratios with (a) a linear *y*-scale, (b) a logarithmic *y*-scale.

Axis Scales

For all variables that include 0 in their plausible range, include 0 on the axis scale to avoid artificially inflating apparent differences. Even a small change can appear huge if the scale begins at a sufficiently high value. In figure 6.22a, the y scale starts at 60%, giving the appearance that the voter participation rate plummeted close to its theoretical minimum, when in fact it was still fully 63% in the latest period shown. When the chart is revised to start the y scale at 0, the possible range of the variable is correctly portrayed and the decline in voter participation appears much more modest (figure 6.22b).

This kind of error crops up most often when presenting small differences between large numbers. If this is your objective, plot the difference instead of the absolute level and report the absolute numbers elsewhere in the document.

Inconsistent Design of Chart Panels

Use uniform scale and design when creating a series of charts or panels to be compared.

Consistent y and x Scales

Show the same range of y values on each panel: panels a and b of figure 6.23 compare knowledge of unlikely (panel a) and likely (panel b) modes of AIDS transmission. However, the y axis in panel b runs from 0 to 100, while that in panel a runs from 0 to 90. Hence bars that appear the same height in fact represent two very different values. For example, knowledge of "working near someone with AIDS" appears to be as good as knowledge of the four "likely" modes of AIDS transmission, when in fact knowledge of "work near" is lower than all of them. When the scales for the two panels are consistent (figures b and c), the relative knowledge levels are displayed correctly.

Occasionally you will have to use different scales for different panels of a chart to accommodate a much wider range of values in one group than another. If so, point out the difference in scale as you compare the panels in the text.

Other Design Elements to Check

- Consistent sizing of comparable charts. Once you have specified a consistent scale for charts to be compared, ensure that the panels are printed in a uniform size on the page, each occupying a half sheet, for example. If one panel is much smaller, a bar of equivalent numeric value will appear shorter

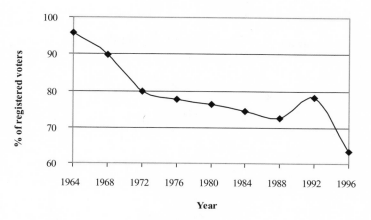

a. Voter participation, U.S. presidential elections, 1964–1996

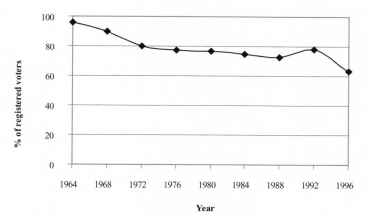

b. Voter participation, U.S. presidential elections, 1964–1996

Figure 6.22. Line charts of same pattern with (a) truncated *y*-scale, (b) full *y*-scale.

Source: Institute for Democracy and Electoral Assistance 1999.

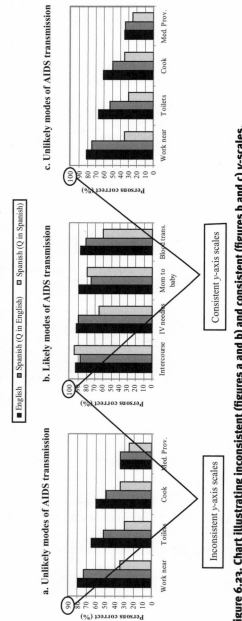

Knowledge of AIDS transmission modes by topic, language spoken at home, and language of questionnaire (Q), New Jersey, 1998

■ English ■ Spanish (Q in English) ▨ Spanish (Q in Spanish)

a. Unlikely modes of AIDS transmission

b. Likely modes of AIDS transmission

c. Unlikely modes of AIDS transmission

Inconsistent *y*-axis scales

Consistent *y*-axis scales

Figure 6.23. Chart illustrating inconsistent (figures a and b) and consistent (figures b and c) *y*-scales.
Source: Miller 2000a.

than on a larger chart, misleading readers into thinking that the value displayed is lower than those in other panels of the chart.

- Consistent ordering of nominal variables, both on the chart axes and within the legend. If panel A sorts countries in descending order of the dependent variable but panel B uses regional groupings, the same country might appear in very different places in the two panels. Or, if you intentionally organize the charts differently to make different points, mention that as you write your description.

- Uniform color or shading scheme (for lines, bars, or slices). Make English-speakers the same color in every panel of a given chart, and if possible, all charts within the same document that compare across language groups.

- Consistent line styles (for line charts). If you use a dotted line for the Northeast in panel A, make sure it is represented with a dotted line in panel B.

- Standardized plotting symbols (for scatter charts involving more than one series). If an asterisk represents males in a chart comparing males and females, use that same symbol in other charts that compare the genders.

- Consistent footnote symbols: if an asterisk denotes $p < 0.01$ on figure x, don't use it to indicate $p < 0.05$ on figure y.

Use of Line Charts Where Bar Charts Are Appropriate
Line Chart for Nominal Variables
Line charts connect y values for consecutive values on the x axis. Reserve them for interval or ratio data—in other words, for variables that have an inherent numerical order and for which absolute difference can be calculated. Do not connect values for nominal categories such as crude oil production by country (figure 6.24). The countries were organized in descending order of the dependent variable, but could equally well have followed alphabetical order or grouping by geographic region, so including a connecting line may encourage readers to mistakenly think about a "slope" for this relationship. For nominal variables, use a bar chart (figure 6.4).

Line Chart for Unequally Spaced Ordinal Categories
A more insidious problem is the use of line charts to connect values for ordinal variables that are divided into unequally spaced categories, as with the income data shown in figure 6.25a. Equal spacing of unequal categories misrepresents the true slope of the relationship

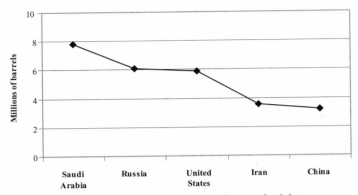

Figure 6.24. Inappropriate use of line chart with nominal data.
Source: U.S. National Energy Information Center 2003.

between the two variables (change in the *y* variable per unit change in the *x* variable). To prevent such distortion, treat the *x* values as interval data by plotting each *y* value above the midpoint of the corresponding income range on an *x* axis marked with equal increments (figure 6.25b).

Coefficients on Categorical and Continuous Variables

Present coefficients or odds ratios for continuous and categorical independent variables in separate charts. The coefficient for a continuous variable like years of age is per one-unit increase in that variable, whereas that for a categorical variable compares one category against another. However, realistic contrasts in the continuous variable might involve changes of several units and hence a larger net effect on the dependent variable. (See chapter 9 for how to interpret coefficients on different types of variables.) Use the approach shown in figure 6.15 to illustrate coefficients for categorical variables, then illustrate the effects of a continuous variable with a line chart like figure 6.11. To compare several continuous variables, plot standardized coefficients to correct for differences in units and distribution.

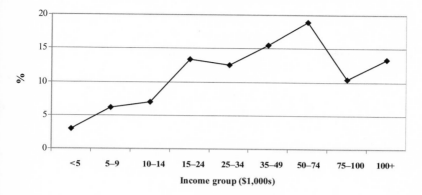

a. Income distribution, percentage of households, United States, 2000

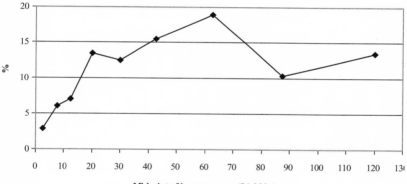

b. Income distribution, percentage of households, United States, 2000

Figure 6.25. Line chart with unequally spaced ordinal variable.
(a) Incorrect *x*-scale, (b) Correct *x*-scale.
Source: U.S. Bureau of the Census 2001c.

▣ CHECKLIST FOR CREATING EFFECTIVE CHARTS

- To choose an appropriate chart type, compare the attributes of
  your topic and data to those summarized in table 6.1.
    Consider type of variables.
    Consider number of variables.
    Establish objective of chart, either
        − composition (univariate), or
        − comparison of values of some other variable across
          groups (bivariate or higher order).
- Evaluate your charts for completeness and consistency.
    Does the title differentiate the topic from those of other
    charts and tables in the same document?
    Is the chart self-contained? Consider
        − context (W's),
        − units for each variable,
        − legend (if needed),
        − definitions and abbreviations, and
        − data sources
    Is the chart organized to coordinate with the narrative?
    Is the design (color, line style, etc.) consistent with similar
    charts in the same document?
    Are the axis scale and printed size consistent with other
    associated charts?
    Does the axis scale include zero? If not, does it encompass
    the plausible range of values for the pertinent variable?
    Is the chart readable in black and white?
- When plotting coefficients from a multivariate model,
    create separate charts for categorical and continuous
        predictors;
    include a footnote to list other independent variables
        controlled in the model, define the reference category,
        or refer to a table with complete model results.

Choosing Effective Examples and Analogies

Examples, analogies, and metaphors are valuable tools for illustrating quantitative findings and concepts. However, choosing effective ones is more complicated than it might first appear. How do you pick analogies that your audience can relate to? How do you avoid selecting numeric contrasts that are too large or too small, or that don't correspond to likely uses of your calculations? As noted in chapter 2, an ideal example is simple, plausible, and relevant to both the issue and audience. Simplicity involves length, familiarity, and wording, while relevance entails considering standard cutoffs and patterns in the field and other contextual issues. Empirical issues such as the range of values in your data and how the variables are measured should also inform your choice of example. I begin this chapter by describing ways to use examples and analogies in quantitative writing, then present criteria to help you choose effective examples.

■ WHY USE NUMERIC EXAMPLES?

Every numeric example performs one of several purposes: to generate interest in the topic of your work, to quantify differences across groups or time periods, to translate complicated statistical or technical findings into more accessible form, or to illustrate the implications of a statistical finding in a broader social or scientific context.

Establish the Importance of Your Topic

Engage your readers' interest by demonstrating the importance of your topic, ideally right at the beginning of the work. Catch their attention with a few choice statistics on the frequency with which some problem occurs or the consequences of that phenomenon. If you show that doing something a new way can save them a lot of money or extend their lives by several years, readers will want to find out more about it. If told that incidence of low birth weight is rising or that it is less common in other similar countries, they will be motivated to continue reading.

Compare to Previous Statistics

To establish the context and comparability of your findings, relate new information to what is already known. Contrast this year's rate of low birth weight with last year's, or compare your findings with results of previous studies. Use quantitative contrasts to assess the extent of similarity or difference between data from different sources. This application of numeric examples is often used in an introduction, a review of the previous literature, or a concluding section of a work.

Explicate Results of Models

In analytic sections of a scientific paper, illustrate results of statistical models. Decipher complicated statistical model results by translating coefficients into substantively meaningful comparisons, such as the effect of a 20-unit increase in blood pressure on risk of hospital admission (see section on per-unit changes below). Generate predicted values of the dependent variable for selected values of key independent variables to contrast common or interesting case examples from your data. Suppose you have estimated a model of birth weight using a range of socioeconomic and behavioral independent variables. To show the effect of quitting smoking, compare predicted birth weight for smokers and nonsmokers with all other characteristics "held constant" at their sample means. Or contrast two or more case examples chosen to represent different but typical profiles from your sample. For instance, low educational attainment and low income tend to occur together, so you might compare birth weight for infants born to less-educated, low-income women against those born to more-educated, higher-income women.

Illustrate Repercussions of Analytic Results

Use examples to assess substantive significance. Multiply the excess risk of low birth weight (LBW) associated with a given risk factor by the total number of such infants to illustrate how many LBW births could be avoided by eliminating that risk factor. Combine estimates of reductions in airborne particulates from a new pollution-prevention technology with information on the respiratory effects of particulates to place the new technology in a broader environmental and health perspective. Use these approaches in a general-interest article or in the analytic or concluding section of a scientific paper.

■ WHY USE ANALOGIES?

Use analogies to help readers grasp the scale of your numbers, understand the shape of an unfamiliar pattern or a relationship between variables, or follow the logic in a multistep calculation. Metaphors, similes, and other related rhetorical devices can also be used to accomplish these tasks; for simplicity I refer to this family of concepts as analogies.

Analogies to Illustrate Scale

Explain very large or very small numbers to audiences that are not conversant with that scale by illustrating those numbers with concrete analogies. To convey the enormity of the world population, the Population Reference Bureau (1999) used the following illustrations of "how much is a billion?"

- "If you were a billion seconds old, you would be 31.7 years of age."
- "The circumference of the earth is 25,000 miles. If you circled the earth 40,000 times, you would have traveled 1 billion miles."

Other dimensions such as weight, volume, or velocity can also be portrayed with analogies. For a nutrition fact sheet or diet guide, relate standard portion sizes to common objects: a standard 4-ounce serving of meat is equivalent to a regulation-size deck of playing cards; a half-cup serving of rice would fill half a tennis ball.

Analogies to Demonstrate Patterns or Relationships

Portray patterns or relationships using descriptors such as "U-shaped" or "bell-shaped." To illustrate a positive association, compare it to how children's age and height move up together. To describe an inverse association, refer to the relationship between higher prices and lower demand. Analogies can also be used to explain more complicated patterns or relationships. In the business section of the *New York Times,* seasonal adjustment of employment rates was related to the mental process many people apply to the way their body weight changes with the seasons (box 7.1). The fact that the analogy was published shortly after the winter holidays probably only increased its effectiveness.

Box 7.1. Analogy for Seasonal Adjustment

From the *New York Times* Job Market section: "Most of us routinely engage in a little seasonal adjustment of our own. Say, for example, you always put on five pounds between Dec. 1 and New Year's Day, and then work it off at the gym over the next six months. When you step on the scale on Jan. 1, you don't say 'Yikes! I'm turning into a blob.' You say 'Here we go again.' But what if, one year, there were a sugar-plum shortage, and you gained only two pounds? You'd probably be relieved. But you'd be even happier if you used economics-style seasonal adjustments, because then you could claim that you actually *lost* three pounds. And so you would have, compared with what you usually weigh at that time of year." (Eaton 2002)

Analogies to Explain Processes or Calculations

To explicate unfamiliar processes or calculations, relate them to well-known ones. If you liken exponentiating and taking logarithms to "doing and undoing" a mathematical calculation and follow with a more elementary example of inverse operations such as multiplication and division, most listeners will quickly grasp the basic idea. Descriptions of more complex calculations can also be clarified by comparison to familiar processes, although they often require longer, step-by-step explanations. Consider the following ways to introduce odds ratios to a nonstatistical audience:

Poor: "If the probability of low birth weight (LBW) among blacks is denoted P_b and the probability of LBW among whites is P_w, the odds ratio of LBW for blacks compared to whites is the odds for the first group divided by the odds for the second group, or $[P_b/(1 - P_b)]/[P_w/(1 - P_w)]$."

An equation full of symbols and subscripts is likely to scare off most nonstatisticians. Even those hardy enough to tackle it will spend a lot of time wading through the notation instead of understanding the logic. For folks who understand odds and odds ratios, just tell them which is the comparison group (e.g., the denominator); the equation is probably superfluous.

Not much better: "Odds ratios are one set of odds divided by another. For example, the odds of low birth weight differ by racial group, so we take the ratio of the odds in one case (e.g., black infants) to the odds in the other case (e.g., white infants). The ratio of to 0.127 to 0.062 equals 2.05, so the odds ratio is 2.05."

The basic logic is in place here, but for an audience not used to thinking about odds, the source of the figures is not clear. Where did the value 0.127 come from? The value 0.062? (See "Odds" in chapter 9 to find out.) Most people will remember that a ratio involves division, but wording such as "ratio of ___ to ___" often confuses nonmath folks. Finally, readers are left on their own to interpret what that value of the odds ratio means.

Best (for a lay audience): "Odds ratios are a way of comparing the chances of some event under different circumstances. Many people are familiar with odds from sports. For example, if the Yankees beat the Red Sox in two out of three games so far this season, the odds of another Yankees victory would be projected as 2-to-1 (two wins against one loss). Now suppose that the chances of a win depend on who is pitching. Last year, the Yankees won two out of three games against the Red Sox when Clemens pitched (2-to-1 odds) and two out of four times when Pettite was on the mound (1-to-1 odds). The *odds ratio* of a Yankees win for Clemens compared to Pettite is 2-to-1 divided by 1-to-1, or 2. In other words, this measure suggests that the odds of a Yankees victory are twice as high if Clemens is the starter. The same logic can be used to estimate how the relative chances of other types of events differ according to some characteristic of interest, such as how much odds of low birth weight differ by race."

This explanation is longer but every sentence is simple and explains one step in the logic behind calculating and interpreting an odds ratio.

For statistically knowledgeable audiences, you needn't explain the calculation, but a brief analogy is an effective introductory device:

"An odds ratio measures how the chances of an event change under different conditions, such as the odds of a Yankees victory if Clemens is pitching compared to when Pettite is on the mound."

◼ CRITERIA FOR CHOOSING EXAMPLES AND ANALOGIES

In chapter 2, I introduced two criteria for choosing effective examples: simplicity and plausibility. Here, I elaborate on those criteria and offer several others—familiarity, timeliness, relevance, intended use, and comparability.

Simplicity

Simplicity is in the eye of the beholder, to adapt the old expression. To communicate ideas, choose examples and analogies to fit your audience, not yourself. What seems obvious to one person may be hopelessly obscure to others. A necessarily thorough explanation for one group may be overkill for another. If you are writing for several audiences, adapt the content and wording of your analogies to suit each group. For most applied audiences, the ideal analogy will be as nonquantitative as possible.

Familiarity

Choose analogies that your audience can relate to their own experience. For adults, you might illustrate the penalties associated with missing a deadline by mentioning the consequences of being late for the income tax return filing date. For children, being tardy for school is a better analogy. If your average reader will need to look up a concept or term to grasp your point, find another analogy.

Timeliness increases familiarity. To introduce the field of epidemiology to a group of undergraduates in the mid-1990s, I used the 1976 Legionnaire's disease outbreak at a convention of the Pennsylvania American Legion—the group from which the disease took its name. I subsequently realized most of my students were still in diapers when that outbreak occurred, which is why my example drew a sea of blank stares. A few years later when the movie *Outbreak* was released, students flocked to me to recount scenes from the movie that illustrated various concepts we were learning in class. Now I scan the popular press shortly before I teach to identify fresh examples of the topics I will cover. Especially for a general audience, pick examples that are current or so famous (or infamous) that their salience does not fade with time.

Vocabulary

Don't obscure your message with a poor choice of words. Use terminology with which your audience is comfortable. Your objective is to communicate, not to demonstrate your own sophistication. Mathematically inclined audiences will understand "asymptotically approaching" and "sigmoid," but others will relate better to "leveling off" and "S-shaped."

Plausibility

Assessing plausibility requires an intimate acquaintance with both your topic and your data. Don't mindlessly apply values gleaned from other studies. For instance, patterns of low birth weight among all infants are unlikely to represent those among infants from low-income families. Review the literature in your field to learn the theoretical basis of the relationships you are analyzing, then use descriptive statistics and exploratory data analytic techniques to familiarize yourself with the distributions of your key variables and identify unusual values.

Sometimes you will want to use both typical and atypical values, to illustrate upper and lower limits or best-case and worst-case scenarios. If so, identify extreme values as such so your audience can differentiate among utopian, draconian, and moderate estimates. See below for more information on sensitivity analyses that compare estimates based on several sets of values or assumptions.

Relevance

A critical facet of a numeric example or comparison is that it be relevant—that it match its substantive context and likely application.

Substantive Context

Before you select numeric values to contrast, identify conventional standards, cutoffs, or comparison values used in the field.

- Evaluations of children's nutritional status often use measures of the number of standard deviations above or below the mean for a standard reference population (Kuczmarski et al. 2000). If you don't use those measures or the same reference population, your findings cannot easily be compared with those of other studies.
- Eligibility for social programs like Medicaid or food stamps is based on multiples of the Federal Poverty Level. If you use purely empirical groupings such as quartiles or standard deviations of the income distribution, your examples will not be directly applicable.

Intended Use

Before you choose examples and specify your model, find out how your intended audience is likely to use the information. Suppose you are studying characteristics that affect responsiveness to a drug rehabilitation program. In an academic journal, you might report estimates from a regression that controls simultaneously for age, sex, and educational attainment. In an issue brief or chartbook, describe patterns for specific age or education groups that correspond to program design features instead.

Comparability
Comparability of Context

In background examples, present data from a similar context (who, what, when, and where). For comparisons, choose data from a context that differs in at most one of those dimensions. If you compare women under age 40 from California in 2000 with people of all ages from the entire United States in 1980, it is hard to know whether any observed differences are due to gender, age, location, or date. Which dimension you vary will depend on the point you want to make: are you examining trends over time, or differences by gender, age group, or location? In each case, cite information that differs only in that dimension, keeping the other W's unchanged.

Comparability of Units

Make sure the numbers you compare are in consistent units and that those units are familiar to your readers. If you are combining numbers from data sources that report different units, do the conversions before you write, then report all numbers in the same type of unit.

Poor: "The 2002 Toyota Prius hybrid (gas/electric) engine requires 4.6 liters of gasoline per 100 kilometers, compared to 33 miles per gallon for a 2002 Toyota Corolla with a gasoline-only engine (www.fueleconomy.gov 2002)."

For some idiosyncratic reason, in the British measurement system fuel economy is reported in terms of distance traveled on a given volume of gasoline (miles per gallon—the higher, the better), but in the metric system the convention is how much gas is required to go a given distance (liters per 100 kilometers—the lower, the better). Hence, this comparison is worse than "apples and oranges." If readers don't pay attention to the units, they will simply compare 4.6 against 33. American and British readers will incorrectly conclude that the gasoline-only engine has better fuel economy, while metric thinkers will conclude that the hybrid is better, but based on incorrect logic.

Better (for those who use British units): "Hybrid (electric/gas) engines improve considerably on fuel economy. For example, the 2002 Toyota Prius hybrid engine gets 52 miles per gallon

(mpg) compared with 33 mpg for the 2002 Toyota Corolla with
a gasoline-only engine."

Better (for the rest of the world): "Hybrid (electric/gas) engines
improve considerably on fuel economy. For example, the 2002
Toyota Prius hybrid engine requires only 4.6 liters of gasoline
per 100 kilometers (L/100 km) as against 7.2 L/100 km for the
2002 Toyota Corolla with a gasoline-only engine."

*Apples to apples or oranges to oranges, as the case may be. No need
for your readers to conduct a four-step conversion calculation.*

■ SENSITIVITY ANALYSES

Sensitivity analyses show how results or conclusions vary when
different definitions, standards, or statistical specifications are used.
Each definition, standard, or specification constitutes a different example and is chosen using the criteria outlined above. Sensitivity
analyses can be used as follows:

- To compare results of several different values of independent
  variables. When projecting future population, demographers
  often generate a series of high, medium, and low projections,
  each of which assumes a different growth rate (figure 6.1).
  Typically, the medium value is chosen to reflect current
  conditions, such as the population growth rate from the past
  year, while the high and low values are plausible higher and
  lower growth rates.
- To compare a new standard or definition against its current
  version. In the mid-1990s, the National Academy of Sciences
  convened a panel of experts to assess whether the existing
  definition of poverty thresholds should be changed to reflect
  new conditions or knowledge (Citro et al. 1996). Their report
  included a table showing what poverty rates would have been
  in each of several demographic groups under both the old and
  new definitions of poverty (table 7.1).
- To compare results with and without imputed values for
  missing data (see "Imputation" in chapter 12).
- To assess sensitivity of results to trimming sampling weights
  (see "Trimming Sampling Weights" in chapter 12).
- To test the effects of different functional forms or other
  aspects of model specification. For example, the age pattern
  of mortality can be modeled using different statistical
  distributions such as the Weibull, Gompertz, or exponential

Table 7.1. Tabular presentation of a sensitivity analysis

Poverty rates (%) by group under current and proposed poverty measures, United States, 1992

	Current measure[b]	Proposed measure[a]		Percentage point change Current vs. proposed	
		Alt. 1	Alt. 2	Alt. 1	Alt. 2
Total population	14.5	18.1	19.0	3.6	4.5
Age					
Children <18	21.9	26.4	26.4	4.5	4.5
Adults 65+	12.9	14.6	18.0	1.7	5.1
Race/ethnicity					
White	11.6	15.3	16.1	3.7	4.5
Black	33.2	35.6	36.8	2.4	3.6
Hispanic	29.4	41.0	40.9	10.6	10.5

Source: Citro et al. 1996

[a]Alternative 1 uses the same income threshold as the current measure, an economy scale factor of 0.75, housing cost index, and a new proposed resource definition. Alternative 2 is the same as alternative 1 but with an economy scale factor of 0.65. See chapter 5 of Citro et al. 1996 for additional information.

[b]Based on the 1992 threshold of $14,800 for a two-adult/two-child family.

functions. A sensitivity analysis might compare overall model goodness-of-fit statistics or robustness of coefficients when different functional forms of the age variable are specified for an otherwise identical model.

For applied audiences, conduct the analysis behind the scenes and describe the findings in nonstatistical language:

"Under the current measure, the 1992 poverty rate for the United States as a whole was 14.5%, compared to 18.1% with a new housing cost index and proposed resource definition recommended by an expert panel of the National Academy of Sciences (Citro et al. 1996, 263)."

Simple comparisons often can be summarized in a sentence or two.

"In every demographic group examined, estimated poverty rates were several percentage points higher under either alternative poverty definition 1 or 2 than under the current poverty definition (table 7.1). Changes were larger under Alternative 2 than Alternative 1 in all but one subgroup."

To present detailed results of a sensitivity analysis, create a chart like figure 6.1 or a table like table 7.1. To compare three or more scenarios for a scientific audience, report the different assumptions for each variant in a column of a table (see "Column Spanners" in chapter 5), a footnote, or an appendix. If the definitions, standards, or statistical specifications are explained in another published source, give a brief description in your document and cite the pertinent source.

■ COMMON PITFALLS IN CHOICE OF NUMERIC EXAMPLES

Failing to examine the distribution of your variables, falling into one of several decimal system biases, or disregarding default software settings can create problems with your choice of examples.

Ignoring the Distributions of Your Variables

Overlooking the distributions of your variables can lead to some poor choices of numeric examples and contrasts. Armed with information on range, mean, variability, and skewness of the major variables you discuss, you will be in a better position to pick reasonable values, and to be able to characterize them as above or below average, typical, or atypical.

Using Typical Values

Make sure the examples you intend as illustrations of typical values are in fact typical: avoid using the mean to represent highly skewed distributions or other situations where few cases have the mean value. If Einstein had happened to be one of 10 people randomly chosen to try out a new math aptitude test, the mean score would have vastly overstated the expected performance of an average citizen, so the median or modal value would be a more representative choice. If half the respondents to a public opinion poll strongly agree with a proposed new law and the other half passionately oppose it, characterizing the "average" opinion as in the middle would be inappropriate; in such a case, a key point would be the polarized nature of the distribution.

Unrealistic Contrasts

Avoid calculating the effect of changing some variable more than it has been observed to vary in real life. Remember, a variable is unlikely to take on the full range of all possible values. Although balance scales include the measurement zero grams, you'd be hard pressed to find any live-born infants weighing that little in a real-world sample. Instead, pick the lowest value found in your data or a low percentile taken from a standard distribution to illustrate the minimum.

If you use the highest and lowest observed values, explain that those values represent upper and lower bounds, then include a couple of smaller contrasts to illustrate more realistic changes. For instance, the reproductive age range for women is biologically fixed at roughly ages 15 to 45 years, on average. However, a woman who is considering childbearing can realistically compare only her current age with older ages, so for women in their 20s, 30s, or 40s, the younger end of that range isn't relevant. Even among teenagers, for whom that entire theoretically possible range is still in their future, few will consider delaying childbearing by 30 years. Hence, comparing the effects of having a child at ages 15 versus 45 isn't likely to apply to many women. A more reasonable contrast would be a 5-year difference—age 15 versus 20, or 25 versus 30, for example.

Out-of-Range Values

Take care when using example values that fall outside the range of your data. This issue is probably most familiar for projecting future values based on historical patterns, but also applies to regression based on a limited age or income range to predict outcomes for other ages or incomes, for example. Accompany your calculations with a description of the assumptions and data upon which they are based.

Decimal System Biases

Ours is a decimal (base 10) oriented society: people tend to think in increments of one or multiples of 10, which may or may not correspond to a realistic or interesting contrast. Before you reflexively use a 1- or 10- or 100-unit difference, evaluate whether that difference suits your research question, taking into account theory, the previous literature on the subject, your data, and common usage. Frequently, the "choice" of comparison unit is made by the statistical program used to do the analysis because the default increment often is 1-unit or 10-unit contrasts.

Single-Unit Contrasts

Even if you have concluded that a one-unit increase is realistic, other contrasts may be of greater interest. Showing how much more food an American family could buy with one dollar more income per week would be a trivial result given today's food prices. A difference of 25 or 50 dollars would be more informative. Even better, find out how much a proposed change in social benefits or the minimum wage would add to weekly income, then examine its effects on food purchases. However, as always, context matters: if you were studying the United States in the early twentieth century or some less developed countries today, that one-dollar contrast in weekly income would be well fitted to the question.

In regression analysis, the coefficient on a continuous independent variable reflects the effect of a one-unit increase in that variable on the dependent variable, such as the association between an additional dollar of income and birth weight (see chapter 9 for an explanation of regression coefficients). Even if a one-unit increase is realistic, other contrasts may be more relevant. For example, in an analysis of biomedical risk factors for hospital admission, my colleagues and I contrasted predicted risk of admission for increments of the independent variables identified using clinical or empirical criteria (table 7.2, adapted from Miller et al. 1998). For blood pressure, for which a 1 millimeter mercury (mm Hg) difference is too small to be clinically meaningful or measured with precision, we compared effects of 20 mm Hg increments—a standard increment in the medical literature. For serum albumin, which lacked established cutoffs related to health outcomes, we compared hospital admission rates for people at the 25th and 75th percentiles (the interquartile range)—a three- to four-unit change depending on the age/sex group (see footnote to table 7.2). By presenting these contrasts, we spared readers the task of identifying substantively meaningful contrasts and the hassle of doing the calculations based on the estimated coefficients (which we reported in a separate table; not shown).

Ten-Unit Contrasts

Some analyses, such as life table calculations, use 10-unit contrasts as the default—a poorly suited choice for many research questions. For instance, infant mortality declines precipitously in the hours, days, and weeks after birth. Ten-day age intervals are too wide to capture mortality variation in the first few weeks of life and too

Table 7.2. Calculated effects of substantively meaningful contrasts based on regression coefficients

Relative Risks of Hospital Admission for Specified Values of Continuous Variables, by Age and Sex, 1987 U.S. NHANES I Epidemiologic Followup Study

Variable	Age 45–64		Age 65 and older	
	Men	Women	Men	Women
Age (years)				
45 versus 50	1.09**	1.04*	NA	NA
65 versus 70	NA	NA	1.20**	1.10**
Systolic blood pressure (mm Hg)				
140 versus 120	1.09**	1.07**	1.02**	1.05**
160 versus 120	1.18**	1.15**	1.05**	1.09**
180 versus 120	1.28**	1.23**	1.07**	1.15**
Cholesterol (mg/dL)				
200 versus 180	1.01	1.01	1.01	0.99
240 versus 180	1.04	1.03	1.04	0.97
280 versus 180	1.07	1.05	1.07	0.95
Serum albumin (g/L)				
25th versus 75th percentiles[a]	0.93**	0.92*	0.90**	0.87**

Source: Miller et al. 1998.
Note: Based on a Cox proportional hazards model that accounts for body weight, smoking, exercise, alcohol consumption, dietary intake, chronic conditions, and the variables shown in table 7.2.
[a] The 25th and 75th percentiles of the albumin distribution differ by age/sex group; for males 45–64: 42 and 46; for females 45–64: 42 and 45; for males and females 65+ : 41 and 45.
*$p < 0.05$ **$p < 0.01$

narrow in the months thereafter. For that topic, more appropriate groupings are the first day of life, the rest of the first week (6 days), the remainder of the first month (21 days), and the rest of the first year (337 days). Although these ranges are of unequal width, mortality is relatively constant within each interval, satisfying an important empirical criterion. Those age ranges also correspond to theory about causes of infant mortality at different ages (Puffer and Serrano 1973;

Mathews et al. 2002). Before you choose your contrasts, investigate the appropriate increment for your research question and do the calculations accordingly.

Digit Preference and Heaping

Another issue is digit preference, whereby people tend to report certain numeric values more than others nearby because of social convention or out of a preference for particular units. In decimal-oriented societies, folks are apt to prefer numbers that end in 0 or 5 (Barclay 1958), rounding actual values of variables such as weight, age, or income to the nearest multiple of 5 or 10 units. When reporting time, people are inclined report whole weeks or months rather than exact number of days; or quarter, half, or whole hours rather than exact number of minutes. These patterns result in "heaping"—a higher than expected frequency of those values at the expense of adjacent ones (figure 7.1).

If you have pronounced heaping in your data, treating the heaped responses and those on either side as precise values may be inappropriate. Instead, analyze data that are grouped into ranges around those preferred digits. For example, if many people who earn between $23,000 and $27,999 report their income as $25,000, looking at small changes within that range may not make sense. Graphs or tabular frequency distributions can help evaluate whether heaping or digit preference is occurring.

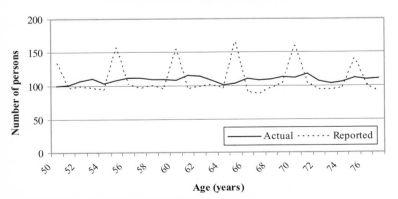

**Hypothetical age distribution
with and without heaping, ages 50 and older**

Figure 7.1. Graphical depiction of data heaping.

Units or Categories of Measurement

Suitable comparisons also are constrained by how your data were collected. With secondary data you are forced to use someone else's choices of level of aggregation and definitions of categories, whether or not those match your research question. If income data were collected in ranges of $500, you cannot look at effects of smaller changes. Even if you pick values such as $490 and $510 that happen to cross category limits, the real comparison is between the two entire categories (<$500 versus $500–$999), not the $20 difference you appear to be contrasting.

■ **CHECKLIST FOR CHOOSING EFFECTIVE EXAMPLES AND ANALOGIES**

- Select analogies or metaphors to fit each intended audience.
    Take into account their knowledge of the topic and
        concepts.
    Choose familiar ideas and vocabulary.
- Tailor each numeric example to fit its objective.
    Establish the importance of the topic.
    Compare against previous findings.
    Interpret your statistical results.
    Demonstrate substantive significance of your findings.
- Consider your numeric contrasts.
    Are they within the observed range of values in your data?
    Are they theoretically plausible?
    Are they substantively interesting—neither too big nor too
        small for real-world conditions?
    Do they apply conventional standards or cutoffs used in
        the field?
    Do they correspond to likely uses of the results?
- Specify whether the values you present are typical or unusual.
- Evaluate your contrasts.
    Check comparability of context (W's) and units.
    Present one or two selected types of quantitative
        comparisons.
- For a sensitivity analysis, explain the alternative input values,
    definitions, or functional forms.

Basic Types of Quantitative Comparisons

One of the most fundamental skills in writing about numbers is describing the direction and magnitude of differences among two or more values. You may need to quantify the size of a difference—whether an election was close or a landslide, for example. You may want to assess the pace of change over time—whether population growth was slow or rapid in recent years, for instance. Or you may want to show whether a value exceeds or falls short of some important cutoff, such as whether a family's income is below the poverty level and if so by how much.

There are several commonly used ways to compare numeric values: rank, absolute difference, relative difference, percentage difference, and z-scores. Another measure—attributable risk—is less familiar to many statistical analysts but is a useful addition to your quantitative toolkit. With the exception of z-scores, which require some basic statistical knowledge, these calculations involve no more than elementary arithmetic skills—subtraction, multiplication, or division. For most authors, the difficult part of quantitative comparison is deciding which aspects are best suited to the question at hand and then explaining the results and their interpretation clearly and correctly. In the sections below, I describe how to choose among, calculate, and describe these measures, which provide the foundation for understanding and writing about numeric contrasts based on regression model results—the subject of the next chapter.

▪ COORDINATING CALCULATIONS WITH PROSE

As with the tools described in the last few chapters, an important aspect of working with quantitative comparisons is to coordinate them with the associated narrative. Think about how you prefer to word your comparisons, then perform the corresponding calculations accordingly. Doing so will spare your readers the confusion of interpreting ratios that you have accidentally described "upside down" or subtraction you have inadvertently explained "backward" (see examples below).

■ CHOICE OF A REFERENCE VALUE

The first step in comparing numbers is to decide which values to compare. Often you will contrast a figure from your own data against numbers or distributions from other sources. For instance, you might compare average children's height for one country against international growth standards, or today's scorching temperature against historic records for the same date and location. In addition, you might contrast several values from within your own data, such as average heights of children from several different countries, or the daily high temperatures over the past week.

Use of Standards and Conventions

As discussed in chapter 4, standards and conventions exist in many fields. A few examples:

- As of early 2003, the year 1984 was used as the baseline or reference value for the Consumer Price Index when calculating inflation (U.S. Bureau of Labor Statistics 2002b).
- National norms for exam scores and physical growth patterns are standard distributions used to evaluate individual test scores or height measurements.
- The federal poverty thresholds (Proctor and Dalaker 2003) are reference values that are commonly used to assess family income data.

If conventions or standards are commonly applied in your field and topic, use them as the reference values in your calculations.

Comparisons Within Your Own Data

If external standards don't exist or you want to provide additional contrasts, pick salient comparison values within your own data. Some guidelines about deciding on a reference value or group for use in basic calculations or multivariate models.

For Basic Calculations

To choose reference values for use in descriptive statistics or simple calculations reported in an introduction or conclusion, consider the following:

- Social norms and considerations of statistical power often suggest comparison against the modal category. In language comparisons within the United States, English speakers comprise a sensible reference group.
- Pick a reference group to suit your audience and research question. For a report to your state's Department of Human Services, national values or those for adjacent states are logical points of reference.
- If there is no standard benchmark date for a temporal comparison, changes are often calculated relative to the earliest value under consideration, sometimes against the most recent value.
- The value for all groups combined is a good comparison value for bivariate comparisons as long as none of the subgroups comprises too large a share of that whole. None of the 50 states is so large that its value dominates the total population of the United States, so the United States is a fine basis of comparison for each of the individual states. However, comparing values for males against those of both sexes combined is a poor choice because males make up half the population, strongly influencing the value for the whole population. Instead, compare males to another subgroup (in this case the only other subgroup)—females.

Choice of a comparison value may depend on data availability.

- The U.S. Census is conducted at 10-year intervals and surveys are conducted periodically, so you may have to compare against the closest census or survey date even if it doesn't exactly match the date of interest.
- Information on small groups or unusual cases may have to be approximated using data on related groups or similar cases.

For Multivariate Models

Choice of a reference value also pertains to multivariate analyses, where you must specify a reference category for each dummy variable in the model (see "Coefficients on Categorical Independent Variables" in chapter 9).

- As in bivariate contrasts, norms and statistical power issues imply comparison against the modal category. In a regression model with several independent variables, specifying the largest racial group as the reference category often makes sense.
- To contrast treatment and control groups, the control group usually serves as the reference category. To approximate a quasi-experimental evaluation of a new math curriculum, specifying the old curriculum as the reference category in a multivariate regression model is a logical choice.
- Likewise, a model to estimate the effect of exposure to some risk factor typically specifies the unexposed group as the reference category. In a multivariate analysis of effects of cigarette smoking on some health outcome, nonsmokers would be specified as the reference category.

The initial choice of a reference group or value may be arbitrary: it might not matter which group or place or date you choose as the basis of comparison. However, once you have selected your reference, be consistent, using it for all bivariate or multivariate analyses addressing a particular question. If you have decided on the Midwest as the reference region, calculate and report values for each of the other regions compared to the Midwest, not the South versus the Midwest and the Northeast versus the West.

If you compare against a standard threshold or other value from outside your data, report its value in the text, table, or chart. For comparisons against standard distributions involving many numbers (e.g., national norms for test scores or physical growth) provide descriptive statistics or a summary chart, then refer to a published source for more detailed information.

Wording for Comparisons

Name the comparison or reference group or value in your description of all numeric contrasts so the comparison can be interpreted. "The sex ratio was 75" doesn't convey whether that is 75 males per 100 females or 75 females per 100 males. The two meanings are not interchangeable.

Before you choose a reference value within your own data, anticipate how you will word the description. If you naturally want to compare all the other regions to the Midwest, make it the reference, then calculate and describe accordingly: "The Northeast is [measure of difference] larger (or smaller) than the Midwest." Without the phrase "than the Midwest," it isn't clear whether the comparison is relative

Table 8.1. Formulas and case examples for different types of quantitative comparisons

	Reference value	Rank based on x	Number of interest	Rank based on y	Absolute difference	Relative difference (ratio)	Percentage difference or percentage change
Formula	x		y		$y - x$	y/x	$[(y - x)/x] \times 100$
Case 1	1	3	2	5	1	2.00	100
Case 2	1	3	26	3	25	26.00	2,500
Case 3	25	2	50	2	25	2.00	100
Case 4	50	1	25	4	−25	0.50	−50
Case 5	50	1	51	1	1	1.02	2

Note: Ranks based on x and y are from highest (1) to lowest.

to the past (in other words, the region grew), to other concurrent estimates of the Northeast's population, or to some other unspecified region.

■ TYPES OF QUANTITATIVE COMPARISONS

There are several types of numeric contrasts, each of which provides a different perspective on the direction and magnitude of differences between numbers. In addition to reporting the values themselves, use rank, absolute difference, relative difference, percentage difference, z-score, or attributable risk help interpret the meaning of those values in the context of your research question. In this chapter, I use those terms for convenience and to relate them to mathematical and statistical concepts used elsewhere. In general, you should avoid technical jargon in your writing, substituting phrases such as those shown in the illustrative sentences throughout this chapter.

Value

The value is the amount or level of the measure for one case or time point: the infant mortality rate (IMR) in the United States in 2000; the current cost of a gallon of gasoline. Always report the value, its context, and its units. However, reporting the value alone leaves its purpose and meaning unclear. Is this year's IMR higher or lower than last year's? By how much? Is that a lot? To answer such questions, include one or more of the following numeric comparisons.

Rank

Rank is the position of the value for one case compared to other values observed in the same time or place, to a well-established standard, or against a historic high or low value. How does this year's IMR in the United States compare to that in other countries in the same year? To its IMR for last year? To the lowest IMR ever observed anywhere? "Seventh lowest," "lowest ever," and "middle of the pack" are examples of rankings. Two identical values share the same rank just as two identical race times or two equal vote tallies constitute a tie. For instance, the values of x for cases 4 and 5 in table 8.1 are both 50, so they share the rank of 1.

Percentile

When many cases are being compared, use percentiles to convey rank. An assessment of a child's height includes his percentile score to show how his height compares to that of all boys the same age. Percentiles are calculated by ranking all of the values and categorizing them into 100 groups each containing an equal share (1/100th) of the distribution (Utts 1999). Values that are lower than 99% of all other values are in the zeroth (or bottom) percentile, while those that exceed 99% of all other values are in the 99th (or top) percentile. The 50th percentile, or middle value, is the median; half of all values are lower and half are higher than the median. Because percentiles encompass all the values in a distribution, they are bounded between 0 and 99: it is impossible to be below the lowest value or above the highest value.

To describe rank in somewhat less detail, report deciles (ranges of ten percentiles), quintiles (one fifth of the distribution, encompassing 20 percentiles), quartiles (ranges of 25 percentiles), or terciles (the bottom, middle, and top third of the distribution).

Wording for Rank

To report rank, select words that describe both relative position and the concept being compared: "fastest," "least expensive," and "second most dense," make it clear that the descriptions pertain to velocity, price, and density, respectively. If you use the words "rank" or "percentile," also mention what is being compared: "Kate's GRE score placed her in the second highest quartile nationwide," or "The United States ranked seventh best in terms of infant mortality."

Rank and percentile do not involve units of their own but are based on the units of the values being compared. If you have already reported the values and their units elsewhere, omit them from your description of rank. If not, rank and value can often be incorporated into the same sentence.

Poor: "Marcus Bigbucks's rank for income is 1."

Although this statement may be correct, it can be restated in a more straightforward and informative way.

Better: "With an income of $27 billion in 2003, Marcus Bigbucks is the richest person in the world."

This version conveys the value, rank, and reference group in easily understood terms.

Advantages and Disadvantages of Rank

Rank is useful when all that matters is the order of values, not the distance between them. In elections, the critical issue is who came in first. Rank in class or quartiles of standard test scores are often used as admission criteria by colleges.

Although rank and percentile both provide information about relative position (higher or lower, faster or slower), they do not indicate by how much one value differed from others. In the 2000 U.S. presidential election, rank in electoral votes identified the winner but was not the only salient information. Bush's small margin of victory over Gore caused much debate and recounting of the popular vote—demands that would not have surfaced had the difference been larger. And some might argue that students at the bottom of the highest quartile and at the top of the second quartile are so similar that they should receive similar college admission offers.

To quantify size of difference between two or more values, use absolute difference, relative difference, percentage difference, or z-score. Their formulas (except z-scores) are presented in table 8.1, along with some numeric examples. Throughout table 8.1, x represents the reference or comparison value and y represents another number of interest.

Absolute Difference or Absolute Change

Absolute difference subtracts the reference value (x) from the number of interest (y), or y minus x. For case 1 in table 8.1, the absolute difference is 1 unit ($y - x = 2 - 1 = 1$). The absolute difference for case 5 is also 1 unit ($51 - 50 = 1$), although both x and y are much higher. Absolute change subtracts an earlier value from a more recent value, such as the U.S. population in 1999 minus its population in 1990. Absolute difference and absolute change can be used for either interval or ratio variables.

Wording for Absolute Difference

An absolute difference or change is computed by subtracting one value from another, so describe it in terms of a difference or margin. Mention the units, which are the same as those for the values being compared.

Poor: "The absolute change was 23.9 million (table 8.2)."
> This sentence reports the magnitude but not the direction of the change, does not explain what concept or cases are being compared, and uses unnecessary jargon.

Better: "In late 1999, the Census Bureau estimated a total U.S. population of 272.7 million persons—an increase of 23.9 million over the 1990 population (column 5 of table 8.2)."
> This version specifies the two cases being compared (their years), mentions the pertinent concept (population) and units (millions of people), and reports the direction and size of the change.

Table 8.2. Application of absolute difference, relative difference, and percentage change to United States population data

Region	(1) Population (millions) 1990	(2) Ratio 1990 (relative to Midwest)	(3) % Difference 1990 (rel. to Midwest)	(4) Population (millions) 1999	(5) Absolute change (millions) 1990–1999	(6) % Change 1990–1999
United States	248.8	NA	NA	272.7	23.9	9.6
Northeast	50.8	0.85	−14.9	51.8	1.0	2.0
Midwest	59.7	1.00	0.0	63.2	3.5	5.9
South	85.5	1.43	43.2	96.5	11.0	12.9
West	52.8	0.88	−11.6	61.2	8.4	15.9

Source: U.S. Census Bureau 1999b.

Advantages and Disadvantages of Absolute Difference

The absolute difference or absolute change is useful when the difference itself is of interest: how much more will something cost and is that amount within your budget? How many more people live in South Florida now than ten years ago and will that additional population overtax water supplies?

However, the absolute difference does not address all questions well. Is an eight-ounce weight loss big? For a premature infant weighing only 3.5 pounds (56 ounces), an eight-ounce weight loss could be life-threatening. For a sumo wrestler weighing 350 pounds (5,600 ounces), an eight-ounce weight loss would hardly be noticeable.

Relative Difference or Change

The relative difference is the ratio of two numbers, the number of interest (y) divided by the reference value (x). If the quantity in numerator (y) is larger than that in the denominator (x), the ratio is greater than 1.0, as in cases 1, 2, 3, and 5 in table 8.1. If the numerator is smaller than the denominator, the ratio is below 1.0, as in case 4 ($25/50 = 0.50$).

By dividing one value by the other, the relative difference adjusts for the fact that a one-unit absolute difference has very different interpretations if both values are very small than if both values are very large. In both cases 2 and 3, the absolute difference is 25 units. However, the relative difference is much larger in case 2 (ratio = 26.0) because the reference value is very small ($x = 1$). In case 3, the reference value is much higher ($x = 25$), yielding a much smaller ratio (2.0). Relative difference can be used for ratio variables but not interval variables: it makes no sense to say that it is 1.25 times as hot today as yesterday, for example.

Wording for Relative Difference

Describe a relative difference in terms of multiples: the value in the numerator is some multiple of the value in the denominator (without using that jargon . . . see table 8.3). Do not just report the ratio in the text without accompanying explanation:

Poor: "In 1990, the Southern numerator was 1.43 times the Midwestern denominator (column 2 of table 8.2)"
The terms "numerator" and "denominator" indicate that the comparison involves division, but the sentence doesn't express what aspect of the regions is being compared.

Table 8.3. Phrases for describing ratios and percentage difference

Type of ratio	Ratio example	Rule of thumb	Writing suggestion[a]
<1.0 (e.g., 0.x) *Percentage difference* = ratio × 100	0.80	[Group] is only x% as ____[b] as the reference value.	"Males were only 80% as likely as females to graduate from the program."
Close to 1.0	1.02	Use phrasing to express similarity between the two groups.	"Average test scores were similar for males and females(ratio = 1.02 for males compared to females)."
>1.0 (e.g., 1.y) *Percentage difference* = (ratio − 1) × 100.	1.20	[Group] is 1.y times as ____ as the reference value. *or* [Group] is y% ____er than the reference value.	"On average, males were 1.20 times as tall as females." *or* "Males were on average 20% taller than females."
	2.34	[Group] is (2.34 − 1) × 100, or 134% ____er than the reference value.	"Males' incomes were 134% higher than those of females."
Close to a multiple of 1.0 (e.g., z.00)	2.96	[Group] is (about) z times as ____.	"Males were nearly three times as likely to commit a crime as their female peers."

[a] Females are the reference group (denominator) for all ratios in table 8.3.

[b] Fill in each blank with an adjective, verb, or phrase to convey the aspect being compared, e.g., "tall," "likely to graduate."

Poor (version 2): "In 1990, the ratio between the South and the
Midwest was 1.43 (column 2, table 8.2)."
*This version doesn't convey what is being measured or which region has
the higher value.*
Better: "In 1990, the South was 1.43 times as populous as the
Midwest (column 2, table 8.2)."
*In this version, it is immediately evident what is being compared, which
region is bigger, and by how much.*

If the ratio is close to 1.0, use wording to convey that the two values are very similar. For ratios below 1.0, explain that the value is
smaller than the reference value. For ratios above 1.0, convey that the
value is larger than the reference value. Table 8.3 gives examples of
ways to explain ratios (including relative risk and odds ratios) without using phrases such as "ratio," "relative difference," "numerator,"
or "denominator."

Common Errors When Describing Ratios

Some cautions: word your explanation to conform to the kind of
calculation you performed. I have seen people subtract to find a 2-
unit difference between scores of 73 and 71, and then state that the
score for the second group was twice as high as for the first. Likewise,
if you divide to find a ratio of 1.03, do not explain it as a "1.03 unit
difference" between the quantities being compared.

Explain ratios in terms of multiples of the reference value, not
multiples of the original units. For example, although the 1990 populations of the South and Midwest were originally measured in millions of persons (column 1 of table 8.2), the ratio of 1.43 does not
mean there were 1.43 million times as many people in the South as
in the Midwest. During the division calculation the millions "cancel," as they say in fourth-grade math class, so there were 1.43 times
as many people in the South as in the Midwest in 1990.

Avoid calculating the ratio with one group as the denominator and
then explaining it "backward" or "upside down": for example, do not
report the relative size of the southern and midwestern populations
in a table as ratio = 1.43 and then describe the comparison as Midwest versus South ("The population of the Midwest was 0.70 times
that of the South").[1] Decide in advance which way you want to phrase
the comparison, then compute accordingly.

Percentage Difference and Percentage Change

Percentage difference is a ratio that expresses the difference between two values in relation to the reference value. Percentage change is a ratio that expresses the amount of change in relation to the original value. A one-unit absolute difference yields a much larger percentage difference with an initial level of 1 (case 1 in table 8.1) than for an initial level of 50 (case 5). To compute percentage difference, divide the absolute difference by the reference value, then multiply the result by 100 to put it in percentage terms: $[(y - x)/x] \times 100$. If you do not multiply by 100, you have a *proportionate* difference or change.

Percentage difference is typically calculated by subtracting the smaller from the larger value, hence such comparisons often yield positive percentage differences. Negative percentage differences usually occur only when several values are being compared against the same reference value, with some falling below and some above that value. For example, in 1990 the Northeast was 14.9% smaller than the Midwest ($[(50.8 \text{ million} - 59.7 \text{ million})/59.7 \text{ million}] \times 100 = -14.9\%$), whereas the South was 43% larger than the Midwest ($[(85.5 \text{ million} - 59.7 \text{ million})/59.7 \text{ million}] \times 100 = 43.2\%$; column 3, table 8.2).

A percentage *change* compares values for two different points in time. Conventionally, a percentage change subtracts the earlier (V_1) from the later value (V_2), then divides that difference by the initial value and multiplies by 100: $[(V_2 - V_1)/V_1] \times 100$.

- If the quantity increased over time, the percentage change will be positive. For the West region: $(V_{1999} - V_{1990})/V_{1990} \times 100 = (61.2 \text{ million} - 52.8 \text{ million})/52.8 \text{ million} \times 100 = 8.4 \text{ million}/52.8 \text{ million} \times 100 = 15.9\%$, reflecting a 15.9% increase in population between 1990 and 1999 (column 6 of table 8.2).
- If the quantity decreased over time, the percentage change will be negative. Between 1990 and mid-1999, the District of Columbia lost 14.5% of its population, decreasing from 607,000 persons to 519,000 in 1999 (U.S. Census Bureau 1999b): $(519 - 607)/607 \times 100 = -88/607 \times 100 = -14.5\%$.

If the time interval is very wide (e.g., several decades or centuries), sometimes the average of the values for the two times is used as the denominator: $(V_2 - V_1)/[(V_1 + V_2)/2] \times 100$. When you report a percentage change, indicate which date or dates were used as the base for the calculation.

A percentage difference is one variant of relative difference: if you know either the ratio or percentage difference between two values, you can calculate the other measure of relative difference:

- For ratios that are greater than 1.0, percentage difference = (ratio − 1) × 100. Conversely, ratio = (percentage difference/100) + 1. A recent article in the *American Journal of Public Health* reported that ready-to-eat cookies being sold in some popular fast-food and family restaurants have 700% more calories than the standard USDA portion size (Young and Nestle 2002)—a ratio of eight times the calories of a "standard" cookie.
- For ratios less than 1.0, percentage difference = ratio × 100. If there are 0.85 northeasterners per midwesterner, then the population of the Northeast is 85% as large as that of the Midwest (column 2, table 8.2).

Wording for Percentage Change or Difference

To describe percentage change or difference, identify the cases being compared and the direction of the difference or change. A percentage difference is expressed as a percentage of the reference value, replacing the units in which the original values were measured.

Poor: "The Western population percentage change was 15.9."
This sentence is awkwardly worded and does not convey which dates are being compared.

Better: "During the 1990s, the population of the West region grew from 52.8 million to 61.2 million persons—an increase of 15.9% (column 6, table 8.2)."
This version reports both value (population in each time period) and percentage change, including direction, magnitude, concepts, and units.

To report a negative value of percentage change or percentage difference, select words to convey direction:

Poor: "In 1990, the populations of the West and Midwest were 52.8 million and 59.7 million persons, respectively, so the percentage difference between the West and the Midwest is negative (−11.6%; column 3, table 8.2)."
Although this sentence reports the correct calculation, wording with negative percentage differences is unwieldy.

Better: "In 1990, the West had 11.6% fewer inhabitants than the Midwest (52.8 million persons and 59.7 million persons, respectively; table 8.2)."

The phrase "fewer inhabitants than the Midwest" clearly explains the direction of the difference in population between regions.

Common Errors for Wording of Percentage Difference

Do not confuse the phrases "*y* is 60% *as high as x*" and "*y* is 60% *higher than x*." The first phrase suggests that *y* is lower than *x* (i.e., that the ratio *y*/*x* = 0.60), the second that *y* is higher than *x* (i.e., *y*/*x* = 1.60). After you calculate a ratio or percentage difference, explain both the direction and the size of the difference, then check your description against the original numbers to make sure you have correctly communicated which is bigger—the value in the numerator or that in the denominator. See also table 8.3 for example sentences.

Watch your math and reporting of units to avoid mixing or mislabeling percentages and proportions. A proportion of 0.01 equals 1%, not 0.01%.

Other Related Types of Quantitative Comparison

Annual Rates

Many annual rates such as interest rates or population growth rates are measures of change over time that are reported in percentage form. However, an annual growth rate cannot be calculated simply by dividing a percentage change over an *n*-year period by *n*. For example, the annual growth rate in the West between 1990 and 1999 is not 15.9%/9 years. The explanation lies in the process of compounding: an interest rate is applied to a successively larger principal each year. The same logic applies to population growth: each year there are more people to whom the annual growth rate applies, so even if that growth rate is constant, the absolute number of additional people rises each year.[2] Between 1990 and 1999, the West region grew at an average annual rate of 1.65%.[3]

Percentage versus Percentile versus Percentage Change

A common source of confusion involves "percentage difference," "difference in percentage points" and "difference in percentiles." Just because they all have "percent-" in their names does not mean they are equivalent measures. If *x* and *y* are expressed as percentages, their units of measurement are percentage points; hence the absolute difference between their values is reported as a difference in percentage points. A rise in the unemployment rate from 4.2% to 5.3% corresponds to an increase of 1.1 percentage points, not a 1.1% difference. The percentage difference in those unemployment rates is (5.3% −

4.2%)/4.2% × 100, which is a 26% increase relative to the initial value.

Percentages and percentiles calculate the share of a whole and the rank within a distribution, respectively. By definition, neither can be less than zero or greater than 100: no case can have less than none of the whole, or more than all of it. In contrast, percentage change and percentage difference measure relative size against some reference value and are not constrained to fall between 0 and 100. If a value is more than twice the size of the reference value, the percentage difference will be greater than 100%, as in case 2 in table 8.1. Similarly, if the quantity more than doubles, the corresponding percentage change will exceed 100%. If a quantity shrinks over time, as did the population of Washington, D.C., in the 1990s, the corresponding percentage change will be less than 0% (negative).

To illustrate how percentage, percentile, and percentage change interrelate, box 8.1 and table 8.4 apply those measures to SAT scores for a fictitious student. The description also illustrates how to integrate several different types of quantitative comparison into a coherent discussion to make different points about the numbers.

Standardized Score or z-Score

Standardized scores, or z-scores, are a way of quantifying how a particular value compares to the average, taking into account the spread in the sample or a reference population (Agresti and Finlay 1997). A z-score is computed by subtracting the mean (μ) from the value for one case (x_i), then dividing that difference by the standard deviation (σ), or $z = (x_i - \mu)/\sigma$. A positive z-score corresponds to a value above the mean, a negative z-score to a lower-than-average value. For instance, on a test with a mean of 42 points and a standard deviation of 3 points, a raw score of 45 points corresponds to a z-score of 1.0, indicating that the individual scored one standard deviation above the mean. Z-scores are best used when the distribution is approximately normal (bell-shaped). Standardized scores are often used to provide a common metric that allows variables with very different ranges to be compared with one another in a regression (see "Standardized Coefficients" in chapter 9).

In addition to correcting for level by subtracting the mean value, z-scores adjust for the fact that a given absolute difference is interpreted differently depending on the extent of variation in the data. Among six-month-old male infants, mean height is 66.99 centimeters (cm) with a standard deviation (σ) of 2.49 cm (Centers for Disease

Box 8.1. Relations among Percentage, Percentile, and Percentage Change

The following description is annotated to indicate whether the numbers are value (denoted "V"), percentage correct (P), rank (R), absolute difference (A), or percentage change (C). Those annotations and the material in brackets are intended to illustrate how the different statistics relate to one another and would be omitted from the description for most audiences.

"The first time he took the SATs, Casey Smith correctly answered 27 out of 43 (V) questions (63% [P]; table 8.4). Compared to all other students who took the test nationwide, he placed in the 58th percentile (R). The next year, he improved his score by 9 percentage points (A) [from 63% of questions correct (P) to 72% correct (P)], placing him in the 70th percentile (R). That change was equivalent to a 14.3% improvement in his score (C) [a 9 percentage-point improvement (A), compared to his initial score of 63% correct (V)]. His rank improved by 12 percentiles (A) [relative to his first-year rank of 58th percentile (R)]."

Table 8.4. Examples of raw scores, percentage, percentile, and percentage change

Comparison of standardized test scores, Casey Smith, 1999 and 2000

	1999	2000
Number of questions correct	27	31
Total number of questions	43	43
Percentage of questions correct	63%	72%
Absolute difference in % correct (vs. 1999)	NA	9%
Percentile (compared to national norms)	58	70
Percentage change in % correct	NA	14.3%

Control 2002). Hence a baby boy who is 2.54 cm shorter than average would have a z-score of -1.02, indicating height roughly one standard deviation below the mean. Among six-year-old boys, however, there is wider variation around mean height (115.39 cm; $\sigma = 5.05$ cm), so a boy 2.54 cm shorter than average (the same absolute difference as for the infant) would be only about half a standard deviation below the norm for his age ($z = -0.50$).

Sometimes the mean and standard deviation used to calculate z-scores are from within your sample, other times from a standard population. For example, international growth standards for children's height-for-age and weight-for-height are used to provide a consistent basis for evaluating prevalence of underweight, overweight, and long-term growth stunting in different populations (Kuczmarski et al. 2000; World Health Organization 1995).

Report the mean and standard deviation of the distribution used to derive the z-scores and whether those figures were derived from within your own data or from an external standard. If an external standard was used, name it, explain why it was chosen, and provide a citation. If you report z-scores for only a few selected cases, also report the unstandardized values for those cases in the text or a table; for more cases, create a graph comparing your sample to the reference distribution.

The units of a z-score are *multiples of standard deviations,* not the original units in which the variable was measured: "With a raw score of 72, Mia scored one standard deviation below the national average."

Attributable Risk

An important issue for many research questions is the substantive significance of the pattern under study. Imagine that you oversee the Superfund cleanup effort and must decide which waste sites to clean up first, given a limited budget. Most people assume that priority automatically should go to removing materials that have a high relative risk—those that drastically increase health risks. However, another important but often ignored determinant of the potential impact of a risk factor is its prevalence—how common it is—in this case measured by the proportion of the population exposed to that material.

To measure the net impact of both prevalence and relative risk, epidemiologists use a calculation called attributable risk, also variously referred to as "attributable fraction" and "population attributable risk." Attributable risk can be thought of as the maximum percentage reduction in the incidence of the outcome if no one were exposed to the suspected risk factor (Lilienfeld and Stolley 1994), and is used to compare the burden of different diseases and preventable risk factors (e.g., World Health Organization 2002). For example, what fraction of cancer cases could be prevented if all exposure to a certain

Table 8.5. Relationship between relative risk, prevalence of risk factor, and attributable risk

Attributable risk (%) for selected values of relative risk (RR) and proportion of the population with the risk factor (p)

p = Proportion of population exposed to risk factor	Attributable risk (%)		
	RR = 2.0	RR = 4.0	RR = 10.0
0.10	9	23	47
0.25	20	43	69
0.50	33	60	82
0.75	43	69	87
0.90	47	73	89

toxic substance were eliminated? What share of low birth weight cases could be averted if no women smoked while they were pregnant?

Although it is little known outside of epidemiology, attributable risk also can shed light on other kinds of research questions. Suppose more students fail a proficiency test under the current math curriculum than under a newer curriculum. Attributable risk calculations can be used to estimate the percentage of failing scores that could be eliminated if the better curriculum completely replaced the current one. Attributable risk is calculated $AR = [p(RR - 1)]/[(p[RR - 1]) + 1] \times 100$, where RR is the relative risk of the outcome for those exposed to the risk factor versus those not exposed, and p is the proportion of the population exposed to the risk factor. Specify the lowest risk category as the reference group for the relative risk (or relative odds) calculation. In the math curriculum example, RR measures the relative risk of failing the exam for students using the current compared to the new math curriculum, and p is the proportion of students using the current math curriculum.

Table 8.5 reveals that both relative risk and prevalence of the risk factor have substantial influences on attributable risk. For instance, an attributable risk of 47% can be obtained by either the combination (RR = 10.0 and p = 0.10) *or* (RR = 2.0 and p = 0.90), two very different scenarios. Risk factors that are both very common and have large relative risks have the largest attributable risk, while those that are both uncommon and have modest effects have the smallest impact (e.g., RR = 2.0, p = 0.10 yield an AR of 9%).

The logic behind attributable risk assumes a causal relationship: that eliminating the risk factor will reduce the probability of the outcome. Consequently, use relative risk estimates based on data from a randomized experiment, or—if you have observational data—from a multivariate model that controls for potential confounding factors. With those caveats in mind, attributable risk is a compelling statistic for journalists and policy makers because it quantifies maximum potential benefits of a proposed solution.

Provide data on the prevalence of each risk factor and its associated relative risk either in tables or in the text and specify the reference group for the relative risk calculations. When comparing attributable risk for several different independent variables, create a table to present relative risk, prevalence, and attributable risk (columns) for each risk factor (rows). For single attributable risk calculations in a results or discussion section, report that information in the text, table, or a footnote.

Poor: "The attributable risk was 9% (RR = 1.4; prevalence = 0.25)."
This version leaves the units ("percentage of what?") and interpretation of attributable risk unexplained, and fails to mention the pertinent risk factor ("prevalence of what?") or outcome ("relative risk of what?").

Better: "Approximately 25% of pregnant women in the United States smoke. Combined with the estimated 1.4-fold increase in odds of low birth weight associated with maternal smoking, this figure suggests that if all pregnant women could be persuaded not to smoke, roughly 9% of low birth weight cases could be eliminated."
Attributable risk is explained in terms of familiar concepts, avoiding introduction of a term that would be used only once. The statistics used in the calculation are cited in the text and units for each number are clearly specified.

For scientific readers who are unfamiliar with attributable risk, include a footnote such as:

"Based on attributable risk calculations: $AR = [p(\text{RR} - 1)]/[(p[\text{RR} - 1]) + 1] \times 100$, where relative risk (RR) = 1.4 and prevalence of smoking (p) = 0.25 (see Lilienfeld and Stolley 1994)."

This footnote names the measure (attributable risk) and gives a reference for additional information. It also relates components of that calculation to specific numeric values and concepts for this research question.

■ CHOOSING TYPE(S) OF QUANTITATIVE COMPARISONS FOR YOUR WRITING

The types of variables you are working with constrain which types of quantitative comparisons are appropriate (Chambliss and Schutt 2003).

- Ratio variables: rank, absolute difference, and relative difference all make sense.
- Interval variables: rank and absolute difference work, but relative difference does not.
- Ordinal variables: only rank can be calculated.
- Nominal variables: the only pertinent comparison is whether different cases have the same or different values, but differences cannot be quantified or ranked.

For variables where several of these contrasts are possible, different types of quantitative comparisons provide distinct perspectives about the same pair of numbers. Always report the value of a variable to set the context and provide data for other calculations, then present one or two types to give a more complete sense of the relationship. To help readers interpret both value and absolute difference, mention the highest and lowest possible values and the observed range in the data. A one-point increase on a five-point Likert scale is substantial[4]—equal to one-fourth of the theoretically possible variation. A one-point increase in the Dow Jones Industrial Average is minuscule—equivalent to a 0.01% change compared to its level of roughly 10,000 points.

The value is also important for putting a relative difference in context: suppose a study reports that a pollutant is three times as concentrated in one river as in another. A very low concentration in both locations (e.g., 1 part per million [ppm] versus 3 ppm) has very different environmental implications than a high concentration in both (e.g., 1% versus 3%). Likewise, reporting the percentage difference or percentage change without the value can be misleading. A 100% increase (doubling) in the number of scooter-related injuries over a three-month period might be considered alarming if the injury rate in the baseline period was already high, but not if there were initially few injuries because scooters were not in widespread use.

The choice of which calculations to include depends on your topic and discipline. Read materials from your field to learn which types of quantitative comparisons are customary in your field. Use those calculations, then consider whether other types of comparisons would add valuable perspective.

- Report results of a race, election, or marketing study in terms of rank and absolute difference.
- Describe time trends in terms of percentage change and absolute difference, substituting ratios to express large changes such as doubling, tripling, or halving.
- Describe variations in risk or probability in terms of ratios. Because the ratio and percentage change are simply mathematical transformations of one another (table 8.3), present only one of those statistics to avoid repetition.
- Likewise, report only one measure of rank (e.g., position, percentile, decile, or quartile) along with information on the number of cases involved in the ranking.
- Convey potential reductions in risk associated with eliminating a risk factor using attributable risk.

■ CHECKLIST FOR TYPES OF QUANTITATIVE COMPARISONS

- Always report the values of the numbers being compared, either in the text itself or in a table or chart.
- Select one or two additional types of quantitative comparisons.
- Report the values and units of the numbers being compared, and specify which value or group is the reference value.
- Interpret your calculations to convey whether the values are typical or unusual, high or low. For trends, explain whether the values are stable or changing, and in what direction.
- Describe results of each quantitative comparison to match its calculation:
    - "Difference" or "margin" of the original units for subtraction
    - Multiples of the reference value for ratios
    - Multiples of standard deviations for z-scores
    - Percentage reduction in risk compared to the reference group for attributable risk; naming the reference group, outcome, and risk factor in your explanation
- Explain standard definitions, constants, or reference data, and provide citations.

Quantitative Comparisons for Multivariate Models

Authors who write about ordinary least squares and logistic regression models encounter some additional quantitative comparisons or different applications of those covered in the preceding chapter. Some of these measures are included in the standard output of most statistical programs:

- Coefficients on continuous and categorical independent variables
- Standardized regression coefficients

Others can be calculated from that output:

- Net effects of interactions or other patterns specified with multiple terms
- Predicted values of the dependent variable for selected values of the independent variables
- Excess risk from analyses of categorical dependent variables
- Change in excess risk across nested models with categorical dependent variables

The material in this chapter assumes a working knowledge of ordinary least squares (OLS) and logistic regression. See Fox (1997) or Gujarati (2002) for detailed information about the derivation and estimation of OLS models, Powers and Xie (2000) or Long (1997) regarding logistic regression and other methods of analyzing categorical dependent variables. Allison (1999) offers an excellent intuitive discussion of OLS models and their interpretation. Throughout this chapter, I mention common terms for these models, their components, and output, with synonyms listed in appendix C.

In this chapter, I review how to interpret the direction and magnitude of coefficients from OLS and logistic regression models. I explain how their interpretation relates to the kind of variable and to basic types of quantitative comparisons, then identify what information you should report as you describe the results. Of necessity, I use the shorthand of equations to explain these concepts and illustrate the terms and arithmetic needed for calculations. To demonstrate how to write about these concepts for various audiences, I include illustrative sentences using as little jargon as possible. More examples of how to write about these statistics without explaining their underlying logic and derivation are shown in chapters 14 (for statistical audiences) and 16 (for nonstatistical audiences).

In a multivariate OLS or logit regression, the coefficient on each variable is calculated holding all other variables in the model constant. Hence it measures the association of an independent variable with the dependent variable, net of the other included variables. This net effect is also known as the "marginal effect," the "incremental contribution," or the "partial regression coefficient."

▓ ORDINARY LEAST SQUARES REGRESSION

Ordinary least squares regression (also known as "OLS" or "linear regression")[1] is used to estimate the association of one or more independent variables with a continuous dependent variable such as birth weight in grams. An OLS model with k independent variables (X_1 through X_k) can be written in general terms:

Equation 9.1a: $Y = \beta_0 + \beta_1 X_1 + \beta_2 X_2 + \cdots + \beta_k X_k + \varepsilon$,

where Y is the dependent variable, β_0 is the intercept (or "constant") term, β_k is the coefficient on the kth independent variable (X_k), and ε is the random error or disturbance term.[2] For a model of birth weight as a function of race/ethnicity, mother's age, and smoking status, equation 9.1a becomes:

Equation 9.1b: Birth weight (grams) = $\beta_0 + \beta_1$Non-Hispanic Black $+ \beta_2$ Mexican American $+ \beta_3$Mother's age (years) $+ \beta_4$Smoker $+ \varepsilon$

In the terminology of chapter 8, the coefficient (or "effect estimate," "parameter estimate", or "beta") from an OLS regression is a measure of absolute difference.[3] Coefficients on continuous and categorical independent variables are interpreted differently from one another.

Coefficients on Continuous Independent Variables
Unstandardized Coefficients
For a continuous independent variable, the unstandardized coefficient is an estimate of the slope of the relationship between the independent and dependent variables: the marginal effect of a one-unit

increase in that independent variable on the dependent variable, holding constant all other variables in the model.

In tables and text that report OLS coefficients, specify the units in which the dependent and independent variables are measured. Unstandardized OLS coefficients are in the same units as the dependent variable: "For each additional year of mother's age, predicted birth weight increased by 10.7 grams (model A, table 9.1)."

If you specify ordinal variables such as attitudinal scales in continuous form, remind readers of the interpretation of a one-unit increase, such as from "somewhat likely" to "very likely" or from "agree" to "agree strongly."

Standardized Coefficients

Standardized regression coefficients adjust for the fact that some variables have a much larger standard deviation than others, hence a one-unit absolute increase means different things for different variables. For example, a one-dollar increase in annual income is much smaller relative to its overall range and scale than a one-year increase in mother's age. Standardized coefficients are also commonly used for psychological or attitudinal scales for which the units have no inherent meaning.

Like standardized scores or z-scores, standardized coefficients are measured in multiples of standard deviations, providing a consistent metric in which to compare coefficients on different variables, and allowing assessment of the relative sizes of the associations of each independent variable with the dependent variable (Kachigan 1991). The standardized coefficient estimates the effect of a one-standard-deviation increase in the independent variable on the dependent variable, where that effect is measured in standard deviation units of the dependent variable. The column of standardized coefficients for model A in table 9.1 shows that a one-standard-deviation increase in mother's age is associated with a birth weight increase of 0.097 standard deviations—or 9.7% of a birth weight standard deviation. In contrast, a one-standard-deviation increase in the income-to-poverty ratio is associated with a change of 19.6% of a standard deviation in birth weight. Standardized coefficients typically are not used for dummy variables or interaction terms (see below), for which a one-standard-deviation increase lacks an intuitive interpretation (Fox 1997).

In the table of multivariate results, report both the unstandardized and standardized coefficients for each independent variable, with columns labeled accordingly. As you describe the standardized

Table 9.1. Standardized and unstandardized coefficients from two ordinary least squares regressions

Estimated coefficients from two OLS regressions of birth weight (grams) by mother's race/ethnicity, socioeconomic status, and smoking characteristics, United States, 1988–1994

Variable	Model A			Model B	
	Coefficient	Standardized Coefficient	t-statistic	Coefficient	t-statistic
Intercept	3,039.8		77.51**	3,042.8	77.18**
Race/ethnicity (ref. = non-Hispanic white)					
Non-Hispanic Black	−172.6	−0.107	−9.86**	−168.1	−5.66**
Mexican American	−23.1	−0.011	−1.02	−104.2	−2.16**
Boy	117.2	0.097	9.76**	117.4	9.78**
Mother's education (ref. = >HS)					
Less than high school (<HS)	−55.5	−0.037	−2.88**	−54.2	−2.35**
High school graduate (=HS)	−53.9	−0.043	−3.64**	−62.0	−3.77**

	Model 1			Model 2	
Interactions: race and education					
Non-Hisp. black × <HS				−38.5	−0.88
Mexican American × <HS				99.4	1.72
Non-Hisp. black × =HS				18.4	0.47
Mexican American × =HS				93.7	1.49
Mother's age at child's birth (yrs.)	10.7	0.097	8.92**	10.6	8.84**
Income-to-poverty ratio (IPR)	80.4	0.196	5.54**	81.4	5.59**
IPR^2	−9.9	−0.143	−4.43**	−10.1	−4.37**
Mother smoked during pregnancy	−194.7	−0.139	−13.52**	−193.9	−13.43**
F-statistic (df)	94.08 (9)			65.59 (13)	
Adjusted R^2	0.082			0.083	

Source: 1988–1994 National Health and Nutrition Examination Survey (NHANES III; U.S. DHHS 1997).

Notes: Coefficients are weighted to national levels using sampling weights provided with the NHANES III (U.S. DHHS 1997).

**$p < 0.01$

coefficients, interpret them in terms of multiples of standard deviations of the dependent variable. Mention the means and standard deviations of the respective variables in the text, or refer to a table of descriptive statistics where they can be found.

Note that the scale (units) of the effect estimate and the associated standard errors and confidence intervals differ between standardized and unstandardized coefficients; hence they must be reported separately for the respective sets of coefficients. In contrast, the sign (direction of the effect), t-statistics, and associated p-values for each independent variable remain unchanged between standardized and unstandardized coefficients, so report those statistics once for both sets of coefficients, as in table 9.1. See chapter 10 for how to choose among different ways of presenting statistical significance.

Coefficients on Categorical Independent Variables

With categorical variables such as race, one category is selected as the *reference* (or "omitted") category and is the basis of comparison for the other categories of that variable. *Dummy variables* (also known as "binary," "dichotomous," or "indicator" variables) are defined for each of the other categories, each coded 1 if the characteristic applies to that case, and 0 otherwise. A dummy variable is *not* defined for the reference group (hence the name "omitted category"), resulting in $(n - 1)$ dummies for an n-category variable. Cases in the reference category will have a value of 0 for each of the dummy variables pertaining to that categorical variable.

For example, in the birth weight analysis shown in table 9.1, race/ethnicity is a three-category variable, with other racial/ethnic groups excluded from the analysis (as noted in box 12.1). Selecting non-Hispanic white infants as the reference group, we define two dummies: "non-Hispanic black" (coded 1 for infants of that race and 0 for non-Hispanic white or Mexican American infants) and "Mexican American" (coded 1 for infants with that trait and 0 for all others). For non-Hispanic whites—the reference category—both the "non-Hispanic black" and "Mexican American" dummy variables equal 0. The OLS coefficients on "non-Hispanic black" and "Mexican American" measure the absolute difference in mean birth weight for infants in the respective groups when each is compared to non-Hispanic whites (the reference category), taking into account the other variables in the model.

In a multivariate model, the reference category is defined by the combination of omitted categories for all categorical variables in the model. (See "Labels for Categorical Independent Variables" in chapter 5 for a review of conventions for identifying reference categories in tables.) In model B (table 9.1), for example, the reference category is non-Hispanic white female infants born to mothers with at least some college who did not smoke. To avoid a reference category that contains very few cases, often the modal category for each variable is chosen as the reference category, although the combination of characteristics should also be considered.[4] (See also "Comparisons Within Your Data" in chapter 8 for more on choosing a reference category.)

In the text, specify the reference group as the basis of comparison as you report the coefficients for categorical variables, and mention the units of the dependent variable. For example, "Non-Hispanic black newborns weighed on average 172.6 grams less than non-Hispanic white newborns (model A, table 9.1)." To reduce chances of misinterpretation, label the dummy variables in your data set, text, tables, and charts to reflect the values they represent, e.g., "non-Hispanic black," not "race."

Nonlinear Specifications for Independent Variables

If the relation between a continuous independent variable and a dependent variable is suspected to be nonlinear, that relation can be specified using polynomial functions, splines, parametric specifications, or logarithmic or other mathematical transformations of the independent or dependent variables (Long 1997; Kennedy 2003). A nonlinear relationship for an ordinal variable can be tested using a series of ordered dummy variables, as with the educational attainment specification shown in table 9.1.

Polynomial Functions

To specify a nonlinear function using a polynomial, include linear and higher-order terms for the independent variable in the model specification: linear and square terms for a quadratic function, those terms plus a cubic term for a cubic function, for instance (Allison 1999; Kennedy 2003). For example, the birth weight models shown in table 9.1 include both income-to-poverty ratio (IPR) and IPR^2 as independent variables, yielding the polynomial $(\beta_{IPR} \times IPR) + (\beta_{IPR^2} \times IPR^2)$. Substituting the estimated coefficients from model B, table 9.1, gives $(81.4 \times IPR) + (-10.1 \times IPR^2)$.

To observe the marginal effect on birth weight of a change in the IPR, multiply the estimated coefficients on those two terms by selected values of IPR, then calculate the difference in the results. Better yet, have a spreadsheet do the cranking—they are good for conducting repetitive, multistep calculations such as these (see appendix D).[5] Note that the intercept and all terms related to other variables in the model will cancel out when you subtract to calculate the difference between values, so you needn't include them in these calculations. For example, to illustrate the nonlinear effects of IPR, plug IPR = 1.0, IPR = 2.0, and IPR = 3.0 into the above formula in turn. Using the coefficients from model B, for IPR = 1.0, we have: (81.4 × 1.0) + (−10.1 × [1.0^2]) or 71.3 grams. For IPR = 2.0, we have (81.4 × 2.0) + (−10.1 × [2.0^2]) = 122.4 grams. Hence the marginal effect of moving from IPR = 1.0 to IPR = 2.0 is an increase of 51.1 grams (= 122.4 − 71.3), holding constant the other variables in the model. Because of the negative coefficient on IPR^2, the marginal effect of moving from IPR = 2.0 to IPR = 3.0 is smaller (30.9 grams). To illustrate the nonlinear pattern, create a graph such as figure 6.11. See box 14.2b for wording to describe this pattern.

Logarithmic Transformations

Another way to model nonlinear relations is to transform the dependent variable (Y), an independent variable (X_k), or both by taking logarithms. If either the dependent or independent variable (but not both) are logged, the specification is called a semilog model (Gujarati 2002). For models of the form $\ln Y = \beta_0 + \beta_1 X_1$ (sometimes referred to as "log-lin" models), $100 \times (e^\beta - 1)$ gives the percentage change in the dependent variable for a one-unit absolute increase in X_1 (Allison 1999).[6]

For models of the form $Y = \beta_0 + \beta_1 \ln X_1$ (sometimes known as "lin-log" models), β_1 divided by 100 gives the absolute change in the dependent variable of a 1% increase in X_1. For instance, the coefficient on logged income-to-poverty ratio in a birth weight model (not shown) is 45.5, hence the effect of a 1% increase in lnIPR is a 0.46 gram increase in birth weight.

If both the independent and dependent variables are logged, e.g., $\ln Y = \beta_0 + \beta_1 \ln X_1$, the model is referred to as a "log-log" or "double-log" model. In such specifications, the coefficient measures relative change in the dependent variable for a given relative change in the independent variable — a concept known in economics as the elasticity (Gujarati 2002). A log-log specification of income in the birth weight model would yield an estimate of the percentage change in birth weight for a 1% increase in income.

Interactions

Interactions (or "effects' modifications") occur when the size or direction of the association of one independent variable with the dependent variable depends on the value of a second independent variable. In GEE lingo, interactions are simply an exception to a general pattern among those variables (see chapter 13). In multivariate models, interactions are specified by including terms for the main effects of the independent variables involved and the interaction between them. As you explain the patterns implied by an interaction, do *not* discuss the direction or size of the individual main effects or interaction terms alone; see boxes 14.2a and 14.2b for illustrations. To portray the overall pattern you must consider the set of terms together, using the calculations described below.

Interactions between Two Categorical Variables

Both models A and B in table 9.1 include two dummy variables for the main effects of race/ethnicity ("non-Hispanic black" and "Mexican American") and two dummies for mother's educational attainment ("<high school" and "=high school"). In model B, four additional dummies specify the interaction: each of the race/ethnicity dummies multiplied by each of the education dummies. For example, the dummy variable for the interaction of Mexican American and less than high school (denoted "Mexican American $\times$ <HS") is coded 1 for infants with *both* of those attributes and 0 for everyone else, including Mexican Americans with high school or more, and people of other races with less than high school. The reference category is the combined reference categories from the two variables involved, in this case "non-Hispanic white" and "at least some college."

To calculate the net effect on birth weight of less than a complete high school education for a Mexican American, add together the coefficients on the two main effects and their interaction: $\beta_{\text{Mexican American}} + \beta_{<\text{HS}} + \beta_{\text{Mexican American} \times =\text{HS}}$. Filling in the estimated coefficients from model B in table 9.1 yields $-104.2 + (-54.2) + 99.4 = -59.0$. Hence, an infant born to a Mexican American mother with less than a high school education is predicted to weigh 59 grams less than an infant in the reference category (in this case, one born to a non-Hispanic white woman with at least some college), controlling for other variables in the model.

For groups in the reference category of one but not both variables in the interaction, calculations involve fewer terms. For instance, the

Table 9.2. Net effects of an interaction

Predicted difference in birth weight (grams) by race/ethnicity and mother's educational attainment, United States, 1988–1994

	Race/ethnicity		
Mother's education	Non-Hispanic White	Non-Hispanic Black	Mexican American
Less than high school	−54.2	−260.8	−59.0
High school graduate	−62.0	−211.7	−72.5
College+	0.0	−168.1	−104.2

Notes: Compared to non-Hispanic white infants born to mothers with at least some college. Weighted to national levels using sampling weights provided with the NHANES III (U.S. DHHS 1997). Based on model B, table 9.1 from analysis of the NHANES III 1988–1994.

effect of less than high school for a non-Hispanic white infant is simply $\beta_{<HS}$ because non-Hispanic whites are the reference category for race/ethnicity. Conduct the analogous calculations to determine the estimated effects of other race/education combinations (table 9.2), each of which measures the absolute difference in birth weight relative to the reference category. Again, a spreadsheet facilitates both the computation and presentation of these patterns (appendix D).

In addition to sparing readers the task of calculating the net effect of the terms in the interaction, a table such as 9.2 supports an "across the columns" and "down the rows" GEE description of the pattern—in this case across race within each education level, and across educational levels within each racial/ethnic group. Alternatively, create a clustered bar chart displaying calculated effects for all possible combinations of the independent variables; put one predictor on the x axis and the other in the legend, facilitating a "within-cluster" and "across-cluster" description; see figure A.2 for an example.

Interactions between Other Combinations of Variable Types

Use the same logic for calculating and interpreting an interaction between a continuous independent variable and a categorical independent variable or between two continuous independent variables, adding together the coefficients on the two main effects and their interaction, after filling in values for the continuous variables. For an interaction between a continuous predictor and a categorical predictor, calculate the pattern across values of the continuous independent variable for each category of the categorical variable.

For example, to evaluate how birth weight is influenced jointly by the income-to-poverty ratio (IPR) and race/ethnicity, calculate the shape of the IPR/birth weight curve for each racial/ethnic group. In the model shown in table 9.3, six terms are needed because birth weight is specified as a quadratic function of IPR. For non-Hispanic black infants (NHB): $\beta_0 + \beta_{\text{non-Hispanic black}} + (\beta_{\text{IPR}} \times \text{IPR}) + (\beta_{\text{IPR}^2} \times \text{IPR}^2) + (\beta_{[\text{NHB} \times \text{IPR}]} \times \text{IPR}) + (\beta_{[\text{NHB} \times \text{IPR}^2]} \times \text{IPR}^2)$. Substituting the respective coefficients from table 9.3, we have: $3{,}005.2 + (-73.1) + (107.9 \times \text{IPR}) + (-13.7 \times \text{IPR}^2) + (-104.1 \times \text{IPR}) + (17.4 \times \text{IPR}^2)$, which can be solved for specific values of IPR as in the section "Polynomial Functions" above. For Mexican Americans, replace the NHB terms with the corresponding main effects and interactions for Mexican American infants. For non-Hispanic white infants, only the intercept, IPR, and IPR^2 terms are needed. Figure 6.12 illustrates this interaction.

Testing Statistical Significance of Interactions

To evaluate statistical significance of an interaction, use both t-tests for individual coefficients and F-tests for the collective contribution of a set of terms to the overall fit of an OLS model.[7] For example, none of the interaction terms between race/ethnicity and mother's education shown in table 9.1 achieve statistical significance as assessed by their t-statistics.[8] However, the difference in F-statistics between model A (without interaction terms) and model B (with interaction terms) is 28.5 $(= F_{\text{model A}} - F_{\text{model B}} = 94.1 - 65.6)$. The critical value for the F distribution with 4 degrees of freedom for the numerator (based on the difference in number of independent variables between the respective models), ∞ degrees of freedom for the denominator (based on the sample size used in the model), and $p = 0.001$ is 10.8.[9] Because 28.5 exceeds that critical value, we conclude that the inclusion of interaction terms improves the overall fit of the model at $p < 0.001$.

The same strategy can be used to test differences in overall fit of other sets of nested models, whether or not they include interactions. See Wonnacott and Wonnacott (1984) or other statistics textbook for more guidance on using the F-test to contrast fit of nested models.

Table 9.3. Results of an ordinary least squares model with an interaction between continuous and categorical independent variables

Estimated coefficients from an OLS regression of birth weight (grams) by race/ethnicity, socioeconomic and smoking characteristics, United States, 1988–1994 NHANES III

Variable	Coefficient	t-statistic
Intercept	3,005.17	73.43*
Race/ethnicity		
(Non-Hispanic White)[a]		
Non-Hispanic Black	−73.08	−1.91
Mexican American	57.69	1.12
Boy	117.10	9.76**
Income–to–poverty ratio (IPR)	107.86	6.30**
IPR^2	−13.65	−5.21**
Interaction: Race and IPR		
Non-Hisp. black × IPR	−104.05	−2.75**
Non-Hisp. black × IPR^2	17.38	2.30*
Mexican American × IPR	−57.34	−1.11
Mexican American × IPR^2	3.75	0.37
Mother's age at child's birth (yrs.)	10.51	8.76**
Mother's education		
Less than high school (<HS)	−57.49	−2.98**
High school graduate (=HS)	−52.15	−3.52**
(College+)		
Mother smoked during pregnancy	−192.57	−13.36**

Source: 1988–1994 National Health and Nutrition Examination Survey (NHANES III; U.S. DHHS 1997).

Notes: Weighted to national levels using sampling weights provided with the NHANES III (U.S. DHHS 1997). F-statistic is 66.03 with 13 df; adjusted R^2 is 0.083.

[a] Reference categories in parentheses.

*$p < 0.05$ **$p < 0.01$

Predicted Value

In forecasting or simulation models, the results of a regression model are typically illustrated by presenting the predicted value of the dependent variable for selected values of the independent variables. Input values can be chosen from within the data set used to estimate the original model or from other data sources to simulate a different time, place, or group. For example, Russell et al. (2004) used two decades of follow-up data from the Epidemiologic Follow-up Study to the 1971–1974 NHANES I to estimate models of hospitalizations, nursing home admissions, and mortality as a function of baseline clinical characteristics such as hypertension and diabetes. They then used updated prevalence data on hypertension and diabetes from the 1988–1994 NHANES III to forecast future patterns of mortality and health care utilization.

Showing predicted values for case examples also can be useful in other applications. For instance, many socioeconomic traits co-vary, so it makes sense to calculate the net effect of changing several independent variables' values together rather than presenting the marginal effect of changing only variable at a time (which is captured by its coefficient). Phillips (2002) used this approach to estimate the extent to which homicide rates for blacks and Latinos could be reduced if structural factors (including percentage divorced, percentage unemployed, and percentage poor) faced by minorities could all be improved to the level observed among whites.

To calculate a predicted value, add together the intercept term and each of the estimated coefficients multiplied by the desired values of the associated variables. For example, predicted mean birth weight for a non-Hispanic white male infant born to a 20-year-old, nonsmoking mother with less than a high school education and family income at 1.5 times the poverty level = $\beta_0 + \beta_{boy} + \beta_{<HS} + (\beta_{age} \times 20) + (\beta_{IPR} \times 1.5) + (\beta_{IPR^2} \times 1.5^2)$. Non-Hispanic white and nonsmoker are reference categories for their respective variables, thus their values are captured in the intercept; likewise the race × education interaction does not figure into the calculation. Substituting the coefficients from model B, table 9.1, we obtain: 3,042.8 + 117.4 + (−54.2) + (10.6 × 20) + (81.4 × 1.5) + (−10.1 × [1.5²]), yielding a predicted birth weight of 3,417.4 grams for an infant with those traits.

Conduct analogous calculations for other combinations of characteristics, choosing case examples based on your knowledge of how independent variables are jointly distributed in your data and which cases would be of greatest interest for your research question and audience.[10] Predicted values of the dependent variable can be reported in the text (for one or two case examples), made into a small supplementary table with predicted values for several case examples arranged and labeled in the rows, or shown graphically with a line chart (for a continuous independent variable) or bar chart (for categorical independent variables or case examples).

▦ COEFFICIENTS FROM LOGISTIC REGRESSION MODELS

Logistic regression (or "a logit model") is used to estimate the effects of several variables on a categorical dependent variable such as low birth weight.[11] For outcomes with a temporal component such as patterns of divorce in a prospective cohort study, survival models (also known as "hazards models," "event history analysis," or "failure time analysis") are used (Cox and Oakes 1984, Allison 1995). In their most basic form, logit models analyze dichotomous (binary or two-category) outcomes such as winning a game or having a low birth weight infant. More advanced forms include multichotomous (also known as "polytomous" or "multinomial") models for categorical variables with more than two possible outcomes, such as win/lose/tie, or very low/moderately low/normal/high birth weight (Powers and Xie 2000). For survival models, multichotomous dependent variables can be analyzed using competing risks analysis (Allison 1995).

A logistic regression with k independent variables (X_k) can be expressed as follows:

Equation 9.2a: $\text{logit}(p) = \beta_0 + \beta_1 X_1 + \beta_2 X_2 + \cdots + \beta_k X_k + \varepsilon,$

where p is the probability of the outcome category under study, bounded between 0 and 1. The logit is defined as the natural log of the odds of the outcome, or $\ln(p/[1-p])$; see "Log-Odds" below. Substituting this expression for $\text{logit}(p)$, we have:

Equation 9.2b: $\ln[p/(1-p)] = \beta_0 + \beta_1 X_1 + \beta_2 X_2 + \cdots + \beta_k X_k + \varepsilon.$

For a logit model of low birth weight (LBW) as a function of race/ethnicity, mother's age, and smoking status:

Equation 9.2c: $\ln[p_{LBW}/(1-p_{LBW})] = \beta_0 + \beta_1$ non-Hispanic Black $+ \beta_2$ Mexican American $+ \beta_3$ Mother's age $+ \beta_4$ Smoker $+ \varepsilon.$

Logit models generate coefficients in the form of log-relative odds. Proportional hazards models yield estimates of the log-relative risk. Here is a quick review of how these measures are defined and interpreted.

Odds

The odds of a categorical outcome divide the probability of the outcome occurring (p) by the probability of it not occurring ($1 - p$) within a given group. For instance, the odds of a non-Hispanic black infant being low birth weight can be written $p(\text{LBW})_{\text{non-Hispanic black}} / (1 - p[\text{LBW}]_{\text{non-Hispanic black}})$, where $p(\text{LBW})$ is the probability of being low birth weight, $(1 - p[\text{LBW}])$ is the probability of *not* being low birth weight, and the subscript (e.g., "non-Hispanic black") identifies the group to which those probabilities pertain. Using the statistics on incidence of low birth weight from table 5.6, we have $p(\text{LBW})_{\text{non-Hispanic black}} = 0.113$, yielding an odds of low birth weight among non-Hispanic blacks of 0.127 ($= 0.113/0.887$).

Odds Ratios or Relative Odds

The odds ratio (OR), or relative odds, is computed by dividing the odds of the outcome for one group by the odds of the outcome for another group. It can be calculated from bivariate tabulations to yield an unadjusted odds ratio, or computed from the coefficient (log-odds) from a multivariate model to yield an adjusted OR; see below. In a multivariate model, the group in the denominator of the odds ratio is the reference category of the independent variable. For example, the odds ratio of low birth weight for black compared to white infants can be expressed:

$$\text{OR} = [p(\text{LBW})_{\text{black}}/(1 - p[\text{LBW}]_{\text{black}})]/[p(\text{LBW})_{\text{white}}/(1 - p[\text{LBW}]_{\text{white}})],$$

where odds for the reference category (non-Hispanic white infants) are in the denominator. Plugging in the rates of low birth weight for the respective racial/ethnic groups from table 5.6 (expressed as proportions) yields an unadjusted relative odds of 2.05 ($= 0.127/0.062$).

Odds ratios are a form of relative difference or ratio, and can be described using the wording for ratios given in table 8.3. "In bivariate tabulations, the odds of low birth weight are roughly twice as high for non-Hispanic blacks as for non-Hispanic whites." If odds are the same in both groups, the OR is 1.0. An OR above 1.0 reflects higher odds in the numerator group than in the denominator group, while an OR below 1.0 indicates lower odds (e.g., a protective effect) for the numerator group.

Log-Odds

The estimated coefficient (β_k) from a logistic regression is the change in the natural logarithm of the odds ratio of the outcome associated with a one-unit increase in the independent variable (X_k). (See below for interpretation of coefficients on categorical independent variables.) The units of logit coefficients are usually referred to as the "log-odds" although technically they are log-*relative* odds. Hence the odds ratio is calculated by exponentiating the logit coefficient: odds ratio $= e^\beta = e^{\text{log-odds}}$, where e is the base of the natural logarithm (2.718). This calculation is sometimes referred to as "taking the antilog" of the coefficient. A negative log-odds corresponds to a lower odds of low birth weight than the reference category (e.g., boys compared to girls; table 9.4), while a positive log-odds corresponds to higher odds (e.g., smokers compared to nonsmokers). Cox proportional hazards models and some parametric hazards models generate estimates of ln(relative risk), which can be exponentiated to yield relative risk. See below for more on the distinction between relative risk and relative odds.

Coefficients on Continuous Independent Variables

As in an OLS regression, the coefficient for a continuous variable in a logit model measures the marginal effect of a one-unit increase in the independent variable on the dependent variable—in this case, the log-odds of low birth weight—controlling for the other variables in the model. In table 9.4, the log-odds on mother's age is -0.008, yielding a relative odds of 0.992 ($=e^{(-0.008)}$). In relative terms, the odds of LBW are 0.992 times as high for each additional year of mother's age. Expressed as a percentage change, the risk of LBW decreases by eight tenths of 1% for a one-year increase in mother's age; see table 8.3 for how to convert a ratio to a percentage change.

Coefficients on Categorical Independent Variables

The logit coefficient for a dummy variable compares the log-odds of LBW in that group to those in the reference category. For instance, the "mother smoked during pregnancy" coefficient of 0.33 translates to an odds ratio of 1.39 ($=e^{(0.33)}$), meaning that infants born to mothers who smoked had 1.39 times the odds of LBW as those born to nonsmokers (table 9.4).

Interaction Effects in Logistic Models

Specify interactions in logit models by including main effects for each of the independent variables and pertinent interaction terms,

Table 9.4. Results of a logistic regression

Estimated odds ratios (OR) and 95% confidence interval (CI) from a logistic regression of low birth weight, NHANES III 1988–1994

	Log-odds (β_k)	Odds ratio (OR)	95% CI for OR
Intercept	−2.03		
Race/Hispanic origin (Non-Hispanic white) [a]			
Non-Hispanic black	0.38	1.46	1.23–1.74
Mexican American	0.36	1.43	1.15–1.78
Boy	−0.02	0.98	0.86–1.12
Mother's education			
Less than high school	0.51	1.67	1.36–2.05
High school graduate (College+)	0.31	1.37	1.14–1.63
Mother's age at child's birth (yrs.)	−0.008	0.99	0.98–1.01
Income-to-poverty ratio (IPR)	−0.26	0.77	0.65–0.91
IPR²	0.019	1.02	0.99–1.05
Mother smoked during pregnancy	0.33	1.39	1.20–1.62

Source: 1988–1994 National Health and Nutrition Examination Survey (NHANES III; U.S. DHHS 1997).
Notes: $N = 9{,}813$. Wald chi-square statistic (df) = 236.68 (9); $-2 \log L = 6{,}130.4$; $-2 \log L$ for null model $= 6{,}377.9$. Low birth weight <2,500 grams or 5.5 pounds. Weighted to population levels using sampling weights from the NHANES III (U.S. DHHS 1997).
[a] Reference categories in parentheses.

just as in OLS models. Calculate the net effect of interactions among categorical independent variables in one of two ways:

- Add together the estimated *log-odds* (β s or logit coefficients) for each of the main effects and the interaction term, then exponentiate that sum. For example, the odds ratio of LBW for non-Hispanic black infants born to mothers with less than high school compared to the reference category $=$
  $e^{(\beta \text{ non-Hispanic black}+\beta<\text{hs}+\beta \text{ [non-Hispanic black}\times<\text{hs]})} =$
  $e^{(0.68+0.60+[-0.45])} = e^{(-0.84)} = 2.29$ (model not shown).

- *Or* multiply the *odds ratios* of LBW for each of the main effects and the interaction term: $(OR_{non\text{-}Hispanic\ black} \times OR_{<hs} \times OR_{[non\text{-}Hispanic\ black \times <hs]}) = 1.98 \times 1.81 \times 0.64 = 2.29$.

Either approach yields an odds ratio, measuring the relative difference between the respective group and the reference category. For interactions involving one or more continuous independent variables, fill in values of those variables as outlined above for OLS models.

The form you use for reporting results of logistic models depends on your audience. Odds ratios are generally easier to explain, but some statistically oriented readers prefer log-odds. (See "Presenting Statistical Significance Information to Match the Measure of Effect Size" in chapter 10 for an important caution.) As with OLS models, clearly convey the units and coding of independent variables, and for categorical independent variables, the reference category. "Non-Hispanic black infants born to mothers with less than a high school education had roughly 2.3 times the odds of LBW of non-Hispanic white infants born to mothers with at least some college."

Predicted Values from Logit Models

Predicted odds of the outcome category under study (e.g., odds of low birth weight) can be calculated from logistic regression models much as for OLS models, exponentiating the sum of the coefficients on the intercept term and independent variables, with independent variables set at the values of interest. For a male, non-Hispanic white infant born to a 20-year-old nonsmoking mother with less than a high school education and family income at 1.5 times the poverty level, the log-odds of LBW can be calculated from the coefficients in table 9.4 as follows: $-2.03 + (-0.02) + 0.51 + (-0.008 \times 20) + (-0.26 \times 1.5) + (0.019 \times 1.5^2) = -2.05$. Exponentiating this sum yields an estimate of the odds of LBW: $e^{(-2.05)} = 0.129$, or a 12.9% chance of low birth weight for an infant with those traits.

An Aside on Relative Risk and Relative Odds

Relative *risk* and relative *odds* (or odds ratios) are often treated interchangeably in written descriptions of model results although they often differ numerically for reasons explained below. *Odds ratios* are derived from coefficients of logit models or calculated from cross-tabulations from a case-control study (Lilienfeld and Stolley 1994). The odds ratio comparing two groups exposed (*e*) and unexposed (*u*) to some risk factor can be written

Equation 9.3: $OR = [p_e/(1 - p_e)]/[p_u/(1 - p_u)]$.

Relative risk is derived by exponentiating coefficients from Cox proportional hazards models or from cross-tabulations from population-based surveys or cohort studies.[12] The ratio of two mortality rates from a cohort study, for example, is an estimate of relative risk. The relative risk for exposed compared to unexposed groups can be written

$$\text{Equation 9.4: } RR = p_e/p_u.$$

The effect estimates from a logistic regression are conventionally expressed in terms of odds ratios for each of the independent variables.[13] However, as either the odds ratio (OR) or the prevalence of the outcome among the unexposed (p_u) increase, odds ratios are an increasingly poor approximation of the corresponding relative risk (Zhang and Yu 1998; Schwartz 2004). (Note that p here has a different meaning than either p-value (chapters 3 and 10) or p in the attributable risk formula shown in chapter 8—another example of why it is important to define each abbreviation in the context of a particular usage.)

As shown in equation 9.5, the corresponding relative risk (RR) can be calculated from an odds ratio and the prevalence of the outcome among subjects without the risk factor of interest (e.g., the unexposed).

$$\text{Equation 9.5: } RR = OR/[(1 - p_u) + (OR \times p_u)]$$

In the comparison of low birth weight for black versus white infants, black race is considered the risk factor, hence p_u is the proportion of white infants who are low birth weight, and the OR and RR compare low birth weight across racial/ethnic groups. Plugging in the estimated odds ratio of low birth weight for non-Hispanic black compared to non-Hispanic white infants of 1.46 (from table 9.4), and the prevalence of low birth weight among non-Hispanic white infants of 0.058 (from table 5.6), we have RR = 1.46/(1 − 0.058) + (1.46 × 0.058) = 1.42. In this case, the odds ratio is a close approximation of the relative risk—the discrepancy is less than 3%.

To identify the circumstances under which the OR provides a reasonable estimate of the RR, table 9.5 shows the relative risks that correspond to different values of the odds ratio and prevalence of the outcome among the unexposed. When prevalence of the outcome is very low, the OR is within a few percentage points of the RR regardless of the value of the odds ratio. However, as prevalence rises above 5%, relative risk and odds ratios diverge substantially, especially for high values of the odds ratio. Suppose a logit model estimated that

Table 9.5. Relationship between relative risk, disease prevalence, and odds ratio

Relative risk (RR) of the disease for exposed versus unexposed persons

Odds ratio (OR) of the disease	Disease prevalence among persons unexposed to the risk factor (p_u) [a]				
	0.01	0.05	0.10	0.25	0.50
1.0	1.00	1.00	1.00	1.00	1.00
2.0	1.98	1.90	1.82	1.60	1.33
4.0	3.88	3.48	3.08	2.29	1.60
6.0	5.71	4.80	4.00	2.67	1.71
8.0	7.48	5.93	4.71	2.91	1.78
10.0	9.17	6.90	5.26	3.08	1.82

Note: $RR = OR/[(1 - p_u) + (OR \times p_u)]$
[a] Prevalence expressed as a proportion of the unexposed population.

the odds ratio of divorce for people married as teens compared to those married at older ages was 4.0, and that divorce occurred in 25% of the latter group (e.g., $p_u = 0.25$). Table 9.4 shows that the corresponding relative risk is 2.29, meaning that the odds ratio overstates the true relative risk by 75%.

If your model estimates high odds ratios (e.g., OR > 3.0) or your outcome is relatively common in the reference group (e.g., prevalence above 10%), calculate the corresponding relative risks using the formula in equation 9.5. If the odds ratio overestimates the relative risk by more than 25%, describe the relative risks instead and explain why you have done so. Even if the estimated odds ratio closely approximates the relative risk, describe it in terms of multiples of odds rather than multiples of risk.

Poor: "The relative odds of low birth weight among blacks are 1.46, meaning that black infants are 1.46 times as likely to be low birth weight as white infants."

Better: "The odds of low birth weight among blacks are 1.46 times as high as for whites."

■ EXCESS RISK AND CHANGE IN EXCESS RISK

For many research questions, it is useful to estimate the extent to which the risk in one group exceeds that in another group, and by how much that extra risk is reduced when other variables are taken into account. For categorical dependent variables such as cancer incidence or low birth weight, these comparisons—known as excess risk and change in excess risk—can be calculated from estimated odds ratios or the equivalent relative risk (table 9.6).[14] For these calculations, specify the lowest risk category as the reference category so the odds ratios (or relative risks) for other groups are greater than 1.0.

Excess Risk

As explained above, relative risk is the ratio of risks in two groups: if the risk is the same in both groups, the relative risk = 1.0. A relative risk above 1.0 reflects higher risk in the comparison group (numerator) than the reference group (denominator). Excess risk uses percentage difference to quantify the higher risk in the comparison group. Suppose you want to estimate the excess risk of cancer among people exposed to electromagnetic fields (EMFs) compared to those who haven't been exposed. For study 1, model I (table 9.6), the relative risk is 2.0 for exposed versus unexposed persons. Substituting that value into the formula in table 9.6 gives [(2.0 − 1.0) × 100], or an excess risk of 100%. Put differently, the estimate from model I suggests that persons exposed to EMFs are 100% more likely than unexposed persons to develop cancer. In study 2, the relative risk is 1.0, indicating equal risk in the two groups, which works out mathematically (and logically) to an excess risk of 0%. Excess risk is expressed as a *percentage difference, compared to the level of risk in the reference group,* and can be explained using the guidelines given in chapter 8 for writing about percentage difference.

Change in Excess Risk

Often multivariate models are used to investigate the degree to which additional variables "explain" the observed differences in risk across groups, such as whether other factors reduce the size of the coefficient on EMFs in a logit model of cancer risk. As an example of how to address this type of question, use a percentage change calculation to compare the excess cancer risks from two models shown in table 9.6: model I with controls only for exposure to EMFs, model II

Table 9.6. Relations among relative risk, excess risk, and percentage change in excess risk

Relations among relative risk (RR), excess risk (ER), and percentage change in excess risk, hypothetical model of exposure to electromagnetic fields (EMFs) on cancer risk.

	Model I EMFs only		Model II EMFs & control variables		Model I vs. II
	Relative risk I	Excess risk I[a] (%) $ER_I =$ $(RR_I - 1.0) \times 100$	Relative risk II	Excess risk II[a] (%) $ER_{II} =$ $(RR_{II} - 1.0) \times 100$	% change in excess risk = $[(ER_{II} - ER_I)/$ $ER_I] \times 100$
Formula	$RR_I{}^b$		RR_{II}		
Study 1	2.00	100	1.00	0	−100
Study 2	1.00	0	1.00	0	0
Study 3	4.00	300	3.00	200	−33
Study 4	1.50	50	1.25	25	−50

[a] Excess risk as a percentage difference in absolute risk compared to the reference category (no EMF exposure).

[b] Subscripts in formulas denote model number. E.g., RR_I is the relative risk from model I.

with the addition of controls for potential confounding factors such as individual and environmental characteristics related to cancer risk. The estimated effect of EMFs from model I is sometimes referred to as the "unadjusted estimate" while the corresponding estimate from model II is the "adjusted estimate."

For study 3 (third row of table 9.6), models I and II yield relative risks of 4.0 and 3.0, respectively, corresponding to excess cancer risks of 300% (model I) and 200% (model II). Applying the percentage change formula from chapter 8, we obtain [(200% − 300%)/300%] × 100, or −33%. In other words, controlling for those variables reduces the estimated excess risk associated with EMF exposure by 33%, bringing it closer to the level of risk in the unexposed (reference) group.

Change in excess risk is calculated as a percentage change *in the excess risk in the original model*, not in the level of risk in the reference group. As with all percentage or percentage change calculations, the best way to figure out "percentage of what?" is to consider the concept—not just the number—in the denominator.

To present excess risk calculations, first report the levels of risk (e.g., cancer incidence rates) in each group in a bivariate table. In the table of multivariate results, present the relative risk estimates from which excess risk and change in excess risk were calculated and specify the reference group. Present and explain the excess risk results in the text. For change in excess risk, state whether a bivariate tabulation or a prior multivariate model was used as the basis of comparison; if a prior model, name it (if reported in a table) or list which variables were controlled.

▩ CHECKLIST FOR QUANTITATIVE COMPARISONS FOR MULTIVARIATE MODELS

As you write about estimated coefficients from regression models, incorporate units, direction, and magnitude of association. See chapter 10 for how to report statistical significance.

- For categorical independent variables, present the coefficients in a table, then express the size of each effect relative to the reference category.
- For continuous independent variables, report the coefficients in a table, then contrast other increments if a one-unit increase is not typical or of interest (see "Single-Unit Contrasts" in chapter 7).

For standardized coefficients, units are multiples of standard deviations, not the units in which the variables were originally measured.

If you transformed the independent variable, consider explaining the effect size in the original units as well as the transformed units (e.g., undoing logarithms).

- For interactions involving a key independent variable, report the associated coefficients on main effects and interaction terms in the table of model results, then supplement with a table or chart presenting the net effect. Do *not* interpret main effects or interaction terms in isolation from one another.
- For polynomial or other multiterm specifications of a key independent variable, report the coefficients in the table of model results, then supplement with a chart illustrating the net effect.
- For ordinary least squares (OLS) regression models, effects are absolute difference measured in the units of the dependent variable.
- For logistic regression models, coefficients are measured in units of log-relative odds of the modeled category of the dependent variable (e.g., *low* birth weight, or *un*insured).

Accompany or replace log-odds with odds ratios, expressed in terms of multiples of odds in the reference category.

Specify which category of the dependent variable was modeled.

- Consider fleshing out interpretation of coefficients with one or more of the following:

Predicted values of the dependent variable for selected values of the independent variables

Excess risk from analyses of categorical dependent variables, expressed as a percentage difference, compared to the level of risk among the unexposed

Change in excess risk across nested models of a categorical dependent variable, expressed as a percentage change relative to that in the unadjusted estimate or coefficient from a simpler model

10

Choosing How to Present Statistical Test Results

When writing about multivariate analyses, the main goal is usually to convey the direction, magnitude, and statistical significance of individual measures of association, and how well the model fits the data. Most computer programs generate a substantial amount of information on each model: one or two measures of effect size (e.g., log-odds and odds ratios), three or four ways to assess statistical significance of each independent variable (e.g., standard errors, test statistics, p-values, and confidence intervals), and several goodness-of-fit statistics for the overall model (e.g., coefficient of determination: F-statistics and adjusted and unadjusted R^2 for an OLS model; likelihood-ratio and Wald chi-square statistics for a logit model).

This plethora of information is included in the statistical output because it may be useful to some quantitative analysts with specific objectives, but you do not need every piece of this information to communicate the model results to others. Unless the objective of your paper or talk is to teach your readers how to calculate and interpret statistics or you need to conduct a specialized analysis, much of the statistical output will be superfluous. Therefore, an important step in writing about multivariate analyses is deciding which of the many pieces of information to report from the computer output of model results, taking into consideration the interests and abilities of your particular audience. Rather than ask readers to apply their statistical skills to obtain their own answers from a litany of statistics, you will select and report one or two measures each of effect size, statistical significance, and model fit, then discuss what they imply for the hypotheses that model is intended to test. (In appendix B, I show output from a logistic regression and suggest how to organize it into a table for an audience familiar with logit models.)

Among the different ways to present results of significance tests — standard errors, confidence intervals, test statistics, p-values, and symbols—there is a tradeoff between the amount of statistical knowledge and effort needed to see the conclusions of those tests and the degree of flexibility in the other hypotheses that readers can examine easily. Consequently, some approaches suit statistical experts but not novices, and vice versa. Nonstatistical readers need only the statistical conclusions and perhaps enough information to verify that you used the correct approach, not the complicated steps to reach those conclusions. On the other hand, statistically oriented readers may want to reconstruct those steps or test different hypotheses, so they require the detailed results. In addition, some approaches are more effective in tables for published papers than in slides for a speech, while others work best in charts or prose.

I begin this chapter with a summary of concepts related to inferential statistics, then describe how to decide which ways of presenting information on effect size and statistical significance best match your audience, objectives, and format. To illustrate the different variants, I use examples from an OLS regression and a logistic regression. The same criteria can be used to select ways to present results of inferential statistical tests for bivariate or three-way associations such as a t-test for a difference in means or a chi-square test for differences in cross-tabulated groups.

■ CONCEPTS BEHIND INFERENTIAL STATISTICS

As background for the discussion of alternative approaches to presenting statistical test results, here is a brief overview of how critical values of test statistics are determined and the role of the null hypothesis, building upon the introduction given in chapter 3. For a thorough treatment of inferential statistics, see Agresti and Finlay (1997) or another introductory statistics textbook.

Deriving the Critical Value for a Statistical Test

Inferential test statistics for each independent variable in a regression are calculated from the estimated coefficient (β_k) and its associated standard error (s.e.).[1] Most statistical software reports the pertinent test statistic as part of standard model output. To evaluate hypotheses about statistical significance using test statistics, you need several additional pieces of information:

- The *statistical distribution* against which the test statistic is to be compared: t-statistics are compared against the t-distribution, χ^2 statistics against the chi-square distribution, and F-statistics against the F-distribution, for example. This may seem self-evident given the names of the statistics, but if those statistics aren't identified in your work, readers may not know which distribution is appropriate. (See table 5.9a for an example.)

- The pertinent number of *degrees of freedom* (df), given the sample size, the model specification, and the assumptions of the statistical test
- The desired level of α (also known as the *significance level* or *Type I error*), which is the probability of falsely rejecting the null hypothesis that the coefficient is equal to zero (H_0: β_k = 0). An α of 0.05 corresponds to a 5% chance ($p < 0.05$) of incorrectly concluding that β_k is statistically significantly different from zero when in fact it is equal to zero; $\alpha = 0.01$ corresponds to a 1% chance, or $p < 0.01$.
- Whether the hypothesis involves a *one- or two-tailed test*. A one-tailed test specifies the expected direction of the difference (e.g., boys are heavier at birth than girls), whereas a two-tailed test hypothesizes that boys and girls have different average birth weights without predicting which sex is heavier. The default setting in most statistical software is a two-tailed test.

These factors together determine the *critical point* or *critical value* against which the test statistic is compared. A test statistic that exceeds the critical value is sometimes described as being in the *critical region*. Figure 10.1 illustrates, for example, how the F distribution

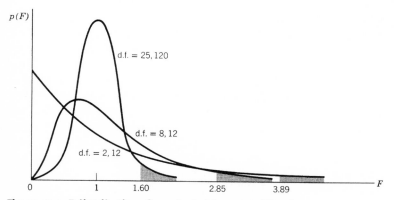

Figure 10.1. *F*-distributions for selected degrees of freedom.
Source: Wonnacott and Wonnacott 1984.

varies with the number of degrees of freedom. See "Interpreting the Test Statistic" below for how to use this information in hypothesis testing.

Most people who have studied basic statistics have been exposed to a handful of important critical values. When the null hypothesis is true,

- a large-sample t-statistic of 1.96 or greater corresponds to $p < 0.05$ with a two-tailed test;
- a t-statistic of at least 2.56 corresponds to $p < 0.01$ for a two-tailed test; and
- a chi-square test with 1 degree of freedom (e.g., for a 2-by-2 cross-tabulation) has a critical value of 3.84.

Unless you are writing for a statistically savvy audience, do not assume that people remember critical values or how to interpret them. Don't drag folks who lack statistical training or recent practice through the steps of calculating test statistics and interpreting critical values. Instead choose one of the simpler approaches to presenting results of statistical tests described below. Even people who routinely work with statistics may not know critical values for other levels of α, number of degrees of freedom, small sample sizes, or one-tailed tests, so report the critical value if any of those issues pertain to your analysis. Or use a method of conveying statistical test results that does not require readers to interpret the test statistic themselves.

Interpreting the Test Statistic

The Null Hypothesis

Interpretation of the test statistic depends on the associated null hypothesis. In most statistical packages, the default is to test the null hypothesis that each coefficient is equal to zero, $H_0: \beta_k = 0$, although other hypotheses can be manually specified (see below). If the test statistic for a coefficient exceeds the critical value, we reject the null hypothesis and conclude that the difference is statistically significant at the pertinent α level. To illustrate, figure 10.2 shows that for $p = 0.05$ and 1 degree of freedom, the critical value for the χ^2 statistic is 3.84. Hence a calculated χ^2 greater than 3.84 with 1 degree of freedom means that there is at most a 5% chance that the null hypothesis is correct.

For example, to assess whether boys' mean birth weight is statistically significantly different from that of girls ($BW_{boys} = BW_{girls}$), we have $H_0: \beta_{boy} = 0$ for the dummy variable "boy" with girls as the reference category. In the large NHANES III sample with $\alpha = 0.01$, using the standard normal distribution (or a t-distribution with more than

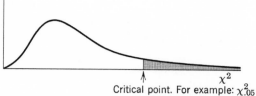

Critical point. For example: $\chi^2_{.05}$
leaves 5% probability in the tail.

Figure 10.2. Critical values for a chi-square distribution. (*continued p. 236*)
Source: Wonnacott and Wonnacott 1984.

120 df) with a two-tailed test yields a critical value of 2.56. The estimated t-statistic for "boy," 9.86 (from table 10.1), is greater than the critical value, hence the difference is statistically significant at $p < 0.01$. The standard output from a regression model includes test statistics and p-values for each coefficient (see appendix B), saving you the effort of looking up the critical value in a statistical distribution table.

Other Hypotheses

As noted above, the default null hypothesis in most regression models is H_0: $\beta_k = 0$. For many research questions and variables, statistical tests of other hypotheses also may be of interest.

- Whether two coefficients in the model are statistically significantly different *from one another,* such as whether $\beta_{<HS}$ is statistically significantly different from $\beta_{=HS}$. The default statistical output contrasts each of those categories against "college+" (the reference category), not against each other.
- Whether the size and statistical significance of a coefficient *changes* when additional variables are introduced into the model, such as how the coefficient on "non-Hispanic black" changes when socioeconomic characteristics are taken into account. This is often the objective of a series of nested models, including a comparison of "unadjusted" (e.g., bivariate) and "adjusted" (multivariate) coefficients on the variable of interest.
- Whether the effect of a covariate *differs across subgroups,* such as whether the association between mother's educational attainment and mean birth weight is the same for infants of different races, time periods, or places. This is one way of testing for an interaction in an OLS model.

TABLE **VII** χ^2 Critical Points

d.f.	$\chi^2_{.25}$	$\chi^2_{.10}$	$\chi^2_{.05}$	$\chi^2_{.025}$	$\chi^2_{.010}$	$\chi^2_{.005}$	$\chi^2_{.001}$
1	1.32	2.71	3.84	5.02	6.63	7.88	10.8
2	2.77	4.61	5.99	7.38	9.21	10.6	13.8
3	4.11	6.25	7.81	9.35	11.3	12.8	16.3
4	5.39	7.78	9.49	11.1	13.3	14.9	18.5
5	6.63	9.24	11.1	12.8	15.1	16.7	20.5
6	7.84	10.6	12.6	14.4	16.8	18.5	22.5
7	9.04	12.0	14.1	16.0	18.5	20.3	24.3
8	10.2	13.4	15.5	17.5	20.1	22.0	26.1
9	11.4	14.7	16.9	19.0	21.7	23.6	27.9

Figure 10.2. *Continued*

In "Testing Other Hypotheses" below, I explain how to conduct and present results of these additional hypothesis tests.

■ PRESENTING EFFECT ESTIMATES

Different statistical models generate different types of effect estimates and offer the option of displaying more than one form, such as unstandardized and standardized coefficients, or log-odds and odds ratios. Rather than repeat the explanations from chapter 9 on how to interpret effect estimates, here I focus on how to choose among the different variants to best suit your audience.

Ordinary Least Squares Regression

Most readers can understand unstandardized coefficients from ordinary least squares models if the variables and their units are adequately labeled. Reserve standardized coefficients for readers who are familiar with their interpretation. A caveat: unstandardized and standardized coefficients are measured in different units (chapter 9). Choose a way of presenting statistical significance that matches the measure of effect size you report, or use an approach that works with either type of measure (see "Presenting Statistical Significance Information to Match the Measure of Effect Size" below).

Logistic Regression

Many audiences find it easier to assess the effect size from logit models using the odds ratio rather than the log-odds because the units of an odds ratio are interpretable as simple multiples or can be easily transformed into percentage differences. Consequently, the odds ratio often is presented instead of, or in addition to, the log-odds, each in its separate column.

Again, remember to pay attention to the units of the effect size to ensure that you select a way of presenting statistical significance that matches those units.

■ PRESENTING RESULTS OF STATISTICAL TESTS

Statistical significance can be assessed using standard errors, confidence intervals, test statistics, p-values, or symbols to denote levels of significance. These approaches differ in terms of the range of hypotheses that can be tested easily, whether additional information is needed to interpret their values, and the statistical knowledge required of your readers. To illustrate the strengths and weaknesses of these approaches, tables 10.1 and 10.2 present information from an OLS model of birth weight and a logistic model of low birth weight, respectively. These tables are far more complicated than those you would use in a paper or presentation. They are shown here to facilitate comparison across all of the different ways of presenting statistical significance, *not* to illustrate effective tables for use with an audience. For each paper or presentation, select at most two ways to present statistical significance (see guidelines below).

In the next few sections I discuss the various approaches to presenting results of statistical tests in descending order of statistical proficiency required of your readers. Calculating and choosing among the different variants requires that you are proficient in all of them so you can work behind the scenes to identify the approach that best suits your audience.

Standard Errors

A standard error measures the extent of variation around the associated estimated coefficient—the standard deviation of the sampling distribution of that estimate. In tables, standard errors can be reported either in a column adjacent to the column with the effect estimate (as in table 10.1), in parentheses below it (see "Portrait versus Landscape Layout" in chapter 5), or as the point estimate $\pm$ the standard error. Label your column to convey which convention you have used. In the text, either report and label the coefficient and standard error (s.e.) separated by a comma (e.g., $\beta_k = 10.7$, s.e. $= 1.2$ for mother's age in the birth weight model shown in table 10.1), or use the $\beta_k \pm$ s.e. format (e.g., 10.7 ± 1.2). The "$\pm$" approach can also be used for confidence intervals (see below), so clearly identify which you are reporting.

Advantages of Standard Errors

One advantage of presenting standard errors is that they give an estimate of the extent of variation or uncertainty around the point estimate. In addition, readers can calculate intervals for different levels of confidence simply by varying the multiplier in the formula (see "Confidence Intervals" below). They also can calculate the test statistic and examine both one-tailed and two-tailed tests. Under certain circumstances, standard errors allow readers to test statistical significance of differences between coefficients, e.g., H_0: $\beta_j = \beta_k$. See "Testing Other Hypotheses" below for calculations and an explanation.

Disadvantages of Standard Errors

Standard errors are a poor choice for communicating results of statistical tests to nonstatistical readers because they involve several intermediate steps before the answer to the hypothesis test is apparent. For the same reason, they don't work well when time is tight (as in a short speech), regardless of audience.

Moreover, standard errors require that you also report covariance information to test significance of differences between coefficients within a given model. If the main hypothesis to be tested is whether $\beta_k = 0$, use one of the other approaches outlined below. If additional hypothesis tests such as $\beta_j = \beta_k$ are of interest, request the pertinent comparison of coefficients when you specify the model. Then report results of that comparison using symbols or footnotes (in tables or charts), or a phrase such as "the difference between coefficients on 'non-Hispanic black' and 'Mexican American' was statistically significant at $p < 0.05$" (in the text).

Confidence Intervals

An alternative way to express results of a statistical test is to present the confidence interval around the estimate. For large samples, the 95% confidence interval (95% CI) is calculated: $\beta_k \pm (1.96 \times \text{s.e.}_{\beta k})$, where 1.96 is the critical value for $p < 0.05$ with a two-tailed test. For other width confidence intervals, substitute the appropriate critical value (e.g., 1.64 for a 90% CI; 2.56 for a 99% CI). The 95% confidence interval is the range between these two values (the *lower* $[\beta_k - (1.96 \times \text{s.e.}_{\beta k})]$ and *upper* $[\beta_k + (1.96 \times \text{s.e.}_{\beta k})]$ *confidence limits,* respectively). In conceptual terms, for 95 out of 100 samples drawn from the same population, the true population mean will fall between the lower and upper confidence limits constructed this way.

There are several approaches to presenting confidence intervals in tables or text.

- Report the confidence interval as a range with a dash between lower and upper confidence limits (e.g., 93.7–140.7 for the coefficient on "boy" in table 10.1). Don't use this variant if the confidence interval involves negative numbers to avoid confusion of the minus sign with the dash.
- Report the lower and upper confidence limits separated by a comma (e.g., −222.9, −166.5 for the "mother smoked during pregnancy" coefficient). Don't use this construction if the numbers themselves include commas (e.g., as thousands' separators).

Table 10.1. Alternative ways of presenting statistical significance for an ordinary least squares regression

Results of an OLS regression of birth weight (grams) by race/ethnicity, socioeconomic and smoking characteristics, United States, 1988–1994

	Coefficient[a] (β_k)	Standard error	Statistical significance information				
			t-statistic	p-value	Symbol[b]	Lower 95% CL[c]	Upper 95% CL
Intercept	3,039.7	39.2	77.51	<.001	**	2,962.9	3,116.6
Race/Hispanic origin (Non-Hispanic white)[d]							
Non-Hispanic black	−172.6	17.5	−9.76	<.001	**	−206.9	−138.3
Mexican American	−23.1	22.7	−1.02	.31	NS	−67.6	21.4
Boy	117.2	12.0	9.86	<.001	**	93.7	140.7
Mother's education							
<High school	−55.5	19.3	−2.88	<.001	**	−93.3	−17.7
=High school	−53.9	14.8	−3.64	<.001	**	−82.9	−24.9
(College+)							

Mother's age at child's birth (years)	10.7	1.2	8.92	<.001	**	8.3	13.1
Income-to-poverty ratio (IPR)	80.5	14.5	5.54	<.001	**	52.1	108.9
IPR^2	−9.9	2.3	−4.33	<.001	**	−14.4	−5.4
Mother smoked during pregnancy	−194.7	14.4	−13.52	<.001	**	−222.9	−166.5

Source: 1988–1994 National Health and Nutrition Examination Survey (NHANES III; U.S. DHHS 1997)

Notes: $N = 9,813$. F-statistic is 94.08 with 9 df; adjusted R^2 is 0.082.

[a]Weighted to population levels using sampling weights from the NHANES III.

[b]Symbols are usually included in the same cell as the coefficient, as in table 9.1, for example. They are shown separately here to convey that symbols are a method of presenting statistical significance, not a measure of effect size. Nonsignificant results would be shown without a symbol.

[c]CL = Confidence limit. The 95% confidence limits are calculated as $\beta \pm (1.96 \times \text{standard error})$.

[d]Reference categories are in parentheses.

$**p < 0.01$ NS: $p \geq 0.05$.

Table 10.2. Alternative ways of presenting effect size and statistical significance for a logistic regression

Results of a logistic regression model of low birth weight, United States, 1988–1994

| Variable | Effect size: coefficient | | | | Effect size: odds ratio (OR)[a] | | | Effect size: Coefficient or OR[b] | | |
	Coefficient (β_k: log-odds)	Std. error	Statistical test results Lower 95% CL[c]	Upper 95% CL	Odds ratio (OR)	Stat. test results Lower 95% CL[c]	Upper 95% CL	Stat. test results Wald chi-square	p-value	Symbol[d]
Intercept	−2.03	0.22	−2.46	−1.60				85.62	<.001	**
Race/Hispanic origin (Non-Hispanic white)[e]										
Non-Hispanic black	0.38	0.09	0.20	0.56	1.46	1.23	1.74	17.98	<.001	**
Mexican American	0.36	0.11	0.14	0.58	1.43	1.15	1.78	10.50	.001	**
Boy	−0.02	0.07	−0.16	0.12	0.98	0.86	1.12	0.061	.80	NS
Mother's education										
<High school	0.51	0.11	0.31	0.71	1.67	1.36	2.05	23.64	<.001	**
=High school	0.31	0.09	0.13	0.49	1.37	1.14	1.63	11.83	.001	**
(College+)										

Mother's age at child's birth (yrs.)	−0.008	0.007	−0.02	0.01	0.99	0.98	1.01	1.46	.23	**
Income-to-poverty ratio (IPR)	−0.26	0.08	−0.42	−0.10	0.77	0.65	0.91	9.86	.001	**
IPR²	0.019	0.015	−0.01	0.05	1.02	0.99	1.05	1.54	.21	NS
Mother smoked during pregnancy	0.33	0.08	0.17	0.49	1.39	1.20	1.62	18.68	<.001	**
Wald chi-square statistic (df)					236.67* (9)					
Diff. in − 2 Log L relative to null model					247.5					

Source: 1988–1994 National Health and Nutrition Examination Survey (NHANES III; U.S. DHHS, 1997).

Notes: N = 9,813. Low birth weight < 2,500 grams or 5.5 pounds. Weighted to population levels using sampling weights from the NHANES III.

[a] Odds ratio = $e^{\text{log-odds}}$ = e^{β}. Also known as relative odds.

[b] Test statistics, p-values, and symbols pertain to both the coefficients (log-odds) and odds ratios.

[c] CL = Confidence limit. The 95% confidence limits for the coefficient (log-odds) are calculated as $\beta \pm (1.96 \times \text{standard error})$. The confidence limits for the odds ratio are calculated $e^{(\beta \pm [1.96 \times \text{standard error}])}$.

[d] Symbols are usually included in the same cell as the coefficient. They are shown separately here to convey that they are a method of presenting statistical significance, not a measure of effect size. Nonsignificant results would be shown without a symbol.

[e] Reference categories are in parentheses.

**p < 0.01   NS: $p \geq 0.05$.

- In tables, create separate, labeled columns for the two confidence limits, as in table 10.1.
- Identify and express the confidence interval as the point estimate ± (1.96 times the standard error) (e.g., 95% CI: −23.1 ± 44.5 for the Mexican American coefficient).

Advantages of Confidence Intervals

Confidence intervals are easy to interpret because there is no need for readers to conduct additional calculations, and comparisons for the null hypothesis are against a straightforward value.

- For an OLS coefficient for which H_0: $\beta_k = 0.0$, assess whether the confidence interval overlaps 0.0. The 95% CI for "Mexican American" is −67.6 to +21.4 (table 10.1), so we cannot reject the null hypothesis. We conclude with 95% certainty that mean birth weight for Mexican Americans is *not* statistically significantly different from that of non-Hispanic whites (the reference category).
- For logit coefficients, again assess whether the confidence interval overlaps 0.0. The 95% CI for "boy" in the logit model of LBW is −0.16, 0.12 (table 10.2), again failing to reject the null hypothesis. We conclude that the log-odds of low birth weight are no different for boys than for girls (the reference category).
- For odds ratios, H_0: OR = 1.0 (e.g., equal odds of the outcome in the groups being compared), evaluate whether both confidence limits are on the same side of 1.0. In table 10.2, the 95% CI for "mother smoked during pregnancy" is 1.20−1.62, so we reject the null hypothesis and conclude that odds of low birth weight are higher among infants born to smokers than to nonsmokers at $p < 0.05$.
- To test hypotheses comparing coefficients from different models, observe whether the respective confidence intervals overlap one another. For example, if the 95% CI for "boy" is 100.2−130.4 for white infants, and the corresponding 95% CI for "boy" is 95.0−145.5 from a separate model for black infants, we would conclude that the gender differences are statistically indistinguishable between whites and blacks at $p < 0.05$ because those CI substantially overlap.

Confidence intervals are also relatively easy to explain to statistical neophytes, especially if presented in graphical form (e.g., figure 6.15) with accompanying descriptions like those in the above examples (see also "Describe the Pattern" in chapter 15 for ways to describe such charts).

Disadvantages of Confidence Intervals

A disadvantage of reporting 95% confidence intervals is that it is difficult to perform tests other than $p < 0.05$ unless the standard error is also reported. Confidence intervals cannot be used to compare coefficients from the same model unless those CI take into account the covariance between the coefficients (see "Testing Other Hypotheses" below). Also, to avoid confusion, stick to one confidence level (such as either 95% CI for all variables *or* 90% CI for all variables).

Test Statistics

Another frequently used approach is to present the test statistic for each predictor. For OLS regression, the test statistic is a t-statistic; for a logistic regression, a χ^2 or z-statistic. In tables, report the test statistic next to or below its associated effect estimate. In the text, report and name the test statistic in parenthesis after the associated effect estimate. "The odds ratio of low birth weight for infants born to mothers who smoked = 1.39 ($\chi^2 = 18.7$)."

Advantages of Test Statistics

For an audience that has some statistical training but isn't interested in performing their own hypothesis tests across models, the test statistic is a relatively user-friendly approach to testing the null hypothesis. By comparing the test statistic with the critical value for the associated distribution and degrees of freedom, readers can assess "how close" an effect is to conventional significance levels, such as when $p = 0.06$. If you elect to show test statistics without other indicators of statistical significance, also report the number of degrees of freedom in the table or in the text as you describe the findings. If the test involves an unusual number of degrees of freedom (other than 1 or ∞) or a one-tailed test, also report the critical value or accompany the test statistic with a symbol to denote statistical significance or lack thereof (see "Symbols" below).

Disadvantages of Test Statistics

Some readers don't know how to interpret a test statistic because they aren't familiar with the concept of a critical value or don't know the critical value for the pertinent distribution and number of degrees of freedom. If that characterizes your audience, avoid test statistics

and use *p*-values or symbols instead. Another drawback is that if readers are interested in comparing coefficients across models, they first
have to derive the standard error from the test statistic and coefficient.
If these other hypotheses are important for your research question, either present the confidence intervals, or conduct the tests yourself and
report the conclusions with a simpler indicator of statistical significance such as a *p*-value or symbol.

p-Values

Another approach is to present the *p*-value for each independent
variable, usually in a column to the right of the effect estimate (in a
table), or in parentheses after the associated effect estimate (in the
text). Report exact *p*-values to two decimal places unless $p < 0.01$, in
which case a third decimal place will suffice.

Advantages of p-*Values*

A *p*-value answers the question "is this variable statistically
significantly associated with the outcome?" without requiring much
work on the reader's part because the test statistic has already been
compared against the critical value. Readers who are familiar with
conventional cutoffs for assessing statistical significance will recognize $p = 0.03$ as "statistically significant" but $p = 0.27$ as not significant. This approach also gives more detail than a simple yes/no
answer provided by the symbol approach described below.

Disadvantages of p-*Values*

A disadvantage of reporting only a *p*-value is that it is difficult to
test hypotheses other than H_0: $\beta_i = 0$. To test whether a coefficient is
statistically significantly different from that in another model, readers would have to "work backward" to estimate the approximate test
statistic and standard error before they could calculate the standard
error of the difference (see below). Also, readers must know the conventional cutoffs for statistical significance.

Symbols Denoting Level of Statistical Significance

The final approach to presenting results of statistical tests is to use
symbols or different formatting to identify statistically significant
coefficients in tables or charts. Include these symbols in the same
table cell as the effect estimate or adjacent to the pertinent portion of
the chart, then define the convention in a footnote. Common variants
include:

- Typographic characters such as an asterisk or dagger (†) to denote $p < 0.01$ or $p < 0.05$. Effects without such symbols are not statistically significant.
- Bold or italics to highlight coefficients that are statistically significant — an effective approach in tables with many numbers, only some of which are statistically significant.
- In color documents or slides, a contrasting color for statistically significant findings.

Symbols are not used to report statistical significance in prose, so use one of the other approaches to report results in the text.

Advantages of Symbols

Symbols or bold or italic formatting are the quickest ways to identify results that reach conventional levels of statistical significance. They also save space because they avert the need for a separate column or row of detailed numbers—an advantage for a small, focused table or one presenting results of several different models.

Disadvantages of Symbols

Symbols make it very difficult for readers to perform their own hypothesis tests. In addition, symbols alone don't allow readers to distinguish effects that approach conventional levels of statistical significance (e.g., $p = 0.06$) from those that do not (e.g., $p = 0.63$).

■ PRESENTING STATISTICAL SIGNIFICANCE INFORMATION TO MATCH THE MEASURE OF EFFECT SIZE

Once you have decided which measure of effect size to report (e.g., standardized versus unstandardized OLS coefficients; or log-odds versus odds ratios), make sure your statistical significance information is in the same units of measurement.

- Test statistics, p-values, and symbols to denote significance levels can be used for any of the measures of effect size (e.g., both unstandardized and standardized coefficients in table 9.1; or both log-odds or odds ratios in table 10.2).
- Standard errors and confidence intervals differ for standardized versus unstandardized OLS coefficients, and for log-odds versus odds ratios. If you elect to present statistical significance with standard errors or confidence intervals, make sure the units of those indicators match the units of the corresponding effect estimate.

Accompany log-odds either with their standard errors or confidence intervals around the log-odds point estimate.

Accompany odds ratios with a confidence interval *converted to the same units as the odds ratio* (see formula in note to table 10.2). The estimated standard errors for logit coefficients are in a different metric (log-odds, not odds ratios), so they cannot be used directly with odds ratios.

Likewise, standard errors for unstandardized OLS coefficients cannot be used directly with the standardized coefficients.

■ TESTING OTHER HYPOTHESES

For some research questions, you may need to test a hypothesis in addition to $\beta_k = 0$.

- To find whether two coefficients in a given model are statistically significantly different *from one another,* such as whether $\beta_{<HS} = \beta_{=HS}$ in the model shown in table 10.1.
- To find whether the size and statistical significance of a coefficient *changes* across nested models, such as whether $\beta_{\text{non-Hispanic black (I)}} = \beta_{\text{non-Hispanic black (II)}}$ in the nested models I and II shown in table 14.3.
- To find whether the effect of a covariate *differs across models estimated for independent subgroups* (stratified models), such as whether $\beta_{<HS}$ is the same for each racial/ethnic group.

Standard Error of the Difference

To formally test statistical significance of differences between coefficients, e.g., H_0: $\beta_j = \beta_k$, divide the difference between the estimated coefficients $(\beta_j - \beta_k)$ by the standard error of the difference to obtain the test statistic, then compare that value against the pertinent critical value with one degree of freedom (Freedman et al. 1998). The standard error of the difference is calculated: $\sqrt{\text{var}\beta_j + \text{var}\beta_k - 2 \times \text{cov}(\beta_j, \beta_k)}$, where $\text{var}\beta_j$ and $\text{var}\beta_k$ are the variances of β_j and β_k, respectively, and $\text{cov}(\beta_j, \beta_k)$ is the covariance between β_j and β_k. The complete variance-covariance matrix for a regression can be requested as part of the output. The variance of each coefficient can be calculated from its standard error (s.e.): $\text{var}\beta_j = (\text{s.e.}\beta_j)^2$.

Differences between Coefficients from Independent Models

Estimated coefficients from *different* models can be considered to be statistically independent of one another, in which case $\text{cov}(\beta_j, \beta_k) = 0$. Hence, changes in coefficients across nested models, comparison of unadjusted and adjusted effects, or differences in OLS coefficients for a given variable in models of independent samples or different subgroups can each be tested without consideration of the covariance between the β s. In these instances, the formula for the standard error of the difference reduces to $\sqrt{\text{var}\beta_j + \text{var}\beta_k}$, which is equivalent to $\sqrt{\text{s.e.}\ \beta_j^2 + \text{s.e.}\beta_k^2}$. For example, $\beta_{\text{non-Hispanic black}}$ decreases by 97.3 between models I and II, table 14.3, from -244.5 in model I to -147.2 in model II. Plugging the associated standard errors into the formula for the standard error of the difference, we obtain $\sqrt{16.7^2 + 17.6^2} = 24.3$. Dividing 97.3 by 24.3 yields a t-statistic of 4.01, so we conclude that the change in coefficients for "non-Hispanic black" between models I and II is statistically significant at $p < 0.01$.

For continuous dependent variables, you can test differences in coefficients across models for different subgroups by estimating separate OLS regression models for each of those subgroups (not shown). Or estimate one model with data from all racial/ethnic groups and include interaction terms like those shown in model B, table 9.1. For categorical dependent variables, estimate one logit model with data from all racial/ethnic groups and include interaction terms.

Differences between Coefficients from the Same Model

Estimates of coefficients from within a regression model are generally not independent of one another, so $\text{cov}(\beta_j, \beta_k) \neq 0$. In such cases, information on the covariance between β_j and β_k must be taken into account when calculating the standard error of the difference or confidence intervals (Freedman et al. 1998; Gujarati 2002). Suppose we want to test $H_0: \beta_{<\text{HS}} = \beta_{=\text{HS}}$. From table 10.1, we have coefficients on $<\text{HS}$ and $=\text{HS}$ of -55.5 and -53.9, for a difference of 1.6. For that model, $\text{var}\beta_{<\text{HS}} = 370.87$, $\text{var}\beta_{=\text{HS}} = 218.79$, and $\text{cov}(\beta_{<\text{HS}}, \beta_{=\text{HS}}) = 137.83$ (output not shown). Plugging those values into the formula for the standard error of the difference yields $\sqrt{370.87 + 218.79 - (2 \times 137.83)} = \sqrt{314.0} = 17.72$. Finally, to calculate the test statistic, divide the difference between $\beta_{<\text{HS}}$ and $\beta_{=\text{HS}}$ by the standard error of the difference: $1.6/17.7 = 0.09$. This value is far below the critical value of 1.96 for a t-test with ∞ degrees of freedom, so we cannot reject the null hypothesis that $\beta_{<\text{HS}} = \beta_{=\text{HS}}$.

To test significance of differences across coefficients within a model, anticipate the contrasts of greatest interest and request tests of those hypotheses when you estimate the model. Do not present the entire variance-covariance matrix for a full regression model—an unwieldy proposition at best. In most statistical software you can request that additional hypotheses be tested when you specify a model. In SAS, if you include TEST $X_j = X_k$ as a statement in the REG procedure, the output will also include test statistics and p-values for the comparison $\beta_j = \beta_k$. For example, the test $\beta_{<HS} = \beta_{=HS}$ for the model in table 10.1 yields an F-statistic of 0.01 with a p-value of 0.93.

Having done this behind-the-scenes work either manually or using a TEST statement, report the results (but not the steps) to your readers: "The difference between coefficients for 'less than high school' and 'high school graduate' is not statistically significant."

"Ballpark" Assessment of Differences between Coefficients

In many cases, you can get an approximate sense of whether two estimated coefficients β_j and β_k are statistically significantly different from one another using only the coefficients and standard errors. Such "ballpark estimates" involve information that is part of standard regression output, without requiring either a formal test of $\beta_j = \beta_k$ or the variance-covariance matrix.

- If the difference between β_j and β_k is clearly swamped by the standard error of either estimate, you can fairly confidently conclude that the null hypothesis is correct, e.g., that $\beta_j = \beta_k$. For example, in table 10.1, the coefficients on <HS and =HS are −55.5 and −53.9, with standard errors of 19.3 and 14.8, respectively. The difference of only 1.6 units is far smaller than either standard error, so it is very unlikely that taking the covariance into account could alter that conclusion. And even if the difference were statistically significant, an absolute difference that small is of trivial interest (see "Substantive Significance" in chapter 3).
- If the difference between β_j and β_k is several times as large as the quantity $\sqrt{\text{s.e.}_{\beta j}^2 + \text{s.e.}_{\beta k}^2}$, you are probably safe concluding that the two coefficients are statistically significantly different from one another unless you have reason to suspect a very large negative covariance between the two variables.

- However, if the difference between β_j and β_k is between one and four times the quantity $\sqrt{\text{s.e.}_{\beta j}^2 + \text{s.e.}_{\beta k}^2}$, calculate the correct standard error of the difference—taking into account the covariance between the two coefficients—before drawing conclusions about the statistical significance of the difference.

■ CHOOSING HOW TO PRESENT STATISTICAL RESULTS FOR YOUR AUDIENCE AND FORMAT

Table 10.3 summarizes alternative ways to present information on statistical significance, along with suggestions about their use for particular audiences and formats. If you are writing for different audiences or formats, you will likely use different approaches in each. Select at most two ways to present statistical significance in each table or chart, choosing approaches that complement rather than duplicate one another. For many purposes, one approach is all that is needed.

- Don't report both standard errors and test statistics, which require roughly the same level of statistical proficiency and offer many of the same advantages for statistical audiences.
- Standard errors and confidence intervals share many of the same attributes, so use only one of those variants in a given table or chart.
- Likewise, reporting both p-values and symbols is largely redundant.

In the text, report statistical significance using the same approach as in the accompanying table or chart. An exception is that symbols should be replaced by the corresponding p-value in the text. Conventions presenting statistical results differ by disciplines and journals, so check before you create your tables.

Table 10.3. Strengths and weaknesses of alternative approaches to presenting statistical significance test results

Approach (Example)	Easy to interpret?	Easy to perform additional contrasts?[a]	Additional information needed to interpret?	Requisite competence w/inferential stats	Best uses	Comments
Standard error (s.e.) (e.g., s.e. = 3.8)	☹	☺☺	Point estimate Degrees of freedom Critical value of test statistic Covariance matrix (to compare coefficients within a model)	Proficient	Tables for statistical audiences	Accompany with symbol or p-value. For logistic models, present only with log-odds. not odds ratios.[b]
Confidence interval (e.g., 8.3 – 13.1)	☺	☺☺	Point estimate Covariance matrix (to compare coefficients within a model)	Familiar	Charts Slides	Facilitates comparison of coefficients for different variables. For odds ratios, report confidence limits in same metric as odds ratio.[b]

			Degrees of freedom / Critical value of test statistic	Proficient / Familiar / Minimal	Tables / Charts	
Test statistic[c] (e.g., $t = 2.57$ or $\chi^2 = 4.22$)	☺	☺	Degrees of freedom Critical value of test statistic	Proficient	Tables for statistical audiences	Accompany with symbol or *p*-value.
p-value (e.g., $p = 0.06$)	☺☺	☺	None	Familiar	Tables	Often used in conjunction with other approaches.
Symbol (e.g., ** $p < 0.01$)	☺☺	☺☺	None	Minimal	Charts/slides for any audience.	Use alone for lay audiences or slides.
					Tables for non-statistical audiences	Use with other approaches for statistical readers.

[a] "Additional contrasts" include comparison of coefficients from nested models or across models for different samples or subgroups. To test across coefficients within one model, the covariance between coefficients is needed; see "Testing Other Hypotheses."

[b] See "Presenting Statistical Significance Information to Match the Measure of Effect Size" and note to table 10.2 for an explanation of consistent units between effect estimate and standard errors or confidence intervals.

[c] Test statistic: *t*-statistic for OLS regression; χ^2 or *z*-statistic for logit regression.

☺☺ Very easy ☺ Somewhat easy ☺ Somewhat difficult (involves at least one step) ☺ Very difficult (involves several steps) ☺☺ Very difficult (involves several steps)

▓ CHECKLIST FOR CHOOSING HOW TO PRESENT STATISTICAL RESULTS

- For each paper or presentation, select one or two ways of presenting statistical significance results to accompany the point estimate, taking into account your audience, format, and objectives.
- Report statistical test results to the fewest possible decimal places needed to convey the finding (see table 4.2).
- In text or tables,

    for audiences with limited statistical training or interest, report p-values or use symbols to denote statistical significance;

    for statistical audiences, report standard errors, confidence intervals, or test statistics, accompanied by p-values or symbols to permit quick assessment of statistical test results.

- For charts, include confidence intervals, error bars, or symbols to denote statistical significance.
- For slides,

    avoid standard errors or test-statistics except in short prose or small tables; replace them with p-values or symbols in large tables;

    present confidence intervals graphically, with a reference line showing the null hypothesis against which to compare effect estimates (see figure 6.15 for an example);

    use color to highlight statistically significant findings.

- For all audiences, if hypotheses or calculations other than H_0: $\beta_k = 0$ are of interest, conduct those tests behind the scenes and report the conclusions of those tests.

Pulling It All Together

PART III

In the preceding chapters, I described a series of tools and principles for writing about multivariate models. In practice, rarely will you use these elements piecemeal. Instead, you will integrate them to create a compelling explanation of the issues you address, complete with the quantitative evidence needed to evaluate those questions. Rather than naming or describing the various principles and tools as you use them, you will simply incorporate them into the narrative. The next few chapters show how to do just that, with illustrative "poor/better/best" examples of introductory, data and methods, results, and concluding sections and abstracts for a scientific paper or grant proposal. I also demonstrate how to design slides and accompanying speaker's notes for a speech—another common and challenging way to present results of a multivariate analysis. Finally, I give guidelines for writing posters, chartbooks, issue briefs or policy briefs, reports, and general-interest articles—other frequently encountered formats for presenting findings to applied audiences. I return often to considerations of audience and format to show how to modify your writing to suit those varied purposes.

Writing Introductions, Conclusions, and Abstracts

Academic papers or scientific reports about a statistical analysis usually follow a prescribed structure, with the text divided into an introduction, literature review, data and methods, results, and discussion and conclusions. Grant proposals follow a similar structure, substituting a description of pilot studies or preliminary findings for the results section and replacing the discussion and conclusions with a section on policy, program, or research implications of the proposed project. In this chapter, I give suggestions on how to write an effective title, then illustrate the structure and contents of introductory and concluding sections and an abstract for a regression analysis of relations among race/ethnicity, socioeconomic status, and birth weight in the United States. The other sections of a scientific article are covered in chapters 12 (data and methods) and 14 (results). For additional guidance on writing scientific papers, see Montgomery (2003), Davis (1997), Hailman and Strier (1997), or Pyrczak and Bruce (2000).

▩ TITLE

The title is the first aspect of your paper or proposal readers will see. Use it to identify the topic, context, and what is new or different about your work—what sets it apart from other related studies. Convey the questions or hypotheses you investigate or the methods you apply, using your research question and context (W's) as starting points. Often, a rhetorical version of your research question or objective works well.

- If you are testing a hypothesis about relations among two or three concepts, use the title to name those concepts or to state your hypothesis about how they are related. For instance, "The Contribution of Expanding Portion Sizes to the US Obesity Epidemic" (Young and Nestle 2002) clearly identifies the dependent and independent variables—obesity and expanding portion sizes, respectively. Reworded as a rhetorical question, the title might read: "The US Obesity Epidemic: How Much Did Expanding Portion Sizes Contribute?"

- If you are describing a trend or other pattern, name the relevant dimensions of the contrast in the title. For example, "Voter Turnout from 1945 to 1998: A Global Participation Report" (Institute for Democracy and Electoral Assistance 1999) indicates both the period to which the analysis pertains and the international scope of the comparison, as well as the topic under study.

- If your work is among the first to advance a new type of study design or statistical method, or to apply a technique to a new topic, mention both the method and the topic in the title. For example, "Dropping Out of Advanced Mathematics: A Multilevel Analysis of School- and Student-Level Factors" captures the dependent variable, statistical method, and different levels of analysis for the independent variables. For a lay audience, replace the name of the method with the question it is intended to answer, such as "Dropping Out of Advanced Mathematics: How Much Do Students and Schools Contribute to the Problem?" (Ma and Willms 1999).

■ ORGANIZING YOUR PROSE

Writing about a statistical analysis is similar to writing a legal argument. In the opening statement, a lawyer raises the major questions to be addressed during the trial and gives a general introduction to the characters and events in question. To build a compelling case, he then presents specific facts collected and analyzed using standard methods of inquiry. If innovative or unusual methods were used, he introduces experts to describe and justify those techniques. He presents individual facts, then ties them to other evidence to demonstrate patterns or themes. He may submit exhibits such as diagrams or physical evidence to supplement or clarify the facts. He cites previous cases that have established precedents and standards in the field and discusses how they do or do not apply to the current case. Finally, in the closing argument he summarizes conclusions based on the complete body of evidence, restating the critical points but with far less detail than in the evidence portion of the trial.

Follow the same general structure as you write your quantitative story line for a scientific paper or grant proposal. The introduction parallels the opening argument; the data and methods and results sections mirror the evidence portion of the trial; and the discussion and conclusions parallel the closing argument. Open by introducing the overarching questions before describing the detailed statistical findings, just as a lawyer outlines the big picture before introducing specific testimony or other evidence to the jury. Describe and justify your methods of data collection and analysis, including why a multivariate model is needed to answer your research question with the data at hand (see "Building the Case for a Multivariate Model" in chapter 14). Systematically introduce and explain the numeric evidence in your exhibits—tables, charts, maps, or other diagrams—building a logical sequence of analyses. Close by summarizing your findings and connecting them back to the initial questions and previous studies of related topics.

As in other types of expository writing, introduce the broad topic or question of the work and then organize the factual material into separate paragraphs, each of which describes one major topic or pattern or a series of closely related patterns. Begin each paragraph with a statement of the issue or question to be addressed, write a sentence or two to sketch out the shape of the contrast or pattern with words, then provide and interpret numeric evidence to document that pattern. To portray the size of each pattern, use selected comparisons such as absolute or relative difference, percentage difference, or excess risk.

As you write, select analogies and descriptive words or phrases to convey the context and scale of those differences. Well-chosen verbs, adjectives, and adverbs sharpen descriptions of patterns and contrasts and can add considerable texture and interest.

■ WRITING AN INTRODUCTION

In your introduction, state the topic and explain why it is of interest. After a general introductory sentence, report a few numbers to establish the importance of that topic. Include information on the prevalence of the issue or phenomenon under study or the consequences of that phenomenon, using one or two selected numeric contrasts to place those statistics in perspective. Cite the source of each fact as you mention it, using the standard citation format for your discipline. End the introduction with a statement of what your study will add to what is already known on the subject, either as a list of questions to be addressed or as one or more hypotheses.

Box 11.1 illustrates how to apply these ideas to the birth weight analysis, with comments keyed to numbered sentences within the narrative.

■ LITERATURE REVIEW

Academic papers, books, and grant proposals usually include a review of the existing literature on the topic to describe what is already known, provide background on the hypothesized relationships among variables, explain applications of new methods to related topics, and report major quantitative findings for comparison with the current study. Instead of writing separate sentences or paragraphs about each previous study, aim for a paragraph or two synthesizing previous findings on each of the major relationships you will examine or applications of methods you will use. Summarize, generalizing where possible about broad similarities and differences in theories or findings from the existing literature, and pointing out appreciable discrepancies among them. Where pertinent, discuss aspects of data or methods that affect interpretation or comparability of others' findings (see chapter 12 for issues to be considered).

Emphasize the direction and approximate size of associations, reporting a few illustrative numbers from other studies. Discuss only findings that are statistically significant and mention when a lack of statistical significance for key variables contradicts theory or other studies (see "Statistical Significance" below). To facilitate comparison of results across studies, report the value as well as quantitative comparisons such as absolute difference, ratio, or percentage change to provide the raw data for those calculations and to help readers interpret the contrasts.

To avoid a long, serial description of detailed findings from each of many studies, use the GEE ("generalization, example, exceptions") technique, explaining where there is and isn't consensus on the topic and identifying questions that remain to be addressed. A dissertation or book can include more comprehensive discussion of individual studies, but should still provide a synthesis of current evidence and theory about the topic.

Poor: "Smith and Jones (date) studied the relationship between race and birth weight in the United States and found [*XYZ*]."

Box 11.1. Using Numbers in an Introduction to a Scientific Paper or Report

"(1) Low birth weight (LBW) is a widely recognized risk factor for infant mortality, neurological problems, asthma, and a variety of developmental problems that can persist into childhood and even adulthood (U.S. Environmental Protection Agency 2002; Institute of Medicine 1985). (2) For example, in 1999, U.S. infants born weighing less than 2,500 grams (5.5 pounds) were 24 times as likely as normal birth weight infants to die before their first birthday (60.5 deaths per 1,000 live births and 2.5 deaths per 1,000, respectively; Mathews, MacDorman, and Menacker 2002). Although they comprise about 7.5% of all births, LBW infants account for more than 75% of infant deaths (Paneth 1995).

"(3) Costs associated with low birth weight are substantial: in 1995, Lewit and colleagues estimated that $4 billion—more than one-third of all expenditures on health care for infants—was spent on the incremental costs of medical care for LBW infants. Higher risks of special education, grade repetition, hospitalization, and other medical costs add more than $85,000 (in 1995 dollars) per low birth weight child to costs incurred by normal birth weight children through age 15 (Lewit et al. 1995).

"(4) Despite considerable efforts to reduce the incidence of low birth weight, the problem remains fairly intractable: between 1981 and 2000, the percentage of LBW infants rose from 6.8% to 7.6% of all infants, in part reflecting the increase in multiple births (Martin et al. 2002). (5) Rates of LBW among black infants have remained approximately twice those among white infants over the same period (13.0% and 6.5% in 2000, respectively). In 2002, black infants weighed on average 264 grams less than their white counterparts (Martin et al. 2003). (6) This analysis uses multivariate regression to assess the extent to which lower mean birth weight among black children in the United States can be explained by socioeconomic, demographic, and behavioral characteristics."

COMMENTS
(1) Introduces the topic of the paper, gives a general sense of its importance with reference to major studies on the topic, and defines the acronym LBW.

(2) Reports statistics on the consequences of LBW, using relative risk and percentage share to quantify mortality differences, and citing original sources of the figures used in those comparisons.

(3) Reports estimates from other studies of the costs associated with LBW, providing further evidence that the topic merits additional study.

(4) Generalizes about trends in LBW over the past two decades and reports numeric facts to illustrate those patterns, with citations of the original data sources.

(5) Presents information about racial differences in LBW and mean birth weight, providing a transition to the research question for this study.

(6) States the research question, mentioning the statistical method, dependent and key independent variables to be used in the analysis.

Michaelson (date) also studied the relationship between race and birth weight and found [ABC]. [Separate descriptions of results from five more studies on the topic.]

Better: "Five out of seven recent studies (authors, dates) of the relationship between race and birth weight in the United States found that [pattern and example]. In contrast, Michaelson (date) found [different pattern and example], while DiDonato (date) . . ."

For literature reviews that address several issues, use subheadings within the section to orient readers. For example, if you are applying a new method to your topic, organize the literature review into one subsection describing previous studies of the topic and another subsection describing the method and previous applications.

In some disciplines, the literature review is a free-standing section or chapter; in others, it is integrated into the introduction. If your literature review is separate from your introduction, place your research questions or hypotheses at the end of the literature review. Acquainting readers with theory and empirical findings from other studies helps substantiate the reasons behind the specific objectives and hypotheses for your analysis or proposed study. Examples of these elements are included in box 11.1.

■ DISCUSSION AND CONCLUSIONS

In the discussion and conclusions section, relate the evidence from your analysis back to the larger research question, comparing broad conclusions against hypotheses posed at the beginning of the work and results from related studies. See also chapter 12 regarding data and methods in the conclusions.

Numeric Information in a Concluding Section

In the concluding section, restate conclusions about the size and statistical significance of associations among the variables in the main research question, and consider extensions that help readers see the importance (or lack of importance) of those findings. To convey the purpose and interpretation of numeric facts or contrasts, introduce them in sentences that place them in their substantive context.

Effect Size

Rather than repeat precise numeric estimates and results of statistical tests from the results section, use verbal descriptions or approximate numeric values, rounding to the nearest whole multiple or familiar fraction.

Causality and Substantive Significance Revisited

To bring your analysis to a close, describe the implications of the associations reported in the analytic portion of the paper. In analyses that ask cause-and-effect type questions, revisit two issues discussed in chapter 3. First, can the associations be viewed as causal? And second, if so, what is the substantive meaning or importance of the findings? As you describe the relationships in your analysis, choose wording that conveys whether you are interpreting those relationships as causal or merely as associations. To assess how much a pattern matters, combine estimates from the analytic portion of the paper with information from other sources. Depending on your topic, these calculations might involve cost effectiveness analysis (e.g., Gold et al. 1996), attributable risk calculations (chapter 7), or other applicable measures of net benefits, costs, or tradeoffs between alternative proposed solutions.

Statistical Significance

Rarely is statistical significance discussed explicitly in the concluding section, and then only for key variables in your research question. Use results of statistical tests in conjunction with substantive considerations to assess which findings to emphasize. Instead of reporting standard errors, test statistics, *p*-values, or confidence intervals, use phrases such as "were statistically significant" or "was not associated."

There are three situations where you should discuss statistical significance in your conclusion:

(1) If your statistical test results *run counter to theoretical expectations,* such as when theory led you to predict a large, statistically significant difference across groups that was not borne out in your study, or vice versa.

(2) If your statistical test results *conflict with those of previous empirical studies.* Perhaps you found statistically significant differences that others had not. Or others may have found statistically significant differences that were not apparent with your data.

In those instances, explicitly mention the discrepant findings regarding statistical significance, using words rather than detailed numeric results. Explain what these findings imply, relating them back to your original hypotheses and the literature that led you to formulate those hypotheses. Discuss possible explanations for the discrepancy of findings across studies, such as differences in study populations, design, or variables.

(3) The third situation in which statistical significance merits discussion is if you observe changes in effect size and statistical significance of key variables in your model when you introduce measures of potentially mediating or confounding factors, particularly those that were not previously available or were poorly measured in other studies. This kind of issue is often the reason for estimating a multivariate model, and should be explained as such in your summary.

Statistical Methods in the Concluding Section

In the discussion, restate the type and purpose of your statistical method or study design to show where your analysis fits in the context of previous studies. For a well-established statistical method or design, simply name it or briefly paraphrase the rationale for using it. For a newer method or one that has not been widely used in your field, include a few sentences to explain why it is needed for your data and research question and how it improves upon other types of analyses. Finally, if the results obtained using that method differ from those obtained using other methods, discuss reasons for those differences and the pros and cons of each approach. See "Data and Methods in the Discussion Section" in chapter 12 for examples.

Citing Other Sources

Unlike the results section, which is devoted almost exclusively to reporting and analyzing data from within your own study, a discussion and conclusions section often incorporates numeric information from other studies. There are several reasons to cite other works in the discussion:

- To evaluate whether the current findings are consistent with previous research
- To provide perspective on the importance of the research question
- To apply numbers from other sources of background information that place the findings of the current study in context
- To compare your results with those obtained with different analytic methods or study designs
- To offer ideas about underlying reasons for observed patterns, generating hypotheses to be tested empirically in later studies (otherwise known as "directions for future research")

Box 11.2 is an illustrative discussion and conclusion section of a scientific paper on racial/ethnic differences in birth weight, summarizing the findings presented in the results section shown in chapter 14.

■ ABSTRACTS AND KEYWORDS

Most scientific papers or proposals require an abstract and keywords to summarize and classify the work. Conference organizers often review abstracts rather than full papers when deciding among submitted papers.

Abstracts

Abstracts are capsule summaries of a scientific paper, grant proposal, research poster, or book. They are often shown on the first page

Box 11.2. Using Numbers in a Discussion and Conclusion to a Scientific Paper

"(1) Consistent with a large body of previous research (e.g., Institute of Medicine 1985), we found a substantial birth weight disadvantage among black infants compared to infants from other racial/ethnic groups in the United States between 1988 and 1994. (2) Although black infants weigh on average 246 grams less than white infants, (3) part of this difference can be attributed to the fact that black infants are more likely to be of low socioeconomic status (SES). Regardless of race, children born into low SES families have lower mean birth weight than those born at higher SES. (4) However, our multivariate analysis shows that differences in family socioeconomic background do not explain the entire difference across racial ethnic groups. When family income, mother's age, and smoking are taken into account, black infants weigh 150 to 200 grams less than their white counterparts; this gap occurs at each level of mother's education.

"(5) The causal role of low socioeconomic status is also brought into question by the relatively high birth weight among Mexican American infants, which is quite close to that of white infants and far above that of black infants. This phenomenon of relatively good health among Mexican Americans despite their low SES is referred to as the "epidemiological paradox" or "Hispanic paradox" and also has been observed for other health conditions (Franzini et al. 2001; Palloni and Morenoff 2001).

"(6) Other possible mechanisms that have been proposed to explain lower mean birth weight among black infants include less access to health care, higher rates of poor health behaviors, greater social stress (Zambrana et al. 1999), intergenerational transmission of health disadvantage (Conley and Bennett 2000), and other unmeasured factors that affect black people more than those of other racial/ethnic origins.

"(7) Reducing the incidence of low birth weight is a key objective of Healthy People 2010 (U.S. DHHS 2000). (8) If the incidence of low birth weight among black infants decreased to the level among white infants, nearly 40,000 of the low birth weight black infants born in 2000 would instead have been born at normal birth weight. That reduction in low birth weight would have cut the black infant mortality rate by more than one-third, assuming the infant mortality rate for normal birth weight infants (Mathews, MacDorman, and Menacker 2002). In addition, an estimated $3.4 million in medical and educational expenses would be saved from that birth cohort alone, based on Lewit and colleagues' estimates of the cost of low birth weight (1995)."

COMMENTS

(1) Generalizes the major finding of the current study and places it in the context of previous research, citing a summary report by a prominent national research institute.

(2) Quantifies the size of the unadjusted black/white difference in mean birth weight.

(3–6) Describes the association between race/ethnicity in cause-neutral language ("found a substantial birth weight disadvantage among," sentence 1), leading into a discussion of causal interpretation. In contrast, the hypothesized causal role of socioeconomic characteristics is clearly conveyed using language such as "attributed to" (sentence 3), "do not explain" (sentence 4). The intentional use of causal language continues into the subsequent paragraph with "causal role" (sentence 5), and "possible mechanisms" (sentence 6).

Sentence 4 names the statistical method and lists which characteristics were taken into control in the analysis of race, socioeconomic status, and birth weight.

Sentences 5 and 6 discuss possible explanatory mechanisms linking race and birth weight, citing published sources of these theories. Sentence 5 mentions the "epidemiological paradox" observed in other health studies and relates it to the current findings. Sentence 6 introduces other theories that can be used to generate hypotheses to be tested in future studies.

(7) Brings the paper full circle, returning to the "big picture" to remind readers of the reasons for addressing this research question. Establishes that lowering the incidence of low birth weight is a major priority identified by experts in the field, and cites the pertinent policy document.

(8) Combines statistics on the excess risk of low birth weight among black infants from the current analysis with information from other published sources about infant mortality rates and costs of low birth weight to estimate how many infant deaths could be prevented and how many dollars saved if the incidence of low birth weight among black infants could be reduced to the same level as among whites. Figures are reported in round numbers: phrases such as "nearly 40,000" and "more than one-third" are precise enough to make the point.

of the associated journal article or research proposal, in the program for a professional conference, or in a list of recently published books. They provide a quick way for readers to familiarize themselves with the topic and findings of a large number of studies, often helping them to decide which articles to read closely, which presentations to attend, or which proposals to review in detail. Abstracts are your opportunity to stand out among competing works, so take the time to write a compelling, accurate summary of your work.

Although the length and format vary by discipline and type of publication, the contents generally include short descriptions of the objectives, data and methods, results, and conclusions of the study. Structured abstracts include subheadings for each of those parts, while unstructured abstracts integrate all those elements into one short paragraph. Consult the instructions for authors for your intended publication for guidelines on structure and length.

Use the W's to organize the information in an abstract.

- In the objectives (sometimes called the "purpose" or "background") section, state what your study is about and, if word count permits, why it is important.
- In the data and methods (sometimes divided into "data sources," "study design," and "data collection and analysis") portion, state the type of study design, listing who, what, when, where, and how for each major data source, mentioning the number of cases, and naming the analytic methods.
- In the results section of the abstract, briefly summarize key findings, including a few carefully chosen numbers and statistical test results.
- In the conclusions (sometimes called "discussion," or divided into "conclusions" and "policy implications"), relate major findings to the initial objectives. For policy-oriented or other applied audiences, include a short phrase or two pointing out policy implications of the findings.

Because it repeats information from all parts of your paper, an abstract is often best written after the paper is complete. Alternatively, draft an abstract early in the writing process to help organize your work, then revise it once you have finished the paper or proposal to make sure it reflects the final version.

Keywords

Keywords are used in online databases of publications and conference presentations, allowing readers to search for papers that match a specified set of topics, methods, or contextual characteristics. As the term suggests, keywords should emphasize key elements of the paper; use the W's as a mental checklist to identify them. At a minimum, include keywords for the dependent variable and main independent variables. Also include location or dates if these are important aspects of your research question, and mention any major restrictions on who was studied. For methodologically oriented papers or audiences, the type of study design and statistical methods are often included as keywords.

Box 11.3 is a structured 150-word abstract and keywords for the analysis of racial differences in birth weight, with numbered comments for each component.

Box 11.3. Structured Abstract and Keywords for a Scientific Paper

Objectives. (1) To assess whether differences in socioeconomic status explain lower mean birth weight among black than white infants in the United States.

Methods. (2) Ordinary least squares regression was used to analyze (3) data from the Third National Health and Nutrition Examination Survey (NHANES III, 1988–1994) for 9,813 children. (4) Birth weight and socioeconomic characteristics were from the parental interview.

Results. (5) Even when socioeconomic status and maternal smoking were taken into account, (6) non-Hispanic black children weighed 150 to 200 grams less than non-Hispanic whites ($p < 0.01$). (7) Girls and children born to less educated, lower income, younger women or to smokers also had lower than average birth weight ($p < 0.01$), but differences for Mexican Americans were not statistically significant.

Conclusions. (8) At all socioeconomic levels, black infants weigh considerably less than infants of other race/ethnicity. (9) Additional research is needed to identify modifiable risk factors to improve birth weight among black infants.

Keywords: (10) birth weight; black race; Hispanic ethnicity; socioeconomic factors; United States.

COMMENTS

(1) Identifies dependent variable, key independent variables, and sets the context.

(2) Specifies the statistical method.

(3) Names the data source, including dates and number of cases.

(4) Identifies the means by which the variables were collected.

(5) Paraphrases use of a multivariate model ("when . . . were taken into account").

(6) States direction, magnitude, and statistical significance of the association between race and birth weight.

(7) Summarizes the direction of association and statistical significance for the other independent variables.

(8) Restates results of the analysis, tying them back to the research question (objective).

(9) Suggests additional research direction and relates it to the underlying policy question ("modifiable risk factors to improve birth weight").

(10) Lists five keywords that identify the dependent and independent variables, and context.

■ CHECKLIST FOR WRITING INTRODUCTIONS, CONCLUSIONS, AND ABSTRACTS

- Write a title that conveys your research question, methods, and key facets of context (W's).
- Apply the principles for good expository writing.
  Organize ideas into one major topic per paragraph.
  Start each with an introductory sentence that identifies the purpose of that paragraph.
  Write transition sentences to show how consecutive paragraphs relate to one another.
- In the introduction,
  introduce the issues to be discussed,
  provide evidence about their importance, and
  state hypotheses; if the literature review is a separate section, put hypothesis after that section.
- In the literature review,
  organize paragraphs by major topic, grouping articles on each topic, rather than writing separately about every article; and
  summarize theory and findings from previous studies of your topics, using the GEE approach to identify similarities and differences.
- In the discussion and conclusion,
  relate your findings back to your original hypotheses and to previous studies, summarizing key numeric findings rather than reporting detailed statistical results,
  illustrate substantive significance of findings (see chapter 3),
  discuss advantages and limitations of your data and analytic approach, and
  identify implications for policy or research.
- In the abstract,
  summarize the objectives, methods, results, and conclusions of your study;
  use the W's to organize the topics; and
  see instructions to authors for guidelines about length and structure of abstract for the pertinent journal or call for proposals.
- For the keywords, select nouns or phrases to identify the dependent and key independent variables, methods, and context of your study.

Writing about Data and Methods

An essential part of writing about multivariate analyses is a description of the data and methods used to generate your statistics. This information reveals how well your measures match the concepts you wish to study and how well the analytic methods capture the relationships among your variables—two important issues that affect how your results are interpreted. Suppose you are writing about an evaluation of a new math curriculum. Having explained why students would be expected to perform better under the new curriculum, you estimate a model based on a sample that includes some students following the new curriculum and some following the old. Because the data were collected in the real world, the concepts you seek to study may not be captured well by the available variables. Perhaps math performance was measured with a multiple-choice test in only a few classes, and quite a few children were absent on test day, for example.

In addition, statistical methods involve certain assumptions that are not always realistic, thus the methods of analysis may not accurately embody the hypothesis you wish to test. For instance, a multivariate regression model estimated from observational data with information on only a few basic demographic and school attributes is unlikely to satisfy the assumption of a quasi-experimental comparison of the two curriculums.

To convey the salience of these issues for your work, write about how the study design, measures, and analytic methods suit the research question, how they improve upon previous analyses of the topic, and what questions remain to be answered with other data and different methods. With this information, readers can assess the quality and interpretation of your results, and understand how your analyses contribute to the body of knowledge in the field.

In this chapter I show how to apply the principles and tools covered in previous chapters to writing about data and methods. I begin by discussing how to decide on the appropriate level of detail for your audience and the type of document you are writing. I then give guidelines about the contents of data and methods sections, mentioning many aspects of study design, measurement of variables, and statistical analysis. In the interest of space, I refer to other sources on these topics. See Schutt (2001) or Lilienfeld and Stolley (1994) for general references on research design, Fox (1997) or Gujarati (2002) on OLS models, Powers and Xie (2000) on logit models, and Wilkinson et al. (1999) for a comprehensive guide to data and methods sections for scientific papers. Finally, I demonstrate how to write about data and methods as you describe your conclusions.

■ WHERE AND HOW MUCH TO WRITE ABOUT DATA AND METHODS

The placement and level of detail about data and methods depend on your audience and the length of your work. For scientific readers, write a dedicated, detailed data and methods section. For readers with an interest in the topic but not the methods, include the basic information as you describe the findings. Regardless of audience, include a discussion of how these issues affect your conclusions. In the paragraphs that follow, I touch briefly on the different objectives of a data and methods section and the discussion of data and methods in a concluding section. Later in the chapter, I give a more detailed look at the respective contents and styles of those sections.

Data and Methods Sections

In articles, books, or grant proposals for scientific audiences, comprehensive, precise information on data sources and statistical methods is expected. In such works, a well-written data and methods section will provide enough information that someone could replicate your analysis: if they were to collect data using your guidelines, they would end up with a comparable study design and variables. If they were to use the same data set and follow your procedures for excluding cases, defining variables, and applying analytic methods, they could reproduce your results.

Data and Methods in the Conclusion

In the concluding section of both applied and scientific papers, emphasize the implications of data and methods for your conclusions. Discuss the strengths and limitations of the data and methods to place your findings in the larger context of what is and isn't known on your topic. Review the potential biases that affect your data and explain the plusses and minuses of the analytic techniques for your research question and data. For an applied audience, skip the technical details and use everyday language to briefly describe how your data and methods affect interpretation of your key findings.

■ HOW MUCH TECHNICAL STUFF?

Scientific papers and proposals devote an entire section to data and methods, sometimes called just "methods" or "methods and materials." One of the most difficult aspects of writing these sections—particularly for novices—is selecting the appropriate level of detail. Some beginners are astonished that anyone would care how they conducted their analyses, thinking that only the results matter. Others slavishly report every alternative coding scheme and model specification from their exploratory analysis, yielding an avalanche of information for readers to sift through. A couple of guiding principles will help you arrive at a happy medium.

First, unless explanation of a particular aspect of the data or methods is needed to understand your analyses, keep your description brief and refer to other publications that give the pertinent details. If your document is the first to describe a new data collection strategy, measurement approach, or analytic method, thoroughly and systematically report the steps of the new procedure and how they were developed. If the method has been described elsewhere, restrict your explanation to the aspects needed to understand the current analysis, then cite other works for additional information.

Second, conventions about depth and organization of data and methods sections vary by discipline, level of training, and length of the work. To determine the appropriate style for your work, read examples of similar documents for comparable audiences in your field. Some general guidelines for common types of writing about multivariate analyses:

- For a journal article or research proposal with a methodological emphasis, provide details on methods of data collection or analysis that are novel, including why they are needed and the kinds of data and research questions for which they are best suited.

- For a journal article or research pro osal with a substantive emphasis, summarize the data and ethods concisely and explain the basic logic of your analytic approach, then return to their advantages and disadvantages in the concluding section. Give less prominence to these issues in both the data and methods and discussion sections than you would in a methodological paper.
- For a "data book" designed to serve as a reference data source, summarize data and methods in the body of the report, with technical information and pertinent citations in appendixes.
- For a book or doctoral dissertation, follow the general guidelines above but take advantage of the additional length to provide more detail and documentation. If quantitative methods aren't a major focus, relegate technical details to appendixes or cite other works.
- For documentation to accompany public release of a data set, give a comprehensive, detailed explanation of study design, wording of questions, coding or calculation of variables, imputation, derivation and application of sampling weights, and so forth, accompanied by citations to pertinent methodological documents. For documentation to accompany a simulation model, define input variables, statistical assumptions, and model specifications. Documentation serves as the main reference source for all subsequent users, so dot all the i's and cross all the t's. For excellent examples, see National Center for Health Statistics (1994) and Westat (1994, 1996).
- For general-interest newspaper articles, chartbo ks, policy briefs, or other summaries of research for an ap lied audience, incorporate the W's (who, what, when, where) and units as you write about the numbers rather than in a separate section, then follow the approach described later in this chapter under "Data and Methods in the Discussion Section" to explain strengths and weaknesses. See chapter 16 for examples of describing data and methods for applied audiences.

■ DATA SECTION

More than any other part of a scientific paper, a data and methods section is like a checklist written in sentence form. Organize the de-

scription of your data around the W's—who, what, when, where—
and two honorary W's, how many and how. If you are using data from
a named secondary source such as the Panel Study of Income Dy-
namics (PSID) or the National Health Interview Survey, identify that
source and provide a citation for published documentation. For applied audiences or brief reports, that citation plus a brief list of who,
what, when, and where is sufficient.

When

Specify whether your data pertain to a single time point (cross-
sectional data), to different samples compared across several points
in time (repeated cross-sections), or to a sample followed over a period of time (longitudinal data), then report the pertinent dates and
units of time.

Where

Identify where your data were collected. For studies of human populations, "where" usually encompasses standard geographic units
such as cities, countries, or continents, or institutions such as schools,
hospitals, or professional organizations. For ecological, geological, or
other natural science studies, other types of places (such as bodies of
water, landforms, or ecologic zones) or other geographic and topo-
graphic attributes (like latitude, longitude, altitude, or depth) may
pertain. If geography is important to your topic, include one or more
maps to orient an unfamiliar audience.

Who

"Who" encompasses several dimensions related to how data were
collected and whether some cases were omitted from your sample because of missing values on one or more variables. Describe the *final
analytic sample* used in your analysis, which may differ from the
sample of cases for which data were originally collected.

Universe or Sample?

Some data sources aim to include the full universe of cases in the
place and time specified, others a subset of those cases. In your data
section, state whether your data include all cases in the specified
place and time as in a census, or a sample of those cases, like a 1%
poll of prospective voters. See "Study Design" and "Sampling" sections below for related issues.

Characteristics

Some research questions pertain to only some subgroups rather than all possible cases in the time and place specified. If you are using secondary data, you might analyze a subset of cases from a larger study. For example, the study described in box 12.1 focuses only on selected racial/ethnic groups and age groups. Indicate whether your analytic sample was restricted to those who meet certain criteria, such as having particular demographic traits, minimum test scores, or a particular disease, and explain why such restrictions suit your research question.

Response Rate and Excluded Cases

Few studies succeed in collecting data on all the cases they sought to study. For instance, some subjects who are selected for a study cannot be contacted or refuse to participate; censuses and surveillance systems overlook some individuals. Report the response rate for your study as a percentage of the intended study sample and consider representativeness of the sample (see below).

In almost every study, some cases have missing or invalid information on one or more variables. Cases that are missing the dependent variable or a key independent variable (birth weight and race/ethnicity, respectively, in the study described below) cannot be used to analyze the association between those variables. To create a consistent analytic sample for bivariate and multivariate analyses, researchers often exclude cases that are missing information on potential mediators, confounders, or background control variables to be included in the multivariate models. Some researchers impute missing values (see "Imputation" below), although this is typically avoided for the main variables in an analysis.

If you exclude cases with missing values, list the variables that formed the basis for the exclusion and report the number and percentage of cases omitted based on those criteria. If a large percentage of cases that otherwise fit your research question are missing data, discuss whether the retained cases are representative of the population to whom you wish to generalize your results (see "Representativeness" below).

Loss to Follow-Up

Studies that follow subjects across time typically lose some cases between the beginning and end of the study. For instance, studies tracking students' scholastic performance across time lose students who transfer schools, drop out, or refuse to participate. Perhaps you started following a cohort of 500 entering ninth graders, but only 250 remain four years later.

Loss to follow-up, also known as attrition, affects statistical analyses in two important ways. First, the smaller number of cases can affect the power of your statistical tests (Kraemer 1987). Second, if those who are lost differ from those who remain, inferences drawn from analysis of the remaining cases may not be generalizable to the intended universe. For example, dropouts are often weaker students than those who stay in school, yielding a biased look at the performance of the overall cohort.

For longitudinal data, provide the following information, and then discuss representativeness:

- The number of cases at baseline (the start date of the study), following the guidelines for response rate and missing data described above.
- The number and percentage of the baseline sample that remained at the latest date from which you use data.
- Reasons for dropping out of the study (e.g., moved away, dropped out of school, died), if known, and the number of cases for each.
- The percentage of initial cases present at each round if you use data from intervening time points, e.g., five sets of observations collected at annual intervals.

A chart can be a very effective way to present this information. For example, in a study of religious practices and beliefs in respondents' last year of life, Idler and colleagues (2001) graphed the total number of respondents remaining in each of the four survey years (the downward-sloping line in figure 12.1) and the number of deaths that occurred in a year following a face-to-face interview (in the brackets). The chart complements the accompanying description of study design and sample size by illustrating both the criteria for identifying cases for their study and the overall pattern of attrition.[1]

Outliers

Occasionally, your data will contain "outliers"—values that fall well outside the range of the other values and can substantially affect estimates based on the full sample. To avoid biasing results, outliers are sometimes excluded from an analysis sample. If an NFL first-round draft pick happened to be part of your sample of 100 recent col-

what was done, including duration of the experiment, how often observations were made, and other details that would allow readers to replicate the experiment and associated data collection.

- Mention whether placebos were used and whether single- or double-blinding was used.

Sampling. For studies that involve sampling, indicate whether the cases were selected by random sampling, quota sampling, convenience sampling, or some other approach. If random sampling was used, specify whether it was a simple random sample or a more complex design involving stratification, clustering, or disproportionate sampling. For complex sampling designs, explain in your methods section how sampling weights were used (see below) and mention statistical techniques that were used to adjust for the study design (e.g., Westat 1996).

Some types of study design require additional information about identification or selection of cases. Cohort studies sample on the independent variable, such as selecting smokers and nonsmokers in a prospective cancer study. Case-control studies sample on the outcome, selecting people with and without lung cancer and then retrospectively collecting smoking information. If the study involved matching of cases to controls, describe the criteria and methods.

Data Sources

Specify whether your data came from a questionnaire, interview, surveillance system (e.g., vital registration or cancer registry), administrative records (e.g., medical or tax records, voters' registration), observation of subjects, physical examination, or other sources, and cite associated data documentation. List other attributes of data collection that could introduce sample selection bias, coding mistakes, or other types of errors. These issues vary considerably depending on the mode of data collection, so read the literature on the methods used to collect your data to anticipate what other information is relevant. A few illustrations:

- If the data are from a survey, was the questionnaire self-administered or from an in-person or telephone interview? Were the data collected orally or in written format?
- If information was extracted from existing records, who identified relevant cases and transcribed data from the

forms: a few people specifically trained for the task, or people who normally work with those records but not for research purposes?

- For scientific measurements, the name and characteristics of the measuring instrument (e.g., type of scale, brand of caliper or thermometer) are often required.

What

Finally, having reported the context, study design, and data sources, describe what variables were measured. If all your variables come from the same source, summarize the W's in one sentence, and don't repeat. If more than one data source is involved, generalize as much as possible about which variables came from which sources. Use panels within tables or create separate tables to organize variables by topic and source, with information about sources of each variable in the title or footnotes.

Poor: "Age, sex, race, marital status, number of children, income, and educational attainment were taken from the demographic section of the questionnaire. Attitudes about [long list] were taken from the attitudinal section of the questionnaire. Medical records provided information about [long list of health items]. Asthma was also asked about on the questionnaire."
This description is unnecessarily long, repeating information that is far more easily organized in a table.

Better: "Demographic characteristics and attitudinal factors (table A) were drawn from the questionnaire and most health indicators from the medical records (table B). An exception was asthma, for which information was available from both sources."
This description coordinates with tables (not shown) that organize variables by data source and major conceptual groupings, eliminating the need to specify the source for every variable individually.

Variables

Except for the most detailed scientific texts or data documentation, limit in-depth descriptions of measures to your dependent and key independent variables. For other, less central variables, refer to another publication that contains information about their attributes or mention them as you describe the chart or table in which they are first shown. The documentation for the NHANES III—the data used in the birth weight analysis reported here—includes a CD-ROM with copies of the field manuals used by data collectors, spelling out in great detail how various aspects of the health examination, nutritional history, and cognitive testing were conducted (NCHS 1994; Westat 1996). Because that information is publicly available, scientific papers that use those data can refer to that source for details.

Raw versus calculated data. Some of your variables may be used exactly as they were collected (raw data), others calculated from one or more variables in the raw data. For variables analyzed in the same units or categories in which they were originally collected, mention their source. If the phrasing of a question could affect how subjects interpreted that question, include the original wording either in a short paragraph within the data section or in an appendix that displays the relevant portion of the data collection instrument. Avoid rephrasing the original, such as substituting "better than average" for "excellent" and "very good," or replacing "HIV" for "AIDS," as the specific wording of items can affect subjects' responses. Wording of very short items can sometimes be incorporated into table headings (see table 5.2).

Poor: "One asthma measure was collected on the mother's questionnaire, the other from medical records."
The questionnaire and medical records could have collected data in any of several ways, each of which has different potential biases, so for most scientific papers a more precise description is needed.

Better (for a lay audience): "Two types of asthma measures were used. The mother's measure was based on the question 'Have you ever been told your child has asthma?,' the doctor's measure on whether a physician wrote 'asthma' on the medical record or checked it on a list of possible diagnoses."

Better (for a scientific audience): "A maternal report of asthma was based on the question 'Have you ever been told your child has asthma?' A doctor's report of asthma was based on (1) checking that diagnosis on a list of possible diagnoses, (2) listing 'asthma' on the open-ended section of the medical record, or (3) listing an IDC9 code of 493 on the open-ended section of the medical record (NCHS 1995)."

For primary data, indicate whether you adopted or adapted the items or scales from other sources or developed your own. For either primary or secondary data, explain whether and how items were pretested, and report on reliability and validity (see below).

To address some research questions, new variables must be created from variables in the original data. Examples include calculating a categorical variable from a continuous one (e.g., an indicator of whether birth weight fell below the cutoff to define "low birth weight," or quartiles of the income distribution), combining categories (e.g., collapsing five-year age groups into ten-year groups), creating a summary variable to aggregate information on several related items (e.g., calculating total family income from wages, salary, alimony, Supplemental Security Insurance benefits, etc.), and creating a scale (e.g., the CESD scale from a series of items related to depressive symptoms).

Explain how new variables were calculated, whether by you or in secondary data, and mention whether that approach is consistent with other analyses. State whether the criteria used in those calculations were based on existing standards or cutoffs (such as the definition of low birth weight, or the list of income components used to calculate overall income), empirical analysis of your data (such as quartiles of the income distribution), or theoretical criteria, then cite the pertinent literature.

Units and categories. Name the subgroups of each categorical variable and the units of measurement for every continuous variable in each table where that variable is reported. Explain units of measurement in the data section only if they are unusual or complex. Mention variables measured in familiar units as you write up corresponding results. Accompany ordinal values that were created from continuous variables with their numeric equivalents, e.g.,

"'High' and 'low' correspond to the top and bottom quintiles of the income distribution, while 'middle' comprises the middle three quintiles."

If ordinal variables were collected without reference to specific numeric values, list the possible responses exactly as they were worded on the original data collection instrument, e.g.,

"How would you rate your health: excellent, very good, good, fair, or poor?"

See "Considerations for Categorical Dependent Variables" below for additional guidelines about specifying coding and categories.

Reliability and validity. Indicators of reliability are used to evaluate consistency of alternate measures of the same concept—whether different questions, different observers, or different time points. Measures of validity consider whether a question or scale captures the concepts it is intended to measure, including face validity, concurrent validity, predictive validity, and construct validity. Report standard statistics on the reliability and validity of your key variables. See Schutt (2001) for an overview of reliability and validity; Morgan et al. (2002) for illustrative wording to report the measures.

Missing Values, Again

In most data sets, information is missing on one or more questions for at least some cases: a subject returned the survey but refused to report income, for example, or information on weight was missing from some medical records. In some instances, you will retain cases that are missing information on one or more variables ("item nonresponse") and either create a missing value category or impute missing values. Report frequency of item nonresponse that affects more than a few cases and explain how you dealt with missing values on individual items (see Westat 1994 for discussion).

Missing value category. One approach to handling missing values for a variable is to create a category of that variable called "missing." This method is best used to avoid excluding cases that lack data on one of several background variables and only if a small share of cases have missing values on any one variable. Report the percentage of cases in the missing value category of each variable in a table of descriptive statistics. Comment on its interpretation in the discussion section if it affects more than a small percentage of cases.

Imputation. Imputation involves filling in values for cases that lack data on a variable based on values of that variable or related variables for cases with valid data. There are several ways to impute (see Westat [1994] or Kalton and Kasprzyk [1986] for reviews of imputation processes and evaluation):

- Assigning a single value (e.g., the sample mean for a continuous variable; the mode for a categorical variable) to all cases with missing values
- Using other characteristics to predict a value for each case, either by calculating separate means within groups or

estimating a regression equation for that variable based on cases with known values

- Filling in the mean value for other items within a scale if a value on one item is missing
- "Hotdecking," or random sorting of the data followed by assigning to each case that has a missing value the value of that variable from the preceding case in the file

Indicate the method, the percentage of cases imputed for each variable, and cite methodological literature that explains and evaluates the approach. If you impute values for more than a small percentage of cases or for key variables in your analysis, briefly summarize sensitivity analyses comparing results based only on cases with known values versus those based on all (imputed and nonimputed) cases or derived from different imputation strategies. Also compare characteristics of those with imputed versus actual data. For example, if income is more likely to be missing for people in certain demographic groups or regions, these differences could bias results. If results are sensitive to imputation, or values are not missing at random, revisit these issues in the limitations section of your discussion.

Representativeness

Describe how well your sample reflects the population it is intended to represent. Limit this comparison to those who qualify in terms of place, time, and other characteristics that pertain to your research question. For instance, if studying factors that influence urban school performance, don't count students from suburban or rural schools among the excluded cases when assessing representativeness—they aren't part of the population to whom you want to generalize your results.

Depending on your audience and the length of your document, there are several ways to report on representativeness.

- At a minimum, report how many and what percentage of sampled cases were included. If the response rate is over 85%, no additional discussion of representativeness may be needed.
- Create a table of bivariate statistics comparing known characteristics of included and excluded cases, or, if statistics are available from the census or other sources, comparing the sample (weighted to the population level; see below) to the target population. Statistically significant differences in these traits help identify likely direction of bias, which you can summarize in the concluding section of the paper.

- Describe reasons for exclusion or attrition, such as whether those who remained in the sample differed from who were lost from the sample by moving away, dropping out of school, or dying.
- Report results of a multivariate analysis of inclusion in the sample or a survival analysis of attrition from the sample, controlling for age, sex, income, or other characteristics, such as those used in Heckman selection models (Heckman 1979, 1998).

Box 12.1 presents an example of a data section for a scientific paper, with phrases numbered to coordinate with the accompanying comments.

▦ METHODS SECTION

In the methods section of a scientific paper, explain how you analyzed your data, including which statistical methods were used and why, a description of your model specification and how you arrived at it, and whether you used sampling weights. See appendix B for pointers on extracting pertinent information for the methods section from your regression output. Focus on the logic and strategy of your analytic approach, saving the description of statistical findings for the results section of your work. See "Building the Case for a Multivariate Model" in chapter 14 for more guidelines and examples.

Types of Statistical Methods

Name the statistical methods used to analyze your data (e.g., analysis of variance, Pearson correlation, chi-square test) and the type of software (e.g., SAS, SPSS, Stata) used to estimate those statistics. For multivariate models, mention the type of statistical model (e.g., OLS or logistic regression, Cox proportional hazards model, multilevel model) and name the dependent variable and its units. If your statistical methods go by different names or are similar to methods in other disciplines, mention the synonyms when writing for an interdisciplinary scientific audience; see appendix C or Maciejewski et al. (2002).

Considerations for Categorical Dependent Variables

For models of categorical dependent variables, specify which category is being modeled and which is the reference category. For a dichotomous (binary) variable with mutually exclusive, exhaustive

Box 12.1. Example of a Data Section for a Scientific Paper

(1) Data were extracted from the 1988–1994 National Health and Nutrition Examination Survey III (NHANES III)—a cross-sectional, population-based sample survey of the noninstitutionalized population of the United States (U.S. DHHS 1997). (2) To reduce recall bias, birth weight questions were asked only about children aged 0 to 10 years at the time of the survey. (3) Our final sample comprised 3,733 non-Hispanic white, 2,968 non-Hispanic black, and 3,112 Mexican American children for whom family income and race/ethnicity were known (93% of that age group in the NHANES III). (4) Children of other racial/ethnic backgrounds (mostly Asian) were excluded because there were not enough cases to study them as a separate group.

"(5) All variables used in this analysis were based on information from the interview of the reporting adult in the household. (6) Consistent with World Health Organization conventions (1950) a child was considered to be low birth weight (LBW) if his or her reported birth weight fell below 2,500 grams or 5.5 lbs. (7) Coding and units of variables are shown in table 5.5, (8) which compares the sample to all U.S. births."

COMMENTS

(1) Names the data source, including dates, and specifies type of study design and target population (where, who), and provides a citation to study documentation.

(2) Mentions potential bias for one of the variables and how it was minimized by the study design (age restrictions).

(3) Reports the unweighted sample size for the three major subgroups in the study, specifies exclusion criteria, and reports the associated response rate.

(4) Explains why children of other racial/ethnic background were excluded from this birth weight analysis. (For other research questions, different criteria would pertain.)

(5) Specifies which sources from the NHANES III provided data for the variables in the analysis. (The NHANES III also included a medical history, physical examination, lab tests, and dietary intake history. Those sources were not used in the birth weight analysis described here.)

(6) Explains how the low birth weight indicator was calculated and gives its acronym, with reference to the standard definition and a pertinent reference.

(7) Directs readers to the table of descriptive statistics for details on units and coding of variables, averting lengthy discussion in the text.

(8) Refers to a table with data to assess representativeness of the sample.

categories, name the category being modeled; the reference category will be implicit.

"Logistic regression was used to estimate odds ratios of low birth weight."

For a survival model, specify what values constitute censoring (Allison 1995). In a model of high school graduation, for example, the value being modeled is "graduating"; students who moved away, died, or were lost to follow-up before graduating would be considered censored.

If you are estimating a model of a multichotomous dependent variable such as a competing risks survival model or an ordered logit model, mention each of the categories in the text and tables of descriptive statistics. For example, a competing risks analysis might classify deaths into those with an underlying cause of heart disease versus cancer versus all other causes. Also clarify whether the categories are exhaustive (e.g., everyone fits into one such category). For instance, in a prospective study, many study subjects may still be living (e.g., censored) at the end of the observation period and hence would not have experienced any causes of death. On the other hand, if cases were drawn from a death registry, every case would have a cause of death, so the categories would be exhaustive.

Weighted Data

Sampling Weights

If your data are from a random sample, they usually come with sampling weights that reflect the sampling rate, clustering, or disproportionate sampling, and which correct for differential nonresponse and loss to follow-up (Westat 1996, sec. 2). Most analyses of such data use the weights to inflate the estimates back to the population level, estimating the total number of low birth weight infants in the United States based on the number in the study sample, for instance. If disproportionate sampling was used, the data must be weighted to correctly represent the composition of the population from which the sample was drawn (e.g., Westat 1996, sec. 1.3). The sample size used to calculate the standard errors for statistical tests should be the unweighted number of cases; verify that your statistical program makes this correction.

Explain when and how you used the sampling weights and refer to the data documentation for background information about the derivation and application of those weights. For analyses of clustered data, name the statistical methods used to correct the standard errors for clustering (e.g., Shah et al. 1996).

Trimming Sampling Weights

In studies that involve complex designs, the range of sampling weights can be considerable, potentially magnifying the influence of an outlier that happened to occur in a cell with a high sampling weight. To reduce the effects of widely varying sampling weights, they are sometimes trimmed, replacing extreme values of sampling weights with less extreme weights (e.g., Ingram and Makuc 1994). For example, cases with sampling weights above the 95th percentile might be assigned the 95th percentile value of the sampling weight, while sampling weights below the 5th percentile are replaced with the 5th percentile value. In the NHANES Epidemiologic Followup Study (NHEFS), trimming the weights at the 5th and 95th percentiles reduced the original 144-fold range in weights to a 16-fold difference.

If you used trimmed weights in your analysis, report how you identified the extreme values and decided on trimming cutoffs, report the number and percentage of cases affected, and cite other studies that used that approach. Report on sensitivity of findings to the trimmed weights in a footnote or appendix.

Choice of Model Specification

Occam's Razor (also known as the principle of parsimony) recommends that "descriptions be kept as simple as possible until proven inadequate" (Newman 1956)—a worthy objective for all expository writing. For multivariate models, this principle suggests choosing the simplest model from among those with equivalent goodness-of-fit (Heylighen 1997), including the fewest possible independent variables and the simplest functional form. Empirical approaches to obtaining a parsimonious model include forward and backward selection techniques, using a specified α level (e.g., $p < 0.05$) to determine whether an independent variable enters or stays in the model (Kachigan 1991).

Alternatively, you might have used theoretical considerations to determine the order and combination in which variables were entered and retained. For example, you might have estimated a series of models that sequentially introduce variables to test whether they mediate or confound the relationship between a key independent variable and the dependent variable (see "Common Reasons for Estimating a Multivariate Model" in chapter 14). Perhaps you started with a model of birth weight that included only race and gender, then introduced family socioeconomic characteristics, then health behaviors. You might have aimed for parsimony in the final model but intentionally kept other variables in the intermediate model to estimate the size and statistical significance of their effects.

For some research questions, it is appropriate to retain independent variables regardless of statistical significance rather than to pursue a parsimonious model. For example, you might need a uniform specification to compare findings across subgroups, time periods, or against previous studies, or in a competing risks model (e.g., for different causes of death), or to contrast the effects of a uniform specification on a series of related outcomes. To allow comparison across a wide range of data sources and dependent variables, all of the authors contributing studies to *Consequences of Growing Up Poor for Young Children* (Duncan and Brooks-Gunn 1997) were asked to estimate identical model specifications, regardless of whether those models were parsimonious. There also may be theoretical concerns like controlling basic demographic traits when analyzing nonexperimental data.

Whether you aimed for the parsimonious model or followed other principles for model specification, summarize the statistical or theoretical criteria used to determine the set of variables in your models. Mention how you evaluated and addressed multicollinearity or serial correlation, and whether you used data reduction techniques such as factor analysis (see pertinent sections below). Also discuss how you decided on the functional form for each variable and whether you tested for interactions among independent variables.

Multicollinearity

High levels of correlation among independent variables (multicollinearity) can affect your regression results. If some of your variables are highly correlated, report the pertinent correlation coefficients in the text, then explain how you evaluated the effects of multicollinearity on your model and decided which variables to include (Fox 1997; Kennedy 2003). If many of your potential independent variables are highly correlated, include a table of correlations as an appendix, then summarize key patterns in the text before explaining how they influenced your model specification.

Serial Correlation

In time series analyses, repeated observations across time for a given case are often highly correlated with one another, a phenomenon known as serial correlation or autocorrelation (Gujarati 2002; Kennedy 2003). For example, monthly observations on body weight over a period of ten years are likely to be highly correlated for each individual: someone who has reached mature height is likely to weigh about the same each month, with minor fluctuations up and down. In your analysis, you are most likely interested mainly in how independent variables such as exercise, diet, and illness affect body weight, taking out the expected high temporal correlation across weight measurements for each case. If this is an issue with your data and topic, present pertinent statistics to demonstrate the extent of serial correlation, mention the statistical corrections you used and how they apply to your particular model, and report the associated measures from the multivariate specification.

Factor Analysis

For analyses involving many correlated items as potential explanatory variables, data reduction techniques such as factor analysis (also known as principal components analysis) are sometimes used to remove redundancy in the data by creating factors that represent sets of related independent variables (Kachigan 1991). For example, variance in a dozen subtests of mathematical and spatial abilities might be condensed down to three distinct factors which could then be used to predict subsequent math and science performance. Explain the statistical methods and criteria, and report factor loading for each of the items or cite another publication that describes this process for the data and topics you analyzed.

Functional Form of Independent Variables

Describe whether you tested quadratic or other polynomial specifications, logarithmic transformations, parametric specifications (Blossfeld et al. 1989; Fox 1997), or splines (also known as piecewise linear models; Gujarati 2002) for one or more independent variables in the model. If you used any of these functional forms, name them and the variables involved, and identify the units of measurement for each such variable. Equations are especially useful for showing polynomials or other specifications involving more than one term for a given independent variable; see below.

Interactions

If you tested for interactions among two or more independent variables, explain which you examined and why, and what statistical or theoretical criteria you used to decide which interactions to retain in your multivariate model. A three-way tabulation demonstrating that the relationship between a key independent variable and the dependent variable varies according to another independent variable is an effective way to show why a particular set of interactions was tested (see box 14.1b).

Equations

Equations are an efficient way of summarizing a model specification to a statistically savvy audience. Using standard notation such as subscripts, superscripts, and other mathematical notation, you can quickly convey the essential features of your regression model.

- Identify the dependent variable and type of statistical model.
- List the independent variables (or theoretical blocks of independent variables) in the model.
- Show any polynomial specifications, logarithmic, or other mathematical transformations of independent variables.
- Identify interactions between two or more variables.

In an equation, the dependent variable is shown on the left-hand side (sometimes known as the "LHS variable"), while the independent variables are on the right-hand side (abbreviated "RHS variables"). If you use abbreviations for your variables in the equation, spell them out in a sentence. For example, equation 12.1 specifies a logistic model of low birth weight as a function of race/ethnicity (the dummy variables "NHB" and "MexAmer"), a quadratic specification of the income-to-poverty ratio (IPR), and interactions between race/ethnicity and IPR.

$$\text{Equation 12.1: logit(LBW)} = \log[p_{LBW}/(1 - p_{LBW})] = \beta_0 + \beta_1 \text{NHB}$$
$$+ \beta_2 \text{MexAmer} + \beta_3 \text{IPR} + \beta_4 \text{IPR}^2 + \beta_5 (\text{NHB} \times \text{IPR}) + \beta_6 (\text{NHB} \times \text{IPR}^2)$$
$$+ \beta_7 (\text{MexAmer} \times \text{IPR}) + \beta_8 (\text{MexAmer} \times \text{IPR}^2) + \varepsilon$$

However, unless the statistical method is new (or at least new to your field or topic) or the model involves one or more multiterm specifications for independent variables, equations are often superfluous. Most of these attributes of the model specification can be inferred from a well-written narrative about the methods, reference to other published documents on the methods, and an adequately labeled table of regression estimates. On the other hand, equations are an important tool in grant proposals involving a multivariate model because proposals rarely have a table of regression results to convey the model specification.

Equations are also an expected feature in economics, statistics, and related fields. Before including equations for other audiences, consider whether they add important information not otherwise available in your document or other publications. Do not repeat statistical logic or derivations that are explained elsewhere unless you are writing for a statistics course and have been asked to do so.

- For new methods, include a complete set of equations to illustrate assumptions, functional form, and derivations of final equations from earlier statistical principles, but only in articles intended for a statistical audience.
- For a method that is new to your field but has been documented elsewhere, include an equation or two to illustrate how the specification applies to your research question and variables. Avoid replicating the complete series of equations that were initially used to derive the original statistical methods; instead refer to other publications that describe that process.
- For other audiences, including academic audiences of nonstatisticians, explain the statistical *concepts* embodied by the method, paraphrasing jargon into less technical terminology of the field into which the research question fits, and using equations as sparingly as possible. See "Giving an Overview of Methods and Variables" in chapter 16 for illustrations.

Box 12.2 is an illustrative methods section for a scientific paper about the birth weight analysis, with phrases numbered to coordinate with the associated comments.

■ DATA AND METHODS IN THE DISCUSSION SECTION

Many of the elements described in the data and methods sections have repercussions for the analysis and interpretation of your results.

Box 12.2. Example of a Methods Section for a Scientific Paper

METHODS

"(1) Bivariate associations were tested using t-tests and chi-square tests. (2) Ordinary least squares regression was used to estimate (a) mean birth weight (in grams) by race/ethnicity, (b) controlling for socioeconomic characteristics and smoking behavior. (3) We estimated a series of models, starting with controls for race/ethnicity and gender, then introducing blocks of conceptually related variables. (4) Interaction terms were introduced to investigate whether the relation between race/ethnicity and birth weight varied by socioeconomic status. (5) Linear and square terms on the income-to-poverty ratio were included to test for a non-linear relationship with birth weight."

(6) "All statistics were weighted to the national level using weights provided for the NHANES III by the National Center for Health Statistics (U.S. DHHS 1997). (7) SUDAAN software was used to adjust the estimated standard errors for complex sampling design (Shah et al. 1996)."

COMMENTS
(1) Identifies the types of statistics used to test bivariate associations.
(2) Specifies the kind of multivariate model, explains why that method is needed, and identifies (a) the dependent variable and its units, and (b) independent variables for that model. Audiences familiar with multivariate models will recognize that "controlling for" identifies the independent variables.
(3) Describes the strategy used in the sequence of models.
(4) Mentions the use of interaction terms and why they were used, and names the variables involved.
(5) Explains why a polynomial specification was tested for the income-to-poverty ratio.
(6) Mentions use and source of sampling weights and cites pertinent documentation.
(7) Names the method and software used to correct for complex study design, with a citation.

Explain these issues by discussing the advantages and limitations of your data and methods in your conclusion.

Strengths

Remind your audience how your analysis contributes to the existing literature with a discussion of the strengths of your data and methods. Point out that you used more recent information than previous studies, data on the particular geographic or demographic group of interest, or improved measures of the key variables, for example. Mention any methodological advances or analytic techniques you used that better suit the research question or data, such as taking a potential confounding variable into account or using survival analysis to correct for censoring.

Rather than repeat the W's and other technical details from the data and methods section, rephrase them to emphasize specifically how those attributes strengthen your analyses.

Poor: "The experimental nature of the study strengthened the findings by eliminating self-selection."

This generality about experimental studies doesn't convey how they affected this particular research question and data source.

Better: "Because subjects were randomly assigned to the treatment and control groups, differences in background characteristics of those who received treatment were ruled out as an explanation for better survival in that group."

This version explains how an experimental design (randomization) improved this study, mentioning the outcome (survival), the predictor (treatment versus control) and potential confounders (background characteristics).

Limitations

Just as important as touting the strengths of your data and methods is confessing their limitations. Many neophytes flinch at this suggestion, fearing that they will undermine their own work if they identify its weaknesses. On the contrary, part of demonstrating that you have done good science is acknowledging that no study is perfect for answering all questions. Having already pointed out the strengths of your study, list aspects of your analyses that should be reexamined with better data or statistical methods, and mention new questions raised by your findings. Translate general statements about biases or other limitations into specific points about how they affect interpretation of your findings.

Poor: "The study sample is not representative, hence results cannot be generalized to the overall target population."
This statement is so broad that it doesn't convey direction of possible biases caused by the lack of representativeness.

Better: "The data were collected using a self-administered questionnaire written in English; consequently the study sample omitted people with low literacy skills and those who do not speak English. In the United States, both of these groups are concentrated at the lower end of the socioeconomic spectrum; therefore estimates of health knowledge from this study probably overstate that in the general adult population."
This version clearly explains how the method of data collection affected who was included in the sample and the implications for estimated patterns of the outcomes under study. Jargon like "representativeness" and "target population" is restated in terms of familiar concepts and the concepts related to the particular research question and study design.

Accompany your statements about limitations with reference to other publications that have evaluated those issues for other similar data. By drawing on others' work, you may be able to estimate the extent of bias without conducting your own analysis of each such issue.

Directions for Future Research

Close your discussion of limitations by listing some directions for future research. Identify ways to address the drawbacks of your study, perhaps by collecting additional data, or collecting or analyzing it differently, and mention new questions raised by your analyses. This approach demonstrates that you are aware of potential solutions to your study's limitations and contributes to an understanding of where it fits in the body of research on the topic.

Box 12.3 is an example discussion of the advantages and disadvantages of the birth weight data, to follow the concluding section presented in box 11.2. By discussing possible strengths and weaknesses consecutively, the first paragraph helps to weigh their respective influences and provide a balanced assessment of the data quality.

**Box 12.3. Data and Methods in the Discussion
of a Scientific Paper**

"(1) This multivariate analysis of a large, nationally representative survey of U.S. children extends previous research on determinants of racial/ethnic differences in birth weight by including family income and maternal smoking behavior—two variables not available on birth certificates, which were the principal data source for many past studies. Although maternal smoking was reported on birth certificates for about 75% of U.S. births during the NHANES III study years, several key states (including California and New York) did not report smoking on their birth certificates (Mathews 2001). Consequently, studies of smoking and birth weight based on birth certificate data from that period are not nationally representative. No states report income on the birth certificate.

(2) A potential drawback of the survey data is that information on birth weight was collected from the child's mother at the time of the survey—up to 10 years after the child's birth. In contrast to birth weight data from the birth certificate, which are recorded at the time of the birth, these data may suffer from retrospective recall bias. (3) However, previous studies of birth weight data collected from mothers reveal that they can accurately recall birth weight and other aspects of pregnancy and early infant health several years later (Githens et al. 1993; Olson et al. 1997). (4) In addition, racial and socioeconomic patterns of birth weight in our study are consistent with those based on birth certificate data (Martin et al. 2002), suggesting that the mode of data collection did not appreciably affect results.

"(5) A useful extension of this analysis would be to investigate whether other Latino subgroups also exhibit the relatively high mean birth weight observed among the Mexican American infants studied here. (6) Inclusion of additional measures of socioeconomic status, acculturation, and health behaviors would provide insight into possible reasons for that pattern."

COMMENTS

(1) Mentions that multivariate analyses were used in this study, controlling for several new variables available in the current data source that were not present in data used in previous analyses.

(2) Points out a potential source of bias in the study data.

(3) Cites previous research evaluating maternal retrospective recall of birth weight to suggest that such bias is likely to be small.

(4) Compares findings about sociodemographic determinants of birth weight from the survey with findings from studies using other sources of birth weight data to further dispel concerns about the accuracy of the survey data, and provides a citation to those studies.

(5) Rather than describing the inclusion of only one Latino group in the study sample as a weakness, suggests that expanding the range of Latino groups would be a useful direction for future research.

(6) Identifies additional variables that could shed light on the underlying reasons for the epidemiologic paradox (explained in box 11.2), again suggesting important ideas for later work.

■ CHECKLIST FOR WRITING ABOUT DATA AND METHODS

- Where possible, refer to other publications that contain details about the same data and methods.
- Regardless of audience, discuss how the strengths and limitations of your data and methods affect interpretation of your findings.

Consider audience and type of work to determine appropriate placement and detail about data and methods.

- For short, nonscientific papers,
  integrate the W's into your narrative,
  name the type of study design, and
  explain briefly how key variables were measured, if this affects interpretation of your findings.
- For scientific papers or grant proposals, include a separate data and methods section.
  Use the W's to organize material on context and methods of data collection.
  Report the analytic sample size, then discuss the response rate, loss to follow-up, extent of missing values on key variables, treatment of outliers, and representativeness.

Define your variables.

    —Include original wording of novel or complex questions, in the text or an appendix for key variables, as you describe results for other variables.

    —Report units, defining them if unusual or complicated.

    —Describe how new variables were created.

    —Explain the imputation process used to fill in missing values.

    —Report on reliability and validity.

Name the statistical methods. For models of categorical dependent variables, name the category being modeled.

Mention whether sampling weights were used, and if so, their source. If you trimmed the weights, explain how and report sensitivity of results.

Explain the analytic strategy used to arrive at your final model or a series of models you present.

    —If you used empirical approaches such as forward or backward selection, state the criteria (e.g., $\alpha = 0.05$).

    —If you used theoretical criteria, describe them.

    —If multicollinearity or serial correlation affect your data, explain how you account for them in your model specification.

Convey your statistical specification, including dependent and independent variables, functional form, and interactions.

    —For statisticians and economists, use equations.

    —For other academic audiences use equations only to illustrate complex (e.g., multiterm) specifications, or new methods or applications.

Suggest ways future research could address the limitations of your analysis.

Writing about Distributions and Associations

Writing about numbers often involves portraying the distribution of a variable or describing the association between two or more variables. These tasks require several of the principles and tools introduced in the preceding chapters: specifying direction and magnitude of association (chapter 2); considering statistical significance (chapters 3 and 10), types of variables, units, and distribution (chapter 4); organizing the text to coordinate with a table or chart (chapters 5 and 6); and using analogies (chapter 7) and quantitative comparisons (chapters 8 and 9). In this chapter, I explain how to combine these concepts to write about common types of univariate, bivariate, and three-way patterns for both statistical and lay audiences. Chapter 14 builds on these examples, with additional examples and critiques of a complete results section for a scientific paper involving a multivariate analysis.

■ WRITING ABOUT DISTRIBUTIONS AND ASSOCIATIONS

Information on distributions of values for single variables or associations among two or three variables provides the foundation of results sections in scientific articles and is included in many general-interest articles. In an article about elementary education, for instance, you might describe the distribution of class sizes, then show how class size, expenditures per student, and student achievement are related to one another. In a basic statistical analysis or report about experimental data, descriptions of distributions and bivariate or three-way associations often constitute the entire analysis. For more advanced statistical analyses such as multivariate regression, this information helps demonstrate why a more complex statistical technique is needed (see "Building the Case for a Multivariate Model," in chapter 14; for guidelines on table or chart layouts to present distributions or associations for different types of variables, see chapter 5 and table 6.1).

■ UNIVARIATE DISTRIBUTIONS

Univariate statistics provide information on one variable at a time, showing how cases are distributed across all possible values of that variable. In a scientific paper, create a table with summary information on each variable, then refer to the table as you describe the data. In a general-interest article or issue brief, report the mean or modal values of your main variables in prose, substituting "average" for "mean" and "most common" for "modal." If you will be comparing across samples or populations, report the frequency distributions using percentages to adjust for differences in the sizes of the samples. One hundred passing scores in a sample of one thousand students reflects a very different share than one hundred passing scores among several million students, for example.

The information you report for a univariate distribution differs for categorical and continuous variables.

Categorical Variables

To show composition of a categorical variable, present the frequency of each category as counts (e.g., number of non-Hispanic white, non-Hispanic black, and Mexican American infants) or percentages (e.g., the percentage of infants in each racial group). Report the modal category, since the mean (arithmetic average) is meaningless for categorical variables: the "average race" cannot be calculated or interpreted. If the variable has only a few categories, report numeric information for each category in the text (see examples below).

For variables with more than a handful of categories, create a chart or table to be summarized in the text. Also consider whether two or more small categories might be combined into a larger category without obscuring a group of particular interest to your analysis.

- In some instances, these combinations are based on conceptual similarity. For example, in a comparison of public, private, and parochial schools, you might combine all parochial schools into a single category regardless of religious affiliation.
- In other instances, these combinations are done to avoid tabulating many rare categories separately. For example, you might combine a disparate array of infrequently mentioned

racial or ethnic groups as "other" even though they share little other than their rarity. In these cases, either explain that "other" includes all categories other than those named elsewhere in the table or chart, or include a footnote specifying what the "other" category includes.

The order in which you mention values of a categorical variable depends on your research question and whether that variable is nominal or ordinal. The criteria described on the next few pages also work for organizing descriptions of bivariate or higher-order associations involving categorical variables (see "Associations" below).

Nominal Variables

For nominal variables, such as race/ethnicity or category of federal budget outlays, use principles such as frequency of occurrence or theoretical criteria to organize numbers within a sentence. Often it makes sense to mention the most common category and then describe where the other categories fall, using one or more quantitative comparisons to assess difference in relative shares of different categories.

Poor: "The distribution of U.S. federal budget outlays in 2000 was 61% for human resources, 12% for interest, 16% for national defense, 6% for other functions, and 5% for physical resources (figure 6.2)."
This sentence simply reports the share of federal outlays in each category, requiring readers to do their own comparisons to identify the largest category and to assess the size of differences in the shares of different categories. The categories are inexplicably listed in alphabetical order—a poor choice of organizing principle for most text descriptions.

Better: "As shown in figure 6.2, over 60% of U.S. federal budget outlays in 2000 were for human services, with national defense a distant second (16%), and net interest third (12%). The remaining outlays were roughly equally divided between physical resources and other functions."
This description uses modal category, rank, and relative share to convey comparative sizes, reporting numbers only to illustrate relative sizes of the three largest categories.

If a particular category is of special interest, feature it early in your description even if it isn't the modal value. For example, in a story on the share of interest in the federal budget, highlight that category although it ranks third among the categories of outlays.

Ordinal Variables

For ordinal variables, the natural sequence of the categories frequently dictates the order in which you report them: young, middle-aged, and elderly age groups, for example. Sometimes, however, you want to emphasize which group is largest or of particular importance in your analysis, suggesting that you mention that group first even if that goes against the normal, ranked sequence of categories. For an article about the influence of the baby boom generation at the turn of the millennium, for instance, discuss that cohort first even though its members are in the middle of the age distribution.

In those situations, begin with a general description of the shape of the distribution, using descriptors such as "bell-shaped" (figures 4.3a and b), "uniform" (figure 4.3c), "U-shaped" (figure 4.3d), or "skewed to the right" (figure 4.3e). Then report frequency of occurrence for the groups you wish to highlight.

Poor: "The age distribution of U.S. adults in 2000 was 8.6% ages 20–24, 8.8% ages 25–29, . . . , and 1.9% ages 85 and older (U.S. Census Bureau 2002d)."
A lengthy list in the text is overwhelming and a poor way to describe the overall distribution. To present values for each age group, put them in a table or chart.

Poor (version 2): "The percentage of U.S. adults who were aged 35–39 was larger than the percentages aged 30–34 or 40–44 (10.3%, 9.3%, and 10.1%, respectively). That age group was also much larger than the oldest age groups (those 80 to 84 and 85+, 2.2% and 1.9%, respectively). Age groups 20–24, 25–29, 45–49 . . . and 75–79 were in between (U.S. Census Bureau 2002d)."
Comparing many pairs of numbers is inefficient and confusing.

Better: "In 2000, the age distribution of U.S. adults was roughly bell-shaped between ages 20 and 55, reflecting the dominant presence of the baby boom cohorts born in the late 1940s through the 1950s (figure 13.1). The largest cohorts were ages 35–39 and 40–44, with 10.3% and 10.1% of the adult population, respectively. After age 55, the age distribution tails off rapidly, revealing the combined effects of mortality and smaller birth cohorts (U.S. Census Bureau 2002d)."
This description uses a familiar shape to summarize the age distribution. By naming the baby boom age groups and mentioning birth cohort size and mortality, it also explains some of the underlying factors that generated the age distribution.

Age distribution of U.S. adults, 2000

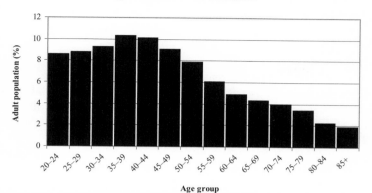

Figure 13.1. Age distribution illustrated with a histogram.
Source: U.S. Census Bureau 2002d.

Continuous Variables

For continuous variables such as income, weight, or age, create a table to report the minimum and maximum values, pertinent measure of central tendency, and standard deviation or interquartile range for the variables used in your analysis. If the distribution is unusual for one of your key variables, portray its distribution in a chart to which you refer in your description. For example, it is easier to observe differences in the shapes of the birth weight distributions for black and white infants from a chart than from a table (e.g., Wilcox and Russell 1986).

If some aspect of the distribution affects how you classify data or conduct your analysis, report the frequency distribution and other statistics according to those classifications. For instance, if you compare outcomes for different quartiles of the income distribution, label each category using the pertinent income range (e.g., "<\$15,000") in tables of descriptive statistics and regression results.

In the prose, give summary statistics rather than reporting information on each case or each value, unless there are very few cases. To report kindergarten class size in a school with four kindergarten classes, for instance, you might list the number of students in each class, followed by the overall average:

"Kennedy Elementary School opened its doors with kindergarten classes of 21, 24, 27, and 28 students, for a mean class size of 25 students."

To describe kindergarten class size for all public schools in a large city, report the range and the mean or median class sizes:

> "On opening day in New York City, kindergarten class sizes ranged from 17 to 31 students, with an average class size of 22.1."

To provide more detail on the distribution of a continuous variable, create a chart, then describe the general shape of the distribution and report specific values of interest as explained above under "Ordinal variables."

Comparing values of a continuous variable against a reference value or cutoff is often informative.

> "New York City schools are making progress toward the city and state goal of limiting classes in the youngest grades to 20 pupils, but more than one-fourth of children in kindergarten through third grade are in classes with more than 25 (Medina 2002)."

■ ASSOCIATIONS

Most quantitative analyses examine patterns of association between two or more variables. Bivariate patterns describe an association between two variables, such as mean class size by type of school (e.g., public, private, and parochial). Three-way associations introduce a third variable—calculating mean class size by geographic region and type of school simultaneously, for instance. Regardless of the types of variables involved, describe both the direction and magnitude of the association. For scientific audiences, also mention names and results of statistical tests. Morgan et al. (2002) provide an excellent guide to reporting results of many types of statistical tests.

Purpose of Describing Associations

Associations give important background information for multivariate analyses in several ways.

- They quantify differences in the dependent variable according to values of an independent variable, such as variation in the percentage of children passing a proficiency test according to school type.
- They describe patterns of association among independent variables, such as whether different regions have similar distributions of school types. Demonstrating such patterns

helps establish the need to control for several independent variables in a multivariate regression (see "Common Reasons for Estimating a Multivariate Model" in chapter 14).

- They evaluate whether the study sample is representative of the target population, such as whether the demographic composition of students in the study schools is the same as in all schools.

Roles of Variables and Causal Language

If you are investigating a potential causal relationship, differentiate between the independent and dependent variables because those roles affect how the statistics are calculated and described. For example, in the relationship between race and birth weight, birth weight is the dependent variable and race is the independent variable, so report mean birth weight by race, not modal race by birth weight. For associations among several similar concepts measured at the same point in time (e.g., scores in a variety of academic subjects, or several concurrent measures of socioeconomic status) or if the causal relationship is ambiguous, avoid causal language.

Types of Associations

The type of statistical procedure and associated statistical test depends on whether you are describing an association between two continuous variables, two categorical variables, or one of each. See Moore (1997), Utts (1999), or another statistics text for more background on the underlying statistical concepts.

Correlations

An association between two continuous variables (e.g., household income in dollars and birth weight in grams) is measured by their correlation coefficient (denoted r). The value of r ranges from -1.0 (for a perfect inverse association) to 1.0 (for a perfect direct association). Variables that are completely uncorrelated have an r of 0.0. Statistical significance is assessed by comparing the correlation coefficient against a critical value, which depends on the number of cases. To describe a correlation, name the two variables and specify the direction of association between them, then report the correlation coefficient and p-value in parentheses:

"Household income and birth weight were strongly positively correlated ($r = 0.85$; $p < 0.01$)."

Table 13.1. Cross-tabulations and differences in means for a dependent variable

Mean birth weight and percentage low birth weight by race/ethnicity, United States, 1988–1994

	Non-Hispanic white (N = 3,733)	Non-Hispanic black (N = 2,968)	Mexican American (N = 3,112)	All racial/ ethnic groups (N = 9,813)
Mean birth weight (grams)[a]	3,426.8	3,181.3	3,357.3	3,379.2
% Low birth weight[ab]	5.8	11.3	7.0	6.8

Note: Weighted to population level using weights provided with the NHANES III (U.S. DHHS 1997); sample sizes are unweighted.

[a] Differences across racial/ethnic origin groups are statistically significant at $p < 0.01$.

[b] Low birth weight <2,500 grams or 5.5 pounds.

Bivariate correlations among many variables are usually reported in a table (e.g., table 5.7). Unless you are testing hypotheses about specific pairs of variables, summarize the correlation results rather than writing a detailed narrative about each bivariate association.

For a scientific audience: "As expected, the different indicators of academic achievement were highly positively correlated with one another, with Pearson correlation coefficients (r) greater than 0.75 ($p < 0.01$ except between mathematics and language comprehension). Correlations between achievement and aptitude were generally lower."
This description uses theoretical groupings (academic achievement and aptitude) to simplify the discussion. Generalizations about correlations among measures within and across those classifications replace detailed descriptions of each pairwise correlation, and exceptions are mentioned. One or two specific examples could also be incorporated.

For a lay audience: "As expected, children who scored well on one test of academic achievement also typically scored well on achievement tests in other subjects. Correlations between achievement and aptitude were generally lower than those among different dimensions of achievement."
This description is similar to that for a scientific audience but replaces names of specific statistical measures with their conceptual equivalents.

Differences in Means across Groups

An association between a continuous variable and a categorical variable can be assessed using a difference in means or ANOVA (analysis of variance). T-statistics and F-statistics are used to evaluate statistical significance of a difference in means and ANOVAs, respectively. To describe a relationship between a categorical independent variable (e.g., race/ethnicity) and a continuous dependent variable (e.g., birth weight in grams), report the mean outcome for each category of the independent variable in a table or simple bar chart, then explain the pattern in the text.

"On average, Non-Hispanic black newborns were 246 grams lighter than non-Hispanic white newborns (3,181 and 3,427 grams, respectively; $p < 0.01$; table 13.1)."

To summarize mean outcomes across several related categorical variables, name the categories with the highest and lowest values, then summarize where values for the other categories fall.

"In the Appleville school district, 2001 SAT II achievement scores were highest on the English language test (mean = 530 out of 800 possible points) and lowest in mathematics (mean = 475). Average scores in science (four subject areas) also fell below the 500 mark, while those for foreign languages (five languages) and social studies (three subject areas) ranged from 500 to 525."

To avoid mentioning each of the 14 test scores separately, this description combines two criteria to organize the reported numbers: an empirical approach to identify the highest and lowest scores, and substantive criteria to classify the topics into five broad subject areas. Mentioning the highest possible score also helps readers interpret the meaning of the numbers.

Use a consistent set of criteria to organize the table or chart associated with your description. To coordinate with the above narrative, create a table that classifies the scores by broad subject area, then use empirical ranking to arrange topics within and across those groupings.

Cross-Tabulations

Cross-tabulations illustrate how the distribution of one categorical variable (e.g., low birth weight status) varies according to categories of a second variable (race/ethnicity). Statistical significance of differences is assessed by a chi-square test. In addition to showing what percentage of the overall sample was low birth weight, a cross-tabulation reports the percentage low birth weight for infants in each racial/ethnic group. Consider this addition to the above description of birth weight patterns by race:

"These gaps in mean birth weight translate into substantial differences in percentage low birth weight (LBW < 2,500 grams), with nearly twice the risk of LBW among non-Hispanic black as non-Hispanic white infants (11.3% and 5.8%, respectively; $p < 0.01$, table 13.1)."

Three-Way Associations

Two common types of associations among three variables are three-way cross-tabulations and differences in means.

Three-way cross-tabulations. Three-way cross-tabulations are used to investigate patterns among three categorical variables. A cross-tabulation of low birth weight (a yes/no variable), race, and mother's education group would produce information about how many (and what percentage of) infants in each combination of race and mother's education group were low birth weight. As with bivariate cross-tabulations, the test statistic is the chi-square.

Differences in means. Differences in means are used to quantify patterns among one continuous dependent variable (e.g., birth weight in grams) and two categorical predictors (e.g., race and mother's education group). If there are three racial groups and three education categories, this procedure would yield nine average birth weight values, one for each combination of race and mother's education (table 14.2). Statistical significance of differences across groups is assessed by an *F*-test from a two-way ANOVA.

Describing associations among three variables is complicated because three dimensions are involved, generating more values and patterns to report and interpret. To avoid explaining every number or focusing on a few arbitrarily chosen numbers, use the "generalization, example, exceptions" (GEE) technique introduced in chapter 2.

■ "GENERALIZATION, EXAMPLE, EXCEPTIONS" REVISITED

To describe a three-way association, start by identifying the three two-way associations among the variables involved. For example, the relationship between race, gender, and labor force participation (figure 13.2) encompasses three bivariate associations: (1) race and gender, (2) gender and labor force participation, and (3) race and labor force participation. Only if there are exceptions to the general pattern in one or more of those bivariate associations does the three-way association need to be considered separately.

In figure 13.2, gender and race are predictors of labor force participation (the dependent variable). If the association between the independent variables (e.g., whether the gender distribution differs by race) is important to your study, explain it before discussing how each of the independent variables relates to the dependent variable. Otherwise, focus on the associations between each of the independent variables and the dependent variable. Begin by describing the race/labor force participation relationship and the gender/labor force participation relationship separately, mentioning the three-way pattern only if the two-way associations cannot be generalized:

Labor force participation
by race and gender, United States, 1998

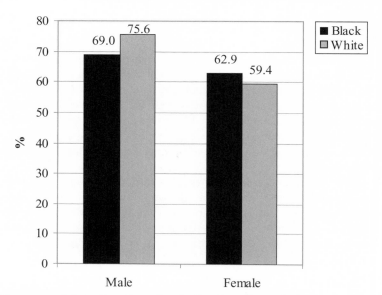

Figure 13.2. Interaction: Exception in direction of association.
Source: U.S. Census Bureau 1999c.

"(1) In the United States in 1998, labor force participation rates were higher for males than for females, regardless of race (figure 13.2). (2) However, the racial pattern differed by gender, (3) with higher labor force participation among white than black males (75.6% versus 69.0%), but lower labor force participation among white than black females (59.4% versus 62.9%; U.S. Census Bureau 1999c)."

The first sentence generalizes the gender pattern in labor force participation, which applies to both races. Phrase 2 explains that the racial pattern cannot be generalized across genders. Phrase 3 describes the three-way association and cites numeric evidence from the chart.

Interactions

In GEE terms, this difference in how race and labor force participation relate is an exception, because no single description of the race/labor force participation pattern fits both genders. In statistical terminology, situations where the association between two characteristics depends on a third characteristic are known as interactions or effects modifications.

Exceptions in Direction, Magnitude, and Statistical Significance

An exception in the *direction* of an association between two groups is fairly easy to detect from a graph of the relationship, as with the pattern of labor force participation by gender and race shown in figure 13.2. Comparing the heights of the respective bars, we observe that male participation is greater than female for both racial groups, but whether black participation is greater than or less than white depends on gender. Exceptions in direction can also occur in trends (e.g., figure 2.1), with a rising trend for one or more groups and a level or declining trend for others.

Exceptions in *magnitude* of association are more subtle and difficult to detect. Consider the relationship between gender, race, and life expectancy shown in figure 13.3: the interaction occurs in the different sizes of the gaps between the gray and black bars in the clusters for the two genders.

Expectation of life at birth by race and gender, United States, 1997

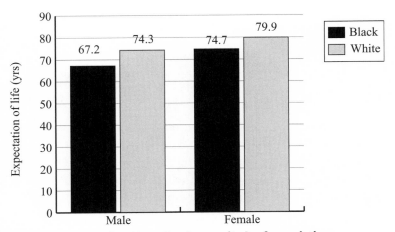

Figure 13.3. Interaction: Exception in magnitude of association.
Source: U.S. Census Bureau 2001c.

"Data from 1997 for the United States show that (1) for both genders, whites outlived blacks (figure 13.3). In addition, (2) females of both races outlive their male counterparts. (3) However, the racial gap is wider for men than for women. Among men, whites outlived blacks by 7.1 years on average, with life expectancies of 74.3 and 67.2 years, respectively. Among women, whites outlived blacks by 5.2 years (life expectancies were 79.9 and 74.7 years; U.S. Census Bureau 2001c)."

In this case, the direction of association in each two-way association can be generalized: the first sentence explains that in all cases, white life expectancy is greater than black, while the second sentence explains that in both racial groups, female life expectancy is greater than male. The third sentence points out the difference in the size *of the two "greater thans."*

For trends, exceptions in size appear as a steeper rise or fall for some groups than for others.

Generalizations and exceptions also apply to *statistical significance.* If most of the patterns in a table are statistically significant, summarize that finding and note any exceptions. Conversely, if most patterns are *not* statistically significant, generalize, identify the few statistically significant associations as exceptions, and report pertinent test statistics or p-values in the text. See box 14.1b for illustrative examples.

Writing about Interactions

The GEE approach is an effective way to describe interactions to either statistical or applied audiences, although you will use slightly different wording for the two. For an audience that is familiar with the statistical meaning of "interaction," use that term as you introduce the pattern:

"Race and gender interact in their relation with labor force participation (figure 13.2)."

For an applied audience, you need not use the term "interaction" at all—a genuine advantage when writing for people who aren't familiar with the statistical meaning of that word. Write:

"The relationship between race and labor force participation depends on gender."

Or

"The relationship between race and labor force participation is different for men than for women."

Having alerted your readers to the fact that the pattern of association escapes a simple generalization, proceed through the rest of the GEE as in the description of figure 13.3 above. See appendix A for a systematic approach to identifying and describing such patterns.

Phrasing for a GEE

As you write a GEE, choose words that differentiate between broad patterns and exceptions.

Wording for Generalizations

To introduce a generalization, use expressions like "in general," "typically," or "by and large" to convey that the pattern characterizes many of the numbers you are summarizing. Phrases such as "virtually all," "in the majority of cases," or "roughly three-quarters of" can enhance the summary by conveying approximately what share of individuals, places, or time periods are encompassed by that general pattern. Often you can work the numeric illustration into the same sentence as the generalization by placing the specific numeric value in parentheses after the pertinent phrase: "Virtually all respondents (98%) . . ." or "In a majority of cases (59%), . . ."

Wording to Introduce Exceptions

To introduce exceptions, use phrases such as "an exception [to that pattern]" or "on the other hand," varying the wording to add interest to your descriptions.

"In seven out of 10 years studied, [pattern and example]. . . .
However, in the other three years, [contrasting pattern]."

If your exception is literally the opposite of your generalization (e.g., falling rather than rising), consider expressions such as "on the contrary" or "conversely." Then describe the shape of the exception:

"Among white persons, male labor force participation exceeded female labor force participation. In contrast, among black persons, female labor force participation was higher than male."

■ CHECKLIST FOR WRITING ABOUT DISTRIBUTIONS AND ASSOCIATIONS

To describe univariate distribution or composition, consider the type of variable.

- For continuous variables, report minimum, maximum, and mean values and a measure of variation, e.g., standard deviation.
- For categorical variables, report modal category and mention selected other categories of interest.
- Coordinate the order in which you mention categories with their sequence in the associated table or chart, using one or more of the organizing criteria described in chapter 5.

To describe a bivariate association, incorporate the following:

- Direction of association
- Selected quantitative comparisons (e.g., absolute, relative or percentage difference) to convey magnitude of association
- Results of statistical tests (e.g., chi-square or t-statistics, or the associated p-values)

To describe a three-way association,

- use the GEE approach to avoid reporting every number or comparison in the text;
- describe exceptions (interactions) of direction, magnitude, and statistical significance.

Writing about Multivariate Models

In this chapter, I illustrate how to write the results section for a scientific paper or technical report that features a multivariate analysis. I begin by addressing how to develop a convincing case for a multivariate model, starting with bivariate associations. This step is also important in a grant proposal that involves an application of a multivariate model, to help convince reviewers that the type of model you chose is appropriate and necessary. Working with the tools introduced earlier in this book, I then explain how to write about multivariate regression results while maintaining a clear narrative related to your research question.

■ BUILDING THE CASE FOR A MULTIVARIATE MODEL

Writing about statistical results is equivalent to the evidence portion of a legal trial. Before you launch into a detailed description of your findings, provide justification for the methods of analysis. As in a legal argument, defend your choice of techniques before you present the associated results. Explain why a simpler method won't suffice to answer your research question with the data at hand. In statistical terms, "if a bivariate test will do, why estimate a multivariate model?"

By and large, results of bivariate tests are easier to describe because they don't require a lot of assumptions or complicated statistical terminology and output. If you can measure the association between one variable and another without a lot of other distracting stuff going on, so much the better. However, multivariate models are needed for research questions or data involving confounding, mediating, or correlation among independent variables, for generating forecasting or simulation models that take many factors into account, or for describing relationships among a set of variables (Allison 1999; Powers and Xie 2000).

Common Reasons for Estimating a Multivariate Model

One frequent application of multivariate analysis is to test hypotheses regarding one or more independent variables, controlling for the other variables in the model. This presumes relationships not only between each of the independent variables and the dependent variable, but among the independent variables as well. If the independent variables aren't correlated with one another, you do not need a multivariate model to estimate their net effects. Correlations among independent variables can occur for any of several reasons—confounding, mediating, or association of several closely related measures of the same concept—each of which has different implications for the interpretation of your findings.

Confounding

Confounding occurs when some other factor is the cause of both the supposed predictor and the purported outcome, or is highly correlated with both. The association of white hair with high mortality cited in chapter 3 is actually due to the fact that each of those factors is associated with old age—age confounds the hair color/mortality relation. Hence if age were introduced into a model with white hair as a predictor and mortality as the outcome using a sample of the general population, both the size and statistical significance of the white hair "effect" would decrease markedly.

Multivariate models often aren't needed for estimating effects of individual variables from experimental data. Such studies involve random assignment of subjects to treatments which equalizes the distribution of other characteristics across treatment groups, substantially reducing the possibility of confounding. For example, subjects in a clinical trial of a medication to prevent skin cancer might be placed in groups based on a coin flip, ensuring that those who receive the treatment are similar to those who receive a placebo in terms of age, occupation, region, or other known risk factors for skin cancer. If bivariate tests reveal no statistically significant differences in the distribution of these potential confounders between treatment and control groups, a multivariate model of the effect of treatment on skin cancer is unnecessary.

In many studies, particularly of social and behavioral phenomena, experimental data are neither feasible nor ethical. People select themselves into "treatment" and "control" groups, so the potential for confounding or reverse causation is considerable. For instance, couples who cohabited before marriage are likely to differ demographically, socioeconomically, and attitudinally from those who did not. To estimate the "effect" of cohabitation on divorce, a multivariate model is required to control for those attributes because they are associated with divorce and could confound the cohabitation/divorce relation.

Mediating

Another reason for estimating multivariate models is to assess possible mediating effects. A mediating variable (or mediating factor) is one that comes between some other independent variable and the dependent variable. Often it is a mechanism by which the first predictor affects the dependent variable, as shown in figure 15.7: in the United States, people of minority race are more likely to be of low socioeconomic status (SES), and low SES is associated with poor health. If SES of minorities increases, their health generally improves. In this instance, SES mediates the relationship between race and health. By estimating models with and without controls for SES, you can evaluate the extent to which SES explains the association between race and health, and how much remains to be explained by other factors.

Describing Relations among a Set of Variables

Some multivariate models are used to estimate the net effects of each of several independent variables that measure different aspects of the same concept and hence are highly correlated with one another. For example, Duncan and colleagues (2002) found that income remained a strong, statistically significant predictor of mortality in the presence of controls for educational attainment and occupation, but neither of those other two SES measures was significant when income was controlled.

Forecasting or Simulation

Multivariate models are also used to predict values of the dependent variable from data on a set of independent variables. For example, data on prices, interest rates, and unemployment rates might be used to build a model to forecast rates of future economic growth. Or information on age, concurrent illness, and stage at diagnosis might be used to predict expected survival time for people diagnosed with cancer. In such models, the principal interest is the predictive value of the overall model, with an emphasis on the fit between predicted and actual values rather than on associations between specific independent variables and the dependent variable. See Kennedy (2003) or other econometrics texts for more on forecasting.

Inappropriate Reasons to Estimate Multivariate Models

A couple of caveats. First, although statistics can demonstrate correlation among variables, they *cannot* be used to determine whether a relation among variables is causal. Put differently, statistical models alone can't help you differentiate between mediating, confounding, reverse causation, or other correlations among independent variables. To determine which of these situations you have—and thus which hypothesis you are testing with your multivariate model—consider the timing of measurement for each of your variables. Even if you have hypotheses about which came first, if the independent variable and dependent variable were measured simultaneously (as in cross-sectional data), the best you can demonstrate is association, not causal order. Also read the literature about the underlying mechanisms that could link the variables you are analyzing. See Davis (1985) or chapter 3 for more on causality and study design.

Second, do not use multivariate models as a fishing expedition to identify "significant" predictors of your dependent variable. The theory behind sampling and inferential statistics implies that on average one out of every twenty independent variables will be statistically significant at $p < 0.05$ by random chance alone, even without a true, underlying relationship. Instead of typing every available variable from your data set into a model and seeing which are statistically significant, use theoretical considerations to guide your choice of specification and the order in which variables are entered into the model, then explain that logic to your readers.

■ STEPS IN DESCRIBING A MULTIVARIATE ANALYSIS

By the time you write your results section, you will have introduced the theoretical basis for the hypothesized relationships and defined the measures of those concepts available in your data. The next steps are to explain where each of the major variables fits into your hypotheses, show bivariate associations to demonstrate the need for a multivariate model, and finally, present and interpret the multivariate regression results. Like an attorney building a legal case, introduce the characters (variables), their hypothesized relationships, and evidence that they are connected in a meaningful way (tests of association).

Organize the results section into paragraphs, each of which addresses one aspect of your research question. Start each paragraph with a sentence that introduces the topic of that paragraph and generalizes the patterns. Then present numeric evidence for those conclusions. A handful of numbers can be presented in a sentence or two. For more complex patterns, report the numbers in a chart or table, then describe the patterns using the "generalization, example, exceptions" (GEE) approach. Refer to each table or chart by name as you describe the patterns and report numbers presented therein.

Explaining the Roles of Your Variables

As you begin your results section, explain the roles of the different variables in your multivariate analyses.[1] Identify the dependent variable, key independent variable, and any potential mediators, confounders, or alternative measures of a given concept by mentioning those relations as you explain the results. Show how general theoretical concepts behind your hypotheses translate into concrete, specific aspects of your research question. In an analysis of who invests in a college education, for example, you might introduce opportunity cost as an important theoretical consideration, then describe the model specification and results in terms of specific measures of opportunity cost related to your topic, such as foregone income while in college and alternative uses for money spent on tuition.

Also distinguish between the key independent variables and other variables in the model, giving less emphasis to general background or control variables that are not central to your hypotheses. Remember that the role of a given variable depends on the research question. Although gender is a control variable in the birth weight analysis presented in this book, it would be the key independent variable in an analysis of gender differences in test scores, and the dependent variable in an evaluation of whether preconception sex selection techniques are effective.

In disciplines such as economics and statistics, equations are commonly used to convey the role of each variable. In other disciplines, model specifications are more often explained verbally, with equations limited to showing how new methods were derived. See chapter 12 for guidelines on when and how to include equations.

Presenting Information on Bivariate Relationships

For multivariate models used to test for mediating or confounding, present information on bivariate associations among your independent variables and dependent variable, including results of statistical tests for associations among those variables. If you suspect interactions involving the main variables of interest, create a three-way table to report the numeric values within each category and to present the results of the associated statistical tests.

Create one or two tables to show:

- The association between the key independent variable and the dependent variable, whether mean values by subgroup (for a continuous dependent variable such as birth weight in grams), distributions, or rates of occurrence (for a categorical dependent variable such as low birth weight). In table 14.1, these associations comprise the top two rows of numbers.
- The associations between the key independent variable and potential confounders or mediators, such as the distribution of socioeconomic characteristics and smoking behavior by racial/ethnic group, shown in the remaining rows of table 14.1.
- The associations between each of the potential confounders or mediators and the dependent variable. In the analysis of birth weight by race, information on birth weight by socioeconomic characteristics and smoking behavior was drawn from other sources, but an additional table could have presented those statistics from the NHANES III data.

An exception: for models intended for forecasting, bivariate associations are less important. In such applications, report descriptive statistics on each of the variables before presenting multivariate results. Tables of descriptive statistics also provide a place to report the unadjusted (raw) values so that readers can assess their level and compare those values with data from other sources. Finally, these tables are a place to report unweighted sample sizes, overall and for major subgroups.

Describing a Bivariate Table Preceding a Multivariate Analysis

Describe the bivariate associations among your key independent variable, dependent variable, and potential confounders or mediators, explaining how those facts substantiate the need for a multivariate model. In the results section, report and describe numeric evidence to test your hypotheses, systematically presenting quantitative examples and contrasts.

Boxes 14.1a and 14.1b show poor and better descriptions of table 14.1, comprising the first step in an analysis of whether socioeconomic or behavioral factors explain racial differences in birth weight. On the pages that follow, I critique the numbered sentences (statements) from those descriptions, identifying the various principles for introducing, organizing, and describing statistical findings.

Poorest: Bivariate tables are omitted.

Unless you are writing a brief statistical report, a talk for a panel of experts, or a forecasting or simulation model, provide the bivariate information. Do not assume that your audience knows either the conceptual relations among your variables or the numeric evidence about those patterns.

Statement 1

Poor: [No introductory sentence.]

By jumping right into a description of the table, this version fails to orient readers to the purpose of that table.

Better: "Table 14.1 presents weighted statistics on birth weight, socioeconomic characteristics, and smoking for the three racial/ethnic groups, along with the unweighted number of cases in each racial/ethnic group. All differences shown are statistically significant at $p < 0.01$."

The topic sentence names the associated table and introduces its purpose, restating the title into a full sentence. It also specifies which statistics are weighted and which are unweighted. The second sentence generalizes about statistical significance for the entire table, echoing the footnote to the table and eliminating the need to report results of statistical tests for each association in the text.

Statement 2

Poor: "Race/ethnicity is strongly related to birth weight and LBW (both $p < 0.01$). Mean birth weight was 3,426.8, 3,181.3, and 3,357.3, for non-Hispanic white, non-Hispanic black, and Mexican American infants, respectively."

This sentence reports but does not interpret average birth weight for each racial/ethnic group, adding little to the information in the table (which it fails to name). It omits the units for birth weight, and presents a string of numbers that is visually difficult to take in.

Better: "On average, non-Hispanic white infants were 246 grams heavier than non-Hispanic blacks and 70 grams heavier than Mexican Americans (3,427 grams, 3,181 grams, and 3,357 grams, respectively). The birth weight difference between Mexican American and non-Hispanic black infants (176 grams) was also

Table 14.1. Bivariate associations among independent and dependent variables

Birth weight, socioeconomic characteristics, and smoking behavior by race/ethnicity, United States, 1988–1994 NHANES III

	Non-Hispanic white (N = 3,733)	Non-Hispanic black (N = 2,968)	Mexican American (N = 3,112)	All racial/ethnic groups (N = 9,813)
Birth weight[a]				
Mean (grams)	3,426.8	3,181.3	3,357.3	3,379.2
% Low birth weight[b]	5.8	11.3	7.0	6.8
Socioeconomic characteristics				
Mother's age				
Mean (years)	26.6	24.2	24.9	26.0
% Teen mother	9.4	22.9	18.4	12.5
Mother's education				
Mean (years)	13.3	11.9	9.1	12.6
% <High school	14.7	30.1	58.4	21.6
% =High school	34.9	41.7	24.5	35.0

Income-to-poverty ratio (IPR) [c]

Mean	2.60	1.39	1.34	2.28
% Poor	14.7	48.5	50.7	23.9
Health behavior				
% Mother smoked while pregnant	26.8	22.9	10.1	24.5

Note: Statistics are weighted to population level using weights provided with the NHANES III (U.S. DHHS 1997); sample size is unweighted.

[a] Differences across racial/ethnic origin groups were statistically significant for all variables shown ($p < 0.01$).

[b] Low birth weight <2,500 grams or 5.5 pounds.

[c] The income-to-poverty ratio (IPR) is family income in dollars divided by the Federal Poverty Threshold for a family of comparable size and age composition. A family with income equal to the poverty threshold (e.g., $17,960 for two adults and two children in 2001; U.S. Census Bureau 2002b) would have an income-to-poverty ratio of 1.0.

Box 14.1a. Description of a Bivariate Table Preceding a Multivariate Analysis: Poor Version

"(1) (2) Race/ethnicity is strongly related to birth weight and LBW (both $p < 0.01$). Mean birth weight was 3,426.8, 3,181.3, and 3,357.3, for non-Hispanic white, non-Hispanic black, and Mexican American infants, respectively. (3) Average educational attainment, percentage of high school graduates, income, percentage in poverty, percentage of teen mothers, and maternal age are all statistically significant ($p < 0.01$). (4) An interesting finding is that smoking shows the opposite pattern of all the other variables ($p < 0.01$). (5) Table 14.2 presents mean birth weight for each combination of race/ethnicity and (6) mother's educational attainment. (7) Among infants born to women with less than complete high school, mean birth weight was 3,300, 3,090, and 3,345 for non-Hispanic whites, non-Hispanic blacks, and Mexican Americans, respectively. [Sentences with corresponding numbers for each racial/ ethnic group among =high school and college+] (8)."

statistically significant. These deficits in mean birth weight translate into substantial differences in percentage low birth weight (LBW < 2,500 grams), with nearly twice the risk of LBW among non-Hispanic black as non-Hispanic white infants (11.3% and 5.8%, respectively). Mexican American infants were only slightly more likely than whites to be LBW (7.0%; relative risk = 1.2; $p < 0.05$)."

The first and second sentences report direction and size of differences in mean birth weight across racial/ethnic groups using absolute difference to assess size, reporting the units of measurement, and separating the string of numbers with text so they are easier to distinguish from one another. The last two sentences quantify differences in low birth weight across racial/ethnic groups using relative risk and reporting the numbers for that calculation. The LBW acronym and definition of low birth weight are repeated from the methods section to remind readers of their meanings. If length is a concern, include either the first two sentences or the last two, anticipating which dependent variable is used in your subsequent multivariate model.

Box 14.1b. Description of a Bivariate Table Preceding a Multivariate Analysis: Better Version

"(1) Table 14.1 presents weighted statistics on birth weight, socioeconomic characteristics and maternal smoking for the three racial/ethnic groups, along with the unweighted number of cases in each racial/ethnic group. All differences shown are statistically significant at $p < 0.01$. (2) On average, non-Hispanic white infants were 246 grams heavier than non-Hispanic blacks and 70 grams heavier than Mexican Americans (3,427 grams, 3,181 grams, and 3,357 grams, respectively). The birth weight difference between Mexican American and non-Hispanic black infants (176 grams) was also statistically significant. These deficits in mean birth weight translate into substantial differences in percentage low birth weight (LBW $<$ 2,500 grams), with nearly twice the risk of LBW among non-Hispanic black as non-Hispanic white infants (11.3% and 5.8%, respectively). Mexican American infants were only slightly more likely than whites to be LBW (7.0%; relative risk $= 1.2$; $p < 0.05$).

"(3) In every dimension of socioeconomic status studied here, non-Hispanic black and Mexican American mothers were substantially disadvantaged relative to their non-Hispanic white counterparts. They were twice as likely as white mothers to be teenagers at the time they gave birth, and two to three times as likely to be high school dropouts. Mean income-to-poverty ratios for black and Mexican American families were roughly half those of white families. (4) In contrast to the socioeconomic patterns, maternal smoking—an important behavioral risk factor for low birth weight—was more common among non-Hispanic white women (27%) than non-Hispanic black (23%) or Mexican American women (10%).

"(5) Does the lower average socioeconomic status (SES) of non-Hispanic black and Mexican American infants explain their lower mean birth weight? To answer that question, table 14.2 presents mean birth weight for the three racial/ethnic groups within each of three socioeconomic strata, (6) defined here in terms of mother's educational attainment. (7) Birth weight increased with increasing mother's education in all racial/ethnic groups. In addition, at all mother's education levels, non-Hispanic black infants weighed 180 to 225 grams less than their white or Mexican American counterparts ($p < 0.01$). In the lowest mother's education group, Mexican American infants slightly outweighed their non-Hispanic white peers, but among infants born to mothers with a high school diploma or higher, non-Hispanic white infants outweighed Mexican Americans, although the difference was not statistically significant.

"(8) These statistics show that even within strata defined by mother's educational attainment, non-Hispanic black race is associated with substantially lower birth weight. However, several other dimensions of SES are also related to minority race. Moreover, studies have shown that low SES is associated with lower birth weight, therefore a multivariate model is needed to disentangle the respective effects of race/ethnicity, SES, and smoking on birth weight. The patterns in table 14.2 also suggest the need to test for interactions between race/ethnicity and educational attainment in the multivariate model."

Statement 3

Poor: "Average educational attainment, percentage of high school graduates, income, percentage poor, percentage of teen mothers, and maternal age are all statistically significant ($p < 0.01$)."
This seemingly simple sentence is plagued by numerous problems.

- Results are listed without differentiating between the dependent (birth weight) and independent variables or drawing a distinction between socioeconomic status (SES) and behavioral characteristics. Combined with the absence of an introductory sentence, this version leaves the results almost completely disconnected from the research question.

- This sentence does not explain that the statistical tests are for differences *across racial/ethnic groups* in each of the SES variables. Because race is not mentioned, readers may mistakenly think that the tests are for association among the SES variables.

- Both the continuous and categorical versions of each SES measure are reported without pointing out that they are merely two different perspectives on the same concept. For example, "% poor" simply classifies family income into poor and non-poor.

Better: "In every dimension of socioeconomic status studied here, non-Hispanic black and Mexican American mothers were substantially disadvantaged relative to their non-Hispanic white counterparts. They were twice as likely as white mothers to be teenagers at the time they gave birth, and two to three times as likely to be high school dropouts. Mean income-to-poverty ratios for black and Mexican American families were roughly half those of white families."

Because most of the remaining numbers in the table deal with associations between race/ethnicity and socioeconomic status, a new paragraph is started to describe those findings. The topic sentence introduces the concepts to be discussed and generalizes the patterns. The next two sentences illustrate the preceding generalization with specific comparisons from the table, using relative differences to quantify racial/ethnic disparities in the three socioeconomic measures.

Statement 4

Poor: "An interesting finding is that smoking shows the opposite pattern of all the other variables."

"Opposite" of what? This sentence does not indicate which patterns smoking is being compared against or mention the direction of any pattern. Neither this nor the preceding sentence mentions that the associations are with race/ethnicity, again keeping the description divorced from the main purpose of the analysis.

Better: "In contrast to the socioeconomic patterns, maternal smoking—an important behavioral risk factor for low birth weight—was more common among non-Hispanic white women (27%) than non-Hispanic black (23%) or Mexican American women (10%)."

This version points out an exception to the generalization that people of color are worse off, reporting the higher smoking rates among whites.

Statements 5 and 6

Poor: "Table 14.2 presents mean birth weight for each combination of race/ethnicity and mother's educational attainment."

By failing to link the description of table 14.2 with previous or subsequent tables, this description leaves readers without a sense of how the evidence in the two tables fits together or how those analyses relate to the overall research question. In addition, the interpretation of mother's educational attainment isn't specified.

Better: "Does the lower average socioeconomic status (SES) of non-Hispanic black and Mexican American infants explain their lower mean birth weight? To answer that question, table 14.2 presents mean birth weight for the three racial/ethnic groups within each of three socioeconomic strata, defined in terms of mother's educational attainment."

Table 14.2. Three-way association among a dependent variable and two independent variables

Descriptive statistics on birth weight (grams)[a] by race/ethnicity and mother's educational attainment, United States, 1988–1994[b]

Mother's education	Mean birth weight	Standard deviation	Unweighted N
<High school			
Non-Hispanic white	3,299.9	51,604.9	596
Non-Hispanic black	3,089.9	28,120.5	903
Mexican American	3,345.2	21,829.7	1662
=High school			
Non-Hispanic white	3,361.5	49,252.6	1309
Non-Hispanic black	3,177.5	28,485.5	1219
Mexican American	3,365.1	20,314.5	712
College+			
Non-Hispanic white	3,506.9	50,155.2	1762
Non-Hispanic black	3,283.4	30,801.6	725
Mexican American	3,384.1	21,161.3	446

[a] Weighted to national level using sampling weights provided with the NHANES III (U.S. DHHS 1997).
[b] Data are from the Third U.S. National Health and Nutrition Examination Survey (U.S. DHHS 1997).

These sentences provide a transition, summarizing the findings in table 14.1 and explaining how they lead to the question addressed in table 14.2. They also help signal a new logical step in the analysis by starting a new paragraph. Mother's educational attainment is identified as an indicator of socioeconomic status, helping orient readers to the purpose of this analysis.

Statement 7

Poor: "Among infants born to women with less than complete high school, mean birth weight was 3,300, 3,090, and 3,345 for non-Hispanic whites, non-Hispanic blacks, and Mexican Americans, respectively. [Sentences with corresponding numbers

for each racial/ethnic group in the high school diploma and
college+ groups.]"

*By simply listing nine birth weight values, this version fails to portray
the size or shape of the two general patterns (birth weight by race and
by education), or relate them to the underlying research question.*

Better: "Birth weight increased with increasing mother's education
in all racial/ethnic groups. In addition, at all mother's education
levels, non-Hispanic black infants weighed 180 to 225 grams less
than their white or Mexican American counterparts ($p < 0.01$). In
the lowest mother's education group, Mexican American infants
slightly outweighed their non-Hispanic white peers, but among
infants born to mothers with a high school diploma or higher,
non-Hispanic white infants outweighed Mexican Americans,
although the difference was not statistically significant."

*This version describes the birth weight patterns by race/ethnicity and
educational attainment using the GEE approach, specifying the direction,
size, and statistical significance of those associations.*

Statement 8

Poor: [No transition to multivariate model].

*By omitting a summary of the findings of tables 14.1 and 14.2, this
description doesn't orient readers about where the different tables and
analyses fit in terms of the overall research question, leaving the
reasons for a multivariate model unclear.*

Better: "These statistics show that even within strata defined by
mother's educational attainment, non-Hispanic black race is
associated with substantially lower birth weight. However,
several other dimensions of SES are also related to minority race.
Moreover, studies have shown that low SES is associated with
lower birth weight, therefore a multivariate model is needed to
disentangle the respective effects of race/ethnicity, SES, and
smoking on birth weight. The patterns in table 14.2 also suggest
the need to test for interactions between race/ethnicity and
educational attainment in the multivariate model."

*This narrative provides a smooth transition to the multivariate model
by reiterating that the bivariate associations among the dependent
variable, key independent variable, and potential mediating factors
were all statistically significant, and gives reasons for testing
interactions in the multivariate specification. It also refers to previous
literature for evidence associating SES and birth weight.*

Explaining How Associations Affect
Your Model Specification Strategy

As you conclude your description of bivariate or three-way associations, explain how those associations influenced your multivariate model specification. For instance, if your analysis includes several highly correlated independent variables, report the correlations and how you handled multicollinearity in arriving at your final model specification. Or, if you used factor analyses as a data reduction technique to create predictors in your model, describe that process. Finally, if a three-way tabulation suggests the need to test for interactions between independent variables, state that as well. See chapter 12 for more on multicollinearity and factor analysis; chapter 9 on interactions.

▓ EXPOSITION OF A MULTIVARIATE MODEL

Having built the case for a multivariate model, present the results. Follow the guidelines in chapter 5 to create tables of multivariate results, structured and labeled to coordinate with your writing. Working from those tables, go systematically through the results, using paragraphs to organize the description, with topic sentences that differentiate among the roles of different variables or blocks of related variables in the model. If you include Greek symbols or other abbreviations in equations and tables, replace or paraphrase them in the text.

At least once, state that the results are from a multivariate model using wording such as

- "net of the other variables in the model,"
- "controlling for other variables in the model,"
- "taking into account other variables in the model,"
- "holding other variables in the model constant," or
- *ceteris paribus* (Latin for "all else equal"; use it only if
  your readers are conversant with its meaning).

If there are only a few other variables or if they can be identified by general conceptual names such as "socioeconomic factors," substitute those names for "other variables in the model" in the above phrases.

Introducing the Model

Begin with a topic sentence that identifies the statistical technique and mentions the major variables involved in the analysis or restates the hypothesis being tested. Explain the purpose of the different variables in your model, organizing them to coordinate with your hypotheses. First, discuss results that address the main hypotheses — the coefficients and statistical significance of the key independent variable and how those coefficients change between the bivariate and multivariate statistics. Then identify and discuss results for mediators or confounders. Report results for control variables much more briefly, using generalizations or lists, or referring to expected effects based on previous research or bivariate findings.

Effects of Individual Independent Variables

A common error among novices is to simply list which factors were and were not statistically significant or to spew out a string of *p*-values without interpreting the coefficients. A sentence summarizing statistical significance or lack thereof can be a fine introductory generalization, but should be followed by a description of direction and size of coefficients for the key independent variables, confounders, or mediators, organized by their roles in the model. If word count is a concern, use one of the approaches recommended below under "Length Considerations" to write a concise description. In the concluding section, return to discuss nonsignificant findings for major variables if theory or previous studies lead you to expect a statistically significant association (see "Statistical Significance" in chapter 11).

Continuous Independent Variables

To interpret effect estimates, mention the units for continuous independent variables along with the results. If a key variable in your model is specified with nonlinear terms or is transformed using logarithms or some other function, consider creating a chart such as figure 6.11 to complement the reported coefficients in the table of model results. In the accompanying narrative, refer to the chart and describe its shape with an analogy or numeric examples.

Categorical Independent Variables

To convey the meaning of categorical independent variables' coefficients, specify the comparison. For dichotomous (two-category) variables the comparison is self-evident, assuming you've named the dummy variable to reflect its identity rather than the general concept of the variable (e.g., "smoker" rather than "smoking status"). For multicategory variables such as race/ethnicity or educational attainment where several comparisons are possible, name the comparison group. Avoid writing about "the reference category."

Describing Interactions

As you describe interactions from a multivariate model, explain the direction and magnitude of the *net effect* of main effect and interaction terms rather than describing them as if they were distinct from one another. The individual main effect and interaction terms have meaning only in relation to each other (see chapter 9). If the interaction involves your key independent variable, present the net pattern in a table (e.g., table 14.4) or chart (figures 6.7 or 6.12), then refer to it in your description.

To illustrate these ideas, boxes 14.2a and 14.2b present poor and better ways to describe the results of model IV in table 14.3, with numbered sentences keyed to the comments below. (Models I through III are discussed under "Comparing a Series of Nested Models" below).

Statement 1

Poor: [no introductory sentence]

By writing immediately about the results for each independent variable, this version leaves the findings in isolation from the research question.

Better: "Ordinary least squares regression shows that even when socioeconomic characteristics and health behaviors were taken into account, non-Hispanic black infants weighed considerably less on average than their non-Hispanic white or Mexican American peers (model IV, table 14.3)."

This version sets the context for the paragraph, identifying the statistical method (OLS), the dependent variable (birth weight), the key independent variable (race/ethnicity), the broad categories of mediators or confounders (socioeconomic characteristics and health behaviors), the general conclusion of the analysis, and the table in which the pertinent results are reported. Despite this plethora of information, the sentence is easy to understand.

Statement 2

Poor: "The beta for non-Hispanic black infants was −168.1 with a standard error (s.e.) of 29.7 (model IV, table 14.3). The effect was statistically significant. The beta for Mexican American was −104.2 ($p = 0.05$).

The results for race/ethnicity are reported in a way that almost defies interpretation, at least without repeatedly consulting the accompanying table.

- The dependent variable isn't mentioned anywhere in the paragraph and the units of "effect" aren't specified.

- "Beta" has different interpretations in different statistical contexts. Translate it into the units and concepts it measures in your analysis to avoid confusion about its interpretation and to emphasize the research question rather than the statistical methods.
- "Effect" isn't much better unless you intend a causal interpretation and specify "effect of __ on ___."
- Which relationship is statistically significant — Mexican American versus non-Hispanic white? Mexican American versus non-Hispanic black? The reference category isn't named, so readers must look in the table to figure out the comparison.

Better: "At every socioeconomic level, non-Hispanic black infants weighed roughly 170 grams less than non-Hispanic whites, as reflected in the statistically significant main effect for non-Hispanic black ($\beta = -168.1$; $p < 0.01$) but lack of significant interactions between black race and mother's educational attainment."

This version generalizes about the birth weight difference between blacks and whites, specifying the direction, size, and statistical significance of the difference, and naming the dependent variable (birth weight) and its units (grams). The comparison group (non-Hispanic whites) is incorporated into the explanation rather than by vague allusion to "the reference category."

Statement 3

Poor [version 1]: "Race/ethnicity and mother's education interact: The main effect of less than high school was −54.2 and the effect of high school graduate was −62.0. The interaction effects for black × < HS and black × =HS were −38.5 and 18.4 (NS). The corresponding interaction terms for Mexican American were 99.4, and 93.7 respectively.

By simply listing the coefficients for the main effects for educational attainment, the two racial/ethnic groups, and the interaction terms, this description doesn't capture their interrelated nature. In addition, the reference category is not identified and "NS" is not defined.

Poor [version 2; not shown in box]: "The effect of mother's education on birth weight for Mexican American infants differs from that of white or black infants. To see the net effect among non-Hispanic black infants of having a mother who did not complete high school, you add together the non-Hispanic black

Table 14.3. Estimated coefficients from a series of nested models

Estimated coefficients from a series of nested OLS models of birth weight (grams) by race/ethnicity, socioeconomic status, and smoking characteristics, United States, 1988–1994

Variable	Model I Infant traits only		Model II Infant traits & SES		Model III Infant traits, SES & smoking		Model IV Infant traits, SES, smoking & interactions	
	Coeff.	s.e.	Coeff.	s.e.	Coeff.	s.e.	Coeff.	s.e.
Intercept	3,367.1**	9.6	2,959.5**	39.1	3,039.7**	39.2	3,042.8**	39.4
Race/ethnicity (Non-Hispanic White)								
Non-Hispanic Black	−244.5**	16.7	−147.2**	17.6	−172.6**	17.5	−168.1**	29.7
Mexican American	−68.4**	21.6	−31.0	22.6	−23.1	22.7	−104.2*	48.3
Boy	116.1**	12.3	114.7**	12.1	117.2**	12.0	117.4**	12.3
Mother's education								
Less than high school			−86.0**	19.3	−55.5**	19.3	−54.2*	23.0
High school graduate			−75.2**	14.9	−53.9**	14.8	−62.0**	16.4
(College+)								

Interactions: race and education

	(1)		(2)		(3)		(4)	
Non-Hisp. black $\times$ <HS							−38.5	43.8
Mexican American $\times$ <HS							99.4	58.0
Non-Hisp. black $\times$ =HS							18.4	38.9
Mexican American $\times$ =HS							93.7	63.0
Mother's age at birth of child (yrs.)			11.3**	1.2	10.7**	1.2	10.6**	1.2
Income-to-poverty ratio (IPR)[a]			95.2**	14.6	80.5**	14.5	81.4**	14.6
IPR^2			−11.5**	2.3	−9.9**	2.3	−10.1**	2.3
Mother smoked during pregnancy					−194.7**	14.4	−193.9**	14.4
F-statistic (df)	102.49 (3)		81.39 (8)		94.1 (9)		65.6 (13)	
Adjusted R^2	0.032		0.065		0.082		0.083	

Note: Weighted to national levels using sampling weights provided with the NHANES III (U.S. DHHS 1997).

[a] Family income divided by the poverty level for a family of that size and age composition.

$* p < 0.05$ $** p < 0.01$

Box 14.2a. Describing Multivariate Model Results: Poor Version

"(1) (2) The beta for non-Hispanic black infants was −168.1 with a standard error (s.e.) of 29.7 (model IV, table 14.3). The effect was statistically significant. The beta for Mexican American was −104.2 (p = 0.05). (3) Race/ethnicity and mother's education interact: The main effect of less than high school was −54.2 and the effect of high school graduate was −62.0. The interaction effects for black × <HS and black × =HS were −38.5 and 18.4 (NS). The corresponding interaction terms for Mexican American were 99.4, and 93.7 respectively. (4) (5) The coefficient for mother's age was 10.6 (s.e. = 1.2), so it had a smaller effect than less than high school (−54.2; s.e. = 23.0). (6) The income-to-poverty ratio had a linear term (81.4) and a square term (−10.1) and both were statistically significant. (7) The smoking effect was negative (−193.9, p < 0.001)."

and <HS main effects and the black × <HS interaction. [Repeat same general idea for black × =HS, and for Mexican Americans at each education level]. . . . So for mothers with less than a high school education, the effect of non-Hispanic black is −260.8 grams, while the effect of Mexican American is −59.0 grams." *This explanation starts out strong, restating the general relationship behind the interaction. However, it goes into far too much detail about the calculations. It also fails to clarify that the comparisons are against non-Hispanic white infants whose mothers have some college, and overlooks comparisons of white infants born to less educated mothers.*

Better: "Birth weight increased with mother's education in each of the three race/ethnicity groups (β = −54.2 and −62.0 grams for less than high school and high school graduates, respectively, when each was compared to college+; p < 0.05). However, gains were much smaller among Mexican Americans than among blacks or whites. As a consequence, the birth weight gap between Mexican American and white infants increased markedly with increasing maternal education. Among infants born to mothers who had not completed high school, Mexican American infants weighed 5 grams less than whites. In the highest education group (mothers with at least some college), the deficit was 104 grams (table 14.4).)

Box 14.2b. Describing Multivariate Model Results: Better Version

"(1) Ordinary least squares regression shows that even when socioeconomic characteristics and health behaviors were taken into account, non-Hispanic black infants weighed considerably less on average than their non-Hispanic white or Mexican American peers (model IV, table 14.3). (2) At every socioeconomic level, non-Hispanic black infants weighed roughly 170 grams less than non-Hispanic whites, as reflected in the statistically significant main effect for non-Hispanic black ($\beta = -168.1$; $p < 0.01$) but lack of significant interactions between black race and mother's educational attainment. (3) Birth weight increased with mother's education in each of the three race/ethnicity groups ($\beta = -54.2$ and -62.0 grams for less than high school and high school graduates, respectively, when each was compared to college$+$; $p < 0.05$). However, gains were much smaller among Mexican Americans than among blacks or whites. As a consequence, the birth weight gap between Mexican American and white infants increased markedly with increasing maternal education. Among infants born to mothers who had not completed high school, Mexican American infants weighed 5 grams less than whites. In the highest education group (mothers with at least some college), the deficit was 104 grams (table 14.4).

"(4) Each of the other socioeconomic characteristics had a statistically significant association with birth weight in model IV. (5) Birth weight increased by an average of 10.6 grams for each additional year of mother's age at the time of the child's birth. (6) The linear and square terms on the income-to-poverty ratio (IPR) demonstrate that as the IPR increased, mean birth weight also increased but at a decreasing rate (figure 6.11). For example, an infant born into a family with income at twice the poverty level (e.g., IPR = 2.0) was predicted to weigh about 50 grams more than an infant born to a family at the poverty level (IPR = 1.0), whereas the corresponding difference between infants born into families at 3.0 and 4.0 times the poverty level was only about 10 grams.

(7) Infants whose mothers who smoked weighed considerably less than those born to non-smokers (-193.9 grams; $p < 0.001$). Although inclusion of the smoking variable improved the overall fit of the model, it did not appreciably alter the race/birth weight relation.

Table 14.4. Net effects of main effects and interaction terms

Predicted difference in birth weight (grams) by race/ethnicity and mother's educational attainment, United States, 1988–1994

	Non-Hispanic White	Non-Hispanic Black	Mexican American
Less than high school	−54.2	−260.8	−59.0
High school graduate	−62.0	−211.7	−72.5
College+	0.0	−168.1	−104.2

Source: Based on multivariate model with controls for gender, IPR and IPR^2, maternal age, and smoking (see model IV, table 14.3).
Notes: Compared to non-Hispanic white infants born to nonsmoking mothers with at least some college. Weighted to national levels using sampling weights provided with the NHANES III (U.S. DHHS 1997).

This version generalizes about the education/birth weight association across racial/ethnic groups, then points out an exception (Mexican American). It then describes the shape and size of the patterns for each racial ethnic group, with reference to a table that presents the net effects of the interaction. Reference categories are specified. The net effect calculations are conducted behind the scenes, avoiding a "teaching statistics" tangent within the presentation of results.

Statement 4

Poor: [No transition sentence.]
The roles of variables aren't distinguished from one another. Instead, the results for all variables in the model are lumped into one paragraph in the order they appear in the table. If the table weren't organized in conceptual order, the description would be even more muddled.

Better: "Each of the other socioeconomic characteristics had a statistically significant association with birth weight in model IV."
The remaining socioeconomic results are described briefly in a separate paragraph with a topic sentence that states the purpose of those variables and identifies the dependent variable again. Statistical significance is summarized up front, eliminating the need to report this information in the text for each variable individually.

Statement 5

Poor: "The coefficient for mother's age was 10.6 (s.e. = 1.2), so it had a smaller effect than less than high school (−54.2; s.e. = 23.0)."
The result for mother's age is reported without pointing out that the effect is per year of age. In addition, the "size" of the effect is misinterpreted relative to the less-than-high-school effect—an error that is more likely when the type of variable and its units are not specified. In this case, mother's age is a continuous variable, whereas educational attainment is categorical, so their effects should not be directly compared (see "Coefficients on Continuous Independent Variables" and "Coefficients on Categorical Independent Variables" in chapter 9).

Better: "Birth weight increased by an average of 10.6 grams for each additional year of mother's age at the time of the child's birth."
The age effect is correctly interpreted as per additional year of age with information on the units of both age and birth weight. Because the pattern of birth weight by mother's education was discussed in detail above (in statement 3), the education coefficients are not interpreted again here.

Statement 6

Poor: "The income-to-poverty ratio had a linear term (81.4) and a square term (−10.1) and both were statistically significant."
By merely reporting the coefficients on income-to-poverty ratio (IPR) and IPR^2, this version leaves readers to figure out the net pattern. Those who aren't mathematically inclined may not know how to do the computations. Even those who routinely work with polynomials must pause to calculate and visualize the shape.

Better: "The linear and square terms on the income-to-poverty ratio (IPR) demonstrate that as the IPR increased, mean birth weight also increased but at a decreasing rate (figure 6.11). For example, an infant born into a family with income at twice the poverty level (e.g., IPR = 2.0) was predicted to weigh about 50 grams more than an infant born to a family at the poverty level (IPR = 1.0), whereas the corresponding difference between infants born into families at 3.0 and 4.0 times the poverty level was only about 10 grams."
The first sentence describes the shape of the relationship between IPR and birth weight and refers to a chart portraying that pattern. The second reports absolute difference in pairs of IPR values at equal increments (one-unit increases in IPR) to help quantify that pattern. If length is an issue, omit the detailed examples.

Statement 7

Poor: "The smoking effect was negative (-193.9, $p < 0.001$)."
Again, no mention of the reference category, dependent variable, or its units.

Better: "Infants whose mothers who smoked weighed considerably less than those born to nonsmokers (-193.9 grams; $p < 0.001$). Although inclusion of the smoking variable improved the overall fit of the model, it did not appreciably alter the race/birth weight relation."
This version mentions the reference category, dependent variable and its units, and conveys direction and magnitude of the association. It also reminds readers that the main goal of this analysis is to investigate reasons for the racial difference in birth weight, not to identify all statistically significant predictors of birth weight.

■ COMPARING A SERIES OF NESTED MODELS

Like nesting Matryoshka dolls, nested statistical models can be thought of as fitting within one another. Starting with the smallest model (fewest independent variables), a series of nested models successively includes more independent variables while keeping those from the preceding models. For instance, the models in table 14.3 are nested because model II adds a new block of variables (SES) and retains all others from model I. Model III adds smoking to model II, while model IV adds interactions between race and mother's education to model III. A model that dropped one variable (e.g., mother's age) and added another (e.g., smoking) to model II would *not* be nested with either model II or model III.

Nested models are often used to test for mediating or confounding. For example, you might start with a model that includes only your key predictor, then introduce potential confounders—individually or in conceptual blocks—to illustrate how the effects' estimates on the key independent variable change when those other variables are introduced, as in the models shown in table 14.3.[2]

To describe a series of nested models, begin with a topic sentence that restates the hypotheses you are testing by comparing those models. Broadly sketch out which variables or sets of variables are included in each model. In your table, name each model according to its contents (e.g., "Race only," "Race + SES") or give it a number (e.g., "Model I"), then refer to each model by name as you discuss it in the text. In the table, report the sample size for the set of models, which should be consistent for all models to be compared—check your output.[3]

As you describe the results, emphasize *changes* in the effect estimates for your key independent variable and in overall model goodness of fit rather than describing each model as if it were the only one in the analysis. If you sequentially describe every coefficient in each of several nested models, your readers will lose sight of the forest for the trees. Instead, show them the big picture—the results of the test for mediating or confounding, or improvement in model fit—using the guidelines below to integrate information on individual effect estimates and model goodness of fit.

Effects of Individual Independent Variables

First, report and interpret the coefficient on the key independent variable in the most basic model, then use one or more quantitative comparisons to illustrate how the size and statistical significance of that coefficient changes when potential mediators or confounders are introduced into the model. Next, describe the coefficients on the mediating or confounding variables from the final, most detailed model. If the key independent variable interacts with a mediator or confounder, explain that interaction as in box 14.2b. Finally, succinctly report results for control variables from the final model, referring where possible to expected patterns based on other studies. Don't report coefficients on control variables from each intermediate model unless they change appreciably when other variables are introduced; in such cases, comment on the direction or size of their change and possible reasons for the change rather than simply reporting their coefficients.

Poor: "In model I, the estimated coefficients on non-Hispanic black, Mexican American, and "boy" were −244.5, −68.4, and 116.1, respectively (all $p < 0.01$). In model II, the estimated coefficients on non-Hispanic black, Mexican American, and "boy" were −147.2, −31.0, and 114.7 ($p < 0.01$ except for Mexican American which was NS), and [reports all of the other coefficients in model II]. In model III, the estimated coefficients on non-Hispanic black, Mexican American, and "boy" were . . . [reports all of the other coefficients in model III]."
By simply reporting each of the coefficients from each model, this description fails to address the main purpose of the series of models — assessing the extent to which SES mediates the race/birth weight

relationship. Readers are left to identify the most important comparisons and to do the calculations themselves. Finally, this version doesn't differentiate among key predictors, mediators, or control variables, yielding a long description that essentially reproduces the table in sentence form.

Better: "Results of a series of nested OLS models shows that socioeconomic characteristics and health behaviors account for part of the racial/ethnic difference in birth weight. When those traits were controlled, non-Hispanic black infants born to mothers with at least some college weighed on average 172.6 grams less than their non-Hispanic white peers ($p < 0.001$; model III, table 14.3), a 30% reduction in the deficit of 245.5 grams from the bivariate tabulations (table 14.1). The corresponding decrease in the birth weight gap between Mexican American and non-Hispanic white infants was 66%, from 69.5 grams to 23.1 grams (tables 14.1 and 14.3, respectively) and was no longer statistically significant ($p = 0.31$)."

This version emphasizes change in size and statistical significance of the race/ethnicity coefficients across models rather than simply reporting them for each model.

- It compares bivariate and multivariate results, using percentage change ("a 30% reduction") to quantify the mediating role of the socioeconomic variables in the association between race/ethnicity and birth weight.
- It measures the adjusted difference between Mexican American and non-Hispanic white infants (23.1 grams) and reports the lack of statistical significance. The phrase "no longer statistically significant" implies that although the bivariate difference was statistically significant, the multivariate is not.

Effects on Overall Model Fit

In the table of results, report the goodness of fit (GOF) statistic and associated number of degrees of freedom for each model. In the text, discuss whether the additional variables yield a statistically significant improvement in model fit, reporting results of tests for difference in model fit based on the F-statistic (OLS models) or -2 log likelihood statistic (logit models). See "Testing Statistical Significance of Interactions" in chapter 9 for an illustration of how to test differences in fit across models.

■ LENGTH CONSIDERATIONS

After you have written a draft description of your multivariate model results, review it for completeness and clarity, then consider whether some material can be condensed. Although it is important to keep your readers oriented to the type of multivariate model and the dependent variable, these needn't appear in every sentence. In addition, some journals have word limits that may force you to shorten your description by summarizing or excluding less central findings. Here are a few guidelines.

The W's Revisited

In the first paragraph pertaining to each multivariate model or series of models, name the type of model, the dependent variable and its units, the general concepts embodied in the independent variables, and the table in which the complete set of model results can be found. If results for more than one model are shown in that table, specify the model number, specification name, or subgroup as you introduce the results. Then remove most other references to these topics in that paragraph, retaining only those needed to maintain clarity, such as incorporating the name and units of the dependent variable as you describe size and direction of individual coefficients. At least once in each subsequent paragraph, mention the model number, the dependent variable, and its units and refer to the accompanying statistical table again. When comparing across models, provide information on how they differ, such as inclusion of additional or different independent variables, or a focus on a different subgroup, time period, or statistical method. This information usually can be incorporated into the description of model results. See "The W's" in chapter 2 for more suggestions.

Provide less detail on results for background or control variables than for your key independent variables, important mediators, or confounders. In very short articles, summarize results for such variables in list fashion, and state whether findings corresponded to expected patterns based on previous literature or bivariate associations. Some journals specify that you omit discussion of background variables entirely, presenting their results only in the tables. In such situations, a well-labeled and organized table is essential, since readers must be able to distinguish the roles of the variables and interpret the associated coefficients without guidance from the text.

[Replaces sentences 4–7 in box 14.2b] "Each of the other
 socioeconomic and behavioral characteristics was associated
 with birth weight in the expected direction (all $p < 0.05$)."
 "Findings for gender, age, and region of residence were consistent
 with those shown in table Q [or with patterns from previous
 studies]."

An alternative is to present only unadjusted (bivariate) and adjusted (multivariate) estimates for the key independent variable of interest—a common approach in biomedical journals. For instance,
create a table showing the unadjusted and adjusted estimates (and associated statistical test results) of racial differences in birth weight,
with a footnote listing which variables are controlled in the multivariate model. In the text, describe the direction, magnitude, and statistical significance of the adjusted effect estimate, and summarize
appreciable changes between the unadjusted and adjusted versions
using comparisons such as percentage change (for OLS coefficients)
or change in excess risk (for odds ratios or relative risks).

"Controlling for age, income, and occupation reduces the
 estimated excess cancer risk associated with electromagnetic
 field (EMF) exposure by 33% compared to the unadjusted
 estimate, bringing it closer to the level in the unexposed
 (reference) group. The adjusted estimate implies that people
 exposed to EMFs have roughly twice the cancer risk of the
 unexposed ($p < 0.01$)."

GEE Revisited

To compare across models for different subgroups, time periods, or
outcome categories, use the GEE ("generalization, example, exceptions") approach to summarize which coefficients are similar in direction, magnitude, and statistical significance instead of writing
piecemeal about every coefficient in every model. Report results to be
compared in one table or in adjacent, similarly structured tables.
Name each model as you introduce it, mention the associated table,
then explain how it relates to results of other models. Generalize
as much as possible about similarities and differences of models
rather than writing a complete description of each model as if it were
isolated from the others in that comparison.

Poor: "Among middle-aged women, diabetes was associated with
 a 3.7-fold greater risk of nursing home admission ($p < 0.05$;

table z). [Description of relative risk for several other risk factors among middle-aged women.] Among elderly women, diabetes was associated with a 1.5-fold greater risk of nursing home admission ($p < 0.05$). [Description of relative risks for other risk factors among elderly women.] [Description of relative risk estimates for diabetes and other risk factors separately for middle-aged and elderly men.]"

Not only does this version result in a very long, repetitive description of the same sets of risk factors for each of four age/sex groups, it fails to identify which risk factors have similar effects in all subgroups and which vary.

"Diabetes increased the risk of nursing home admission in all four age/sex groups ($p < 0.05$); relative risks ranged from 1.5 among elderly women to 3.7 among middle-aged women (table z). [Summary of other results for the four age/sex groups, organized by risk factor, and pointing out (where relevant) patterns that fall along age group or sex lines.]"

This version addresses a key objective of this type of analysis: whether various risk factors have similar associations with nursing home admission for each of the age/sex groups under study. A side benefit is that the narrative will likely be shorter and easier to follow than the poor version.

To compare results across different types of statistical specifications, such as logit versus probit models or linear probability models, or different parametric specifications of a baseline hazard, comment on the similarity of direction and statistical significance of coefficients for the independent variables, again generalizing to the extent possible before pointing out exceptions. To compare magnitude of effect sizes across different types of models, first convert them into a consistent metric (e.g., all probabilities).

■ CHECKLIST FOR WRITING ABOUT MULTIVARIATE MODELS

In the methods section of a scientific paper, explain the following.

- Theoretical reasons why a multivariate model is needed for your data and research question.
- The methods, dependent variable and its units or coding, and the roles of other variables.
- How you arrived at your model specification (see chapter 12).

In the results section, include the following steps.

- Present bivariate and three-way associations among your dependent, key independent, and other variables. For simulation or forecasting models, univariate statistics on each of the variables are sufficient.
- Organize your tables, charts, and prose to identify the roles of different variables and models.
- Create separate paragraphs to describe each step of the analysis.

  Write introductory sentences to identify the purpose of each paragraph.

  Write transition sentences to tie the steps of the analysis together.

- Report the direction, magnitude, and statistical significance of results.
- Emphasize results for key variables or contrasts that relate to your main hypotheses.
- To compare across models for different subgroups or specifications, minimize repetition by using the GEE approach to summarize similarities and differences.

Speaking about
Multivariate Analyses

Speeches are a common means of communicating results of multivariate analyses. Although many of the principles described throughout this book apply to speaking about quantitative analyses, there are a few important modifications that will improve your speeches about multivariate analyses or help you translate written documents into spoken form. The first section of this chapter includes a quick overview of time and pacing, use of visual materials, and speaker's notes, with an emphasis on aspects of public speaking that pertain specifically to conveying quantitative information. The second section describes how to create slides for a speech about a multivariate analysis, including text, tabular, and graphical slides. The third section explains how to write speaker's notes to accompany your slides, including my infamous "Vanna White" technique for succinctly but systematically describing a table or chart. The last section provides guidance on rehearsing your speech to make sure it is clear and fits within the allotted time. See Briscoe (1996) for guidance on preparing slides, Montgomery (2003) or Hailman and Strier (1997) for suggestions on speaking to scientific audiences, and Nelson et al. (2002) for recommendations on speaking to applied audiences.

■ CONSIDERATIONS FOR PUBLIC SPEAKING

Three factors together determine how you will design and deliver a speech: your topic, your audience, and the time available to you. Leave out any of those elements as you plan and your talk will not be as successful. For example, the appropriate depth, pace, types of materials, and language for describing results of an analysis of the relationship between exercise, diet, and obesity are very different for a five-minute presentation to your child's fifth-grade class than for a ten-minute talk to a school board nutrition committee or a half-hour presentation to a panel of experts at the National Institutes of Health.

First identify the few key points you want your listeners to understand and remember, taking into account both your topic and audience. Then consider time and pacing before you design the visual materials and speaker's notes.

Time and Pacing

Most speeches have been allocated a specific amount of time, whether five minutes, fifteen minutes, or an hour or longer. There are tradeoffs between the length of time, the amount of material, and the pace at which you must speak. Reduce the range and depth of coverage rather than speeding up your delivery, especially for an audience that is not accustomed to quantitative information. Better to cut detail than to rush an explanation of your central points or fail to leave time for questions and discussion.

Although each person reads a written document at his own pace, members of your listening audience all receive the material at the same rate—the pace at which you show the slides and explain them. During a speech, individuals cannot take extra time to examine a chart or table, or go back to reread an earlier point. Set the tempo to meet the needs of your typical listener rather than aiming to please either the least or most sophisticated members of your audience. Even for scientific audiences, avoid moving at too rapid a clip. If you present results of many different models in a short talk, the findings blur together and the purpose of each gets lost. Decide which results relate to your main objectives, then introduce and explain them accordingly.

Visual Accompaniment

For speeches of more than a few minutes, visual materials focus your audience's attention and provide a structure to your speech. Slides also help listeners recall facts or concepts to which you refer. In the absence of visual reminders, spoken numbers are easily forgotten, so if specific values are important, put them on a slide. This point is doubly true for comparisons, patterns, or calculations: even if you elect not to create slides for every facet of your talk, do provide charts and tables for your audience to follow as you describe key patterns or findings so they don't have to try to envision them as you speak.

A complete set of slides guides you through your material in a logical order and reminds you where you were if you stopped to answer questions from the audience. Some speakers like to create slides for each component of their talks, mixing text slides for introductory, background, and concluding material with charts and tables of results. However, some speakers prefer a less formal approach, with slides only of essential tables and charts. Even if you use a comprehensive set of slides in some situations, you may want only selected slides in others. For example, although I usually create slides for the whole talk for short professional presentations, I rarely use that approach when teaching. I've found that putting every aspect of a lecture on slides discourages student participation, so I generally create slides only of tables, charts, or equations that I plan to discuss. Working from a written outline or notes, I then introduce each topic, interweaving questions that require students to supply details from readings, describe patterns in the charts or tables, practice calculations, or provide illustrative anecdotes for the points under discussion.

To decide among these different approaches, consider the available time and your own experience, style, and desired extent of interaction with your audience.

Speaker's Notes

Effective slides reduce full sentences into short phrases and reduce complex tables and charts into simpler versions. Accompanying speaker's notes include full sentences and paragraphs to introduce, flesh out, and summarize the information on each slide, and to provide the wording of transitions between slides. For a "generalization, example, exceptions" (GEE) description of a chart or table, speaker's notes are a place to store clear, concise, well-organized explanations that you have tested on similar audiences. Notes can prompt you about which aspects of tables or graphs to emphasize, or remind you of good examples or analogies to reinforce points on the slide. Perhaps most important, speaker's notes are a reminder *not* to simply read the material on your slide out loud—a truly deadening way to give a presentation. More detailed guidelines on writing speaker's notes are given below.

■ SLIDES TO ACCOMPANY A SPEECH

Slides focus and direct your audience and display the facts and patterns mentioned in the speech. With the advent of computerized presentation software such as PowerPoint, it is easy to produce text, tabular and graphical slides, and accompanying speaker's notes. Such software automatically formats the material with large type, bullets, and other features that enhance readability and organization. Once the slides have been created, it is simple to reorganize text within and across slides, adding or removing material to create longer or shorter versions of talks, or making other revisions. Depending upon available audiovisual equipment, these materials can be projected from a computer directly onto an auditorium screen, printed onto overhead transparencies or slides, or printed as paper handouts.

Recently, a backlash has emerged against the use of PowerPoint and other presentation software, stating that these programs have lead to inferior content and organization of slides, overreliance on fancy graphics, and substitution of rote reading of slides for other, more engaging means of presentation (Tufte 2003, Schwartz 2003). Used poorly, any tool—whether a hammer, paintbrush, or presentation software—can be used to produce substandard work. With appropriate training and good technique, however, these tools can help create exemplary results. Below are guidelines on how to create effective slides for a speech, whether or not you elect to use presentation software.

Organizing Your Talk

For a speech to an academic audience, organize your talk with sections that parallel the sections of a scientific paper: an overview and introduction, review of the key literature, description of your data and methods, results, and conclusions. Below are illustrative slides for the sections of a scientific talk about racial/ethnic and socioeconomic differences in low birth weight based on the material in the previous few chapters. These slides can also be used as the basis for a research poster at a scientific conference, or modified to create a chartbook about your findings. For a talk to an applied audience, devote less time to previous literature or data and methods, focusing instead on the purpose, results, and conclusions of your study. See chapter 16 for more suggestions about posters, chartbooks, and communicating to applied audiences.

Introduction, Overview, and Literature Review

In the introduction, familiarize your audience with your topic: what are the main issues you will be investigating and why are they interesting and important? Incorporate some background statistics about the consequences of the issue under study (figure 15.1) or provide some figures on the frequency with which it occurs (figure 15.2).

Consequences of Low Birth Weight (LBW)

- Premature death
  - 24 times as likely as normal-weight infants to die in infancy.

- Other health problems
  - In infancy
  - In childhood
  - In adulthood

- Developmental problems
  - Physical
  - Mental

Note: LBW < 2,500 grams (5.5 pounds)

Figure 15.1. Introductory slide: Bulleted text on consequences of issue under study.
Sources: Martin et al. 2002; U.S. Environmental Protection Agency 2002; Institute of Medicine 1985.

For speeches of 20 minutes or more, consider starting with an overview slide which outlines the topics you will cover (figure 15.3).

Unless you have half an hour or more for your speech, devote much less attention to reviewing the published literature on your topic than you would in a written description of the same study. Often you can incorporate a few essential citations into your introduction. If a comparison of individual articles is important, consider summarizing their key conclusions on your topic in tabular form (e.g., figure 15.4).

Data and Methods

Introduce your data, starting with the W's (who, what, when, where, and how many), type of study design, and response rates for your data sources (figure 15.5). Define your variables on one or more slides in the data and methods section. If you define them as you present the results, viewers tend to focus on the numeric findings rather than listening to how the variables were measured and defined. Create

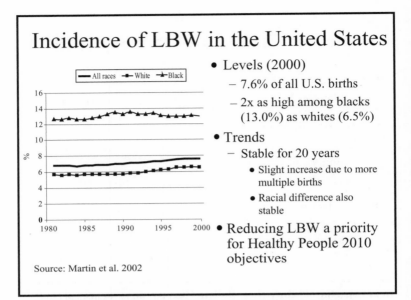

Figure 15.2. Introductory slide: Chart and text on incidence of issue under study.

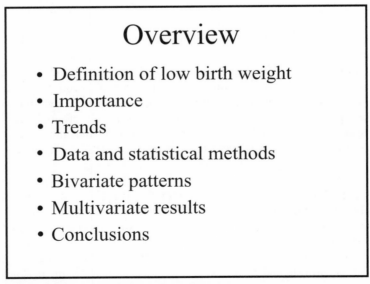

Figure 15.3. Slide outlining contents of speech.

Previous Studies of Race & Birth Weight

Article	Type of study & data source	RR of LBW: black/white	Comments
Smith & Jones (1999)	Sample survey; birth certificates	2.2*	Nationally representative; controlled education
Williams (2000)	Retrospective survey; maternal questionnaires	3.8*	Study in state X; no controls for SES[†]
Travis et al. (1990)	Prospective study; medical records	1.5	Women enrolled in prenatal care clinics in NYC; low SES only

RR: Relative risk.
[†] SES: Socioeconomic status
* $p < .05$.

Figure 15.4. Slide with tabular presentation of literature review.

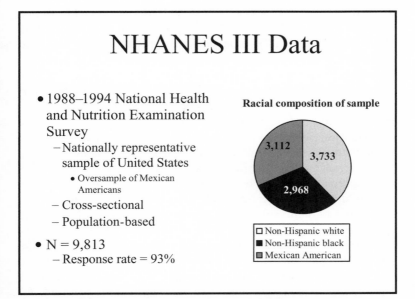

Figure 15.5. Slide describing data source using text and a pie chart.

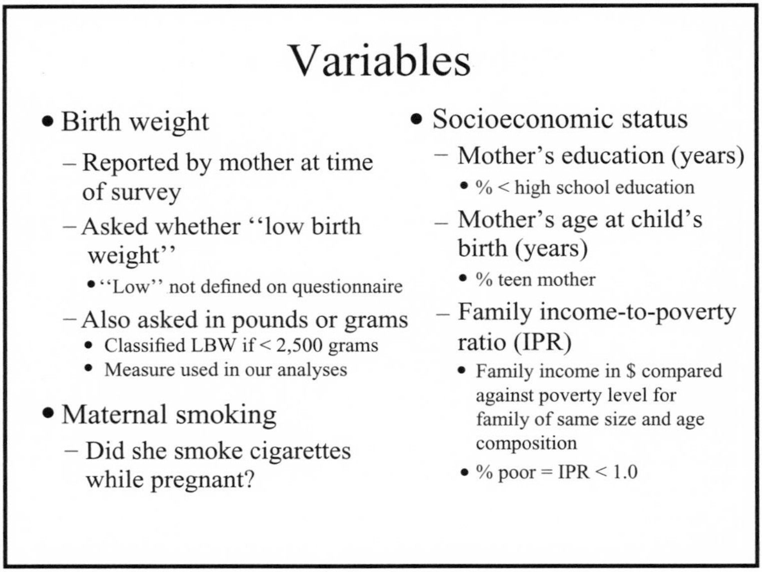

Variables

- **Birth weight**
  - Reported by mother at time of survey
  - Asked whether "low birth weight"
    - "Low" not defined on questionnaire
  - Also asked in pounds or grams
    - Classified LBW if < 2,500 grams
    - Measure used in our analyses

- **Maternal smoking**
  - Did she smoke cigarettes while pregnant?

- **Socioeconomic status**
  - Mother's education (years)
    - % < high school education
  - Mother's age at child's birth (years)
    - % teen mother
  - Family income-to-poverty ratio (IPR)
    - Family income in $ compared against poverty level for family of same size and age composition
    - % poor = IPR < 1.0

Figure 15.6. Slide describing major variables in the analysis.

a text slide listing the variables classified into conceptual blocks (figure 15.6), then use those groupings as you explain your model specifications (see below). For variables such as income or age that could be defined or classified in any of several ways, mention units and explain how your measures of those concepts are defined.

Consider including a schematic diagram to illustrate how your variables are hypothesized to relate to one another (figure 15.7)—showing mediating or confounding relations, for example.

To introduce your multivariate model, include a text slide naming the statistical method, the dependent variable, and whether the analysis was weighted using sampling weights (figure 15.8). For continuous dependent variables, indicate the units in which that variable is measured. For categorical dependent variables, also explain coding (e.g., concepts or numeric cutoffs used to define categories) and which category is being modeled (e.g., *lack* of insurance; *low* birth weight). Omit or use equations sparingly on slides for a speech unless the focus of your talk is on derivation of a new method and the talk is aimed at a statistical audience. Instead, explain model specifications verbally or with reference to tables or charts of results; see chapter 12 for other ideas about substitutes for equations.

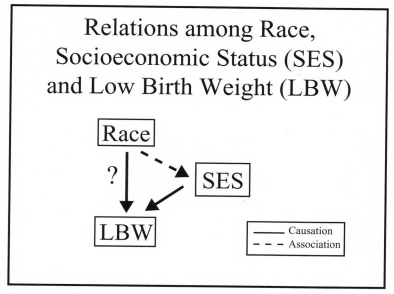

Figure 15.7. Slide with schematic diagram of hypothesized relationship among major variables in the analysis.

Model Specifications

- Linear regression of birth weight in grams
- Logistic regression of low birth weight (<2,500 grams)
- All models weighted to national level using sampling weights from NHANES III

- Model I
  - Race/ethnicity and gender
- Model II
  - Model I + Socioeconomic status (SES)
    - SES includes maternal age, education, family income-to-poverty ratio (IPR).
- Model III
  - Model II + maternal smoking

Figure 15.8. Slide describing model specification for linear and logistic regressions and series of nested models.

If you are presenting a series of nested models, list the set of variables in each model on a methods slide before you present the results, explaining what hypotheses are to be tested by that progression of models (e.g., figure 15.8). If you are presenting separate models for one or more subgroups, list those groups and define if needed.

Results

Start with slides describing the bivariate associations among your key independent variable and dependent variable (figure 15.9) and between the key independent variables and potential mediators or confounders (15.10). To facilitate a GEE summary, the relationships between each of the three socioeconomic variables and race/ethnicity are presented in one clustered bar chart (figure 15.10) rather than as three different bar charts each on a separate slide.

After presenting the bivariate or three-way patterns among key variables, include a transition sentence in your speaker's notes summarizing why those patterns justify a multivariate model, using rhetoric like that in "Building the Case for a Multivariate model" (chap-

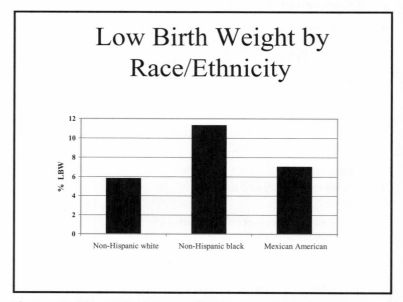

Figure 15.9. Slide of bivariate association between key independent variable and dependent variable.
Source: U.S. DHHS 1997.

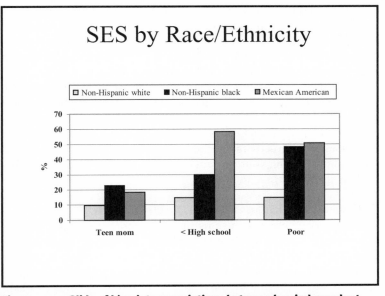

Figure 15.10. Slide of bivariate associations between key independent variable and potential mediators.
Source: U.S. DHHS 1997.

ter 14). Unless you present only the estimates for the key independent variable in the different models (without the effect estimates for the other independent variables), create separate slides to address differ-ent aspects of your hypotheses, each with a title related to the specific relation shown therein (see examples below). For each slide of multi-variate results, include a footnote listing what else was controlled in the model or indicate that results were based on a specification de-scribed on an earlier slide.

For your first slide of multivariate results, focus on the key inde-pendent variable. Report size, direction, and statistical significance in models with and without controls, using a chart or simple table to show how these change across models. If your model includes inter-actions or polynomials involving that variable, show the net patterns in a chart or small table. On separate slides, show the estimated ef-fects of mediating or confounding variables, either in charts, small fo-cused tables, or text slides. To present results for several categorical independent variables on one slide, create a chart with confidence in-tervals around the coefficients or odds ratios. If your model includes both continuous and categorical independent variables, create separate graphs to avoid inappropriate comparisons of their coefficients, such as those in point (5) for box 14.2a. Summarize findings for control variables in a text slide or simple table. See "Adapting Tables and Charts for Slides" below for illustrative examples.

On text or tabular results slides, indicate statistical significance with color and/or symbols rather than detailed standard errors, test statistics or p-values. If your audience is interested in contrasts beyond those in H_0: $\beta = 0$ (e.g., whether $\beta_{<HS} = \beta_{=HS}$), present results of those contrasts directly rather than asking viewers to perform mental calculations during your presentation (see "Testing Other Hypotheses" in chapter 10).

Conclusions

Summarize your conclusions in one or more text slides such as figure 15.11, relating the findings back to your original research question or hypotheses, pointing out new questions that arise from your results, and discussing the policy and research implications of those findings. See "Data and Methods in the Discussion Section" in chapter 12 for more ideas.

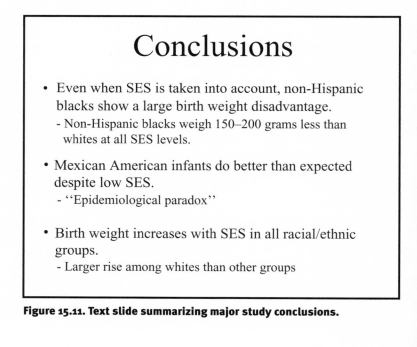

Conclusions

- Even when SES is taken into account, non-Hispanic blacks show a large birth weight disadvantage.
  - Non-Hispanic blacks weigh 150–200 grams less than whites at all SES levels.

- Mexican American infants do better than expected despite low SES.
  - ''Epidemiological paradox''

- Birth weight increases with SES in all racial/ethnic groups.
  - Larger rise among whites than other groups

Figure 15.11. Text slide summarizing major study conclusions.

General Guidelines for Slides

"KISS"

"Keep it simple, stupid," to reiterate one of the principles from chapter 2. Design each slide to concentrate on one or two major points, with title and content to match. Doing so divides your material into small, readily digestible chunks that are easier to organize into a logical, straightforward sequence. Simple, uncluttered slides have another advantage: each can be covered in a minute or two—a much better way to maintain your audience's attention than showing the same crowded slide for several minutes while you slog through each of its contents.

How Many Slides?

Figure on an average of one slide per minute, then err on the low side to avoid rushing and to permit time for questions or discussion. Although a simple text slide can often be covered in 30 seconds, those showing complex patterns or several specific facts may require several minutes apiece. If you are drafting a talk from a written document, start by creating one slide for each major paragraph or topic to be discussed. For short talks, be parsimonious in selecting what material to cover: a 15-minute talk obviously cannot accommodate one slide for every paragraph and statistical model in a 30-page document. Determine which parts of the paper are essential for introducing and answering the key points you have identified for your audience and time limit, then design slides accordingly.

Slide Formats

Like written documents, slides can include text, tables, graphs, diagrams, maps, and other types of graphical images. To enhance the visual appeal of your slides and introduce texture into your talk, vary the design of your slides to include a combination of these elements.

Slide Titles

Good titles guide listeners through your talk, introducing the specific purpose of each slide and orienting listeners to the different sections of the talk. To outline a new speech or revise an existing talk for a new audience, write the titles for each of your slides before you fill in the body of the slide. Give each slide a short, specific title to identify the objective or content of that particular slide. General titles such as "Introduction" or "Results" tend to be ignored if they are repeated for several consecutive slides. The title features prominently on each slide—at the top in large type. Take advantage of that size and position: write informative titles! For instance, although the slides shown in figures 15.1 through 15.3 all comprise parts of the introduction, their titles clearly identify which facet of the introductory material is covered in the respective slides.

Some speakers like to title each slide with a concluding point or rhetorical question related to the slide contents. For example, the title to figure 15.2 could be replaced with "LBW Stable over Past Two Decades" or "Has LBW Declined over Time?" Alternatively, put a title such as "Incidence of LBW" on the slide, then paraphrase it into a concluding point or rhetorical question as you introduce the slide.

Text Slides

Text slides can be used throughout a presentation, as an outline (figure 15.3), in the introduction (figure 15.1), in the data and methods section (figure 15.6), and in the discussion and conclusions (figure 15.11). Text slides also work well to summarize a few key points from previous studies, state hypotheses, list major results, or provide an executive summary. As you design each text slide, put vital numbers in a prominent position in large type, and make sure to report and explain them before they are used in any calculations or discussion. A NASA presentation about possible explanations of damage to the shuttle *Columbia*'s wing during its fatal flight placed critical numeric information in a footnote on the last slide where it was easily overlooked, making it hard to follow the logic of the investigation or understand its conclusions (Schwartz 2003).

Resist the urge to cut and paste sentences from a written document or speaker's notes into your slides. Instead, simplify your paragraphs and sentences into bulleted text phrases, aiming for no more than six bullets per slide and no more than six to ten words or numbers per bullet (Briscoe 1996; Fink 1995). These guidelines force you to plan simple, focused slides, and enhance readability by permitting large type and ample white space.

Bullets. Create a separate bullet for each concept, definition, or fact. Revise sentences into bulleted format in the following ways.

- Include only the essential words from each sentence — nouns, verbs, adjectives, and adverbs.
- Look for commas or the words "and" or "or" to identify clauses or elements of a list, each of which can become its own bullet item.

- Substitute common mathematical symbols such as $<$, $>$, $=$, $\#$, or $\%$ for their equivalent phrases.
- Use arrows to convey directionality and causation.
- Eliminate most other words from the slide.
- Cast all bulleted points in the same syntax. If one is a sentence, make all sentences. Make all bullet points either active or passive, and use a consistent tense throughout. It's much easier to take in and remember points conveyed in a consistent, predictable form.

After you have drafted a bulleted version of a sentence or paragraph, review it to see whether more words can be eliminated without loss of meaning, or if additional words are needed to maintain clarity. Full sentences can be used in the accompanying speaker's notes.

Indenting. Use indenting to organize the material on a slide, presenting supporting facts or clusters of related information under one heading. In figure 15.6, socioeconomic status (SES) is one of several conceptual blocks of variables in the analysis. Indented below the bullet "socioeconomic status" is a list of the different SES measures, with one variable per bullet. Indented yet again beneath each of the SES measures is the categorical version used in this study to indicate low SES.

Observe how these principles improve the introductory slide shown in figure 15.12.

Poor: Figure 15.12.

The slide includes the full text sentences from the introductory paragraph of the paper upon which the talk is based. Although each sentence is given its own bullet, the sentences crowd the slide and encourage viewers to read rather than listen. The title of the slide describes its position in the talk but does not identify the contents or issues addressed.

Better: Figures 15.1 and 15.2.

These slides include the essential information from the poor version but are more succinct and better organized. The titles clue listeners into the specific topics and purposes of the slides. Clauses are broken into separate lines, with supporting information indented.

For an academic audience, mention citations in the bullets or as footnotes. For lay audiences, omit citations except for public figures or widely recognized authorities (e.g., the Centers for Disease Control).

> # Introduction
>
> - "Low birth weight," which is defined as a weight of less than 2,500 grams or 5.5 pounds, is a widely recognized risk factor for infant mortality and a variety of other health and developmental problems through childhood and even into adulthood (Institute of Medicine, 1985).
> - In 1999, U.S. infants born weighing less than 2,500 grams (5.5 pounds) were 24 times as likely as normal birth weight infants to die before their first birthday (Mathews, MacDorman, and Menacker, 2002).

Figure 15.12. Example of a poor introductory slide.

Another example, this time from the data and methods:

Poor: Figure 15.13
Again, paragraphs are pasted directly from the paper onto a slide, resulting in an overcrowded slide that is difficult to read.
Better: Figure 15.5
The information from figure 15.13 is broken up into manageable pieces. Racial composition of the sample is presented in a pie chart and the W's and other background information on the data source for the analysis are organized using bullets and indenting.

Diagrams, Maps, and Graphic Images
In many cases a picture is worth a thousand words—a particularly valuable saving in a timed speech. Schematic diagrams can help viewers understand hypothesized relationships among variables (e.g., figure 15.7), using different types of arrows to illustrate association and causation. Timelines can portray the sequence of events under study or illustrate the number and timing of data collection points in a longitudinal study (e.g., figure 12.1). If your topic has an important geographic component, include one or more maps to present statistics

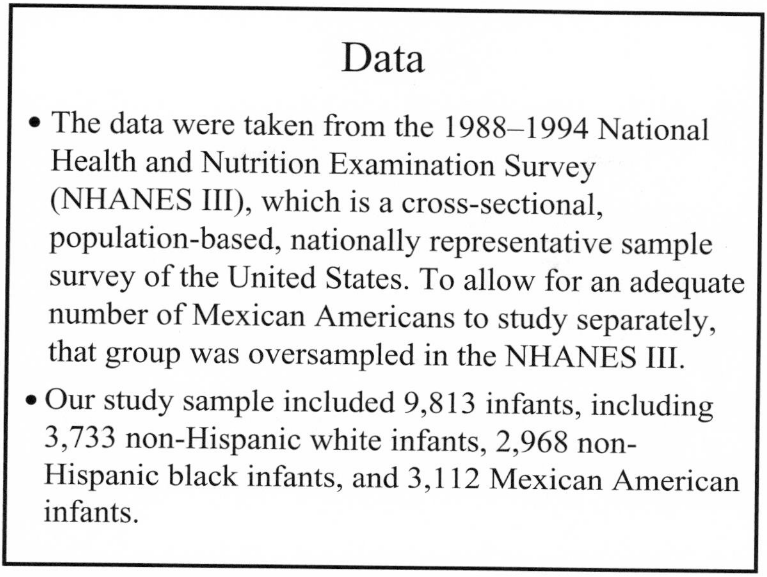

Data

- The data were taken from the 1988–1994 National Health and Nutrition Examination Survey (NHANES III), which is a cross-sectional, population-based, nationally representative sample survey of the United States. To allow for an adequate number of Mexican Americans to study separately, that group was oversampled in the NHANES III.

- Our study sample included 9,813 infants, including 3,733 non-Hispanic white infants, 2,968 non-Hispanic black infants, and 3,112 Mexican American infants.

Figure 15.13. Example of a poor data slide.

such as population density or pollution levels for each area, or to show where the sites you discuss are located relative to hospitals, rail lines, or other features that pertain to your research question. Photographs of people or places can provide a richness difficult to capture in words.

Adapting Charts and Tables for Slides

Use slides with tables, charts, or other graphical material in both brief, general speeches and longer, in-depth presentations. Simple tables of numeric results work well for both scientific and applied audiences. For a scientific talk, a table that organizes and compares key literature on your topic can be very effective (e.g., figure 15.4).

Rather than use tables or charts that were designed for a written document, adapt them to suit a slide format. If your table or chart includes information on more than a few variables, it is impossible to discuss all the patterns simultaneously, so don't ask your viewers to ignore most of a large table or complex chart while you describe one portion. Instead, create two or more slides with simpler tables or charts, each of which includes only the information needed for one

Results

Estimated coefficients from a series of OLS models of birth weight (grams) by race/ethnicity, socioeconomic status and smoking characteristics, United States, 1988–1994

Variable	Model I Infant traits only		Model II Infant traits & SES		Model III Infant traits, SES, & smoking	
	Coeff.	s.e.	Coeff.	s.e.	Coeff.	s.e.
Intercept	3,367.1**	9.6	2,959.5**	39.1	3,039.7**	39.2
Race/ethnicity						
(Non-Hispanic White)						
Non-Hispanic Black	−244.5**	16.7	−147.2**	17.6	−172.6**	17.5
Mexican American	−68.4**	21.6	−31.0	22.6	−23.1	22.7
Boy	116.1**	12.3	114.7**	12.1	117.2**	12.0
Mother's education						
Less than high school			−86.0**	19.3	−55.5**	19.3
High school graduate			−75.2**	14.9	−53.9**	14.8
(College+)						
Interactions: race and education						
Non-Hisp. black × <HS						
Mexican American × <HS						
Non-Hisp. black × =HS						
Mexican American × =HS						
Mother's age at birth of child (yrs.)			11.3**	1.2	10.7**	1.2
Income-to-poverty ratio (IPR)[1]			95.2**	14.6	80.5**	14.5
IPR^2			−11.5**	2.3	−9.9**	2.3
Mother smoked during pregnancy					−194.7**	14.4
F-statistic (df)	102.49 (3)		81.39 (8)		94.1 (9)	
Adjusted R^2	0.032		0.065		0.082	

Note: Weighted to national levels using sampling weights provided with the NHANES III (U.S. DHHS 1997)
[1]Family income divided by the poverty level for a family of that size and age composition.
[a]p < 0.05   [aa]p < 0.01

Figure 15.14. Example of a poor results slide using a table from the paper.
Source: U.S. DHHS 1997.

comparison. Although many publishers set limits on the number of charts or tables in a published document, such restrictions don't affect speeches, so take advantage of that flexibility by creating chart and table slides that concentrate on one or two straightforward relationships apiece.

First, identify the patterns you plan to discuss from a given table or chart, then design simplified versions that focus on one or two major points (or one GEE) apiece. Replace standard errors or test statistics with symbols or formatting to identify statistically significant results (see chapter 10).

Poor: Figure 15.14

The type size for the table, which was copied and pasted directly from the accompanying paper, is far too small for a slide. Even if you circle or highlight the numbers to which you refer, it is difficult for viewers to find (let alone read) those numbers and their associated labels. Do you really plan to discuss all those coefficients and standard errors during your

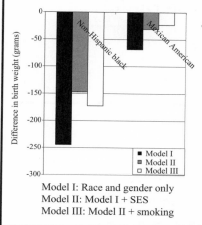

Mediating Effects of SES

- Controlling for SES reduces birth weight gap between non-Hispanic white and other infants:
  —— Deficit reduced by 40% for non-Hispanic black infants
    • 245 grams vs. 147 grams*
  —— Deficit reduced by 55% for Mexican American infants
    • 68 grams vs. 31 grams

Model I: Race and gender only
Model II: Model I + SES
Model III: Model II + smoking

Compared to non-Hispanic white infants born to women with at least some college

*Difference between Models I and II significant at $p < 0.01$.

Figure 15.15. Results slide: Chart to illustrate change in estimated coefficients from nested models.
Source: U.S. DHHS 1997.

talk? To describe the coefficients, you would have to ask viewers to wade through a lot of microscopic print to find the few numbers that pertain to each point.

Better: Figures 15.15, 15.16, and 15.17

The results from the table have been transformed into three separate slides, each of which presents data for one aspect of the story. Although this approach results in more slides, it takes no longer to describe because the amount of material is unchanged. It may even save time, because less guidance is needed to find the pertinent numbers for each comparison. The title of each slide names the variables or relationships in question. Symbols or confidence intervals present statistical significance, and other variables in the model are listed in footnotes. Speaker's notes would introduce each slide by identifying the role of the variables before describing the pattern and the findings on the topic at hand.

- Figure 15.15 uses a clustered bar chart to show how the birth weight deficit between non-Hispanic black and Mexican

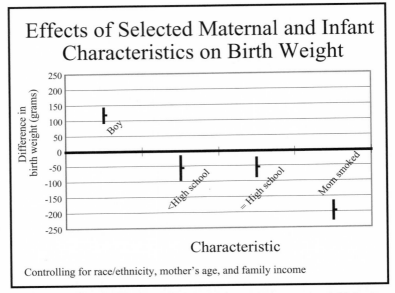

Figure 15.16. Results slide: High/low/close chart to present coefficients from categorical independent variables.
Source: U.S. DHHS 1997.

American infants and non-Hispanic white infants changes across nested models.

- Figure 15.16 portrays the estimated coefficients and confidence intervals for the categorical independent variables from model III.
- Figure 15.17 illustrates the nonlinear relationship between the income-to-poverty ratio (IPR) and birth weight, depicting the net effect of the linear and square terms on IPR from model III.

Mixed Format Slides

If your charts or tables are fairly clear-cut (e.g., a 2-by-2 table, or a pie, single-line, or simple bar chart), consider a "chartbook" layout: a table, chart, or other image occupies one side of the slide, with bulleted text annotations on the other side (e.g., figure 15.2 or figure 15.5). Put more complicated tables or charts alone on a slide, then describe

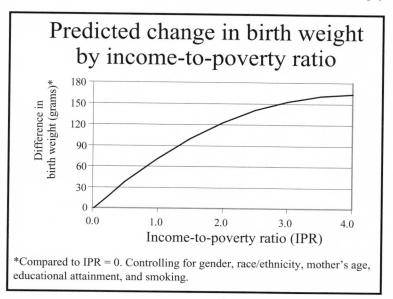

Figure 15.17. Results slide: Chart to show net effect of nonlinear specification of a continuous independent variable.
Source: U.S. DHHS 1997.

the pattern in your speaker's notes or make an additional slide with a short written summary.

■ **DESIGN CONSIDERATIONS**

Substance over Style

Don't give in to the temptation to let the features available in presentation software packages carry your show. Fancy, multicolored background designs, animated text, or sound effects might impress your audience for a moment or two, but if they distract from your story line or substitute for correct, clearly presented material, they will do more harm than good. Whatever time you put into creating a dog-and-pony show is taken away from selecting and organizing the information and writing a clear narrative.

Focus on the substance, not the style, of the slides. First, get the content and organization right, just as you would for a written description of the same material. After you have practiced and revised your talk (see below), consider adding a bit of color or animation *only if they enhance your presentation.*

Color

That said, judicious use of color can enhance communication appreciably, giving you another tool for conveying information. For instance, use red type to identify all of the statistically significant findings in tables or text slides, leaving nonsignificant effects in a neutral shade. Once you have explained that color convention, your viewers will quickly be able to ascertain results of all your statistical tests without further explanation. Use a consistent color scheme for all charts within a talk. If non-Hispanic blacks are represented in black in a pie chart illustrating sample composition, for example, use black for that group in all subsequent charts (whether pie, bar, or line charts) that compare patterns across racial/ethnic groups.

A caution about creating handouts from color slides: some color combinations and lighter colors do not reproduce well in grayscale—the typical color scheme for photocopied handouts. To make sure the handouts convey the same information as the projected slides, follow the guidelines in chapter 6 about using color in charts, then review them in black and white on-screen or in print before making copies. Or if your budget and equipment permit, make color handouts.

Type Size

Use a large type size on all slides—at least 18 point type—and avoid fussy calligraphic fonts. For your slides to be of value, they must be readable in the back row. If you aren't sure about the size of the room in which you'll be speaking, err on the generous side when you select your type size (see Zelazny 2001 for specific guidelines). If material you had planned for a single slide will fit only if you use small type, divide that material across several slides until the contents can be displayed with readable type. Ditto for words used to label charts and tables. Even with large type, slides can be difficult to read from the rear of a large auditorium. For such situations, consider printing handouts of your slides; some presentation software can print several slides per page with space for listeners to take notes.

Symbols and Annotations

As you adapt charts or tables for your slides, omit any features such as symbols, reference lines, or other annotations that you don't explain or refer to during your speech. Unless you mention them, they distract your viewers and clutter the slide. Conversely, you may want to add symbols to charts and tables as you modify them for use on slides. For example, your audience won't have time to digest detailed standard errors or test-statistics during your talk, so replace them with symbols for $p < 0.05$ or $p < 0.01$ to save space and reduce the amount of data on the slide. Include footnotes or legends to explain the symbols.

■ HANDOUTS

A question that often arises is whether to hand out statistical tables like those from the printed paper. (By now, you've probably figured out not to give such tables to lay audiences.) Unless I am presenting at a long seminar where active audience discussion of detailed results is expected, my preference is to distribute such tables after the presentation. This approach gives readers the full set of numbers to peruse at their leisure without getting distracted during the talk. If you want to give handouts for viewers to follow along with a shorter speech, include copies of the most critical slides. Coordinate the handouts with your slides so you and your viewers are looking at the same set of materials as you speak.

Poor (for a short speech): A paper handout of a detailed statistical table, unaccompanied by any slides.

Although you could try to describe each number's position (e.g., "in the fourth row of variables, sixth column labeled 'coeff.' under model III, do you see the value −172.6?"), without a slide, you don't have anything to point at to guide your viewers.

Poor (version 2): A paper handout of a detailed table (e.g., table 14.3) accompanied by simplified slides such as 15.15 through 15.17.

If the table and the slides don't look alike, you will squander even more time guiding readers to the portion of their handout that corresponds to the material on each slide. If you use a handout, make it match your slides, or distribute the detailed tables at the end for later inspection.

Better: Slides 15.15 through 15.17, shown on the screen and reproduced in a handout.

By dividing the analytic points across several slides, you can describe each issue in turn, referring to numbers that you point out on a simple table or chart.

■ WRITING SPEAKER'S NOTES

Having created slides that present the essential textual and graphical elements of your talk, write speaker's notes to fill in the details and transitions among slides. Although you can draw heavily on the content and organization of a paper or book when formulating these notes, avoid recycling large blocks of text in your speech. Rarely will you have time to read an entire paper in the time available. Even if time permits, reading a document out loud is a poor substitute for a speech.

Speaker's Notes to Suit Your Style

The notes can be adapted to suit your speaking style and level of experience. If you are a novice, are uncomfortable inventing sentences in front of an audience, or have a tendency to be long-winded, you may do best with a full script. The wording for such notes can be pirated largely from the corresponding written paper or article, cutting some of the detail (such as citations) and rephrasing into the first person. For figure 15.5, a script might read:

> "We used data from the 1988–1994 National Health and Nutrition Examination Survey, also known as NHANES III, which is a cross-sectional, population-based, nationally representative sample of the United States. To allow for an adequate number of Mexican Americans to study separately, that group was oversampled in the NHANES III. We excluded infants of racial and ethnic groups not shown on this slide because we did not want to group them with any of these three groups and there were not enough of them to analyze as a distinct group. As shown in the pie chart, our study sample comprised nearly ten thousand infants, approximately equally distributed among the three racial/ethnic groups studied."

If you are at ease speaking extemporaneously and are able to keep yourself on schedule, you may need only a list of additional points to make or items to underscore. For the same slide, such notes might read:

> "To allow for an adequate number of Mexican Americans to study separately, that group was oversampled in the NHANES III."
> "As shown in the pie chart, our study sample comprised approximately equal numbers of the three racial/ethnic groups studied."

Before reading those notes, restate the information in the title and bullets into two or three complete sentences. Using selected reminders takes more practice than working from notes that comprise the full speech because you must remember where each typed note fits within the overall description of each slide. Key your notes to your slides to coordinate the spoken and visual components of your speech. Some presentation software programs allow you to type speaker's notes for each individual slide. If you write your notes longhand or in a word processor, write the number of the slide, table, or chart in the margin next to the associated text to remind yourself when to change slides. Do yourself a favor and print your speaker's notes in large type so you won't have to squint to read them as you deliver your speech.

Explaining a Chart "Live"

Tables, charts, maps, and other diagrams offer real advantages for presenting numeric patterns. Unfortunately, many speakers devote far too little time to describing such slides. They put up the slide, state "as you can see, . . . " and then describe the pattern in a few seconds before moving on to the next slide. As the slide disappears, many listeners are still trying to locate the numbers or pattern in question and have not had time to digest the meaning of the statistics. This disease plagues rookie and veteran speakers alike: Beginners may not want to spend very long on a chart out of fear that they will run out of time (or because they just want to get their talks over with). Experts forget that not everyone is conversant with their chart or table layouts or may be too uppity to explain such rudiments.

Although it may appear to save time, failing to orient your listeners to your charts or diagrams reduces the effectiveness of your talk. If you designed the chart and wrote the accompanying talk, you know it well enough to home in quickly on the exact number or table cell or trend line you wish to discuss. Give your audience the same advantage by showing them where to find your numbers and what questions they address before you report and interpret patterns.

Introduce the Topic

First, state the topic or purpose of the table or chart, just as you do in the introductory sentence of a written paragraph. Rather than read the title from the slide, paraphrase it into a full sentence or rephrase it as a rhetorical question. For figure 15.10:

"This slide examines racial and ethnic patterns in each of three indicators of low socioeconomic status. In other words, 'Does socioeconomic status vary by race?'"

Explain the Layout

Second, explain the layout of the table or chart. Don't discuss any numbers, patterns, or contrasts yet. Just give your audience a chance to digest what is where. For a table of several multivariate models, show which model is in which column, then name the major variables in the rows. For a chart, identify the concepts and units on the different axes and in the legend, mentioning the color or shading of bars or line styles that correspond to each major group you will discuss. For maps or other diagrams, point out the location of different features and explain the meaning of legend items or other elements such as arrows, symbols, or scales.

Use a "Vanna White"[1] approach as you explain the layout, literally pointing out the applicable portion of the table or chart as you mention it. Point with a laser pointer, pen, or finger—it doesn't matter. The important thing is to lead your viewers' eyes across the key features of the slide before reporting or interpreting the information found there. At first this may seem silly or awkward, but most audiences follow and retain the subsequent description much more easily than if you omit the guided tour.

Below, I use bracketed comments to describe the Vanna White motions that accompany the surrounding script; they are there to guide you, not to be spoken as part of the presentation. For figure 15.10:

"Across the bottom [wave horizontally at the *x* axis], there is one cluster for each of the three socioeconomic characteristics—teen motherhood, incomplete high school, and poverty [point quickly at each label in turn]. Each racial/ethnic group [point to the legend] is displayed with a different color bar, and the height of a bar [gesture vertically along the *y* axis] shows the percentage of that racial or ethnic group with the associated characteristic."

For figure 15.17:

"The income-to-poverty ratio is shown on the *x* axis, ranging from zero to four times the poverty level. The *y* axis shows the increment in birth weight relative to infants in families with an income-to-poverty ratio of 0, controlling for the other variables in the model, which are listed at the bottom of the slide."

In the next step, you will give a specific example and introduce the bar colors for each subgroup. For lay audiences, "*x* axis" and "*y* axis" may be fuzzily recalled jargon. Instead, use phrases like "across the bottom" or "on the vertical axis," respectively.

If you are explaining a chart with more than three or four nominal variables or categories, mention the organizing principle you have used rather than simply naming each of the categories. As always, coordinate the narrative with the layout of the chart.

> "In figure 6.5, the different AIDS transmission topics are shown on the horizontal axis [point] grouped into "likely" modes on the left [wave at that group of clusters] and "unlikely" modes on the right [gesture]. Within those groupings, the topics are arranged in descending order of average score [wave along the tops of the bars within one group of clusters]."

Describe the Patterns

Finally, having introduced your audience to the purpose and layout of the table or chart, proceed to describe the patterns it embodies. Use the GEE approach, starting with a general descriptive sentence followed by specific numeric examples and exceptions (where pertinent). Again, gesture to show comparisons and point to identify specific values, naming the associated colors or shading schemes for each group the first time you mention it, as shown in the following description of figure 15.10.

> "Regardless of which dimension of socioeconomic status we examine, non-Hispanic black infants, illustrated with the black bar, and Mexican American infants—the dark gray bar [point at legend]—are far more likely than their non-Hispanic white counterparts, in light gray [point at legend element], to be born into low SES families. The black and dark gray bars are higher than the light gray bar in each of the three clusters. For example [gesture at the right-most cluster], infants of color are more than three times as likely to be poor as their white counterparts [point to the respective bars as you mention them]."

For figure 15.17:

> "As the income-to-poverty ratio (abbreviated IPR) increases, birth weight also increases, but at a decreasing rate. For example, predicted birth weight is about 50 grams heavier for infants born into families at twice the poverty level than for those at the

poverty level [point to IPR curve between IPR = 0 and 1]. In contrast, an increase in IPR from 3 to 4 is associated with a predicted increase in birth weight of only about 10 grams [gesture along curve between IPR = 3 and 4]."

As you describe your charts, tables, or other graphics, point to and explain the purpose of features such as reference lines or regions, colors, symbols, or other annotations. For example,

"In figure 15.16, the reference line at $y = 0.0$ [wave along reference line] helps distinguish the factors that are associated with higher birth weight, such as male gender [point to vertical line for "Boy"], from those associated with lower birth weight, such as maternal smoking during pregnancy [point to line for "Mom smoked"]. The 95% confidence interval for each coefficient is shown with the vertical line extending above and below the respective point estimate [wave vertically along one such line]. None of the 95% confidence intervals on this slide cross the reference line [wave horizontally along reference line] corresponding to the null hypothesis of no difference in birth weight between groups, hence all the coefficients shown here are statistically significant at $p < 0.05$."

"In table *yyy*, relationships that were statistically significant at $p < 0.05$ are shown in orange and are marked with asterisks [point to the footnote on the slide that defines the asterisk]. For example, the difference in average math scores between boys and girls was statistically significant [point to pertinent cells], but most other comparisons in the table were not."

Until you are confident that you can recall your Vanna White description, include it in your speaker's notes, either in full sentences or as circles and arrows on a hard copy of the chart, numbered to help you recall the order in which you plan to explain each feature.

■ PRACTICE, PRACTICE, PRACTICE

After you have drafted your slides and accompanying notes, practice your presentation, first alone and then with a test audience. If someone else wrote the speech and made the slides, all the more reason to review and practice. Rehearsal is particularly important for slides involving tables or charts, which are usually more complex than simple text slides. Likewise for slides explaining methods, especially if you have not worked previously with those methods or explained multivariate models to that type of audience.

Time how long the entire talk takes, anticipating that you will become somewhat faster with practice (and adrenaline). If you will be using a Vanna White approach, rehearse speaking and gesturing at the associated chart until you are comfortable coordinating those two actions. Evaluate the order in which you've covered the material, making sure you define terms, acronyms, and symbols before you use them, and that your results are in a logical order with good transitions to convey where they fit in the overall story.

If you exceeded the allotted time by more than a minute or two, identify which sections were too long and assess what can be condensed or eliminated. Some sections will require more time than others, so you may have to omit detail or simplify explanations in other parts of your talk, taking into account what your audience knows (and needs to know). If you finished well under time, think about where additional material or explanation would be most useful. If you were under time but rushed your delivery, slow down.

Revise the coverage, level of detail, and order of material to reflect what you learned from your dry run. If you make substantial revisions, practice on your own again before you enlist a test audience. To assist yourself in pacing your talk, insert reminders in your speaker's notes to indicate where you should be at certain time points so you can speed up or slow down as necessary during your talk. As you are introduced at the talk, write down the actual start time and adjust these time points accordingly.

Dress Rehearsal

Once you have a draft of slides and notes that you are comfortable with, rehearse your talk in front of a colleague or friend who represents your audience well in terms of familiarity with your topic, data, and multivariate methods. If you differ substantially from your prospective listeners on those dimensions, it is difficult to "put yourself in their shoes" to identify potential points of confusion. A fresh set of eyes and ears will be more likely to notice such issues than someone who is jaded from working closely with the material while writing the paper or drafting the slides and talk.

Before you begin your dress rehearsal, ask your guinea pig audience to make notes on the following aspects of your talk:

- Were the objectives of your talk plainly identified?
- Were the purpose and interpretation of your numeric examples evident?
- Were your definitions of terms and concepts easy to grasp? Did you define terms before you used them?
- Did you use jargon that could be replaced by terms more familiar to this audience?
- Was the type of model, the dependent variable, and its units or coding clearly identified?
- Were the model specifications and associated hypotheses easily understood?
- Were your descriptions of tables or charts clear and not too rushed? Was it easy to see where your numeric examples came from in those tables or charts? To follow the patterns you described?
- If you were over time, what material could be omitted or explained more briefly? If under time, where would more information or time be most beneficial?
- Was the amount of time for each section about right? If not, which sections need more or less emphasis?

Go over your reviewers' comments with them, then revise your talk and slides accordingly. Practice yet again if you make appreciable changes.

■ CHECKLIST FOR SPEAKING ABOUT NUMBERS

Before you plan your speech, consider your topic, audience, and amount of time, pacing the talk for the average listener and allowing time for questions and discussion.

- Slide format and content: adapt material from your paper, following the same sequence of major topics.

    For a scientific audience, include an introduction, literature review, data and methods, results, discussion, and conclusions.

    For applied audiences, omit the literature review and condense the data and methods.

    Write a simple, specific title for each slide.

    Replace full sentences with bullets.

    Simplify tables and charts to focus on one major question per slide.

Create no more than one slide per minute, fewer if slides involve tables or charts.

- Speaker's notes: decide whether you need a full script or selected notes. In either case, follow these steps:

  Write an introductory sentence.

  Note aspects of the slide you want to emphasize.

  Include analogies or examples you will use to flesh out the material.

  Write a Vanna White description of charts or tables.

  –Paraphrase the purpose of the slide.

  –Explain the layout of the table (contents of rows and columns) or chart (axes, legend), with notes about which elements to point to for each sentence.

  –Describe the pattern, listing which illustrative numbers you will point to as you speak.

  Write a summary sentence.

  Insert a transition to the next slide.

- Other design considerations:

  Use at least 18 point type for titles and text; smaller for footnotes.

  Consider using color to emphasize selected points or terms, or to indicate statistical significance.

- Rehearsing your talk. First alone, then with a critic familiar with your intended audience, evaluate the following:

  Order and relative emphasis of topics

  Definitions of terms

  Level of detail

  Introductions and explanations of charts and tables

  Coordination of spoken and visual materials

  Time to complete the talk

Writing for Applied Audiences

Many potential audiences for results of multivariate analyses are "applied audiences"—people who raise questions that can be answered using such models, but who are interested principally in the answers rather than the technical details of how they were obtained. Writing about multivariate analyses for applied audiences is a routine task for statistical consultants, policy analysts, grant writers, and science writers; academics and other researchers also must do so when addressing funding agencies or others from outside the research community.

Earlier in this book, I explained how to write papers or reports describing multivariate analyses to audiences with training in those statistical methods. In this chapter, I illustrate how to translate findings of those same analyses so they are comprehensible to a wide range of people, but without "dumbing down" the models themselves. I begin by discussing audience considerations, then cover how to adapt tables, charts, and text for different formats commonly used for applied audiences, including posters, chartbooks, reports, and issue briefs. I also illustrate how to write an executive summary, which can be used to accompany reports or chartbooks. These formats are also effective ways to present results of more elementary inferential or descriptive statistics; see examples under specific formats below. For an in-depth review of different formats and considerations for communicating to applied audiences, see Nelson et al. (2002).

For most people, statistical analysis is not the end in itself, but rather a tool—a way to address questions about relationships among the concepts under study. For complex statistical analyses to be genuinely useful and interesting to an applied audience, make your results accessible to people who understand the substantive context of your analysis, whether or not they "do statistics" themselves. A few common examples:

- Policy analysts must explain results of their models to experts in government or nonprofit agencies—professionals who are well-versed in the issues and their application, but few of whom are skilled statisticians. Their principal interest is in the findings and how to interpret and apply them, along with reassurance that you know how to use the statistical models correctly.

- Economic consultants have to communicate results of their models to professionals in corporations, community development agencies, and other settings. Again, their clients bring many other pertinent types of knowledge to the table but may not know much about statistics.

- Grant writers must explain their models to nonstatistical reviewers at charitable foundations as well as to both statistical and substantive reviewers at scientific research institutes such as the National Science Foundation. Nonstatistical reviewers will be interested in why a multivariate model is needed to analyze the issues at hand and how the results can be applied, rather than in the detailed statistical specifications.

- Science writers have to communicate findings to readers of the popular press.

For people trained in multivariate analysis, nonstatistical audiences are often the most difficult to write for. Most of us who use these methods learned about them in courses that emphasized understanding statistical assumptions, estimating models, interpreting statistical tests, and assessing coefficients and model fit. Sensibly, the material in these courses is conveyed using a teaching style, with the expectation that the audience (students) will repeat each of these steps, demonstrating mastery by working with equations written in statistical notation and identifying the relevant numbers for formal hypothesis testing.

Readers with training in regression methods can work from such shorthand and do much of the interpretation themselves, given the statistical output from the model. However, nonstatisticians cannot be expected to extract the information they want from such raw materials, any more than most of us can create artisanal bread from a bag of ingredients. We expect bakers to make bread for us regardless of our expertise in (or ignorance of) their techniques. Most of us wouldn't be able to replicate their work even given a detailed recipe and we don't want a lecture on how to bake every time we buy a loaf of bread. Likewise, applied audiences expect us to put our results in a format they can appreciate regardless of their proficiency (or lack thereof) with multivariate statistical methods. Few of them could reproduce our analyses even given meticulous instructions and they don't want a sermon on multivariate statistics every time they hear about the results. Just as we would be grateful for some interesting serving suggestions for an artisanal loaf of bread, applied audiences will welcome basic guidance about how to understand and apply multivariate model results.

■ ASSESSING YOUR AUDIENCE

There is a wide range of statistical training and interest among applied audiences.

- Some readers want to review the assumptions and methods behind the models, just as some people want to learn alongside an experienced baker which ingredients or techniques yield bread that suits their tastes. If you are creating a model to forecast growth rates in a particular industry, explain to your client which assumptions and variables you plan to include so they can give you feedback about whether those specifications are consistent with their understanding of the subject.

- Some readers want to hear a bit about the analytic approach, just as some people want to know the ingredients and baking techniques their baker uses so they can assess whether it follows the latest nutritional guidelines. If you are writing about determinants of student achievement for a group of professional educators who have heard of multivariate models and have a general sense of why they are important, mention that such a model was estimated and which variables were included.

- Some readers want to know only what questions you addressed and what you concluded, just as some people simply want to enjoy their bread without worrying about its nutritional content or how it was made. If you are giving a five-minute speech to your neighborhood association, concentrate on the concepts and findings, not the statistics, assumptions, or variables.

Before you adapt your writing, assess the interests, statistical abilities, and objectives of your audience. If you will be presenting your findings to several different audiences, plan to create several different versions.

■ WRITING FOR APPLIED AUDIENCES

In general, writing for an applied audience involves greater prominence of the research question, reduced emphasis on technical details of data and methods, and translation of results to show how they apply to real-world issues of interest to that audience. Your main objective is to write a clear, well-organized narrative about your research question and answers. Explain in plain English what you did, why you did it that way, and what it means. Briefly introduce the topic and why it necessitates a multivariate model, then report the results of your models using table and chart formats that are familiar to that audience. For very short formats such as issue briefs or general-interest articles, some of these topics will be omitted; see pertinent sections below.

With the exception of analytic reports or posters for statistical audiences, translate all jargon and every statistical concept into colloquial language, and resist the urge to include equations or Greek symbols. For readers who are interested in the technical details, provide a citation to the scientific papers or reports on your analysis.

Explaining the Need for a Multivariate Model

For most applied audiences, keep your description of the statistical methods brief, emphasizing what your model did that could not have been answered with simpler techniques. Incorporate the specific concepts you study into your explanation.

Poor: "To adjust for confounding by socioeconomic factors and health behaviors, we use multivariate logistic regression to estimate relative odds of low birth weight, with race/ethnicity as our key independent variable."
Don't confuse or repel nonstatisticians with unfamiliar with terms like "confounding," "multivariate logistic regression," "relative odds," and "key independent variable."

Better: "Because chances of low birth weight are affected by socioeconomic factors and behaviors like smoking, our analyses correct for differences in those traits when estimating the racial/ethnic patterns described here."

This version clarifies the concepts and relationships and provides a sense of why the analysis is needed, without relying on off-putting jargon.

Giving an Overview of Methods and Variables

As you present numeric information, rephrase statistical terminology to focus on the underlying ideas, provide the definition of a measure or variable, or show how the concepts apply to your particular topic. For instance, a *New York Times* article about a model to predict age-related changes in runners' marathon times wrote:

> "'I'm right now at the age where things are getting worse in a bigger way,' said Dr. Fair, using colloquial language to describe the increase in the second derivative on his chart" (Leonhardt 2003).
> *This excerpt phrases the statistical concept in everyday language, then ties that wording to the more technical language that statisticians would use.*

To report a type of statistic that is unfamiliar to your audience, embed the definition in your explanation:

Poor: "The sensitivity of the new screening test for diabetes is 0.90."
   People who do not routinely study screening tests may not know what sensitivity is or how to interpret the value 0.90.
Better: "The new screening test had a sensitivity of 0.90, correctly identifying 90% of diabetics."
   This version clarifies both the metric and purpose of "sensitivity."

To explain a statistical method or assumption, replace technical terms with familiar names that illustrate how that general concept applies to your particular research question and data:

Poor: "The data structure can be formulated as a two-level hierarchical linear model, with students (the level-1 unit of analysis) nested within schools (the level-2 unit of analysis)."
   While this description would be fine for readers used to working with this type of model, nonstatisticians may be confused by terminology such as "level-1" and "unit of analysis."
Better (for a nonstatistical but academic audience): "The data have a hierarchical (or multilevel) structure, with students clustered within schools."

By replacing "nested" with the more familiar "clustered," identifying the specific concepts for the two levels of analysis, and mentioning that "hierarchical" and "multilevel" refer to the same structure, this description relates the generic class of statistical model to this particular data analysis.

Better (for a lay audience): "To try to disentangle the contributions of students' and schools' characteristics to the problem of dropping out of school, we used models that incorporated information at both levels."

This version emphasizes the purpose of the analytic approach in the context of the research question at hand. Neither the name nor technical attributes of the statistical method would be of use or interest to most lay audiences.

Explaining Effect Estimates

To explain effect estimates (coefficients) from your models, emphasize the direction and size of the association, incorporating units of measurement and using colloquial language to explain whether the difference is measured in absolute or relative terms.

- "For each additional year of maternal age, predicted birth weight increased by 10.7 grams," instead of "Beta was 10.7."
- "Infants born to smokers had 1.4 times the chances of low birth weight of those born to nonsmokers," instead of "Log-odds of low birth weight for smokers were 0.33."

See chapters 8 and 9 for additional wording recommendations.

Explaining Interactions or Multiterm Patterns

Just as for statistical audiences, present the net effects of interactions or variables involving more than one term; charts are especially effective. Use the "generalization, example, exceptions"(GEE) approach, which is easily understood by most audiences because it emphasizes the substantive patterns before illustrating them with numbers from the associated table or chart. See "Writing about Interactions" in chapter 13 for examples and suggested wording.

Adapting Tables and Charts

Simplify tables and charts, replacing standard errors or test statistics with *p*-values, symbols, or color to denote statistically significant findings (see chapter 10). If your model involves unfamiliar variables or complex mathematical transformations, paraphrase them or replace with a more familiar version. For instance, many lay readers

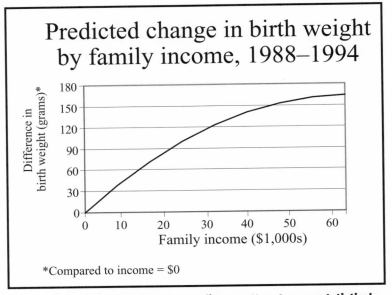

Figure 16.1. Line chart to display a nonlinear pattern to a nonstatistical audience.
Note: Based on multivariate model with controls for gender, race/ethnicity, mother's age, educational attainment, and smoking status. For illustrative purposes, this figure uses the 1999 poverty threshold of $16,895 for a family of two adults and two children. Data are from U.S. DHHS 1997.

will relate better to income in dollars than to the income-to-poverty ratio (IPR), so figure 16.1 converts the IPR into the equivalent income for a family of two adults and two children based on the 1999 Federal Poverty Level, with a footnote to explain that translation. The shape of the association between income and birth weight is the same as that shown in figure 6.11, but will be easier to grasp for readers who aren't conversant with the definition or value of the poverty level.

Statistical Significance

For applied audiences, keep the discussion of statistical significance simple, stressing the conclusions as they apply to your particular research question, not the computational process or logic. No matter how carefully you try to phrase it, a discussion of the purpose and interpretation of statistical tests may confuse readers who are not trained in statistics. Instead of reporting standard errors or test statistics, use statistical tests as a screen for what you report and how you discuss findings. Or paraphrase the concepts behind the statistics into everyday language.

Poor: "In 1997, the mean score on the mathematics test for fourth graders in School A was 62.7% correct. The mean score on the same test in School B was 72.0% correct. The standard error of the difference in means was 2.9. Because the differences in means (9.3 percentage points) is more than twice the standard error of the difference, we conclude that the difference cannot be attributed to random variation in scores at the two schools."
This description puts too much emphasis on the logic behind the statistical test. Skip the statistics lesson and just report whether the difference between the two schools' test scores is statistically significant.

Better: "On a mathematics test given to fourth graders recently, students in School B achieved a lower average score than students in School A (62.7% and 72.0% correct, respectively). The chances of observing a difference this big in our study if there were no real difference between groups was less than one in a thousand."
This description reports the two scores and suggests that they represented different levels of achievement. Statistical significance is worded without reference to technical concepts such as p-values or test statistics.

If, contrary to previous evidence, the difference is not statistically significant, write:

"In 2001, Schools A and B achieved similar average math scores on a standardized mathematics test given to fourth graders (71.7% and 72.0% correct, respectively). These results run counter to findings from 1997, which showed appreciably better performance in School A than in School B. The difference in the schools' current scores could easily have occurred by chance alone."
This version explains that in 2001 the two schools' scores were very close, and that the recent pattern differs from what was previously observed. Statistical significance is implied by the phrase "appreciably better scores" in the earlier study, and lack of statistical significance in the new study by the phrase "chance alone."

Substantive Significance

To convey the substantive importance of your findings, place them in perspective by providing evidence about how they relate to some real-world outcome such as costs or benefits, for the status quo and other alternatives.

Poor: "The association between math curriculums and test scores was not very substantively significant."

Most people won't know what "substantively significant" means. In addition, this version omits both the direction and size of the association, and doesn't help readers assess whether the change is big enough to matter.

Better: "Is the new math curriculum worth the investment? Probably not: the half-point average improvement in test scores translates into only a small (5%) increase in the number of students who pass the test or who master important fourth-grade math skills such as multiplication or division. Implementing the new curriculum would cost an estimated $40 million, which could otherwise be spent on items such as reducing class sizes, yielding larger educational gains."

This version gets straight to the point: is the improvement under the new curriculum big enough to make a meaningful difference? A rhetorical question is an effective way to make this kind of argument, particularly in spoken formats.

▪ GENERAL DESIGN CONSIDERATIONS

A few general guidelines for organization, length, and design apply to most formats for applied audiences. In later sections, I discuss how these considerations pertain to each of the different formats.

Organizing the Material

The W's are an effective way to organize the elements of reports, posters, or chartbooks.

- In the introductory section, describe what you are studying and why it is important.
- In the data and methods section, list when, where, who, and how the data were collected, how many cases were involved, and how the data were analyzed.
- In the body of the work, explain what you found, using tables or charts accompanied by short prose descriptions or text bullets.

- In the conclusion, explain how your findings can be applied to real-world issues or future research.

Briefs and general-interest articles are rarely divided into these formal parts; see sections below for information on how to organize them.

Text Length and Style

The amount and style of text varies from concise, bulleted phrases in a chartbook, to short paragraphs and bullets in a research poster or issue brief, to many more pages in a full report. Generally, these formats are written in a less academic style than research articles or scientific reports, with shorter sentences, less jargon, and few formal citations.

Color

Posters, chartbooks, and briefs are often printed in two or three colors to enhance their appeal and to convey information such as differences across groups or statistical significance of findings. However, they are frequently photocopied into black and white, whether for a grayscale handout based on a poster or chartbooks or for broader distribution of briefs. Plan for this eventuality by designing these documents so they can be interpreted in black and white. See "Use of Color" in chapter 6 for additional suggestions.

■ COMMON FORMATS FOR APPLIED AUDIENCES

Common formats for presenting statistical results to applied audiences include posters, policy or issue briefs, chartbooks, reports, and general-interest articles. Executive summaries are often included at the beginning of reports and chartbooks. Below I describe the audiences, contents, and layouts for each of these formats, with detailed suggestions for posters and issue briefs. I then show how chartbooks, reports, general-interest articles, and executive summaries can be created by adapting elements of the other formats. In the closing section, I explain how to assess which format is best suited to your specific audience or objectives. Examples from a variety of topics and types of studies illustrate how these types of documents can be used to report elementary statistics and reference data as well as multivariate models. The length, structure, and contents of each format vary depending on the client, conference, or publication, so check the applicable guidelines before writing.

Posters

An assortment of posters is a common way to present results to viewers at a professional conference. Posters are a hybrid form— more detailed than a speech but less than a paper, more interactive than either. Different people will ask about different facets of your research. Some may conduct research on a similar topic or with related data or methods. Others will have ideas about how to apply or extend your work, raising new questions or suggesting other contrasts, ways of classifying data, or presenting results. In addition, presenting a poster provides excellent practice in explaining quickly and clearly why your research is important and what it means—not a bad skill to apply when revising a speech or paper on the same topic.

By the end of an active poster session, you may have learned as much from your viewers as they have from you, especially if the topic, methods, or audience are new to you. For example, at David Snowdon's first poster presentation on educational attainment and longevity using data from the Nun Study, another researcher returned several times to talk with Snowdon, eventually suggesting that he extend his research to focus on Alzheimer's disease, which lead to an important new direction in his research (Snowdon 2001).

Audiences

Preparing a poster means more than simply cranking out pages to be tacked onto a bulletin board in a conference hall. It also involves writing an associated narrative and handouts and preparing short answers to likely questions, all of which should be adapted to the audience. In contrast to chartbooks and issue briefs, which are generally written for nonstatistical audiences, posters are used for both statistical and nonstatistical audiences. For instance, the annual meeting of the American Public Health Association draws both academics who estimate multivariate models and public health practitioners who typically do not. In such situations, use nontechnical vocabulary, examples, types of charts, and means of presenting results of statistical tests on the poster, saving the methodological details and statistical tables for handouts (see below).

Contents and Organization of a Poster

Research posters are organized like scientific papers, with separate pages devoted to the background, objectives, data and methods, results, and conclusions. Because viewers read the posters at their own pace and at close range, more detail can be included than in slides for a speech, but less detail than in a full written document. Be selective, concentrating on one or two issues in the poster. Do not simply post pages from the full paper. Adapt them, using the formatting ideas listed below under "Other Design Considerations." See Briscoe (1996) and Davis (1997) for more recommendations about designing research posters.

Number and Layout of Pages

To determine how many pages you have to work with, find out the dimensions of your assigned space and design your poster to fit that space. A trifold presentation board (3' high by 4' wide) will hold roughly a dozen pages, organized into three panels. The left- and right-hand panels each hold about three pages, while the wider middle panel can accommodate another half-dozen. See figure 16.2 for a suggested layout.

- In the left-hand panel, set the stage for the research question, stating why the topic is important, summarizing major empirical or theoretical work on related topics, and stating your hypotheses or research questions, as in the material shown in figures 15.1, 15.2, 15.4, and 15.7. Include a one-page abstract of your project.
- In the middle panel, briefly describe your data source, variables, and methods as in figures 15.5, 15.6, and 15.8, then present results in tables, charts, or bulleted text, using charts like those in figures 15.9 and 15.10 (bivariate associations) and 15.15 through 15.17 (multivariate findings). Alternatively, enlarge the type size on tables 14.1 (bivariate) and 14.3 (multivariate), display the statistically significant results in color in lieu of standard errors, and accompany the tables with bulleted annotations.
- In the right-hand panel, summarize your findings and relate them back to the research question or project aims, discuss strengths and limitations of your approach, identify research or policy implications, and suggest directions for future research, as in figure 15.11.

An 8' by 4' bulletin board can accommodate several additional pages, allowing you to go into somewhat more depth and to present results of additional models.

Regardless of whether you will be mounting your poster at the conference or ahead of time (see "Some Practical Advice" below), plan how the pages are to be arranged. Experiment by laying them out

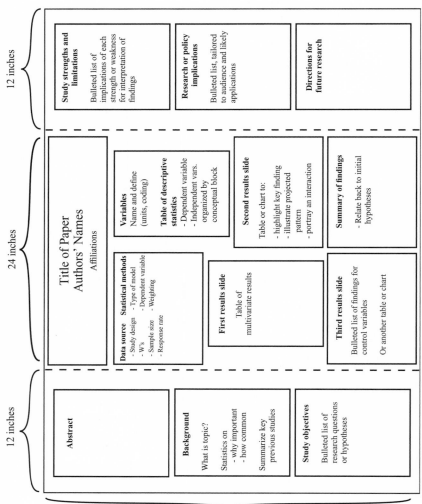

Figure 16.2. Example layout for a research poster.

on a large table marked with the dimensions of your overall poster. Shuffle the pages around to try different arrangements, then number the backs of the pages or draw a rough sketch to work from as you arrange the pages on the board.

Other Design Considerations

A few other issues to keep in mind as you design your poster pages.

- Write a short, specific title that fits on one or two lines in a large type size. The title will be potential readers' first (and sometimes only) glimpse of your poster, so make it interesting and easy to read from a distance—at least 48 point, ideally larger.
- Print all text, tables, and chart labels in at least 14-point type to enhance ease of reading. Take advantage of the smaller type size by combining the contents of two slides onto a single page. For example, the descriptions of data and variables from figures 15.5 and 15.6 could comprise one poster page.
- Modify tables and charts to simplify presentation of statistical test results (see chapter 10).
- Make judicious use of color to differentiate among groups in charts or to highlight statistically significant results in tables. Use a clear, white, or pastel background for all pages, with most text in black or another dark color, and a bright, contrasting shade for points you wish to emphasize.
- If there is space, accompany charts and tables with a narrative explanation. Use a "chartbook layout" such as figure 15.2, with a chart or simple table on one side of a landscape page, accompanied by bulleted annotations on the other.

Use presentation software to create your pages or adapt them from related slides, facilitating good page layout with adequate type size, bulleted text, and page titles. Such software also makes it easy to create matching handouts (see "Handouts" below and in chapter 15).

Oral Introduction to a Poster

Prepare a brief overview to introduce the purpose, findings, and implications of your work. Keep it short—a few sentences that highlight what you are studying and why it is important. After hearing your introduction, listeners will either nod and move along, or comment on some aspect of your work that intrigues them. You can then tailor additional discussion to the individual listener, adjusting the focus and amount of detail to suit their interests. Gesture at the pertinent slides as you make each point, using "Vanna White" scripts to introduce and explain your tables or charts (see "Explaining a Chart 'Live'" in chapter 15). Also prepare short answers to likely questions about various aspects of your work, such as why the work is important from a research or policy perspective, or descriptions of data, methods, and specific results. Think of these as modules—succinct descriptions of particular elements of your research that you can choose among in response to questions that arise.

Handouts to Accompany a Poster

For conference presentations, prepare handouts to distribute to interested viewers. Handouts can be created from slides printed several to a page by your presentation software along with a cover page containing the title, abstract, and your contact information. Or package an executive summary or abstract with a few key tables or charts.

Some Practical Advice

A few pointers to help your poster session go smoothly:

- Find out well in advance how the posters are to be mounted so you can bring the appropriate supplies.

   If the room is set up for table-top presentations, trifold poster boards are essential because you won't have anything to attach a flat poster board or pages to.

   If you have been assigned a bulletin board, bring pushpins or a staple gun, even if the conference is supposed to provide them.

- If you are using a presentation board or a large, single-sheet presentation, mount the pages before going to the conference.[1] You will be more likely to achieve evenly spaced, level alignment if you are not rushed. Cover the finished product or carry it in a mailing tube so it won't get mussed on your way to the conference, and bring extras of your mounting materials (glue sticks, rubber cement) for last-minute repairs or adjustments.

- If you must pin pages to a bulletin board provided at the conference venue, arrive early enough to allow ample time to mount the pages. It may take longer than you'd expect.

- Consider bringing a bottle of water (with a cap, in case you accidentally kick it over). You might not have easy access to water during your poster session.

- Bring pens and paper to jot down questions, comments, and names and addresses of viewers who ask for a copy of your paper. Also bring an envelope or folder to hold business cards of people who prefer to request copies of your paper that way. Much less stuff to lug to or from the conference than bringing numerous copies of the paper . . .

Issue and Policy Briefs

Issue and policy briefs are just that—short summaries of how your research findings apply to some real-world issue or policy. Often structured around a set of questions, they are intended for legislators, advocates, and others interested in your topic but not the technical details of your models. See Musso et al. (2000) for additional guidelines about writing briefs, DiFranza et al. (1996) for pointers on communicating policy-related research to the media and other lay audiences.

Audiences for Briefs

Many issues and policies are of interest to a variety of audiences or stakeholders who represent a range of perspectives and potential applications of your research findings. As you write your brief, put yourself in the shoes of each likely audience and explain how your questions and findings apply to them. For instance, in their series of issue briefs on children's mental health, Warner and Pottick (2004) identify parents and other caregivers, service providers, and policy makers as parties who are likely to be interested in their findings, then describe how each group might best respond to the study findings (box 16.1). If your topic is relevant to several diverse audiences, consider writing different briefs that address their respective interests and viewpoints.

Contents

Introduce the topic and why it is of concern to the intended audience. Don't make them decipher for themselves how your analyses fit their questions. Instead, *you* figure it out before you write, then explain accordingly. Often, applied readers' questions will affect how you specify your model or code your data, so plan ahead by familiarizing yourself with their interests and likely applications of your research results; see "Substantive Context" in chapter 7.

Title. Write a title that convinces potential readers that your brief merits their attention. Make it like a newspaper headline—informa-

Box 16.1. Excerpt from an Issue Brief

From "More Than 380,000 Children Diagnosed with Multiple Mental Health Problems" (Warner and Pottick 2004):

"HOW WE SHOULD RESPOND TO THE FINDINGS"
"Preventing multiple psychiatric problems may be as important as treating them. Prevention means focusing on why co-occurring disorders develop and eliminating the factors that put the children at risk for them. If multiple problems can't be prevented, they should be detected early and treated promptly in order to minimize the substantial burden of psychiatric illness, and encourage positive outcomes.

"Parents and other caregivers are in the best position to observe a child's symptoms and describe them in detail to service providers so that diagnoses are accurate. They should advocate vigorously for their child, making sure that the assessments are thorough, and that treatment reflects the latest research on co-occurring disorders.

"Service providers must stay up-to-date with research on how co-occurring disorders develop and the best ways to treat them. They should also offer support programs for families and caregivers to help them respond to the special needs of these children and to reduce their risk of developing chronic mental illness as adults.

"Policymakers should encourage clinical trials that include children with multiple diagnoses and ensure that community-based mental health programs offer child psychiatrists who are expert in co-occurring disorders."

tive and enticing—and incorporate the key question or main conclusions of your study.

- Instead of "Spending Patterns of People with and without Health Insurance," write "What Do People Buy When They Don't Buy Health Insurance?" (Levy and DeLeire 2002).
- Instead of "Prevalence of Multiple Mental Health Problems among Children," write "More than 380,000 Children Diagnosed with Multiple Mental Health Problems" (Warner and Pottick 2004).

If you report a numeric finding in your title, keep in mind that readers may latch onto it as a "factoid" to summarize your conclusions, so select and phrase it carefully (McDonough 2000).

Briefs are often organized around a series of questions that your audience is likely to ask, with results of your study interpreted to answer those questions. Again, those familiar W's are a handy checklist for identifying relevant questions and organizing your brief:

- Why is the issue important?
- What were your main findings?
- How many people or institutions or countries are affected? Who and where?
- How do your findings apply to the issue or policy at hand?
- How do they correspond to proposed or existing policies? What modifications or new solutions do your results suggest?

Create a paragraph heading for each key question, then present the associated findings in a simple chart, accompanied by short, straightforward descriptions. Limit your design to no more than two charts per page. For some questions, incorporate a few numeric facts in lieu of a chart, providing enough background information that readers can interpret those facts.

Sidebars. Incorporate basic contextual information (W's) into the narrative. If additional information on the data or methods is important, include it in a sidebar and provide a citation to a published paper or report where interested readers can find the technical details. Avoid a lengthy description of methods or models, substituting a short phrase like "when [summary of other concepts] are taken into account," or "holding other factors [short list] constant," to convey that a multivariate model was the basis of your results.

Glossary. In some cases, you will use technical terms in an issue brief to tie your findings to other similar works or if there is no suitable everyday synonym. For instance, you may use a specific measurement technique that is widely used in the field and should be referred to by its usual name. If you use such terms in your brief, provide a glossary. Limit it to no more than a handful of terms, replacing other technical language with more familiar wording in the body of the text.

Length and Format

As their name suggests, issue and policy briefs are generally very short. They are intended for people who can't devote much time to reading about any one topic, often because they must familiarize themselves with many different subjects. A 2001 survey of government policy makers showed that they prefer summaries of research to be written so they can immediately see how the findings relate to issues currently facing their constituencies, without wading through a formal research paper (Sorian and Baugh 2002). Complaints that surfaced about many research reports included that they were "too long, dense, or detailed," or "too theoretical, technical, or jargony." On average, respondents said they read only about a quarter of the material they receive for detail, skim about half of it, and never get to the rest.

To ensure that yours is among the material they read and remember, keep it short and specific, explaining the major questions and answers in plain language, and using charts or bullets to highlight major findings. Common styles for briefs include one-page memos, those that cover both sides of a single page, or simple bifold (e.g., four-page) or trifold (six-page) documents.

Figure 16.3 shows a sample layout for a two-page issue brief, modeled after those designed and written by Pottick and Warner (2002; Warner and Pottick 2004) with example titles and section headings and suggested placement of elements such as the sidebar and glossary. Positioning of charts may vary from the design shown here. For example, charts might appear on both the first and second pages, next to the accompanying description. Longer briefs can accommodate more findings, each described in a short paragraph and identified by a clear subheading or question. If space permits, leave a blank area for a mailing label to facilitate distribution. For briefs that are part of a series, add a banner for the series title.

Chartbooks

Chartbooks present numeric information in a format that is easily accessible to a wide range of audiences. Longer than issue briefs, they accommodate more detailed results on a given topic, or findings on a wider range of topics within a single document. For example, progress toward the national Healthy People 2010 objectives for variety of specific health issues is presented in a chartbook issued periodically by the Office of Disease Prevention and Health Promotion (U.S. DHHS 2000). The Social Security Administration publishes annual chartbooks that describe income levels and sources among the elderly in the United States (U.S. SSA 2003).

Contents

Begin the chartbook with a brief narrative introduction to the purpose and methods of the work, then present results in a series of

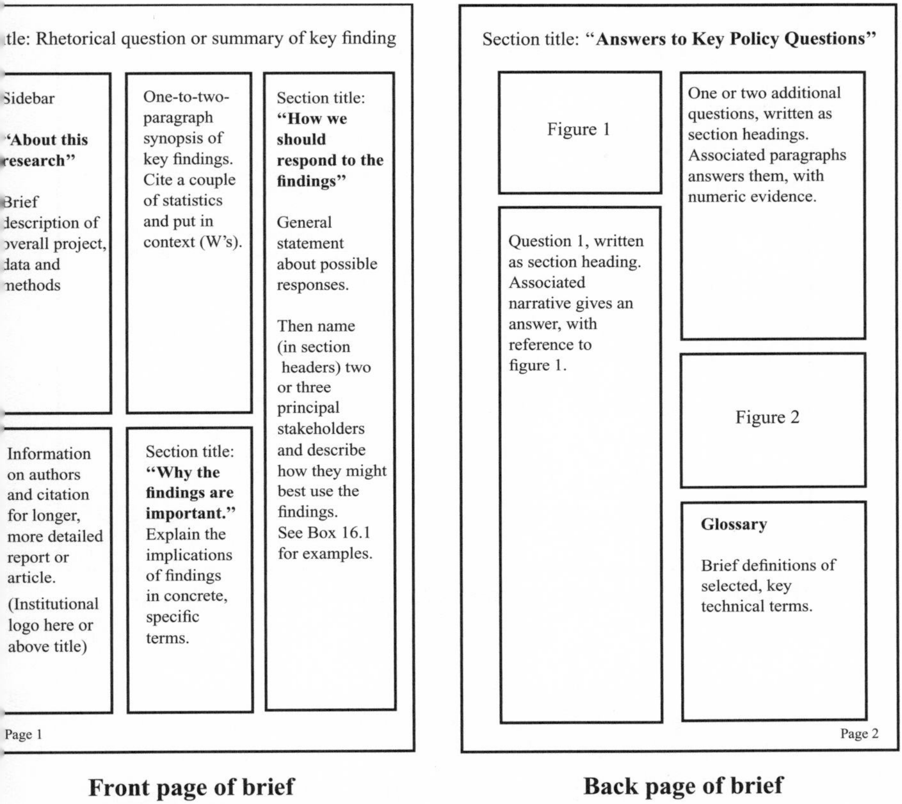

tle: Rhetorical question or summary of key finding			Section title: "**Answers to Key Policy Questions**"	
Sidebar "**About this research**" Brief description of overall project, data and methods	One-to-two-paragraph synopsis of key findings. Cite a couple of statistics and put in context (W's).	Section title: "**How we should respond to the findings**" General statement about possible responses. Then name (in section headers) two or three principal stakeholders and describe how they might best use the findings. See Box 16.1 for examples.	Figure 1 Question 1, written as section heading. Associated narrative gives an answer, with reference to figure 1. Figure 2	One or two additional questions, written as section headings. Associated paragraphs answers them, with numeric evidence.
Information on authors and citation for longer, more detailed report or article. (Institutional logo here or above title)	Section title: "**Why the findings are important.**" Explain the implications of findings in concrete, specific terms.		**Glossary** Brief definitions of selected, key technical terms.	
Page 1			Page 2	

Front page of brief **Back page of brief**

Figure 16.3. Example layout for a two-page issue brief.
Note: Text shown on the diagram in bold type with quotation marks would
be included verbatim in the issue brief. Other text on the diagram gives
guidelines about general topics to include in the brief.

charts, each addressing one aspect of the topic. Place each chart on a
separate page, accompanied by two or three bullets summarizing the
patterns. For charts presenting results from a multivariate model, include a footnote listing what other variables were controlled in the
model. Follow the results section with a short summary of findings
and discussion of policy implications and directions for future work,
using either a bulleted list (e.g., figure 15.11) or paragraph format. For
readers interested in the technical details, include an appendix at the
end of the chartbook or cite the associated statistical paper.

Data and Methods

Data sources

- 1988–1994 National Health and Nutrition Examination Survey (NHANES III)
  - Nationally representative sample of United States population
    - Oversample of Mexican Americans
  - Cross-sectional
  - Population-based

- N = 9,813
  - 3,733 non-Hispanic white
  - 3,112 Mexican American
  - 2,968 non-Hispanic black

- Information on all variables used here taken from household survey portion of the study

Statistical methods

- Linear regression of birth weight in grams
- Logistic regression of low birth weight (<2,500 grams)
- Weighted to national level with sampling weights from NHANES III
  - Corrected for complex survey design
- Models include controls for
  - infant gender
  - race/ethnicity
  - family income-to-poverty ratio
  - mother's age
  - mother's educational attainment
  - mother's smoking during pregnancy
- Also tested whether birth weight patterns by race differed by mother's educational attainment.

Figure 16.4. Example data and methods summary for a chartbook.

Layout and Format

The design of each chartbook page is similar to the design of a slide for a speech, and follows many of the same guidelines for an effective title and length and organization of text bullets. Type size can be smaller than that in slides (e.g., 12-point type), accommodating more information on each page. A chartbook about the birth weight study might include an executive summary like that in box 16.3 (below), a short description of data and methods (figure 16.4), and results presented in charts like those in chapter 15. For simple charts, provide annotation on the same page as the chart (e.g., figure 15.2). For charts that require a full page, place accompanying annotations on a facing page.

As you design the chartbook, include and explain reference lines, bars, or other elements to help readers interpret the values you show. See comment 3 in box 16.2 below for an illustration.

Reports

There are two general types of reports—analytic reports and those that are principally designed for descriptive purposes or to present reference statistics. Analytic reports to government or nonprofit agencies, foundations, or corporate clients are typically structured much like a scientific paper, with an introduction, review of previous studies, data and methods, results, discussion, and conclusions. Include a one- to two-page executive summary in lieu of an abstract. Reduce the level of detail and technical language in your description of previous studies and data and methods, relegating details about data sources, model specifications, and tables of multivariate results to technical appendixes. Summarize key findings in the text, accompanied by simplified tables and charts. See also Hailman and Strier (1997) for guidelines.

Descriptive reports or those that serve as reference data sources are often written using a variant of a chartbook format that includes both tables and charts. For example, the Department of Health and Human Services' annual report to Congress on indicators of welfare dependence (U.S. DHHS, Office of Human Service Policy 2003) divides the information into major topic areas, each of which comprises a section of the report. Start each section with a two- or three-page prose introduction to the measures, data sources, and questions covered in that section, then present tables and charts, each annotated with several text bullets or a brief paragraph describing the patterns. Use tables to report precise numeric values, charts to portray approximate composition, levels, or trends in the outcomes under study.

General-Interest Articles

General-interest articles typically aren't divided into the formal parts that characterize a scientific paper. Instead, write a coherent, logical story line with numeric facts or patterns as evidence, incorporating information about context, data, and methods into the body of the narrative. In multipage articles, consider using subheadings to guide readers through the different topics within your work. If you include charts or tables, keep them simple and focused, then describe and interpret a sample number or two in the text or a sidebar.

To illustrate, box 16.2 shows an excerpt from a two-page article in the *New York Times* about the physical impact of the planes that hit the Twin Towers on September 11, 2001 (Lipton and Glanz 2002). The article includes some fairly technical information, but is written for an educated lay audience. I have accompanied the excerpt with annotations and the figure (16.5) from their article to show how the authors made effective use of explanations, charts, and analogies. Without those elements, readers who aren't familiar with physics,

Box 16.2. Using Numbers in a General-Interest Article: Impact of the Planes on the Twin Towers, September 11, 2001

" . . . (1) The government's analysis put the speeds [on impact] at 586 m.p.h. for the United flight and 494 m.p.h. for the American one. In both cases, the planes were flying much faster than they should have been at that altitude: The aviation agency's limit below 10,000 feet is 287 m.p.h. . . .

"(2) The energy of motion carried by any object, called the kinetic energy, varies as the square of its velocity, so even modest differences in speed can translate into large variations in what the building had to absorb. That means that while the United jet was traveling only about a quarter faster than the American jet, it would have released about 50% more energy on impact. . . . Even at a speed of only about 500 m.p.h., a partly loaded Boeing 767 weighing 132 tons would have created about three billion joules of energy at impact, the equivalent of three-quarters of a ton of T.N.T."

After (3) presenting the respective speeds in a simple bar chart (figure 16.5), the authors explain that both jets were traveling at speeds that exceeded the Boeing design speed limit at 1,500 feet, and the United jet exceeded even the design cruise speed at 35,000 feet. Such speeds threatened the structural integrity of the planes even before they struck the buildings, because "(4) The lower the plane goes, . . . the thicker the air becomes, so the slower the plane must travel to avoid excessive stress."

COMMENTS

(1) Reports the actual speeds of each plane, then compares them against a cutoff (the FAA limit for flights at that altitude) to help readers understand the meaning of those numbers.

(2) Explains in lay terms how differences in speed translate into differences in energy on impact, paraphrasing the meaning of "kinetic energy." The next sentence reports results of calculations to illustrate how much more energy the second plane released, applying the general formula given in the preceding sentence. The third sentence reports results of calculation of absolute energy generated by the second plane and compares its units of measurement (joules) against a more familiar quantity.

(3) Uses a bar chart to illustrate speeds of the two planes and how they compare to industry design speeds, then explains that the planes were traveling too fast for conditions by comparing their speeds against the design speed limit at both the altitude where the planes were flying and cruise altitude.

(4) Uses colloquial language to explain the physical principles why the design speed is slower for lower altitudes.

Impact speed of 9/11 flights and comparison speeds

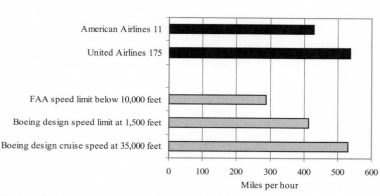

Figure 16.5. Bar chart to accompany a written comparison.
Source: Lipton and Glanz 2002.
Note: FAA = Federal Aviation Administration

engineering, or airline regulations would find it hard to grasp the purpose or interpretation of the numbers in the article.

Executive Summaries

Executive summaries are one- to two-page synopses of a study. They give an overview of the key objectives, methods, findings, and implications of the work that can be read and understood in a few minutes by busy executives or others who must digest the main points from many documents quickly. They are similar in general content and structure to abstracts, but emphasize the questions and answers of the study, with less detail on methods or statistical test results. To make the information easily accessible, executive summaries are often written in a bulleted format with short, simple sentences (box 16.3).

Choose the numbers you report carefully; they are often chosen as "sound bites" to characterize conclusions of the entire work.

▓ SUMMARY

The types of documents used to present statistical results to applied audiences all share certain attributes that help make the numeric information accessible and useful to nonstatisticians.

- They emphasize substantive questions and answers over statistical models and findings.
- They replace technical terms with their colloquial equivalents.
- They use simplified charts or tables to present numeric findings and associated statistical test results.
- They include limited (if any) technical information on statistical methods and data, placing that material in appendixes (for descriptive reports or chartbooks) or sidebars (for briefs), and referring to the associated scientific article for details.

Exceptions to these generalizations include posters for a research audience and analytic reports, in which data and methods are described in the body of the work and results are presented with technical detail similar to that in a scientific paper.

The different formats described in this chapter vary substantially in terms of the audiences and objectives for which they are best suited. In some instances, one of these formats will work best:

- Issue briefs or policy briefs, which are written for applied audiences who need to see what your findings mean for an issue or policy of interest to them without reading a long, detailed, statistical report.
- General-interest articles, which are written for lay audiences, with a more essay-like structure, few citations, and descriptions of a handful of numeric facts or patterns.

In other instances, you will choose among two similar variants:

- Posters and speeches, which are visual and spoken versions of the same material and can be used for similar audiences at professional conferences.
- Chartbooks and descriptive reports, which differ principally in whether they illustrate general patterns (charts in either format) or present precise values (tables in reports). Reports also typically include more prose than do chartbooks, using full paragraphs in place of bulleted text.

Box 16.3. Example of an Executive Summary

Background
- Low birth weight (LBW) is a widely recognized risk factor for infant mortality and poor child health.
- Although only 7.5% of all births are LBW, such infants account for more than 75% of infant deaths.
- Rates of LBW among black infants are approximately twice as high as for white infants (13.0% and 6.5% in 2000). Black infants weigh on average about 260 grams less than white infants.
- Low socioeconomic status (SES) is also associated with lower mean birth weight and higher rates of LBW.

Study Objective
- To assess whether lower average SES of non-Hispanic black infants in the United States explains why they have lower mean birth weight than non-Hispanic white infants.

Data and Methods
- Data on 9,813 children were taken from the 1988–1994 National Health and Nutrition Examination Survey (NHANES III) — a cross-sectional, population-based sample survey of the United States.
- Birth weights were collected in parental interviews about children aged 10 or younger at the time of the survey.
- Statistical models were used to estimate racial differences in mean birth weight, taking into account gender, family income, mother's age, educational attainment, and smoking behavior during pregnancy.

Key Findings
- Regardless of race, children born into low SES families have lower mean birth weight than those born at higher SES.
- At each socioeconomic level, black infants weigh 150 to 200 grams less than whites.

Conclusions
- Further research is needed to investigate possible reasons for higher LBW among blacks. These include:
    less access to health care,
    higher rates of poor health behaviors,
    greater social stress, and
    intergenerational transmission of health disadvantage.

■ **CHECKLIST FOR WRITING FOR APPLIED AUDIENCES**

- When writing for an applied audience, determine which format is most appropriate, taking into account
  - whether readers need or want input into model assumptions or variables,
  - the level of statistical training among expected readers,
  - the likely application of results, and
  - the amount of time readers have to digest findings.
- Emphasize questions and answers rather than statistical methods.
- Replace technical language with familiar synonyms that convey the underlying concepts. Incorporate definitions into the description of findings, or provide a glossary.
- Simplify charts and tables to focus on one pattern at a time and to emphasize key patterns only. Use footnotes to list other variables controlled in the model.
- Adapt your presentation of statistical results, using p-values, symbols, or formatting to convey results of statistical tests (see chapter 10).

APPENDIX A

Implementing "Generalization, Example, Exceptions" (GEE)

One of the basic principles for describing a relationship among two or more variables is to summarize, characterizing that association with one or two broad patterns. In chapter 2, I introduced a mantra, GEE, for "generalization, example, exceptions," to use as a guide on how to write an effective summary. Generalize by stepping back to look at the forest, not the individual trees, describing the broad pattern rather than reporting every component number. Illustrate with representative numbers to portray that general pattern. Finally, if the general pattern doesn't fit all your data, identify and portray the exceptions. For inexperienced writers, this can seem like a daunting task.

In this appendix, I sketch out six steps to guide you through implementing a GEE. After creating a chart and table to present data on the variables in the pattern, proceed through several intermediate steps to identify and characterize the patterns for your final written description. The notes, calculations, and scribbles generated in those steps will not appear in the final written narrative, but are an important part of the analytic process involved in writing a succinct but thorough summary.

■ STEP 1: DISPLAY THE DATA IN A TABLE AND A CHART

Even if you plan to use a table or prose in your document, the chart version may help you see patterns in your data more easily as you write your GEE. It doesn't have to be pretty—even a hand-drawn version will work fine for this purpose—as long as it is an appropriate type of chart for the task, is drawn to scale, and is labeled well enough that you can recognize the variables and assess approximate numeric values. In both table and chart, organize nominal variables or items in a logical order, using empirical or theoretical criteria (see "Organizing Tables to Coordinate with Your Writing in chapter 5), facilitating an orderly comparison in the subsequent steps of the GEE.

■ STEP 2: IDENTIFY THE DIMENSIONS OF THE COMPARISON

Identify the dimensions of the comparison—one for each variable or set of variables in your table or chart. In a table, the rows and columns each comprise one dimension; panels of rows or spanners across columns often indicate the presence of additional dimensions. In a chart, the axes and legends each comprise one dimension. Vary only one dimension of the chart or table at a time, keeping the others constant.

In a multiple-line trend chart like figure A.1, there are two separate comparisons:

(1) *Moving left to right along one line.* In figure A.1, this comparison shows how the variable on the *y* axis (price of housing) varies with time (the *x* variable), within one region (value of the *z* variable, shown in the legend).

(2) *Moving (vertically) across lines.* This comparison shows how price (the *y* variable) varies across regions (the *z* variable), at one time point (value of the *x* variable).

In a three-way table, there are two comparisons:

(1) *Moving down the rows within one column.* Table A.1 shows how AIDS knowledge (in the interior cells) varies by row (topic) within one language group (column).

Median sales price of new single-family homes, by region, United States, 1980–2000

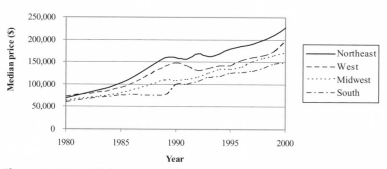

Figure A.1. Generalizing patterns from a multiple-line trend chart.
Source: U.S. Census Bureau 2001a.

Table A.1. Generalizing one pattern within a three-way table

Percentage of respondents answering AIDS transmission questions correctly, by language spoken at home and language used on the questionnaire, New Jersey, 1998

| | Language spoken at home and language used on questionnaire | | |
Mode of transmission	English	Spanish/ English ques.	Spanish/ Spanish ques.
Likely modes of transmission			
Sexual intercourse with an infected person	93.6	87.5	95.0
Sharing needles for IV drug use*	92.4	90.6	65.0
Pregnant mother to baby*	89.5	75.0	80.0
Blood transfusion from infected person*	87.5	81.3	60.0
Mean percentage of "likely" questions correct*	91.7	83.6	75.0

Source: Miller 2000a.
*Difference across language groups is significant at $p < 0.05$.

(2) *Moving across the columns within one row.* Table A.1 shows how AIDS knowledge varies by column (language of respondent) for one topic (row).

■ STEP 3: CHOOSE A REPRESENTATIVE EXAMPLE

Having identified each of the dimensions of comparison, choose one representative example as the basis for each generalization.

- For a comparison across a series of related outcomes a good starting point is a summary measure (e.g., in table A.1, the mean percentage of "likely" questions correct) that combines results for the various component variables. Lacking a summary measure, pick a value of particular interest or start at one end of the axis, column, or row (the best-answered or worst-answered topic, in table A.1).

Box A.1

Generalization 1: Down the rows. On the summary measure of knowledge of "likely" modes of AIDS transmission in table A.1, English speakers score higher than Spanish/English speakers, who in turn score higher than Spanish/Spanish speakers. The difference in mean percentage of "likely" questions correct is statistically significant, as indicated by the asterisk at the end of the row label (see note to table).

Check: Does the pattern in the row showing the mean percentage of correctly answered questions apply to the other rows? In other words, does the generalization from the summary row fit each of the component questions?

Answer: The generalization fits all but the sexual intercourse question, for which the Spanish/Spanish group did best. In addition, the difference across language groups in knowledge of sexual intercourse as a likely means of AIDS transmission is not statistically significant. Hence that question is the exception to the general pattern, in terms of both direction and statistical significance.

Generalization 2: Across the columns. Among English speakers, the best understood "likely" AIDS transmission topic was transmission via sexual intercourse, followed by sharing IV needles, transmission from pregnant mother to baby, and blood transfusion. (Note that the question topics were arranged in the rows in descending order of correct answers for the English-speaking group, facilitating this description.)

Check: Does this same rank order of topics apply to the other language groups? In other words, does the generalization from the summary column fit each of the other columns?

Answer: Spanish/English speakers did best on the needles question and least well on the mother to baby. Among Spanish/Spanish speakers, the rank order of the two middle questions is reversed. In this analysis, number of Spanish speakers is small, so these exceptions would not be emphasized.

- For a comparison across groups, a good starting point for a representative value is the overall sample (e.g., all language groups combined). Alternatively, use the modal (most common) group—English speakers, in table A.1—or a group of particular interest for your research question.

Follow steps 4 and 5 to ensure that your example is in fact representative of a general pattern. If not (e.g., if it turns out to be an exception), try again with a different example until you've found one that is generalizable.

■ STEP 4: CHARACTERIZE THE PATTERN

Using your example value, describe the shape of the pattern, including direction, magnitude, and, for a scientific audience, statistical significance. Make notes in the margins of your table or chart or on an accompanying page. Don't worry about writing complete sentences at this stage. Abbreviate concepts to use as a basis for your written description with short phrases, upward- or downward-pointing arrows, and <, =, or > to show how values on different categories, topics, or time points relate to one another.

Direction

For *trends* across values of an ordinal, interval, or ratio variable such as time, age, or price, describe whether the pattern is

- level (constant) or changing;
- linear (rising or falling at a steady rate), accelerating, or decelerating;
- monotonic or with a change of direction (such as a notable "blip" or other sudden change).

For *differentials* across categories of a nominal variable such as religious affiliation, political party, or gender, indicate which categories have the highest and lowest values and where other categories of interest fall relative to those extremes, as explained in chapter 13.

Magnitude

Use one or two types of quantitative comparisons (chapter 8) to calculate the size of the trend or differential. If the calculations involve only a few numbers and basic arithmetic (e.g., a ratio of two numbers, or a percentage change), include those calculations in your notes, including units. For more complex or repetitive calculations, such as confidence intervals for each of a dozen independent variables, save your work in a spreadsheet, then annotate it to indicate which calculations correspond to which aspects of the GEE for your own future reference.

Scribble down descriptive words or phrases to depict the size of the variation. Is the trend steep or shallow? Is the differential marked or minuscule?

Statistical Significance

Note patterns of statistical significance on your table or chart, particularly if it does not include symbols to indicate which results are statistically significant. Are most of the associations in the table statistically significant? If so, generalize that finding. If most are not, the lack of statistical significance is your generalization. Finally, if only some portions of your table or chart have statistically significant findings, try to identify what they have in common so you can summarize the patterns to the extent possible.

▥ STEP 5: IDENTIFY EXCEPTIONS

If parts of your table or chart depart appreciably from the generalization you have made in the steps above, they are exceptions. Exceptions come in three flavors: direction, magnitude, and statistical significance. A few more illustrations:

Exceptions in Direction

In figure A.1, median sales prices dipped in the early 1990s in the West, but continued upward or remained level in the other regions—an example of a different direction of trend. The West was the exception. In 1980, sales prices in the Northeast were slightly below those in the West ("Northeast < West"), an example of a contrasting direction of a differential (cross-sectional comparison). In all subsequent years, the Northeast had the highest prices ("Northeast > West"). The year 1980 was the exception.

Exceptions in Magnitude

In figure A.2a, the difference across racial groups is much larger among the non-poor than in the other two income groups (compare brackets 2 and 3 to bracket 4). Generalize based on the two income groups for which the racial gap in ER use is similar (poor and near poor), and then point out that the non-poor are the exception.

Exceptions in Statistical Significance

In table A.1, the sexual intercourse question is the only one for which the language difference in AIDS knowledge is not statistically significant. For that table, statistical significance is the rule (generalization) and lack of statistical significance is the exception.

On the printed copy of your table or chart, circle or otherwise mark exceptions to your general pattern. If your table or chart is complicated, consider using color coding (highlighter) to shade which parts share a common pattern and which deviate from that pattern.

a. Relative odds of emergency room visits for asthma, by race and income, United States, 1991

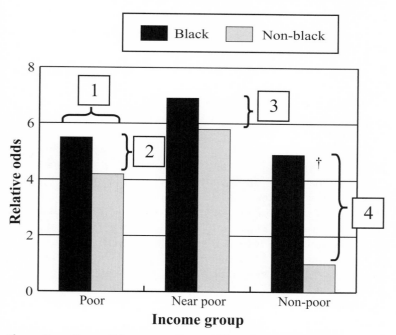

Figure A.2a. Generalizing one pattern within a three-way chart: Within clusters.

Source: Miller 2000b.

Notes: Taking into account mother's age, educational attainment, and marital history; number of siblings; presence of smokers in the household; low birth weight (<2,500 grams) and preterm birth (<37 weeks' gestation).
†Difference across racial groups significant at $p < 0.05$ for non-poor only.

Box A.2a

Generalization: Among the poor (the left-most cluster of figure A.2a), use of the emergency room is greater for blacks than non-blacks (bracket 1).

    Check: Does the same pattern apply in the other clusters? Does that description fit the near poor? The non-poor?

    Answer: Yes, ER use is higher among blacks than non-blacks in all three income groups. However (exception), the racial difference is much smaller among the poor and near poor (brackets 2 and 3) than among the non-poor (bracket 4) and is only statistically significant among the non-poor (see figure note).

■ **STEP 6: WRITE THE DESCRIPTION**

Working from your notes and calculations, write a systematic description of the patterns. For relationships among three or more variables, organize the GEE into one paragraph for each type of comparison—e.g., one for the pattern "across the columns," another for "down the rows."

Start each paragraph with a topic sentence that identifies the main concepts or variables in the comparison. Provide a verbal sketch of the general pattern, selecting verbs and adjectives to convey direction and magnitude. Follow with one or more sentences relating the results of your quantitative comparisons, reporting the raw data from which they were calculated or (if many numbers are involved), referring to the associated table or chart. Finally, describe and document any exceptions. See "Phrasing for a GEE" in chapter 13 for suggested wording to differentiate general patterns from exceptions.

Figures A.2a and b, table A.1, and the associated text boxes illustrate how to identify the dimensions, select a starting point for each generalization, and test the generalization for exceptions of direction and magnitude.

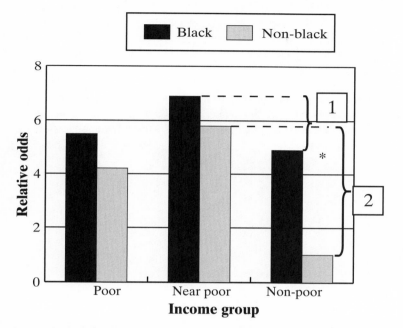

b. Relative odds of emergency room visits for asthma, by race and income, United States, 1991

Figure A.2b. Generalizing a second pattern within a three-way chart: Across clusters.
Source: Miller 2000b; data are from U.S. DHHS 1991.
Notes: Taking into account mother's age, educational attainment and marital history; number of siblings; presence of smokers in the household; low birth weight (<2,500 grams) and preterm birth (<37 weeks' gestation).
*Difference across income groups significant at $p < 0.05$ for non-blacks only.

Box A.2b

Generalization: Among blacks (the black-shaded bars in figure A.2b), emergency room use is highest among the near poor and lowest among the non-poor.

Check: Does that pattern apply to non-blacks (the other bar color) as well?

Answer: Yes, non-blacks exhibit the same income/ER use pattern as blacks. However (exception), the drop in ER use between near poor and non-poor is much smaller among blacks (bracket 1) than among non-blacks (bracket 2), and is only statistically significant among non-blacks (see figure note).

Translating Statistical Output into Table and Text

Regression output from standard statistical packages includes a great deal of information, some of which you will include in a table of model results, some of which belongs in the methods section, and some that you will omit from all but the most technical papers. Rarely will you organize or label the contents of your final table as it appears in the statistical output. Instead, use the criteria in chapter 10 to decide which variants of effect size and statistical significance are best suited for your audience, then organize and label that material into a table, following the guidelines in chapter 5. To illustrate, figure B.1 contains the PROC LOGISTIC output from SAS for the model shown in table B.1, with each piece of information identified by a letter keyed to the figure notes and the text below.

Items A through F of the output (figure B.1) provide general background on the model. In the title or notes to the table, incorporate the type of model (E), dependent variable (A, termed "response variable" in the SAS output), which value was modeled (F, for categorical dependent variables), and the fact that the analysis was weighted with sampling weights (D), then report the sample size (C) in a row or note (table B.1). Explain the binary nature of the dependent variable (B) in the methods section along with a succinct verbal summary of items A and C through F, as in box 12.2. For a continuous dependent variable in an OLS model, report units in body text and table in lieu of item F.

Items G through J are measures of overall model goodness-of fit (GOF). Column G gives three different measures of model fit for the model with intercept only (the null model); Column H reports these same measures for the model with intercept and covariates (independent variables). Panel I shows the model GOF statistics, while panel J presents the difference in each of those statistics between the null model and the model with covariates. Present one or two GOF statistics and their difference against the null model and the associated difference in number of degrees of freedom, as in table B.1.

The parameter estimates and associated statistical test results for each of the independent variables in the model are in the two panels labeled "Analysis of Maximum Likelihood Estimates" (items K through P in figure B.1) and "Odds Ratio Estimates" (items Q through

Table B.1. Table of logistic regression results created from computerized output

Logistic regression model of low birth weight, 1988–1994, U.S. National Health and Nutrition Examination Survey (NHANES III)

	Log-odds	Odds ratio (OR)	95% CI for OR
Intercept	-2.03**	0.14	0.09–0.21
Race/Hispanic origin (Non-Hispanic white)[a]			
Non-Hispanic black	0.38**	1.46	1.23–1.74
Mexican American	0.36**	1.43	1.15–1.78
Boy	-0.02	0.98	0.86–1.12
Mother's age at child's birth (yrs.)	-0.008	0.99	0.98–1.01
Income-to-poverty ratio (IPR)	-0.26**	0.77	0.65–0.91
IPR^2	0.02	1.02	0.99–1.05
Mother's education			
Less than high school	0.51**	1.67	1.37–2.05
High school grad (College+)	0.31**	1.37	1.14–1.63
Mother smoked during pregnancy	0.33**	1.39	1.20–1.62
Wald chi-square statistic (df)		236.7* (9)	
-2 Log L		6,130.4	
-2 Log L for null model		6,377.9	
$N = 9,813$			

Notes: Low birth weight $<2,500$ grams or 5.5 pounds. $N = 9,813$. Weighted to population levels using sampling weights from the NHANES III (U.S. DHHS, 1996).
[a] Reference category in parentheses.
*$p < 0.05$ **$p < 0.01$

S). Column K contains the variable names (or acronyms) used in the data set and program, several of which are fairly cryptic because the software program limits them to no more than eight characters. For your table, translate each variable label into a longer, more descriptive phrase that readers can understand without referring to the text.

```
THE LOGISTIC PROCEDURE MODEL INFORMATION
Data Set                              work.temp
Response Variable                     (A) lbw: birth weight <2500 grams
Number of Response Levels             (B) 2
Number of Observations                (C) 9813
Weight Variable                       (D) normwt
Sum of Weights                        9812.1352158
Model                                 (E) binary logit
Optimization Technique                Fisher's scoring


Response Profile
Ordered                Total          Total
Value       lbw      Frequency       Weight
1            1          1237          980.8466
2            0          8576
(F) Probability modeled is lbw = 1.


Model Convergence Status Convergence criterion (GCONV=1E-8)
satisfied.
MODEL FIT STATISTICS    (G) NULL MODEL       (H) MODEL W/ COVARIATES
                                                 LISTED BELOW
Criterion               Intercept Only       Intercept & Covariates
(I)
AIC                        6379.903              6150.433
SC                         6387.095              6222.347
−2 Log L                   6377.903              6130.433


(J) Testing Global Null Hypothesis: BETA=0
Test                    Chi-Square      DF      Pr > ChiSq
Likelihood Ratio         247.4710        9       <.0001
Score                    252.6384        9       <.0001
Wald                     236.6794        9       <.0001
```

Figure B.1. SAS computer output from a logistic regression model.
Source: U.S. DHHS 1997.
(A) Identifies the dependent variable (response variable): "lbw: birth
weight <2500 grams." (B) Indicates that the dependent variable is binary:
"Number of Response Levels: 2." (C) Reports the unweighted sample size:
"Number of Observations: 9813." (D) Shows that the procedure is weighted
and identifies name of sampling weight variable: "Weight variable: normwt."
(E) Identifies the statistical model specification: "Model: binary logit."
(F) Section shows distribution of values of the dependent variable, and
identifies which value was modeled: "Response profile . . . probability
modeled is lbw = 1." (G) Column label identifies the null model ("Intercept
only," without covariates). (H) Column label identifies model with intercept
and covariates. (I) Row labels identify three different model fit statistics:
AIC, SC, and −2 Log L. (J) Section reports model goodness-of-fit compared
to null model (item G above) with 9 degrees of freedom, one for each covariate
in the model. Reports associated p-value for the null hypothesis that beta
(β) = 0.

```
Analysis of Maximum Likelihood Estimates
                                       (N)           (O)          (P)
(K)             (L)       (M)       Standard        Wald
Parameter       DF      Estimate     Error       Chi-Square   Pr > ChiSq
Intercept       1       -2.0259      0.2189        85.6181       <.0001
BOY             1       -0.0169      0.0683         0.0610       0.8049
BLACK           1        0.3784      0.0892        17.9774       <.0001
mexamer         1        0.3608      0.1113        10.5038       0.0012
HYA2            1       -0.00806     0.0066         1.4654       0.2261
DMPPIR          1       -0.2644      0.0842         9.8565       0.0017
pir2            1        0.0185      0.0149         1.5398       0.2146
LTHS            1        0.5106      0.1050        23.6374       <.0001
HS              1        0.3111      0.0904        11.8288       0.0006
momsmok         1        0.3314      0.0767        18.6828       <.0001

   Odds Ratio Estimates
                      (Q)         (R)          (S)
                     Point          95% Wald
   Effect          Estimate    Confidence Limits
   BOY              0.983       0.860      1.124
   BLACK            1.460       1.226      1.739
   mexamer          1.434       1.153      1.784
   HYA2             0.992       0.979      1.005
   DMPPIR           0.768       0.651      0.905
   pir2             1.019       0.989      1.049
   LTHS             1.666       1.356      2.047
   HS               1.365       1.143      1.630
   momsmok          1.393       1.199      1.619

(T) Association of Predicted Probabilities and Observed Responses
Percent Concordant      63.9        Somers' D      0.289
Percent Discordant      35.1        Gamma          0.292
Percent Tied             1.0        Tau-a          0.064
Pairs               10608512        c              0.644
```

Figure B.1. (*continued*)
(K) Column reports the variable names used in SAS model specification.
(L) Column reports the number of degrees of freedom (DF) associated
with parameter estimate in the associated row. (M) Column reports the
estimated logit coefficients (β = log-odds) for each independent variable
(covariate) in the model. (N) Column reports the standard errors of the
estimated coefficients for each independent variable. (O) Column reports
the test statistics (Wald chi-square; χ^2) for the estimated coefficient for
each independent variable. (P) Column reports the *p*-values for test of each
estimated coefficient against the null hypothesis (β = 0). (Q) Column
presents the estimated odds ratios for each independent variable;
calculated e^β = $e^{\text{log-odds}}$ = Exp(value in column M).(R), (S) Columns
present the lower and upper 95% confidence limits around the estimated
odds ratios. (T) Section reports additional model goodness-of-fit statistics:
concordance or predicted probabilities and observed responses.

Use the criteria in chapter 10 to choose the best way to present effects' estimates (reported in column M [log-odds] and Q [odds ratios]) and one or two ways of assessing statistical significance (arrayed in columns N [for log-odds] or O or P [for either measure of effect size] or R through S [for odds ratios]), to suit your audience. (Table B.1 is designed for statistically proficient readers.) In your tables and text, round the values to two decimal places for odds ratios, test-statistics, and associated confidence intervals, three decimal places for log-odds, standard errors, and p-values less than 0.01 (see table 4.2).

Item T contains additional fit statistics that summarize how well the observed responses compare to the predicted probabilities of the dependent variable. These measures are typically used to evaluate models intended for prediction or forecasting. See Kennedy (2003) for how to report and interpret concordance statistics.

APPENDIX C

Terminology for Ordinary Least Squares (OLS) and Logistic Models

Table C.1. Terminology for components of ordinary least squares and logistic regression models

Terms and synonyms	Definition/Purpose	Examples[a]	Comments
Dependent variable Outcome variable Explained variable Regressand Left-hand side variable (LHS variable)	The variable whose value is estimated as a function of the independent variables	Birth weight, grams (OLS model) Low birth weight (logistic model)	In a "cause/effect" hypothesis, the dependent variable is the variable affected and the independent variables are the hypothesized causes.
Independent variable Predictor variable Explanatory variable Regressor Right-hand side variable (RHS variable)	Variables used to explain or predict the dependent variable	Race/ethnicity, smoking	Can be causal, mediating, confounding, or control (see "Common Reasons for Estimating a Multivariate Model" in chapter 14).
Control variable Covariate	Background variables included as independent variables, but not of central interest to the research question	Male gender	In some disciplines, these terms are used to describe all independent variables in a model.

Term	Definition	Examples	Notes
Continuous variable	A variable measured in integer or ratio units	Integer: mother's age (years) Ratio variable: income-to-poverty ratio	Both independent and dependent variables can be continuous. OLS models are used for continuous dependent variables (see table C.2).
Categorical variable	A variable classified into mutually exclusive and exhaustive nominal or ordinal categories	Ordinal variable: mother's education Nominal variable: Race/ethnicity	Both independent and dependent variables can be categorical. Logistic or other categorical data analysis techniques are used for categorical dependent variables (see table C.2).
Binary variable Dichotomous variable Dummy variable Indicator variable	Categorical variable with two values. Used to compare categories of nominal or ordinal variables.	Gender (male/female) Mother's smoking (yes/no) "Non-Hispanic black" and "Mexican American" in comparison of birth weight across racial/ethnic groups	For an *n* category variable there will be (*n* − 1) dummy variables included in a regression model. See chapter 9 for an explanation of calculation and interpretation.
Multichotomous variable Polytomous variable	Categorical variable with more than two values	Race/ethnicity Mother's education	

(continued)

Table C.1. (continued)

Terms and synonyms	Definition/Purpose	Examples[a]	Comments
Reference category Omitted category	Used in calculation and interpretation of effects of dummy variables in OLS and logistic models	"Non-Hispanic white" infants, in comparison of birth weight across racial/ethnic groups	The category of an ordinal or nominal variable against which other categories are compared in the regression model. The category for which *no* dummy variable is included in the regression model.
Interaction Effect modification	When the effect of one independent variable on the dependent variable varies according to the value of another independent variable	The relationship between educational attainment and birth weight is different for each of the three racial/ethnic groups.	In a multivariate OLS or logistic model, composed of main effect and interaction terms (see below). See chapter 9 for calculations and interpretation; chapter 14 for illustrative prose description.

Term	Definition	Example	Comment
Main effect	The independent effect of one of the variables in an interaction	For the race-by-education interaction, the dummy variables on race/ethnicity and on educational attainment	Main effects and interaction terms must be considered together to ascertain net effect of each independent variable on the dependent variable. See chapter 9 for calculations and interpretation; chapter 14 for illustrative prose description; appendix D for an example spreadsheet to do computations.
Interaction term / Interaction regressor	The coefficient on an interaction term created by multiplying two or more other variables	For the race-by-education interaction, the dummy variables on race/ethnicity, dummies indicating non-Hispanic black *and* less than high school	

[a] Examples are taken from specifications shown in table 10.1 for an OLS model of birth weight; table 10.2 for a logistic model of low birth weight (LBW). These variables could have other roles for different research questions.

Table C.2. Names of common multivariate ordinary least squares and categorical dependent variable models

Terms and Synonyms	Definition/Purpose	Example Application	Comments	Citations
Multivariate model Multiple regression	General class of models that control statistically for effects of several variables simultaneously to describe or predict values of a dependent variable	Relationship between race/ethnicity, socioeconomic status, health behavior, and infant health	Includes OLS models, logit, probit, log-linear, and related models.	Fox 1997 Allison 1999 Powers and Xie 2000
Ordinary least squares regression OLS regression Linear regression[a]	One type of multivariate model for a continuous dependent variable	Relationship between race/ethnicity, socioeconomic status, health behavior, and birth weight in grams	Dependent variable can be interval or ratio.	Fox 1997 Allison 1999
Logistic regression Logit regression	One type of multivariate model for a categorical dependent variable	Relationship between race/ethnicity, socioeconomic status, health behavior, and prevalence of low birth weight	Dependent variable can be nominal or ordinal. Can also be analyzed using probit, linear probability, or log-linear models.[b]	Long 1997 Powers and Xie 2000

Multinomial regression Multinomial logit model Multichotomous model Polytomous model Competing risks model (survival models only)	One type of analysis of a categorical dependent variable with three or more categories	Relationship between race/ethnicity, socioeconomic status, health behavior, and risk of very low vs. moderately low vs. normal vs. high birth weight	Multichotomous dependent variables also can be analyzed using log-linear models or ordered logit or probit models.[b]	Powers and Xie 2000
Survival model Hazards model Event history analysis Failure time analysis Competing risks model (multichotomous outcome)	Analysis of categorical dependent variables with a temporal component	Relationship between cohabitation history, socioeconomic factors, and risk of divorce	Includes Cox proportional hazards models, proportional odds models, and parametric hazards models. Also can be estimated using logit, probit or log-linear models.[b]	Allison 1995 Cox and Oakes 1984.

[a] In some disciplines, the term "linear regression" is used to refer to the functional form of the relationship between the independent and dependent variables.

[b] Units and interpretation of coefficients from probit, log-linear, or linear probability models are different from those described here for logit models. See Powers and Xie (2000) or other textbooks on models for categorical dependent variables.

Table C.3. Terminology for statistical output from ordinary least squares and logistic regression models[a]

Terms and Synonyms	Definition/Purpose	Examples[b]	Comments
Intercept Constant	Value of the dependent variable for reference category (of categorical variables) and with all continuous variables at their means	*Model of birth weight (grams):* Intercept = 3,039.8 *Model of low birth weight:* Intercept = −2.03	Sometimes denoted α in models with one independent variable; β_0 in models with several independent variables (Long 1997).
Coefficient Parameter estimate Effect estimate Beta (β) Point estimate Log-odds (logit model only)	Estimated effect of an independent variable. For continuous variables, an estimate of the slope of the relation between the predictor and dependent variable. For categorical variables, the difference between categories of that variable.	*Model of birth weight (grams):* Boy (categorical): 117.2 Mother's age (continuous): 10.7 *Model of low birth weight:* Boy (categorical): −0.02	See chapter 9 for an explanation of units and interpretation for different types of models and variables.
t-statistic (OLS regression) *z*-statistic or Wald chi-square statistic (logistic regression) Chi-square statistic (Cox model)	Test statistic for an independent variable	*Model of birth weight (grams):* Boy (categorical): $t = 9.76$ *Model of low birth weight:* Boy (categorical): $\chi^2 = 0.06$	See chapter 10 for other output related to inferential statistics, such as standard errors, *p*-values, and confidence intervals.

Degrees of freedom (df)	Used in conjunction with test statistic and pertinent statistical distribution to determine p-value for the coefficient or overall model.	Coefficient on each independent variable in birth weight model: 1 df Overall model: 9 df	See Fox (1997) for OLS models; Powers and Xie (2000) for logistic models.
R^2; adjusted R^2 (OLS regression) −2 log likelihood (logistic regression); often written "−2 log L"	Measure of overall model goodness-of-fit. Use to compare against null model or across nested models (see comments).	Model of birth weight (grams): Adjusted R^2: 0.08 Model of low birth weight: −2 log likelihood relative to null model: 247.5 with 9 df	R^2 measures proportion of variance explained in an OLS model. To formally compare fit of several models, compare F-statistics (Wonnacott and Wonnacott 1984). For logit models, a "pseudo-R^2" can be calculated (Powers and Xie 2000).
Overall model chi-square statistic (logistic regression; hazards models)			

[a] See Maciejewski et al. (2002) for terminology for other types of multivariate models.
[b] From table 10.1 for OLS model of birth weight; table 10.2 for logistic model of low birth weight.

APPENDIX D

Using a Spreadsheet for Calculations

A spreadsheet is an invaluable tool for computing and presenting many of the comparisons described in chapter 9 for multivariate model results. Useful applications include calculating predicted values of the dependent variable for independent variables that were specified using a polynomial, mathematical transformation, or spline; figuring out net effects of an interaction; and calculating excess risk and change in excess risk. Doing these calculations in a spreadsheet has several advantages.

- You can copy formulas to different parts of a spreadsheet, ensuring that repetitive calculations are done consistently for different input values. (See note on absolute and relative addresses below for considerations when copying formulas.)
- You have a record of the calculations and a means to update them quickly by filling in new numeric values, should you decide to respecify your model.
- You can easily create a chart to preview or present the results, eliminating the need to type or copy them into another program.
- You can program the spreadsheet to calculate absolute difference, relative difference, or percentage difference between computed values for use in your narrative description of the above-mentioned patterns.

■ CALCULATE A PATTERN FROM COEFFICIENTS ON A POLYNOMIAL

A spreadsheet is an ideal way to calculate a pattern based on a polynomial because the computation involves applying the same formula repetitively to different input values of the independent variable. For example, to calculate the predicted pattern of birth weight from the linear and square terms on the income-to-poverty ratio (IPR), use the following formula: Predicted birth weight (grams) $= \beta_0 + (\beta_{IPR} \times IPR) + (\beta_{IPR^2} \times IPR^2)$. Filling in the estimated coefficients (β's) from model B, table 9.1, yields $3{,}042.8 + (81.4 \times IPR) + (-10.1 \times IPR^2)$. Instead of manually plugging alternative values of IPR into a calculator, create a spreadsheet like that shown in figure D.1, which was created in Microsoft Excel 97. Rows are numbered in the leftmost (shaded) column of

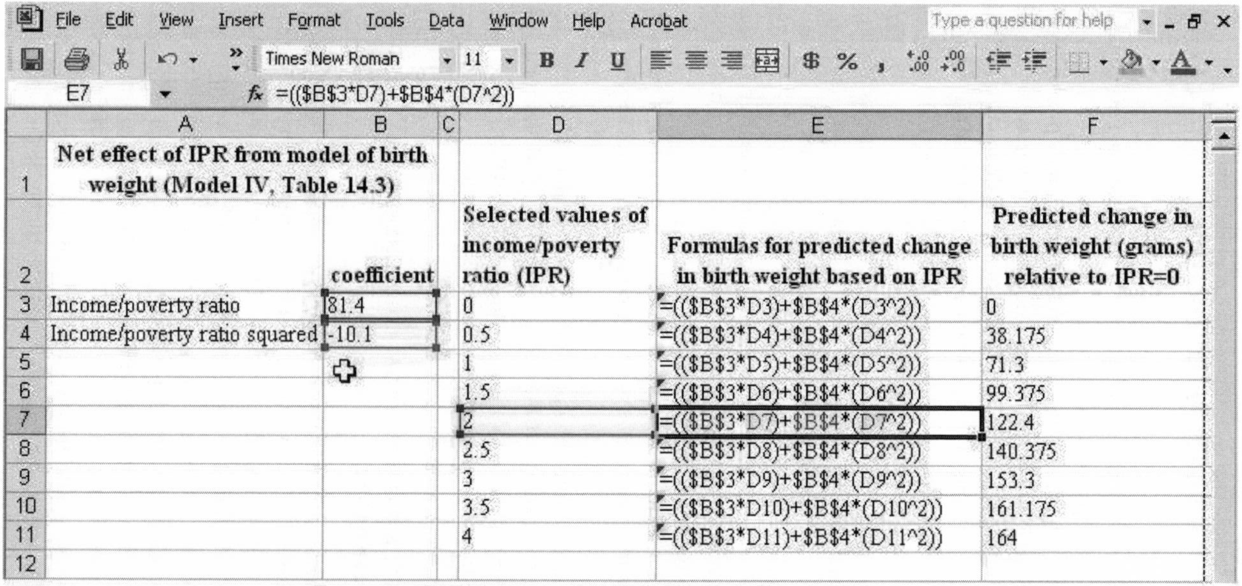

	A	B	C	D	E	F
1	**Net effect of IPR from model of birth weight (Model IV, Table 14.3)**					
2		**coefficient**		**Selected values of income/poverty ratio (IPR)**	**Formulas for predicted change in birth weight based on IPR**	**Predicted change in birth weight (grams) relative to IPR=0**
3	Income/poverty ratio	81.4		0	=(($B$3*D3)+$B$4*(D3^2))	0
4	Income/poverty ratio squared	-10.1		0.5	=(($B$3*D4)+$B$4*(D4^2))	38.175
5				1	=(($B$3*D5)+$B$4*(D5^2))	71.3
6				1.5	=(($B$3*D6)+$B$4*(D6^2))	99.375
7				2	=(($B$3*D7)+$B$4*(D7^2))	122.4
8				2.5	=(($B$3*D8)+$B$4*(D8^2))	140.375
9				3	=(($B$3*D9)+$B$4*(D9^2))	153.3
10				3.5	=(($B$3*D10)+$B$4*(D10^2))	161.175
11				4	=(($B$3*D11)+$B$4*(D11^2))	164
12						

Figure D.1. Spreadsheet to calculate predicted pattern from a polynomial.

Notes: Based on model IV, table 14.3. "^" indicates exponentiation; "$" an absolute address; see notes to appendix D for explanation. Data are from U.S. DHHS 1997.

the spreadsheet, while columns are identified by letter names in the shaded row below the toolbars. Formulas within the spreadsheet use cell addresses comprised of the column letter and row number to refer to the cells that hold estimated coefficients or other numbers needed for the calculations.

In figure D.1, columns A and B contain the pertinent variable labels and estimated coefficients from the multivariate model, while column D includes a range of plausible values of the IPR, running from 0 to 4 in increments of 0.5. The formulas in rows 3 through 11 of column E tell Excel where to find the coefficients—the IPR term in cell B3, the IPR^2 term in cell B4—and how to apply them to the selected values of IPR (in column D) in the pertinent row.[1] For example, the formula in cell E7 (with the dark border around it in figure D.1) calculates the predicted change in birth weight (relative to IPR = 0) for IPR = 2.0. The three cells that contribute input values to the formula—cells B3, B4, and D7—are highlighted with a frame and square markers at each corner in figure D.1. This feature allows you to verify that the formula is calling on the correct input values.

Notice that the formulas in all the rows of column E are identical except for the row number in which the IPR value is to be found, meaning that the same coefficients are combined mathematically the same way in each row.[2] Consult the manual for your spreadsheet program to learn how to program the formulas, which may have a different syntax for expressing cell addresses and formulas than that used in the Excel illustrations shown here.

Column F holds the results of those calculations[3]—in this case, the predicted difference in birth weight in grams for each of the specified values of IPR relative to IPR = 0, based on the estimated coefficients from model B in table 9.1. These calculated values could then be presented in a chart such as figure 6.11—easily produced by most spreadsheet programs—or pasted into a table.

■ CALCULATE NET EFFECTS OF AN INTERACTION

Figure D.2 shows coefficients and formulas used to calculate net effects of an interaction between race/ethnicity and mother's education from model B, table 9.1. Column B contain the estimated coefficients for each independent variable in the model (labeled in column A). In rows 2 through 5 of columns D through G are the labels and formulas to calculate estimated differences in birth weight com-

Net effect of interactions between race/ethnicity and mother's education from model of birth weight (Model IV, Table 14.3)

			Formulas for difference in birth weight by race/ethnicity & mother's education, relative to non-Hispanic white, college+		
OLS model of birth weight (grams)				non-H White	Non-H Black	Mex Amer
Variable	Coefficient		Less than high school	=B14	=B7+B14+B19	=B8+B14+B20
Intercept	3042.8		High school grad	=B15	=B7+B15+B21	=B8+B15+B22
Race/ethnicity			College+	=B6	=B7	=B8
(Non-Hispanic White)						
Non-Hispanic Black	-168.1		Difference in birth weight (grams) by race/ethnicity & mother's education, relative to non-Hispanic white, college+		
Mexican American	-104.2					
Boy	117.4			non-H White	Non-H Black	Mex Amer
Mother's age at birth of child (yrs.)	10.6		Less than high school	-54.2	-260.8	-59
Income/poverty ratio	81.4		High school grad	-62	-211.7	-72.5
Income/poverty ratio squared	-10.1		College+	0	-168.1	-104.2
Mother's educ. attain.						
Less than high school	-54.2					
High school grad	-62					
(College+)						
Mother smoked	-193.9					
Interactions						
Non-Hispanic black * <HS	-38.5					
Mexican American* <HS	99.4					
Non-Hispanic black * = HS	18.4					
Mexican American*=HS	93.7					

Figure D.2. Spreadsheet to calculate net effects of an interaction.
Notes: Based on model IV, table 14.3. Data are from U.S. DHHS 1997.

pared to non-Hispanic white infants born to mothers with at least some college (the reference category).

Laying out the calculations as a grid with a column for each racial/ethnic group and a row for each educational attainment group creates a cell for each possible combination of the two independent variables involved in the interaction. Each of those cells contains the formula to combine the estimated coefficients that apply to cases with the pertinent combination of race and education. For example, cell F3 (highlighted with the dark border in figure D.2) holds the formula to compute the net effect for non-Hispanic blacks (column F) with less than high school (row 3). See "Interactions" in chapter 9 for an explanation of the logic behind these formulas.

The coefficients for the main effects of non-Hispanic blacks (cell B7) and Mexican Americans (cell B8) are each included only in the formulas for the respective racial/ethnic group, shown in columns F and G, respectively. Likewise, the main effects for less than high school (cell B14) and high school grad (cell B15) appear only in the formulas for their respective educational attainment groups—rows 3 and 4 of columns E through G. Coefficients on interaction terms between race and education (cells B19 through B22) are included in only one formula apiece—the one referring to the corresponding race/education combination. For example, the non-Hispanic black × <HS interaction term (from cell B19) shows up only in the formula calculating birth weight for that group, located in cell F3.

NOTES

CHAPTER 2

1. See Best 2001.
2. See chapter 3 for further discussion of various dimensions of "significance" that come into play when assessing quantitative relations.
3. Another aspect of association—statistical significance—is covered in chapter 3.

CHAPTER 3

1. The fifth criterion—specificity—is most applicable to the study of infectious disease. It concerns the extent to which a particular exposure (e.g., the measles virus) produces one specific disease (measles).

CHAPTER 4

1. Temperature in degrees Kelvin has a meaningful absolute zero value and can be treated as a ratio variable, but is rarely used by anyone other than physical scientists in technical documents.
2. When categorical variables are entered onto a computer, each group is often assigned a numeric code as an abbreviation. Do not treat those values as if they had real numeric meaning. It makes no sense to calculate "average gender" by computing the mean of a variable coded 1 for male and 2 for female. For categorical variables, the appropriate measure of central tendency is the mode, not the mean.
3. To generalize, "__ % of [concept in the denominator] is [concept in the numerator]."
4. Sometimes the geometric mean is used instead of the arithmetic mean. It is computed as the nth root of the product of all values in the sample, where n is the number of values in the calculation. If you use the geometric mean, explicitly name it to avoid confusion.
5. In the phrase "significant digits," the term "significant" has a different meaning from the statistical interpretation discussed in chapter 3. Here, it refers to precision of measurement and how that affects the appropriate number of digits in measured values (raw data) and calculations.

CHAPTER 5

1. Breakdowns of non-Hispanic blacks and non-Hispanics of other races could likewise be indented under the respective headings. Those data were not available in the current source (U.S. Census Bureau 1998).
2. For example, there were 3,112 Mexican American infants in the NHANES III sample, of whom 7.0% were low birth weight (table 5.6). Hence $3,112 \times 0.070$, or roughly 218 Mexican American infants in the sample were LBW.

3. However, if a response is missing for a substantial share of cases, show the distribution of both "yes" and "no," as well as "don't know" or other missing values.

CHAPTER 6

1. A pie chart can present two categorical variables simultaneously by cross-tabulating them. E.g., a single pie showing gender and age distribution might have slices for males under 20, males 20 and older, females under 20, and females 20 and older, four mutually exclusive categories. Univariate slices (e.g., one slice for <20 and another for males) cannot be shown in the same pie chart because some people are both <20 and male.

2. Ninety-five percent confidence intervals are the standard, corresponding to a p-value of 0.05. If you use a different confidence level such as 90% or 99%, include that information in the chart title.

CHAPTER 8

1. Changing the reference group in a two-group calculation merely involves "flipping over" the ratio to calculate its reciprocal: a ratio of 1.43 southerners per midwesterner is equivalent to 0.70 midwesterners per southerner.

2. With negative growth rates (yes, they are called that, not "shrinkage rates"!), the base population or principal, becomes successively smaller across time.

3. For annual compounding, calculate the annual interest rate (r) using the formula $\log(1 + r) = \log(P_2/P_1)/n$, where P_1 and P_2 are the populations at times 1 and 2 respectively, n is the number of years between P_1 and P_2, and "log" indicates base 10 logarithms. For continuous compounding use $r = \ln(P_2/P_1)/n$, where "ln" indicates natural logarithms (Barclay 1958; Nicholson 1985).

4. A Likert scale is a common way of collecting attitudinal data on surveys. Subjects are asked to express agreement or disagreement on a five-point scale.

CHAPTER 9

1. In some disciplines, the term "linear regression" is used to refer to the functional form of the relationship between the independent and dependent variables rather than to regression models involving continuous dependent variables.

2. In some disciplines, the intercept term is denoted α.

3. In some disciplines, $\hat{\beta}_k$ is used to denote the estimated coefficient, to distinguish it from the true but unknown population value of β_k. I use the notation β_k for estimated coefficients throughout this book.

4. For example, suppose the modal categories for age and marital status in your study sample are 15-to-19-year-olds and married people, but few of

the 15-to-19-year-olds are married. In that case, it may be preferable to change the omitted category for either marital status or age group to comprise a more typical combination.

5. Most statistical software can do these calculations for you based on the array of estimated coefficients; see your software manual.

6. For models of the form $\ln Y = \beta_0 + \beta_1 X_1$, when β_1 is small, $\beta_1 \times 100$ is a close approximation of percentage change in Y for a one-unit increase in X_1 (Wooldridge 2003). However, as β_1 increases above 0.5, the approximation increasingly deviates from the true percentage change. For example, when $\beta_1 = 0.10$, the approximation understates the true percentage change by only one half a percentage point. When $\beta_1 = 0.50$, the difference is nearly 15 percentage points (or a relative understatement of 23% of the true value).

7. The corresponding statistics for a logistic model are the z-statistics (for individual coefficients) and the -2 log likelihood statistic (for overall model fit).

8. Models that include many interaction terms may be affected by multicollinearity, which can explain why the t-statistics indicate a lack of significance even if the F-statistic indicates statistical significance.

9. For the F-statistic, more than 40 degrees of freedom is generally treated as ∞ (infinite) df. See a statistics textbook for a table of F-statistics.

10. Selecting case examples relates to the distribution of explanatory characteristics among cases in the sample (e.g., associations among independent variables), not to interactions among independent variables in their association with the dependent variable. For example, although non-Hispanic blacks are more likely than others to have been born to teen mothers (reflecting a different age distribution in that racial/ethnic group), race and mother's age do not necessarily interact in their association with birth weight.

11. Probit models, log-linear models, and linear probability models can also be used to analyze categorical dependent variables, but the interpretation of their effect sizes differs from that of logit models. See Powers and Xie (2000) for an excellent review of different types of categorical data analyses.

12. The risk of an event is $p/1$, where p is the probability of the event occurring, expressed as a proportion.

13. Logistic regression models are used to model chances of a categorical outcome because they have the desirable statistical property of forcing the estimated probability of the outcome to be bounded between 0 and 1. OLS and linear probability models do not have that property (Aldrich and Nelson 1984; Schwartz 2004).

14. To quantify extent of disadvantage or change in disadvantage across models of continuous outcomes, use the percentage difference and percentage change calculations explained in chapter 8. For instance, apply those cal-

culations to the coefficients from the OLS models in table 9.1 to assess the size of the birth weight deficit (in grams) for black compared to white infants, and the change in that deficit across models with and without interaction terms.

CHAPTER 10

1. The t-statistic for a coefficient in an OLS model is $\beta_k/\text{s.e.}_{\beta k}$, while the Wald chi-square statistic from a logit model is $(\beta_k/\text{s.e.}_{\beta k})^2$.

CHAPTER 12

1. In addition to the deaths that occurred within a year of each survey date, other cases were lost from the sample due to other forms of attrition (e.g., moving away or refusing to participate) or death in intervening years (Idler et al. 2001).

CHAPTER 14

1. For some journals, descriptions of the role of each variable and model belong in the methods section; for others, in the results section.
2. Sometimes the most basic model will include only the main independent variable, simply translating the bivariate relation into a regression format. Other times it will also include standard background control variables (e.g., gender in the birth weight model) that are not of central interest to your research question.
3. Often, sample size changes because different numbers of cases have valid values on the different covariates, hence when a new independent variable is introduced that has missing values, sample size drops. If different samples are used to estimate different models, changes in the estimated coefficients could be due to compositional changes between samples rather than to the introduction of additional variables. To avoid this error, run the full set of models—as well as descriptive statistics on those variables—using the set of cases that have valid data on *all* variables that are used in any model. Or include dummy variables for missing values or control variables to avoid losing too many cases (see chapter 12).

CHAPTER 15

1. The "Vanna White" moniker is in honor of the longtime hostess of the TV game show *Wheel of Fortune,* who gestures at the display to identify each item or feature as it is introduced.

CHAPTER 16

1. Organizations that produce many poster presentations often have equipment to produce large, single-sheet posters rather than individual pages to be pinned up.

APPENDIX D

1. The "^" symbol is the operational symbol for exponentiation in Excel. For example, "D7^2" (in the formula in cell E7) means to take the numeric value in cell D7 and square it (raise it to the second power.)

2. In an Excel spreadsheet, the "$" symbol in the cell addresses that refer to the estimated coefficients indicates an "absolute address." When a $ is used and the formula is copied across rows or columns, the formula refers to the same exact cell to find the numbers used in each calculation. In the absence of a $, when a formula is copied across rows, the row number will be changed to refer to a relative address. For example, relative addresses are used to ensure that the input value of IPR changes to reflect the current row: in cell E3, the formula takes the IPR value from cell D3, in cell E4, the formula takes the IPR value from cell D4, etc. See Courter and Marquis (1999) or the manual for your spreadsheet program for an explanation of absolute and relative addresses and when each is appropriate.

3. Usually, a spreadsheet displays the computed values in the cell where you have typed the formula. For illustrative purposes, in figures D.1 and D.2 I have shown the formulas and numeric results separately, so you can see both versions and how they relate to the other cells in the spreadsheet.

REFERENCE LIST

Abramson, J. H. 1994. *Making Sense of Data: A Self-Instruction Manual on the Interpretation of Epidemiologic Data.* 2nd ed. New York: Oxford University Press.

Agresti, Alan, and Barbara Finlay. 1997. *Statistical Methods for the Social Sciences.* 3rd ed. Upper Saddle River, NJ: Prentice Hall.

Aldrich, John H., and Forrest D. Nelson. 1984. *Linear Probability, Logit, and Probit Models.* Beverly Hills, CA: Sage Publications.

Allison, Paul D. 1995. *Survival Analysis Using the SAS System: A Practical Guide.* Cary, NC: SAS Institute.

———. 1999. *Multiple Regression: A Primer.* Thousand Oaks: Sage Publications.

Alred, Gerald J., Charles T. Brusaw, and Walter E. Oliu. 2000. *Handbook of Technical Writing.* 6th ed. New York: St. Martin's Press.

Anderson, Robert N. 2001. "Deaths: Leading Causes for 1999." *National Vital Statistics Reports* 49 (11). Hyattsville, MD: National Center for Health Statistics.

Anderson, Robert N., and Harry M. Rosenberg. 1998. "Age Standardization of Death Rates: Implementation of the Year 2000 Standard." *National Vital Statistics Report* 47 (3). Hyattsville, MD: National Center for Health Statistics.

Barclay, George W. 1958. *Techniques of Population Analysis.* New York: John Wiley and Sons.

Benson, Veronica, and Marie A. Marano. 1998. "Current Estimates from the National Health Interview Survey, 1995." *Vital and Health Statistics* 10 (199). Hyattsville, MD: National Center for Health Statistics.

Best, Joel. 2001. *Damned Lies and Statistics.* Berkeley: University of California Press.

Birch and Davis Health Management Corporation. 2000. NJ KidCare enrollment database. (May 30).

Blossfeld, Hans-Peter, Alfred Hamerle, and Karl Ulrich Mayer. 1989. *Event History Analysis: Statistical Theory and Application in the Social Sciences,* Hillsdale NJ: Lawrence Erlbaum Associates.

Briscoe, Mary Helen. 1996. *Preparing Scientific Illustrations: A Guide to Better Posters, Presentations, and Publications.* 2nd ed. New York: Springer-Verlag.

Centers for Disease Control. 1999. "Notice to Readers: New Population Standard for Age-Adjusting Death Rates." *Morbidity and Mortality Weekly Review* 48 (06): 126–27. Available at http://www.cdc.gov/mmwr/preview/mmwrhtml/00056512.htm.

———. 2002. "Compressed Mortality File: U.S. 1999."

Centers for Medicare and Medicaid Services, Office of the Actuary, National Health Statistics Group, Department of Health and Human Services. 2004. "Table 1. National Health Expenditures, Aggregate and Per Capita Amounts, Percent Distribution, and Average Annual Percent Growth, by Source of Funds: Selected Calendar Years 1980–2002." Available at http://cms.hhs.gov/statistics/nhe/historical/t1.asp.

Chambliss, Daniel F., and Russell K. Schutt. 2003. *Making Sense of the Social World: Methods of Investigation.* Thousand Oaks, CA: Sage Publications.

Citro, Constance F., Robert T. Michael, and Nancy Maritano, eds. 1996. *Measuring Poverty: A New Approach.* Table 5–8. Washington, DC: National Academy Press.

Conley, Dalton, and Neil G. Bennett. 2000. "Race and the Inheritance of Low Birth Weight." *Social Biology* 47 (1–2): 77–93.

Cornoni-Huntley, J., D. B. Brock, A. M. Ostfeld, J. O. Taylor, and R. B. Wallace, eds. 1986. *Established Populations for Epidemiologic Studies of the Elderly: Resource Data Book.* NIH Publ. no. 86–2443. Bethesda, MD: National Institute on Aging.

Courter, Gini, and Annette Marquis. 1999. *Microsoft Office 2000: No Experience Required.* Alameda, CA: Sybex.

Cox, D.R., and D. Oakes. 1984. *Analysis of Survival Data.* Monographs on Statistics and Applied Probability. New York: Chapman and Hall.

Davis, James A. 1985. *The Logic of Causal Order.* Quantitative Applications in the Social Sciences 55. Thousand Oaks, CA: Sage Publications.

Davis, James A., Tom W. Smith, and Peter V. Marsden. 2003. *General Social Surveys, 1972–2000: Computer Codebook.* 2nd ICPSR version. Chicago, IL: National Opinion Research Center.

Davis, Martha. 1997. *Scientific Papers and Presentations.* New York: Academic Press.

DiFranza, Joseph R., and the Staff of the Advocacy Institute, with assistance from the Center for Strategic Communications. 1996. *A Researcher's Guide to Effective Dissemination of Policy-Related Research.* Princeton, NJ: The Robert Wood Johnson Foundation.

Duncan, Greg J., and Jeanne Brooks-Gunn, eds. 1997. *Consequences of Growing Up Poor for Young Children.* New York: Russell Sage.

Duncan, Greg J., Mary C. Daly, Peggy McDonough, and David R. Williams. 2002. "Optimal indicators of socioeconomic status for health research," *American Journal of Public Health* 92 (7): 1151–57.

Eaton, Leslie. 2002. "Job Data May Show a False Positive." *New York Times,* February 10, Job Market section.

Fink, Arlene. 1995. *How to Report on Surveys.* Thousand Oaks, CA: Sage Publications.

Fox, John. 1997. *Applied Regression Analysis, Linear Models and Related Methods.* Thousand Oaks, CA: Sage Publications.

Franzini, L., J. C. Ribble, and A. M. Keddie. 2001. "Understanding the Hispanic Paradox." *Ethnicity and Disease* 11 (3): 496–518.

Freedman, David, Robert Pisani, and Roger Purves. 1998. *Statistics,* 3rd ed. New York: W. W. Norton.

Githens, P. B., C. A. Glass, F. A. Sloan, and S. S. Entman. 1993. "Maternal Recall and Medical Records: An Examination of Events during Pregnancy, Childbirth, and Early Infancy." *Birth* 20 (3): 136–41.

Glanz, James, and Eric Lipton. 2002. "The Height of Ambition." *New York Times,* September 8.

Gold, Marthe R., Joanna E. Siegel, Louise B. Russell, and Milton C. Weinstein, eds. 1996. *Cost-Effectiveness in Health and Medicine.* New York: Oxford University Press.

Gujarati, Damodar N. 2002. *Basic Econometrics.* 4th ed. New York: McGraw-Hill/Irwin.

Hailman, Jack P., and Karen B. Strier. 1997. *Planning, Proposing, and Presenting Science Effectively: A Guide for Graduate Students and Researchers in the Behavioral Sciences and Biology.* New York: Cambridge University Press.

Heckman, James J. 1979. "Sample Selection Bias as a Specification Error." *Econometrica* 47 (1): 153–61.

———. 1998. "Characterizing Selection Bias Using Experimental Data." *Econometrica* 66 (5): 1017–98.

Heylighen, Francis. 1997. "Occam's Razor" in *Principia Cybernetica Web,* ed. F. Heylighen, C. Joslyn, and V. Turchin (Principia Cybernetica, Brussels). Available online at http://pespmc1.vub.ac.be/OCCAMRAZ .html. Accessed February 2003.

Hoaglin, David C., Frederick Mosteller, and John W. Tukey. 2000. *Understanding Robust and Exploratory Data Analysis.* New York: John Wiley and Sons.

Idler, Ellen L., Stanislav V. Kasl, and Judith C. Hays. 2001. "Patterns of Religious Practice and Belief in the Last Year of Life." *Journal of Gerontology* 56B (6): S326–S334.

Ingram, Deborah D., and Diane M. Makuc. 1994. "Statistical Issues in Analyzing the NHANES I Epidemiologic Followup Study." *Vital and Health Statistics* 2: 121.

Institute for Democracy and Electoral Assistance. 1999. "Voter Turnout from 1945 to 1998: A Global Participation Report." Available online at http://www.int-idea.se/Voter_turnout/northamerica/usa.html. Accessed January 2003.

Institute of Medicine, Committee to Study the Prevention of Low Birthweight. 1985. *Preventing Low Birthweight.* Washington, DC: National Academy Press.

James, David R., and Karl E. Taeuber. 1985. "Measures of Segregation." In *Sociological Methodology,* edited by Nancy Tuma, 1–32. San Francisco: Jossey-Bass.

Johnson, Kirk. 2004. "Colorado Takes Steps to Polish Thin and Fit Image." *New York Times,* February 1. Front section.

Kachigan, Sam Kash. 1991. *Multivariate Statistical Analysis: A Conceptual Introduction.* 2nd ed. New York: Radius Press.

Kalton, G., and D. Kasprzyk. 1986. "The Treatment of Missing Survey Data." *Survey Methodology* 12 (1), 1–16.

Kennedy, Peter. 2003. *A Guide to Econometrics,* 5th ed. Cambridge MA: MIT Press.

Kleinbaum, David G., Lawrence L. Kupper, Keith E. Muller, and Azhar Nizam. 1998. *Applied Regression Analysis and Other Multivariate Methods.* 3rd ed. Pacific Grove CA: Duxbury Press.

Kolata, Gina. 2003. "Hormone Studies: What Went Wrong?" *New York Times,* April 22, Science sec.

Kornegay, Chris. 1999. *Math Dictionary with Solutions: A Math Review.* 2nd ed. Thousand Oaks, CA: Sage Publications.

Kraemer, Helena C. 1987. *How Many Subjects? Statistical Power Analysis in Research.* Thousand Oaks, CA: Sage Publications.

Kuczmarski, Robert J., et al. 2000. "CDC Growth Charts: United States." *Advance Data from Vital and Health Statistics.* No. 314. Hyattsville, MD: National Center for Health Statistics.

Lanham, Richard. 2000. *Revising Prose.* 4th ed. New York: Longham.

Leonhardt, David. 2003. "For Aging Runners, a Formula Makes Time Stand Still." *New York Times,* October 28.

Levy, Frank. 1987. *Dollars and Dreams: The Changing American Income Distribution.* New York: Russell Sage Foundation.

Levy, Helen, and Thomas DeLeire. 2002. "What Do People Buy When They Don't Buy Health Insurance?" Northwestern University/University of Chicago Joint Center for Poverty Research Working Paper 296 06–26–2002.

Lewit, Eugene, L. Baker, Hope Corman, and P. Shiono. 1995. "The Direct Cost of Low Birth Weight." *Future of Children* 5 (1).

Lilienfeld, David E., and Paul D. Stolley. 1994. *Foundations of Epidemiology.* 3rd ed. New York: Oxford University Press.

Lipton, Eric, and James Glanz. 2002. "First Tower to Fall Was Hit at Higher Speed, Study Finds." *New York Times,* February 23.

Logan, Ralph H. 1995. "Significant Digits." Available online at http://members.aol.com/profchm/sig_fig.html. Accessed January 2003.

Long, J. Scott. 1997. *Regression Models for Categorical and Limited Dependent Variables.* Thousand Oaks, CA: Sage Publications.

Ma, Xin, and J. Douglas Willms. 1999. "Dropping Out of Advanced Mathematics: How Much Do Students and Schools Contribute to the Problem?" *Educational Evaluation and Policy Analysis* 21: 365–83.

Maciejewski, Matthew L., Paula Diehr, Maureen A. Smith, and Paul Hebert. 2002. "Common Methodological Terms in Health Services Research and Their Symptoms." *Medical Care* 40: 477–84.

Mack, Tim. n.d. "Plagues since the Roman Empire." Available online at http://www.ento.vt.edu/IHS/plagueHistory.html#justinian. Accessed January 2002.

Martin, Joyce A., Brady E. Hamilton, Stephanie J. Ventura, Fay Menacker, and Melissa M. Park. 2002. "Births: Final Data for 2000." *National Vital Statistics Reports* 50 (5).

Martin, Joyce A., Brady E. Hamilton, Paul D. Sutton, Stephanie J. Ventura, Fay Menacker, and Martha L. Munson. 2003. "Births: Final Data for 2002." *National Vital Statistics Reports* 52 (10).

Mathews, T. J., and Brady E. Hamilton. 2002. "Mean Age of Mother, 1970–2000." *National Vital Statistics Report* 51 (1). Hyattsville, MD: National Center for Health Statistics.

Mathews, T. J., Marian F. MacDorman, and Fay Menacker. 2002. "Infant Mortality Statistics from the 1999 Period Linked Birth/Infant Death Data Set." *National Vital Statistics Reports* 50 (4). Hyattsville, MD: National Center for Health Statistics.

McDonough, John. 2000. *Experiencing Politics: A Legislator's Stories of Government and Health Care.* Berkeley, CA: University of California Press.

Medina, Jennifer. 2002. "Report Finds Drop in Average City Class Size." *New York Times,* September 20, sec. B.

Miller, Jane E. 2000a. "Differences in AIDS Knowledge among Spanish and English Speakers by Socioeconomic Status and Ability to Speak English." *Journal of Urban Health* 77 (3): 415–24.

———. 2000b. "Income, Race/Ethnicity, and Early Childhood Asthma Prevalence and Health Care Utilization." *American Journal of Public Health* 90 (3): 428–30.

———. 2004. *The Chicago Guide to Writing about Numbers.* Chicago: University of Chicago Press.

Miller, Jane E., Louise B. Russell, Diane M. Davis, Edwin Milan, Jeffrey L. Carson, and William C. Taylor. 1998. "Biomedical Risk Factors for Hospitalization." *Medical Care* 36 (3): 411–21.

Monmonier, Mark. 1993. *Mapping It Out: Expository Cartography for the Humanities and Social Sciences.* Chicago: University of Chicago Press.

Montgomery, Scott L. 2003. *The Chicago Guide to Communicating Science.* Chicago: University of Chicago Press.

Moore, David S. 1997. *Statistics: Concepts and Controversies.* 4th ed. New York: W. H. Freeman and Co.

Morgan, Susan E., Tom Reichert, and Tyler R. Harrison. 2002. *From Numbers to Words: Reporting Statistical Results for the Social Sciences.* Boston: Allyn and Bacon.

Morton, Richard F., J. Richard Hebel, and Robert J. McCarter. 2001. *A Study Guide to Epidemiology and Biostatistics.* 5th ed. Gaithersburg, MD: Aspen Publishers.

Musso, Juliet, Robert Biller, and Robert Myrtle. 2000. "Tradecraft: Professional Writing as Problem Solving." *Journal of Policy Analysis and Management* 19 (4): 635–46.

National Institutes for Health, Office of Human Subjects Research. 2002. *Regulations and Ethics.* Available online at http://206.102.88.10/ohsrsite/guidelines/guidelines.html. Accessed January 2003.

Navarro, Mireya. 2003. "Going beyond Black and White, Hispanics in Census Pick 'Other.'" *New York Times,* November 9.

NCHS (National Center for Health Statistics). 1994. "Plan and Operation of the Third National Health and Nutrition Examination Survey, 1988–1994." *Vital and Health Statistics* 1 (32).

————. 1995. "International Classification of Diseases, Ninth Revision, Clinical Modification." 5th ed. NCHS CD-ROM no. 1. DHHS pub. no. (PHS) 95–1260.

————. 2002. "Policy on Micro-Data Dissemination." Available online at http://www.cdc.gov/nchs/data/NCHS%20Micro-Data%20Release%20Policy%204–02A.pdf. Accessed January 2003.

Nelson, David E., Ross C. Brownson, Patrick L. Remington, and Claudia Parvanta, eds. 2002. *Communicating Public Health Information Effectively: A Guide for Practitioners.* Washington, DC: American Public Health Association.

Newman, J.R., ed. 1956. *The World of Mathematics.* Vol. 2. New York: Simon and Schuster.

Nicholson, Walter. 1985. *Microeconomic Theory.* New York: Holt, Rinehart and Winston.

Nicol, Adelheid A. M., and Penny M. Pexman. 1999. *Presenting Your Findings: A Practical Guide for Creating Tables.* Washington, DC: American Psychological Association.

NIST (National Institute of Standards and Technology). 2000. "Uncertainty of Measurement Results." In *The NIST Reference on Constants, Units, and Uncertainty.* Available online at http://physics.nist.gov/cuu/Uncertainty/index.html. Accessed January 2004.

Olson, J. E., X. O. Shu, J. A. Ross, T. Pendergrass, and L. L. Robison. 1997. "Medical Record Validation of Maternally Reported Birth Characteristics and Pregnancy-Related Events: A Report from the Children's Cancer Group." *American Journal of Epidemiology* 145 (1): 58–67.

Omran, Abdel R. 1971. "The Epidemiologic Transition: A Theory of the Epidemiology of Population Change." *Milbank Memorial Fund Quarterly* 49 (4): 509–38.

Palloni Alberto, and J. D. Morenoff. 2001. "Interpreting the Paradoxical in the Hispanic Paradox: Demographic and Epidemiologic Approaches." *Annals of the New York Academy of Sciences* 954: 140–74.

Paneth, Nigel. 1995. "The Problem of Low Birth Weight." *Future of Children* 5 (1).

Peters, Kimberley D., Kenneth D. Kochanek, and Sherry L. Murphy. 1998. "Deaths: Final Data for 1996." *National Vital Statistics Report* 47 (9). Available online at http://www.cdc.gov/nchs/data/nvsr/nvsr47/nvs47_09.pdf. Accessed January 2003.

Phillips, Julie A. 2002. "White, Black, and Latino Homicide Rates: Why the Difference?" *Social Problems* 49 (3): 349–74.

Pollack, Andrew. 1999. "Missing What Didn't Add Up, NASA Subtracted an Orbiter." *New York Times,* October 1.

Population Reference Bureau. 1999. "World Population: More than Just Numbers." Washington, DC: Population Reference Bureau.

Pottick, Kathleen J., and Lynn A. Warner. 2002. "More than 115,000 Disadvantaged Preschoolers Receive Mental Health Services." *Update: Latest Findings in Children's Mental Health.* New Brunswick, NJ: Institute for Health, Health Care Policy, and Aging Research. 1 (2). Available online at http://www.ihhcpar.rutgers.edu/downloads/fall2002.pdf. Accessed May 2004.

Powers, Daniel, and Yu Xie. 2000. *Statistical Methods for Categorical Data Analysis.* San Diego CA: Academic Press.

Preston, Samuel H. 1976. *Mortality Patterns in National Populations.* New York: Academic Press.

Proctor, Bernadette D., and Joseph Dalaker. 2002. "Poverty in the U.S., 2001." *Current Population Reports.* P60–219. Washington, DC: U.S. Government Printing Office.

———. 2003. "Poverty in the United States: 2002." *Current Population Reports.* P60–222. Washington, DC: U.S. Government Printing Office.

Puffer, Ruth R., and Carlos V. Serrano. 1973. *Patterns of Mortality in Childhood.* Washington, DC: World Health Organization.

Pyrczak, Fred, and Randall R. Bruce. 2000. *Writing Empirical Research Reports.* 3rd ed. Los Angeles: Pyrczak Publishing.

Quality Resource Systems, Inc. 2001. *Area Resource File.* Available online at http://www.arfsys.com/.

Radloff, L. S., and B. Z. Locke. 1986. "The Community Mental Health Assessment Survey and the CES-D Scale." In *Community Surveys of Psychiatric Disorders,* edited by M. M. Weissma, J. K. Myers, and C. E. Ross. New Brunswick, NJ: Rutgers University Press.

Russell, Louise B., Elmira Valiyeva, and Jeffrey L. Carson. 2004. "Effects of Prehypertension on Admissions and Deaths: A Simulation," *Archives of Internal Medicine* 164: 2119–24.

Schemo, Diana Jean, and Ford Fessenden. 2003. "Gains in Houston Schools: How Real Are They?" *New York Times,* December 3.

Schutt, Russell K. 2001. *Investigating the Social World: The Process and Practice of Research.* 3rd ed. Boston: Pine Forge Press.

Schwartz, John. 2003. "The Level of Discourse Continues to Slide." *New York Times,* Week in Review, September 28.

Schwartz, Sharon. 2004. "A Quirky Measure of Effect: On the Interpretation of Odds Ratios," manuscript, Columbia University.

Shah, B. V., B. G. Barnwell, and G. S. Bieler. 1996. *SUDAAN User's Manual, Release 7.0.* Research Triangle Park, NC: Research Triangle Institute.

Slocum, Terry A. 1998. *Thematic Cartography and Visualization.* Upper Saddle River, NJ: Prentice Hall.

Snow, John. 1936. *Snow on Cholera.* New York: The Commonwealth Fund.

Snowdon, David. 2001. *Aging with Grace: What the Nun Study Teaches Us about Leading Longer, Healthier, and More Meaningful Lives.* New York: Bantam Books.

Strunk, William, Jr., and E. B. White. 1999. *The Elements of Style.* 4th ed. Boston, MA: Allyn and Bacon.

Sorian, Richard, and Terry Baugh. 2002. "Power of Information: Closing the Gap between Research and Policy." *Health Affairs* 21 (2): 264–73.

Tufte, Edward R. 1990. *Envisioning Information.* Cheshire, CT: Graphics Press.

———. 1997. *Visual Explanations: Images and Quantities, Evidence and Narrative.* Cheshire, CT: Graphics Press.

———. 2001. *The Visual Display of Quantitative Information.* 2nd ed. Cheshire, CT: Graphics Press.

———. 2003. *The Cognitive Style of PowerPoint.* Cheshire, CT: Graphics Press.

Tukey, John W. 1977. *Exploratory Data Analysis.* New York: Addison-Wesley Publishing Co.

University of Chicago Press. 2003. *The Chicago Manual of Style: The Essential Guide for Writers, Editors, and Publishers.* 15th ed. Chicago: University of Chicago Press.

U.S. Bureau of Labor Statistics. 2002a. "U.S. Economy at a Glance." Available online at http://www.bls.gov/eag/eag.us.htm. Accessed March 2002.

———. 2002b. "Consumer Price Indexes: Frequently Asked Questions." Available online at http://www.bls.gov/cpi/cpifaq.htm. Accessed March 2002.

U.S. Census Bureau. 1998. "Households by Type and Selected Characteristics: 1998." Available online at http://www.census.gov/population/socdemo/hh-fam/98ppla.txt.

———. 1999a. "Comparison of Summary Measures of Income by Selected Characteristics: 1989, 1997, and 1998." Available online at http://www.census.gov/hhes/income/income98/in98sum.html.

———. 1999b. "State Population Estimates and Demographic Components of Population Change: April 1, 1990, to July 1, 1999." Available online at http://www.census.gov/population/estimates/state/st-99–2.txt.

———. 1999c. "Table 650. Civilian Labor Force Participation and Rates, with Projections, 1970–2006." *Statistical Abstract of the United States, 1999.*

Available online at http://www.census.gov/prod/99pubs/99statab/sec13.pdf.

———. 2000a. "Annual Projections of the Total Resident Population as of July 1: Middle, Lowest, Highest, and Zero International Migration Series, 1999 to 2100." Washington, DC: Population Estimates Program, Population Division. Available online at http://www.census.gov/population/projections/nation/summary/np-t1.pdf.

———. 2001a. "Table 940. Median Sales Price of New Privately Owned One-Family Houses Sold by Region, 1980–2000." *Statistical Abstract of the United States, 2001.* Available online at http://www.census.gov/prod/2002pubs/01statab/construct.pdf.

———. 2001b. "Money Income in the United States: 2000." *Current Population Reports.* P60–213. Washington, DC: U.S. Government Printing Office.

———. 2001c. "Table 118. Expectation of Life and Expected Deaths by Race, Sex, and Age: 1997." *Statistical Abstract of the United States, 2000.* Available online at http://www.census.gov/prod/2001pubs/statab/sec02.pdf. Accessed

———. 2002a. "Poverty 2001." Available online at http://www.census.gov/hhes/poverty/threshld/thresh01.html. Accessed October 2002.

———. 2002b. "No. 310. Drug Use by Arrestees in Major United States Cities by Type of Drug and Sex, 1999." *Statistical Abstract of the United States, 2001.* Available online at http://www.census.gov/prod/2002pubs/01statab/stat-ab01.html. Accessed January 2004.

———. 2002c. "Table 611. Average Annual Pay, by State, U.S. 1999 and 2000." *Statistical Abstract of the United States, 2002.*

———. 2002d. "2000 Detailed Tables: Sex by Age, U.S. Summary File SF1." Available online at http://factfinder.census.gov/. Accessed September 2002.

U.S. DHHS (Department of Health and Human Services). 1991. *Longitudinal Follow-up to the 1988 National Maternal and Infant Health Survey.* Hyattsville, MD: National Center for Health Statistics.

———. 1997. *National Health and Nutrition Examination Survey, III, 1988–1994.* CD-ROM Series 11, no. 1. Hyattsville, MD: National Center for Health Statistics, Centers for Disease Control and Prevention.

———. 2000. *Healthy People 2010: Understanding and Improving Health.* 2nd ed. Washington, DC: U.S. Government Printing Office, November 2000. Available online at http://www.healthypeople.gov/Document/tableofcontents.htm#under. Accessed May 2004.

———, Centers for Disease Control and Prevention. 2002. *Z-score Data Files.* Hyattsville, MD: National Center for Health Statistics, Division of Data Services. Available online athttp://www.cdc.gov/nchs/about/major/nhanes/growthcharts/zscore/zscore.htm. Accessed January 2003.

————, Office of Disease Prevention and Health Promotion. 2001. *Healthy People 2010.* US GPO Stock no. 017-001-00547-9. Washington, DC: U.S. Government Printing Office. Available online at http://www.health.gov/healthypeople/. Accessed September 2002.

————, Office of Human Service Policy. 2003. *Indicators of Welfare Dependence: Annual Report to Congress 2003.* Washington, DC. Available online at http://www.aspe.hhs.gov/hsp/indicators03/. Accessed May 2004.

U.S. Environmental Protection Agency. 2002. *Cost of Illness Handbook.* Available online at http://www.epa.gov/oppt/coi/. Accessed September 2002.

U.S. National Energy Information Center. 2003. "Crude Oil Production. Table 2.2. World Crude Oil Production, 1980–2001." http://www.eia.doe.gov/pub/international/iealf/table22.xls. Accessed January 2004.

U.S. Office of Management and Budget. 2002. *Budget of the United States, Fiscal Year 2003, Historical Tables.* Table 3.1. Available online at http://w3.access.gpo.gov/usbudget/fy2003/pdf/hist.pdf. Accessed June 2002.

U.S. Social Security Administration. 2003. *Income of the Aged Chartbook, 2001.* Baltimore, MD. Available online at http://www.ssa.gov/policy/docs/chartbooks/income_aged/2001/index.html. Accessed May 2004.

Utts, Jessica M. 1999. *Seeing through Statistics.* 2nd ed. New York: Duxbury Press.

Ventura, Stephanie J., Joyce A. Martin, Sally C. Curtin, and T. J. Mathews. 1999. "Births: Final Data for 1997." *National Vital Statistics Report* 47 (18). Hyattsville, MD: National Center for Health Statistics.

Warner, Lynn A., and Kathleen J. Pottick. 2004. "More than 380,000 Children Diagnosed with Multiple Mental Health Problems." *Latest Findings in Children's Mental Health.* New Brunswick, NJ: Institute for Health, Health Care Policy, and Aging Research 3 (1). Available online at http://www.ihhcpar.rutgers.edu/downloads/winter2004.pdf. Accessed May 2004.

Westat. 1994. "National Health and Nutrition Examination Survey III, Section 4.1: Accounting for Item Non-Response Bias." *NHANES III Reference Manuals and Reports.* Washington, DC: U.S. Department of Health and Human Services, Public Health Service, Centers for Disease Control and Prevention, National Center for Health Statistics.

————. 1996. "National Health and Nutrition Examination Survey III, Weighting and Estimation Methodology." In *NHANES III Reference Manuals and Reports.* Hyattsville, MD: U.S. Department of Health and Human Services, Public Health Service, Centers for Disease Control and Prevention, National Center for Health Statistics.

Wilcox, Allen J., and Ian T. Russell. 1986. "Birthweight and Perinatal Mortality: III. Towards a New Method of Analysis." *International Journal of Epidemiology* 15 (2): 188–96.

Wilkinson, Leland, and Task Force on Statistical Inference, APA Board of Scientific Affairs. 1999. "Statistical Methods in Psychology Journals: Guidelines and Explanations." *American Psychologist* 54 (8): 594–604.

Wolke, Robert L. 2002. *What Einstein Told His Cook: Kitchen Science Explained.* New York: W. W. Norton.

Wonnacott, Thomas H., and Ronald J. Wonnacott. 1984. *Introductory Statistics for Business and Economics,* 3rd. ed. New York: John Wiley & Sons.

Wooldridge, Jeffrey M. 2003. *Introductory Econometrics: A Modern Approach.* 2nd ed. Mason, Ohio: Thomson South-Western.

World Bank. 2001a. "Health, Nutrition, and Population Statistics." Available online at http://devdata.worldbank.org/hnpstats/. Accessed February 2002.

———. 2001b. *2001 World Development Indicators: Health Expenditure, Service, and Use.* Available online at http://www.worldbank.org/data/wdi2001/pdfs/tab2_15.pdf. Accessed January 2002.

World Health Organization. 1995. *Physical Status: Use and Interpretation of Anthropometry.* WHO Technical Report Series 854. Geneva: WHO.

———. 2002. "Quantifying Selected Major Risks to Health." In *World Health Report 2002: Reducing Risks, Promoting Healthy Life.* Geneva: WHO.

———, Expert Committee on Maternal and Child Health. 1950. Public Health Aspect of Low Birthweight. WHO Technical Report Series, Number 27. Geneva: WHO.

www.fueleconomy.gov. 2002. "1985–2001 Buyer's Guide to Fuel Efficient Cars and Trucks." Available online at http://www.fueleconomy.gov/feg/index.htm. Accessed October 2002.

Young, L. R., and M. Nestle. 2002. "The Contribution of Expanding Portion Sizes to the US Obesity Epidemic." *American Journal of Public Health* 92 (2): 246–49.

Zambrana, R. E., C. Dunkel-Schetter, N. L. Collins, and S. C. Scrimshaw. 1999. "Mediators of Ethnic-Associated Differences in Infant Birth Weight." *Journal of Urban Health* 76 (1): 102–16.

Zelazny, Gene. 2001. *Say It with Charts: The Executive's Guide to Visual Communication.* 4th ed. New York: McGraw-Hill.

Zhang, J., and K. F. Yu. 1998. "What's the Relative Risk? A Method of Correcting the Odds Ratio in Cohort Studies of Common Outcomes." *Journal of the American Medical Association* 280:1690–91.

Zinsser, William. 1998. *On Writing Well: The Classic Guide to Writing Nonfiction.* 6th ed. New York: HarperCollins Publishers.

INDEX